A Jew in America

A Jew in America

My Life and a People's Struggle for Identity

Arthur Hertzberg

HarperSanFrancisco
A Division of HarperCollins*Publishers*

HarperCollins books may be purchased for educational, business, or sales promotional use. For information please write: Special Markets Department, HarperCollins Publishers, Inc., 10 East 53rd Street, New York, NY 10022.

HarperCollins Web site: http://www.harpercollins.com
HarperCollins®, ✿®, and HarperSanFrancisco™ are
trademarks of HarperCollins Publishers, Inc.

FIRST EDITION
Designed by Joseph Rutt

Library of Congress Cataloging-in-Publication Data
Hertzberg, Arthur.
A Jew in America : my life and a people's struggle for
identity / Arthur Hertzberg.
p.cm.
Includes index.
ISBN 0–06–251710–4 (cloth : alk. paper)
ISBN 0–06–251712–0 (paperback)
1. Hertzberg, Arthur. 2. Jews—United States—Biography.
3. Jews—United States—Identity. 4. Rabbis—United States—Biography.
5. Zionists—United States—Biography. 6. United States—Biography.
7. United States—Ethnic relations. 8. Hertzberg, Arthur—Political activity.
I. Title.
E184.37.H47   2002
973'.04924'0092—dc21   2002068715
02 03 04 05 06 ❖ RRD(H) 10 9 8 7 6 5 4 3 2 1

W hen I was a child of eleven, my father told me a Hasidic story. In a village in the far corner of a sparsely inhabited province, the new wheat in the fields nearby could not be eaten. It was infected by a red bacillus that made madmen and madwomen out of those who ate from this harvest. The wise men of the village met to find a way of dealing with this disaster. They decided to set aside, from the remains of the previous year's harvest, enough wheat with which to feed one person for the whole of the coming year. Let all the rest eat the infected new wheat. They would go mad but they would survive, and at the end of the year this one man would be left as the standard of sanity. All the rest would be able to abandon their madness by emulating him when the next, and healthy, crop came up from the earth.

Even at the age of eleven, I understood that my father was telling me a truth about himself, the very same truth that the author of this story a century and a half earlier, Rabbi Nachman of Bratslav, had told about himself: the saving grace of times gone mad is the lonely person who keeps his sanity. I was moved by this story because my father was telling me what he expected of me, but I was not at all sure, even as a child, that the story ended there. A couple of years later, when I was turning into a teenaged contrarian, I reminded my father of the story and asked him, Are you sure that the one person who stayed sane really survived the year in a town of madmen? My father's face turned dark and somber, but he did not reply, so I added a somewhat more cheerful sentence: Being a lone voice of sanity may not be fatal, but it is certainly a difficult and embattled task. At that point, my father spoke up: You have no choice; you must defend what you know is right.

At various turning points in my life, this story has come back to me, both to haunt me and to give me courage. At the age of seventeen, as a sophomore at Johns Hopkins, I could not help repeating this tale to myself as I heard the opening lecture in a course in American history. The professor was explaining the famous thesis about the uniqueness of American society that had been offered a half century earlier by Frederick Jackson Turner: those who came to the New World had the wilderness in front of them. They could leave their previous lives and commitments behind and reinvent themselves on the frontier of Western civilization. If things went bad in Philadelphia, or New York, or Boston, they could move west to virgin land. If necessary they could move farther, and keep moving and moving. The existence of the frontier was the shaping element for Americans. It created the country of second chances.

But I could not help asking another question: if millions of immigrants came to America to reinvent themselves, by what compass did they steer? This question has existed from the very beginning of American society. I have had personal experience of the responses that dominated in this century. In the early 1900s newcomers to America were badgered to give up the ways that they had brought with them, to assimilate into the culture and manners of the White Anglo-Saxon Protestant majority. Some immigrants fought back by imagining American society as a "melting pot" out of which a new model of human conduct would emerge. These new men and women would be fashioned from elements of all the cultures and traditions that had come to the New World. But, in essence, the melting pot was another version of the demand for assimilation. All of the various elements in America, old and new, would be allowed in to claim that they had contributed something to the making of the new Americans, but, in the process of melting in, each of the traditions would disappear.

By the middle of the century, another image of American society was proposed, that of "cultural pluralism." This country would become the home of many "hyphenated Americans." Cultural pluralism is, by now, the accepted official doctrine of American society, but what are these minority cultures in their American version? To be sure, many Italians have heard about Garibaldi and can identify Dante, and many Hispanics know something of the work of Cervantes, and Jews, of course, even those who do not read the Bible very much, take a proprietary interest in sacred scripture. But America is much more aware of ethnic restaurants than of ethnic study groups—and so are the various ethnic groups themselves. I must report that I am not a Jew because I like bagels or Borscht Belt humor. My most serious act as a Jew is that I continue to study the literature that our kind has been producing for thirty centuries and I measure my conduct, day by day, by the standards that these books teach. This is the compass by which I steer.

My experience points away from assimilation and the melting pot, and away from the shallow version of cultural pluralism. It points to living traditions of people who are rooted in their past. These living traditions, I learned from my parents, are a way of reaching universal compassion. They need not—and should not—be a call to war on other traditions. I was taught to see Judaism not as a curtain shutting out others but as a window on the world. I have insisted all my life that being a Jew is rooted in the values that you affirm and not in the enemies that you fight.

Like my father, I do have the bitterness of someone who has fought for principles in a world that has resisted them, but this is not the book of a bitter rabbi. I have won more battles than I have lost. I have kept my zeal for helping people. I remained a rabbi in congregational life for forty years to do good for individual people, even as I chafed at some elements in the congregation that thought they owned me.

As a public figure, I have managed to be a factor in the public life and politics of the Jewish community in the United States, of Israel, and of the American community as a whole. In reverse order: In America, I was one of the makers of the racial revolution, both in the South and in the North. In Israel, I helped to found Peace Now and have remained for decades, especially since 1967, a man of the Left on a wide variety of issues and, especially, a proponent of peace through compromise with the Palestinians. Within the American Jewish community, I have consistently opposed those who equate being Jewish with anti-anti-Semitism. Jewishness will survive, and will have a right to survive, only as long as it affirms and takes risks for virtue. We Jews must keep asking ourselves, over and over again, What decencies do we uphold? What can we do to make the world better?

I was very much surprised by the role that I played at the beginning of the 1970s in defining the dialogue between Jews and Christians. In 1971 I was chair of the Jewish delegation, representing all of the Jewish world both in the Diaspora and in Israel, at the first encounter ever with an official delegation from the Vatican that was sent to meet with us. The achievement of that first meeting was that the two delegations agreed that we would speak to each other, always, as equals, with respect and candor. We would not sweep our differences under the rug, but we would work hard to understand each other. This definition of the relationship had enabled me and, of course, other participants in the dialogue to say uncomfortable things to the Church about the various roles that it played during the Holocaust and yet retain friendships with prelates and scholars of the Roman Catholic community. I remain hopeful that Jewish and Christian leaders have made a profound transition in the past several decades toward a strong partnership in the work for a more decent and a more peaceful world.

As a religious believer I have not remained a fundamentalist. My religious practice has always been deeply traditionalist. I have tried to show the way toward a nonfundamentalist definition of Judaism that emphasizes its moral teaching and its passion for justice for all of mankind. I am proudest of the fact that in this journey I have never lost my connection with any part of the Jewish community. I remain intimately tied to the Hasidic community of my youth and to all of the other schools of thought within Judaism. These connections can be maintained only if one really loves and admires all of the clashing schools of thought, believers and secularists alike, and it remains clear that one continues to learn from all of them.

On the political scene, nationally and internationally, I have insisted all my life that the prime teaching of the Jewish tradition, as I understand it, commands me to defend the defenseless. That means that whether they are Blacks in America, or Palestinian refugees in the camps or under Israeli occupation, or the poorest of the poor in America or elsewhere in the world, it is my moral duty to be on their side. Judaism commands me not to be a false prophet flattering power but a disciple of those ancient preachers who stood in the marketplace or the precincts of the Temple in Jerusalem and defied the kings in the name of justice.

As a scholar I have consistently wrestled, in many permutations, with one overarching subject: the new and very difficult encounter between Jews and the largely Christian majority society in which they have lived during the past two or three centuries—that is, in the modern era. As a scholar, whether writing about Zionists, or the Enlightenment, or the relationship between Jews and other Americans, I have invariably refused to accept the conventional opinions. Though I wrote the first book on Zionist ideology after the creation of the state of Israel, I challenged the dominant Zionist notion that this historic event would make an end of the Diaspora. In my next book, *The French Enlightenment and the Jews,* published in 1968, I confronted the accepted idea that the Enlightenment was the prime source of Western liberalism and the teacher of the doctrine of human equality. On the contrary, I found in some of the leaders of the Enlightenment the racial arrogance that allowed them to dislike Jews and ignore Blacks. These views were not very popular among the unqualified admirers of the men of the Enlightenment. On the relationship between Jews and other Americans, I have insisted in innumerable essays and, ultimately, in 1989 in a book that Jews, like all other American minorities, still had an uneasy relationship to the American majority.

Is there anything in my life that is relevant for those who will be fashioning the future? In American society as a whole, which is becoming ever more complicated and ever more plural, it is absolutely clear that the doctrines of a century ago—assimilation to WASP-dom or its gentler vision of the idea of American society as a melting pot—are dead. The future of America will be made by those who will hold fast to their traditions and their memories, to the cultures that they brought with them from all over the world, but who will understand that the old wars of religion and the old ethnic angers are redundant and dangerous. We cannot raise the next several generations of the many ethnic and religious communities on chauvinism or by demanding that they abandon their traditions. My family lived out and taught this vision of America long before it became conceivable.

The task of the inquiring mind is to ask all the questions, especially those that seem closed, over again. The path to the future is best seen by eyes that are not blinkered and do not blink. It is so much easier, so most of us think most of the time, to live by the accepted clichés and not upset people by raising questions, but I have not been able to live that way. I am a Jew, and, thus, my kind was set in motion by the Patriarch Abraham. He was the first to break with idolatry, to insist that there is only one God. When Abraham came to this conviction, he was alone in the world. He had to make all the decisions of his life all by himself, steering by his own compass. Many centuries later, the Greek philosopher Aristotle taught that we dare not live the unexamined life. There is no alternative to the difficult journey of questioning and self-questioning. I hope that this book will encourage others to stay on such a path. This book is the memoir of one who has made this journey.

Arthur Hertzberg

A Jew in America

My parents were immigrants, but they were different. The vast majority of newcomers who had been arriving in America since the beginning of its history left Europe in order to break with the past and to become new men and women in the New World. My parents had brought their past along with them. They held on to it with pride and even with defiance. They had not come to America to forget their ancestors, who had been writing commentaries on the Talmud and the Kabbalah for centuries. My father was a rabbi and a Hasid ("pious one") who was profoundly learned in classic Jewish texts. My mother was totally selfless. She kept an open house for the hungry and hopeless even in the years when she had little with which to feed her children. Growing up in such a home, I have never ceased feeling inadequate—I have not attained the learning of my father or the charity of my mother—but I am ever more aware that I have always looked at the world through their eyes.

The past that my parents brought with them stretched back through many generations. My father remembered, and he taught his children to remember, that we were descendants of Elimelech of Lizhansk and his nephew Zvi Elimelech of Dinov (after whom my father was

named). They were among the founding figures of the Hasidic movement in Judaism one and a half centuries earlier. This new religious fervor erupted in Eastern Europe in the late 1700s to teach that the service
of God demands more than formal obedience to the ritual laws. God
requires our hearts and our moral passion for justice for people who
seem to be of no consequence. There were also eminent rabbinic scholars in our ancestry leading back to some of the commentators in the sixteenth century on the classics of Jewish law. It was at once exhilarating
and intimidating to hear from my father, and sometimes my mother,
that an author of a weighty classic of the sacred literature in the Middle
Ages or early modern times was an ancestor.

My parents taught that these ancestors still lived. They were
immediately present in my grandfather—my father's father, Avraham
Herzberg—and his four brothers. Each was more pious than the other,
and together they were known everywhere in their region, eastern Galicia, as the "Five Books of Moses." After his marriage in Dinov to my
grandmother, Breindel, Avraham Herzberg was given a modest dowry
and a commitment from her parents that they would support the young
couple for several years so that he could spend all his time studying the
sacred books. After a few weeks he ran away, and he was soon found in
the court of the Hasidic rebbe of Belz. For the rest of his life, he came
home only for special occasions, such as when his two sons were born.
He spent his life being a *yoshev* ("dweller") in Belz. Such people were
intimately connected to their teacher, much more so than the majority
of the rebbe's adherents who came for an occasional visit. The *yoshvim*
made sure that they were present whenever the rebbe spoke, and they
were always alert to every one of his actions. They tried to fathom the
deep meaning that the rebbe was conveying by the way he stood, or sat,
or, especially, by the attitude of his body at prayer. It was their special
merit to share in the very food that he ate. To be a *yoshev* in Belz was,
therefore, much more enticing to Avraham Herzberg than to go home
to Dinov to study in isolation or, later, to Lubaczow, the town of his
family, to help his young wife run the little store on the square from
which she was barely making a living. Avraham Herzberg wrote a contract with his wife that half of the stake he was acquiring in heaven
would be hers, in return for which she would run the small store in
Lubaczow that supported him, her, and their two young sons.

One of the things to which my grandfather Avraham devoted himself at the court of the rebbe of Belz from the mid-1890s to 1914 was to be the rebbe's librarian and the Talmud teacher of the rebbe's children. As librarian he edited and published a kabbalistic manuscript in the rebbe's collection. The book is so rare that the next time I saw it outside of my father's library was in Gershom Scholem's hands in Jerusalem in 1971. Occasionally, Avraham Herzberg would come home to Lubaczow to visit his wife, and once he suddenly found himself alone in the house with an eight-year-old niece, the daughter of one of his brothers. To build a wall against sexual temptation, the Talmud had prescribed strict prohibitions against *yichud*—that is, being alone with an unmarried woman. Grandfather could not wait to walk out the door, because by crossing the room he would be prolonging, by a few seconds, the period of transgression, so he jumped out of a second-story window. Fortunately, he landed on soft dirt and did not hurt himself, but even in his family, and among the pious in town, this jump became part of the local folklore. It added to the legend of the "Five Books of Moses." Sometimes this honorific was translated into a more relaxed, and mocking, description of the brothers as *meshuge frum*—crazy pious.

But that was only part of the essence of the man. There was the matter of how he died. My father, Zvi Elimelech, found it difficult to talk of his father. He felt guilty all his life that he was gone from Lubaczow in 1915 when his father died at the age of forty-two. This guilt was unreasonable. My father could not have been there. He was then a soldier in the Austro-Hungarian army, fighting on the front against the invading Russian army.

In 1915, eastern Poland was a major battleground of the First World War. The Austro-Hungarian army crumbled, and the Germans were forced to intervene to stop a Russian advance. When the Germans recaptured Lubaczow they found that hundreds of people were near death with cholera. The army doctors had neither the medicine nor the personnel with which to take care of the sick, so they ordered that they be abandoned, most probably to die. Everyone in Lubaczow obeyed the order except my grandfather. He would not walk away from the sick. Within days he contracted the disease, and he was soon dead. The others had saved their lives by leaving. Some were, no doubt, upset with themselves, but they could assure themselves that they had no choice.

Did not the Talmud teach obedience to secular authorities: "The law of the state is the law"? My grandfather had not taken refuge in this maxim. He chose to disobey the military doctors, so he tended the sick, and he died among them. And so I was named after him.

Avraham Herzberg's elder son, my father, had been born in 1894, and he was drafted into the Austro-Hungarian Army in 1914. The Austrian authorities had found him in Oświęcim, which the Germans renamed Auschwitz in the next war. My father had been there for several years studying with its famous rabbi, Joshua Bombach, who ordained him just before the First World War broke out. He served all four years of the war until the Central Powers (Germany and Austro-Hungary) were completely defeated and the Austro-Hungarian Empire disintegrated. The Austrian army made no exceptions for young rabbinic scholars, so he began as a frontline soldier and was wounded twice in battle, but he talked little about combat. His favorite subject was the world before the war, which he regarded as a kind of golden age for Jews in the Austro-Hungarian Empire, and he loved to tell peaceful tales of his work as a soldier after he was no longer fit for combat. If it is true that children look back through a golden haze at the youth of their parents, it is certainly true in my case.

Let me tell three stories from the days of my father's youth. He was wounded for the first time in 1915 at the battle of Tarnopol in Galicia (southeastern Poland) as the Russians were advancing against the Austrians. He later took several bullets in a leg, and soon infection set in and he was evacuated to one of the large military hospitals in Vienna. The doctors there decided that his leg had to be amputated, but he resisted that conclusion. A volunteer nurse who was working in the hospital, a very Westernized Jewess, took an interest in him and fought his cause. There seems to have been some remnant of a supply of natural rubber that could be used to treat the leg, but the doctors had no intention of using it on him. The nurse intervened very forcefully, and my father's leg was saved. He later discovered that she was a daughter of the Austrian Baron von Rothschild. This story came back to me with particular force lately when I found myself writing an essay about the meaning of the Rothschild family in the life of Jews. I did not know until I had finished the essay why I had always felt so warm about the Rothschild tradition of concern for Jews in trouble.

When my father was discharged from the military hospital in Vienna, he was sent to Warsaw, which was then the center of the military government of the Central Powers for the territory of the Russian czar that they were then occupying. In Warsaw, my father's job was to work in the office that censored the civilian mail that came through the central office. He read the letters in Hebrew, and especially those that were written in rabbinic Hebrew, to make sure that these languages were not being used by Russian spies as means of communication. Very often, these letters were from one rabbi to another and concerned matters of Jewish religious law and practice or of interpretations of the fine points of the Talmud. My father told me that he could not resist the temptation to write in the margin, very often, some comment of his own on the subject at hand. Of course, he never got an answer, because he did not dare tell them who he was, but he could not resist the role of arguing with, or even correcting, these learned gentlemen.

The most memorable story about his military service he seldom told, but when he did, he was always, again, passionate and angry. In the summer of 1916, the Russians mounted their last offensive on the eastern front. The Cossacks drove through the small towns of Galicia, and everywhere they made a particular point of murdering Jews. The Austro-Hungarian command decided to evacuate the Jews who were in the path of the Russians into the hinterland, in Slovakia and Hungary. My father was assigned to be the military escort on such a refugee train. When the train arrived at the first town in Slovakia, the local Jewish community was well represented on the platform. They had brought food and large cauldrons of soup with which to feed the hungry Jews. These Slovakians were ultra-Orthodox, so they refused to give any food to those people on the train who were no longer wearing traditional Hasidic garb and whose wives had abandoned the custom of shaving their hair and wearing cloth caps or scarves to cover their heads. Without a moment's hesitation, my father, in military uniform, but wearing his beard and side curls as a Hasid should, walked over to the leader of the community and pointed his gun at this worthy's head. He said to him in unmistakable Yiddish that if this discrimination did not stop in thirty seconds he would blast that man's head off. Of course, it stopped.

Why do these stories live with me? (I shall soon tell many others of my father's life in America.) The Talmud taught me, and I know that this is true, that "the deeds of the fathers are a sign for their children." I have all my life found my way toward people who would save the leg of strangers. I have certainly had opinions, and published them and acted on them, even when, and sometimes especially when, they were not popular. I have never put a gun to anyone's head, but I have stood up to attempts to punish me in order to shut me up. I well remember that my father was fired by the small synagogue in Baltimore of which he was the rabbi in 1941 because he dared criticize Franklin Delano Roosevelt, who was then the "king of the Jews," for doing so little to protect them from the Nazis. That very night the board of the synagogue met and fired him. I was never fired, but I was stopped many times from preferment, and I have had to fight some bitter battles against enemies who wanted to shut me up.

Almost inevitably, I know less about my mother's childhood and youth, because women from Hasidic homes were simply not allowed to have much of a biography—and yet I was told enough so that her early years are part of my emotional life. Her mother died when she was seven, leaving behind three children, of which she was the eldest. Even after her father remarried, she continued to mother her siblings. She always spoke well of her stepmother, who treated the stepchildren with as much warmth and kindness as she gave to those who were soon born to her. But this good and even saintly stepmother died within a few years. Her father remarried again when my mother was already in her teens, and, in my mother's telling, this woman was selfish and angry. She resented my grandfather's children, and, what was worse, she had a hand in the first great defeat in my mother's life. The Hasidim often permitted their daughters, as they never permitted their sons, to attend public elementary schools, but it usually stopped there. My mother wanted to go on to high school, but her father, fearing the "heresies" that she might learn, forbade it. His third wife was particularly vehement—and so my mother used her intelligence to read voraciously in Yiddish, Polish, and German, and eventually, in the United States, in English.

When she was orphaned at seven, my mother had presumed that it was her task to keep the family together, and she did it over and over again throughout her life, for herself and for others. When dozens of teenaged refugees arrived in Baltimore after 1945, she became the mother for many of them. The very last picture I have of her was taken three days before her death. She got up out of a sickbed to attend the wedding of one of these refugees because she, and my father, had become his closest family. They were the adopted parents of all of his circle. I have always suspected that she was at least as bright, intellectually, as my father, who was universally respected and even revered as a profound and widely learned rabbinic scholar. I have no doubt that, even though I am a religious traditionalist, I have fought for years for the equality of women in the synagogue because of the memory of my mother. She was herself always Orthodox, but toward the end of her life she was beginning to wonder whether change would not be for the good. My father would not come to the actual service on a Friday night when my wife, Phyllis, and I celebrated the Bat Mitzvah of our elder daughter, Linda. (He did come to the reception on Sunday.) But my mother did come to the synagogue service. At the end of it, she walked over to me—proud that her first granddaughter had conducted much of the service in flawless Hebrew— and said to me, "Perhaps this is, indeed, worth having."

Even more than my father, she navigated for us the transition into the new land of America. She found the balance between her deep loyalties to the classic, Hasidic, code in which she had been raised and what she became, and what she helped her children become, in the New World. She faced the Holocaust, in which her father and all of her siblings and their families were murdered, and never talked of it. She simply dedicated her life to the survivors who came to her. I did not need to see Brecht's *Mother Courage* on the stage. I saw her—I still see her— every day. I can describe something of her life, but to this day I do not understand where she found the power to keep going. I suspect that, like Job, she would not allow God to drive her away from Him. She affirmed herself by rebuilding the good, day after day.

I was five years old in 1926 when I left Poland for the United States, and I remember little, but four scenes have never left me. On the way to school one day, I was surrounded and pushed by several children of the neighborhood, who shouted at me in Polish that I was a *Parshive zhid* ("dirty Jew"). They were many, and I was one; I was small for my age, and they seemed huge. I ran home to my mother.

About the same time, I saw my mother cry. She was alone. My father had gone to New York in 1923, to bring the rest of the family as soon as he could earn the means, and he had left her behind with two children. I was the elder of the two little boys. I remember this brother only as a child sitting in my mother's lap with a very red, burning face. He was feverish—and then he was gone. The loss was never explained to me. This child was almost never mentioned by my mother and never by my father—but I know that they did not, and could not, forget this part of themselves that was buried in Lubaczow. They did not want to scare their living children with the thought of the death of the young, but they always lit a candle for my brother Isaac on the eve of Yom Kippur.

My own memory goes back, dimly, to the age of three, to Lubaczow. My father had already gone to America. Thus, I know that he was not the man who wrapped me in a large tallith (prayer shawl) and carried me to the heder (the special room in which Jewish boys were instructed in the holy language and the sacred texts). It was a well-established ritual that little boys were brought to the heder on their third birthday and began the study of the Hebrew alphabet by licking honey from the page on which the first letter, the aleph, was imprinted. I remember feeling overwhelmed by the large tallith in which I was wrapped and a bit afraid when he who carried me tilted down to the printed page. I was not sure he was holding me tight enough that I would not fall. Yes, the honey was sweet, but it seems to have brought with it some discomforts.

The event that I best remember happened when I was five. It took place at the railroad station of Lemberg. For Jews, this city has remained Lemberg until this day, and not Lwów, as the Poles call it, or Lviv, as the Ukrainians named it, because Jews were happiest there under the Austrians, who gave them the most protection from the anti-Semites. My father had left Poland because he had been superbly trained to be a rabbi in the tolerant Austrian regime but there was no room for him in the more anti-Semitic Poland in the 1920s. My mother's father, on the other hand, was a high official of the Jewish community in Lemberg; he was in charge of the slaughter of animals for kosher food, and, in addition, he was preeminent among the adherents of the Hasidic rebbe of Belz who dominated the Jewish community of that area in Galicia. He wanted my mother to remain in Poland, and he hoped to persuade my father to come back from New York. As a child of five, I was, of course, unaware of this battle, but I was aware that we were going on a far journey where I would meet that mythic figure whom I did not remember, my father. When the day of our departure finally came, my grandfather accompanied us (my mother, my father's mother, and me) to the railroad station to take the long train ride to the port city of Antwerp in Belgium to board the *Lapland*, a ship sailing for New York. I recall that I was wearing new shoes for this occasion and that I felt more festively dressed up than ever before in my life. I was looking forward to the future. My grandfather was crying because, as he said quite openly, he never expected to see us again. As the train pulled out, he was running beside it on the platform until it pulled away. My last sight of him became an image that I could never forget. As he ran, he was holding his round satin hat on his head with his right hand. His black caftan was flying behind him, because somehow its buttons had been opened, and his long gray beard was half over his left shoulder—and the tears in his eyes were becoming wetter as he ran. I did not cry for him then, at the age of five, because I was so pleased with my new shoes and so eager to meet my father. But every time through the years that I have cried for him, for his family, and for his world, the image that I see is this Hasid trying to make his grandchild remember him. I do remember my grandfather, in many more ways, I suspect, than I will ever be able to explain to myself even in this confession.

No doubt, I retain some memory of other events during the first five years of my life, but these have remained beneath the surface of consciousness. The scenes that I have chosen to remember tell me of hurts in the old country, of the pain of parting, and of the duty that I assumed at three to study the sacred texts. These are my memories of Poland: sorrow and duty. But as the train pulled out from the station in Lemberg, the five-year-old child thought that he was on the way to joy, to America. I knew from my new clothes, and my grandfather's resistance to our going, that my mother and I were on the way to a different world. But I had already begun my life in Yiddish, within the world of Galician Hasidim, as a child of a rabbinic house. I did not know then that I would never break with my first five years.

Two weeks later, we arrived in New York Harbor. We were kept aboard the day of our arrival because it was July 4 and no one was working in the port. On the dock, on July 5, 1926, the man who told me that he was my father had a black spade beard, and he wore a modern suit and not a black caftan. The prescribed apron with fringes (zizith), which my grandfather in Lemberg and all other Hasidic men I knew wore as a visible outer garment above their shirts, was out of sight; my father wore it invisibly under his shirt and jacket. He had "Americanized" to some degree in the two and a half years that he had already spent in the United States. I do remember what happened next, but I did not understand what I saw. The story was told to me in detail by my mother after my grandmother's death five years later, in 1930, in Baltimore, and was confirmed, ruefully, by my father. I remember that my grandmother, Breindel, leaned down and put her ear to my father's stomach. I do remember becoming puzzled by the gesture when it happened, but I was five, and so much was happening that I did not ask what it meant. My father's mother had put her ear to her somewhat Americanized son's stomach and told him that she was listening for the squeal of pigs. He was, of course, shocked and asked why she was doing this. She answered that after a couple of years in America she wanted to know how much pig he had, inevitably, eaten so far. She was reflecting the absolute consensus in her world in Eastern Europe that the United States was by its very nature a *treife medineh*—that is, an irreligious country where true Jewish piety was inherently impossible. For her, on that dock in New York, America was not the "last best hope of man." On the contrary, it was a devastatingly difficult challenge to the authentic faith of the Jews.

My life did change radically when we arrived in the United States. In Lubaczow, I had roamed freely in the town square, from a house that opened onto the street. Now suddenly we were on the fourth floor of a tenement on Third Street on the East Side of New York, and I was not allowed to go down to the sidewalk by myself. My mother had little time for me. My father demanded her attention, and she had gone to work in a sweatshop to help make a living. In the new country, I was in the charge of my grandmother.

To learn English, and to begin to find my way in the new country, I was soon enrolled in kindergarten in the nearest public school. I did not understand the teacher because, though the East Side was then peopled almost entirely by Jewish immigrants and their children, she had not a word of Yiddish. The inevitable soon happened. I could not make my teacher understand that I had to go to the toilet, and I was too much in awe of authority to simply walk out of the room. I was sent home to my grandmother in disgrace, and I was so ashamed that I never went back to that school. I have, indeed, always suspected that I studied languages voraciously in high school and college so that I would never again find myself, almost anywhere in the world, in the situation where I could not ask somebody the way to the toilet.

We did not stay on the East Side very long. After a year, it was clear that my father's freelance writing for the Yiddish papers and my mother's work in the sweatshop were not enough to earn a living. We moved to Youngstown, Ohio, where my grandmother's younger brother owned a large dry-cleaning concern. My father, the European rabbi, Hasid, and scholar of the Talmud, tried to make himself over into a presser in a plant that dry-cleaned clothes. Of course, he could not. Within a year we were off to Baltimore, where another uncle was equally prominent in a dry-cleaning business. He helped my father and his younger brother Itche (Isaac), who had come to the United States earlier, in 1919, to open a cleaning store together. This enterprise soon failed. Customers resented that this store was closed on Sabbaths and the Jewish holidays. My father could not be made over; he returned to his true calling, of rabbi and teacher of the classic religious texts.

My Americanization began in Youngstown, where I entered the first grade. By then, I understood enough English to know what was going on in class, but I also knew that I was different. On the East Side of New York in 1926, one could imagine that the world was as Jewish as it had seemed to be in Lubaczow. In Youngstown, I suddenly knew that I was part of a small minority among the Gentiles—but I also discovered that I was in a minority among the Jews. I was no more a stranger in America than any other immigrant child, but my family did not behave like any other Jewish family in town. A number of other relatives worked for Uncle Dave's cleaning plant, and they had all been brought up in Europe in the deepest Orthodoxy, but my father was the only one who refused to work on the Sabbath. The other Jewish children, even those who went to synagogue on Sabbath morning, went off to the

movies that afternoon, usually to see silent pictures in which Tom Mix
played the cowboy hero. I was almost the only Jewish child in
Youngstown who was not permitted to disregard the Sabbath and take
part in this very American activity.

Resolutely, and even bitterly, my father refused to give in to the environment. To the end of his days, he thought of himself as a Galician
Hasid and a rabbi in exile. His sharpest sense of alienation came not
from the American Gentiles, whom he found to be far more decent and
liberal than the Poles, but from American Jews. In their masses, they
were becoming ever less faithful to the tradition, and most of them
were, in any event, unlearned in its literature. He was not going to allow
his household to be swept into this Jewish immigrant culture. My
English soon became American, and I even played with the other Jewish children whom I got to know in the afternoon classes at the synagogue, but I was different—and lonely.

Very early in our stay in Youngstown, my grandmother was introduced
to the rabbi of the local Reform temple. This gentleman, of course, wore
no beard, spoke no Yiddish, did not eat kosher food—that is, he did not
observe the biblical laws that forbade such food as shrimp and lobster—
and was clearly no scholar in the classic Jewish texts, but he was a Ph.D.
or, perhaps, the possessor of an honorary doctorate. In any case, he was
usually addressed not as rabbi but by the supposedly more honorific
title *Doctor*. My grandmother turned to her brother and said, "I understand why this gentleman is more doctor than rabbi, because it is obvious that Judaism is very ill in America. It requires doctors."

Many years later, in the late 1980s, I wrote a book called *The Jews in
America,* in which I maintained that the Jewish experience in the new
land was not a history of unalloyed success. The Jews had, indeed,
risen to very high position in American life; by the 1980s they had
very nearly become the new American elite. But what had happened
to their Judaism? Many had barely inherited any serious links to the
Jewish religion and tradition, and many of those who were not
estranged no longer knew very much about their heritage. The most
telling phrase that I use in that book was the insistent description of
the new land by the European Jewish religious and cultural elite of a
century ago as a *treife medineh*. I know that this book was my homage
to my grandmother.

My sense of otherness lessened a little because we moved to Baltimore in the late fall of 1928. I remember being on the train the night of the presidential election in which Herbert Hoover won over Alfred Smith. The conductors were relaying results as they picked them up at every stop. It was clear to me that Smith had lost the election because he was Roman Catholic and that only Protestants could be considered for the presidency of the United States. Even a child who was not quite eight could reach the obvious conclusion that a Jew would be a much less likely candidate. I had been brought to the new land of freedom and equality, of far greater opportunity than in Poland, but I would have to watch my step. This was not yet the land where I could always be sure that I would not be chased down the street by those who wanted to take their revenge on the killers of Christ.

The east side of Baltimore was, of course, far smaller than the immigrant ghetto in New York, and here we were not the only Orthodox family in the neighborhood. On the contrary, East Baltimore was almost a shtetl, an urban reenactment of a Jewish village in Eastern Europe. It even possessed its own Jewish parochial school. I was enrolled in that school, and I stayed there for the next five years. After the seventh grade, when our school failed to add another class, I went on to public school. The Hebrew Parochial School in Baltimore was in those days a very close approximation of an East European heder, an Orthodox Jewish school for the study of Bible and prayer book, leading to the Talmud. We arrived at eight to say morning prayers together, and we stayed in school until five thirty in the evening. From about nine to three, with a few short breaks, we studied the traditional curriculum of sacred texts in Hebrew. The language of instruction was Yiddish. Shortly after three, a few Gentile women arrived to instruct us. They were public-school teachers who were moonlighting to make a few extra dollars in their after-school hours. They taught us a subject that was called "English" by the administrators of the parochial school.

There were perhaps two hundred students in that school. We were a very small minority among the thousands of Jewish children in Baltimore. There were other minorities. Some Zionist parents sent their children to afternoon classes in which the language of instruction was Hebrew. A few schools in Baltimore belonged to the secularist Jewish labor movement; Yiddish and Yiddish literature were taught in classes that met after the public-school day had ended. But the overwhelming mass of the young received their supplementary Jewish education in Sunday schools or afternoon schools in which the language of instruction was English and the culture was American. The best of these students were very likely to write essays about the "Jewish contribution to America." We, the students in the parochial school, were preparing ourselves to understand the Talmud. We were hoping that we would be able to attain at least the lowest rung of the learning of the great European yeshivot.

When I entered public school in my thirteenth year, I thought that I was finally arriving in America, but I was not. Aside from the teachers, the only connection that I could make with other students was with Jews, and with one Gentile, the son of an Orthodox priest who spoke Greek at home as I spoke Yiddish. I was on loan to America for a few hours each day from a piece of Galicia that had been cast up, despite itself, in Baltimore. This sense of myself was all the more intense because my father woke me at six every morning to study Talmud with him, and he was waiting to continue with the text when I returned from school. My parents never helped me with my homework in public school. They had not been educated in America, and they presumed that their son, who could understand the Talmud, would master the less arduous disciplines (they had no doubt that they were less arduous) of secular learning.

I knew that I was the only Jewish teenager in Baltimore who was receiving such intensive instruction at home. Often I felt put upon and resentful; I wished that my parents were conventional American Jews who would content themselves with pride in the grades I was getting at public school. More often, I knew that I was being given more than most sons get from their fathers. I even began to understand that he was teaching me Talmud and Hasidic literature because he hoped that I would do what he could not do. He, the Yiddish-speaking immigrant rabbi of a small Baltimore synagogue, could not succeed in making America respect classic Jewish learning. He wanted me to grow up to tell the Jewish immigrants of America that the dream of most of the immigrants—of material success—was an illusion, even for those who did succeed. Even if they had millions, Jews who were bereft of Jewish learning were poor. I was to speak for him in the world that he could not enter.

So long as I lived at home, through high school and college at Johns Hopkins, my father devoted enormous energy to teaching me something of his great learning and much of his passion. His congregants saw only the fiercely Orthodox side of his character and commitment. I knew better than anyone that he was not a conventional Orthodox rabbi and Hasid. He had been born into that faith, and he remained fiercely committed to it, but he had re-earned his faith in serious encounters with the best minds among the heretics. Behind the many volumes of rabbinic literature in his library, he kept translations into Hebrew or Yiddish of Spinoza, Marx, and Darwin, along with Tolstoy, Dostoyevsky, and even Balzac. He argued fiercely against these godless writers, but he respected them. He was at one with the rabbis of the Talmud eighteen centuries earlier, who had known, and argued against, the "wisdom of the Greeks." In college, I encountered some other Jews who were not caught up in the quest for success. One of my classmates went off to fight in the Spanish Civil War; another was already a poet. A teacher in his early thirties was an authority on Greek literature. I was not the only student at college who wanted to become a scholar or a writer, with no hope of becoming rich, but part of me remained very alone. Not one of them, and almost no one else among my classmates, knew the Jewish classics. I was almost as lonely as I had been in Youngstown when I was the only child in town who did not go to the movies on Sabbath afternoon.

A child does not have to be told that his parents have little. One winter—I must have been nine or ten—I chose not to tell my mother that there were holes in my shoes, because I knew that she did not have the money to send me to the cobbler. I found some matchbox covers and put them over the holes. This improvisation did not keep my feet dry, but I persisted straight through that winter in keeping quiet about my discomfort. I did not want to make my mother cry.

The economic situation did not really get much better when my father left the cleaning business after a year and turned to his rabbinic training as the source of a living for the family. He became the rabbi of one of the small synagogues not too far from where we lived in the center of the Jewish ghetto, but the laity paid him, as best I can remember, a salary of eleven dollars a week, once every third or fourth week. I think that Uncle Max helped a little, and I know that Mr. Linsk, who owned the grocery store across the street, let us run up a bill to the unbelievable amount of seven hundred dollars until, finally, my parents found a way of paying it off. The greatest help for many years was my father's younger brother, whom I always called Uncle Itche. He remained a bachelor much longer than he should have, living with us while he worked at various jobs. Uncle Itche contributed most of what he earned to the upkeep of our family.

It was a weekly struggle for my parents to find a way to buy a chicken, and make the chicken soup derived from it, for the Sabbath. On Friday night we chanted the prescribed songs asserting that Sabbath was the day of delight, but my mother often looked grim with stress and exhaustion and my father was visibly angry—and yet, they always found room at their table for strangers who had less than they did.

Somehow, my father managed to keep adding to his library of holy books, and the Sabbaths and holidays were always celebrated with some festiveness. Years later, probably in college, I read Chekhov's play *The Cherry Orchard*, about a family of Russian aristocrats who had lost their money. They continued to live in their orchard and to behave according to the manners of their class. I was shaken when I read Chekhov. He could have written the play in Yiddish about my family.

During my childhood in Baltimore, my parents told me stories without number about my ancestors, and the world that I had missed. When I was old enough to understand, I was given an explanation of why my father, my grandparents' eldest son, appeared on official documents under the hyphenated name Fisch-Herzberg, with the addition that he was an illegitimate child acknowledged by his father. The notion that my grandparents could be guilty of such conduct was totally beyond belief, so I wanted to know why my father was listed as a "bastard." The answer was that my grandparents had, of course, been married in a very Orthodox religious ceremony but had been denied a civil marriage license. The Austrian government had decided to "civilize" the Jews of Galicia (the province of southeastern Poland that the Austrians controlled) by making it a precondition for a marriage license that the groom prove that he had attended at least four years of public school. The vast majority of the pious families in Galicia defied the order; they would not allow their children to be affected by the slightest breath of heresy. For a number of years, until the "evil decrees" were repealed, Hasidic marriages were not registered by the state. Children were given birth certificates in the name of both parents, with the unequivocal addition "bastard recognized by his father."

Very early in my life, I stopped believing in the myth that Jewish families and communities lived in stability. There had been too many pogroms, and too many expulsions, for many families to have remained in the same place generation after generation. This was also true of my own family. My great-great-grandfather had not been a Galician Jew, and he was not even a Herzberg. He had come as a child, together with a younger brother, from Russia. At that time, in the 1830s, the government of the czar was drafting twelve-year-old children, and especially Jewish children, into the army for a term of enlistment of twenty-five years. The undisguised purpose was conversion: to take young boys away from their parents and put them into an environment that was dominated by the Russian Orthodox church. The parents of these two boys—the family name was Frischerman—decided to avoid this tragedy by sneaking their sons across the border into Galicia, where no such draconian laws existed. On a very dark night, they were taken to an unguarded field at the border and pointed in the direction of the first village on the other side. The boys were instructed to ask the first Jew they met for an aunt who lived in a nearby town, where her husband was the rabbi. His family name was Herzberg, and so that worthy suddenly acquired two additional "sons." Through bribery, the young boys were given documents that established that they had been born in Galicia and that they were children of the uncle to whom they had been sent. Many years later, my father gave me a book in Hebrew about the Frischerman family; there is no mention of two children who were smuggled across the border. Nevertheless, I believe the story. Why would anyone in that generation or the next, in largely anti-Semitic Eastern Europe, want to tell the story in print, even in Hebrew, of two young boys who had suddenly appeared as additional children of a Galician rabbi? There can only be the evidence of a tale handed down in our family.

I never went to a Jewish camp, and my family never spent a single day on vacation in the Borscht Belt of the Catskills. My father kept me busy at home all summer studying the Talmud. Occasionally, when we were studying a particularly brilliant passage by one of the commentators on the Talmud who was an ancestor, my father would look at me. I knew the question that was on his mind: would his eldest son ever write a single incisive, and startling, line in rabbinic Hebrew that would suggest that he really was a descendant of these originals?

As I got older, I learned that these ancestors were not merely names. I began to know what they represented, what they had taught. In the eighteenth century, when the American colonists were fighting their war against the British, an ancestor of my father's mother had been a principal figure in the controversy between the Hasidim and the Misnagdim that tore apart the Jews of Eastern Europe. Through my great-grandmother Zelda (the mother of my father's mother), a formidable matriarch who was still alive in her nineties in Dinov, Galicia, when I was growing up in Baltimore, I was a descendant of the founder of the dynasty of Hasidic rebbes who had lived in Dinov since the middle years of the nineteenth century. The first rebbe, Zvi Elimelech, had insisted that the *tzaddik*, the Hasidic leader, had supernatural qualities and that the adherents of the *tzaddik* were connected to God through the agency of their righteous leader. The uncle of the first rebbe in Dinov, Elimelech of Lizhansk, had been a disciple of Dov Ber of Mezritsch, the immediate heir of the founder of the Hasidic movement, the Baal Shem Tov. Elimelech of Lizhansk had brought the new teaching of Hasidism, that God should be encountered by finding holiness in the flow of everyday life, to southern Poland. The many stories about the austerity of his personal life had been repeated for generations, and they kept being retold in my family. The regimen of conduct that he had prescribed, a short document of two or three pages that was known as the Tsetel Koton, a list of instructions on how to live a moral and pious life, had become standard teaching among the Hasidim.

Because such families had been intermarrying with each other for many generations, there was hardly a Hasidic or rabbinic authority of the past few centuries who was not some kind of relative. When I was young, I had trouble sorting out the genealogical complexities, but it was drummed into me that I had been born into *yichus*, into an elite that expected its members to possess serious learning in the classic Jewish texts and to maintain and defend the religious and moral norms that it had inherited from its forebears. But I was growing up in a new land, in America and not in Poland. I had even begun to doubt some of the absolutes that undergirded the writings and lives of my ancestors. In the Tsetel Koton of Elimelech of Lizhansk, he had been particularly obsessed by fear of women, and he had recommended that men keep their minds and hearts pure for the service of God by limiting their connection to women to the very minimum necessary for procreation. I even knew that my ancestor had not really added any exaggerations of his own to the image of the female as the source of temptation, because, in the twelfth century, Maimonides had ruled that a woman who was seen outside her house more than once a month was suspect of loose conduct.

Zvi Elimelech of Dinov intrigued me because he had declared war against Moses Schreiber, the rabbi of Bratislava, who had an equally large, and equally deserved, reputation as an uncompromising defender of the faith. Schreiber lived in a region where Jews, too, tended geese and stuffed them to force them to produce large livers out of which foie gras could be made. Schreiber had permitted the practice, but my ancestor was in vehement opposition. I was pleased to find that one of the arguments advanced by Zvi Elimelech of Dinov was that geese should be protected from the pain that they suffered when penned in such fashion that they could barely move, but I was much less comfortable with Zvi Elimelech's repeated insistence, elsewhere in his teachings, that married women who did not shave off all the hair on their heads and cover their bare skulls with a cloth cap were behaving with unforgivable lasciviousness. This could not be true, not in America and in the twentieth century. My mother, and equally pious Jewish women such as the wife of Rabbi Jacob Ruderman, the head of the ultra-Orthodox school of Talmud, the Ner Israel Yeshivah, in Baltimore, had given up this practice. I admired the fierceness of my ancestors, and I was enthralled by the brilliance of their arguments and the soaring passion of their rhetoric, but I could not enlist in many of their battles.

Living by the terms of the tradition was taken for granted in our home. My father never asked me whether I believed in God, and neither did my mother. He often wanted to know whether I had said my morning prayers, so that I would then be free to study Talmud with him before I went to school. When this study session was nearing the end, my mother would ask whether I was ready to wash my hands—that is, to perform the required ritual of purification so that I could eat breakfast. My sharpest memory of my grandmother is of the day I came back from school and suggested that I wanted to go out with my playmates and become "American" like them. I wanted to join them in walking away with an apple or two from the fruit stand on the corner, while one of us distracted the owner of this pushcart. My grandmother replied, with ice in her voice, "A Jew doesn't do such things."

I knew that I had to learn the ways of the new land, but the signals were ambiguous.

The push to assimilate came from my Aunt Frieda. She had come to the United States some years before our arrival, and she had worked very hard to lose the stigma of being an immigrant. When she took me to be enrolled in kindergarten, she could not bring herself to register me as Abraham Herzberg, the name that was given me when I was born; she Americanized my first name to Arthur and put a *t* into the second, so that it would be pronounced more easily. Aunt Frieda even tried to complete the process by renaming my parents, but my father resolutely refused to become Herman instead of Zvi Elimelech and my mother was never at peace with Anna instead of Nechama. Neither of them ever adopted the *t* in the middle of the second name. The changes that Aunt Frieda made in our names did stick to me, because they were on the school register. I think of her every time I sign my name.

Aunt Frieda was not an ideologue. She was not engaged in a conscious effort to disappear into the Gentile majority. On the contrary, the kitchen in her home was kosher, and she read a newspaper every day in Yiddish, but she would not speak Yiddish on the street. She wanted to be accepted as an American lady, and she was very upset with me when she thought she heard the lilt of Yiddish in my English. My Aunt Frieda believed that one was allowed to be a Jew in private but not in public. She was not the only adult I knew who wanted to avoid being foreign. Most Jewish immigrants wanted to learn the language of the new country, to make their way in the "golden land." My mother went to classes in English, and my father taught himself to read the Baltimore *Sun*, but this was not the same as Aunt Frieda's passion for Americanism. My parents had learned Polish when they were children, to navigate in a society in which the majority were Poles, but it had never entered their heads that their Jewish tradition was backward and that they were bereft of manners and virtues, which they needed to learn from Polish culture. They had no sense in East Baltimore either that Jewish ways were inferior to American manners.

But I did want to become an "American." My breakout began with a matter of ritual. I knew that good Jews were forbidden to carry anything outside the house on the Sabbath. That meant that even a handkerchief could not be put in your pocket; it could be taken outdoors only if you tied it around some part of your body and made it an article of clothing. Boys under thirteen, who had not yet attained their Bar Mitzvah, were exempt from this rule, but those who were being brought up in pious families started to obey the injunction at a younger age. One Sabbath day I found that I had left the handkerchief in my pocket. It was no sin to have done this inadvertently, but I did not immediately tie the handkerchief around my wrist.

I was studying the Five Books of Moses with the standard commentary by Rashi, in the Hebrew Parochial School, in which I had been enrolled at the age of seven, when we arrived in Baltimore. On Sabbath afternoons I listened in at synagogue when my father taught the Ethics of the Fathers. I had already heard many times the teaching in those texts: be as exact in your obedience to a minor commandment as to a major one, because you do not know what the reward may be for any act of obedience. I would soon learn, even as I resolutely kept the handkerchief in my pocket on Sabbath, that the commandments were ordained by God—so the Talmud taught—in order to purify human character. A bit later, I became aware of a vast literature that had been composed through the centuries to explain the reasons for the commandments that God had given—all 613 of them, according to the commonly accepted count that was derived from a close analysis of the biblical text. All of the authorities agreed that some of the commandments could not be explained. They existed because God wanted to test man's faith. This was how Maimonides had justified the biblical prohibition that Jews may not eat the meat of pigs: this meat was nourishing and good, but Jews could not eat it because God, for reasons of His own, had chosen to forbid it. To obey is to display one's faith in God. Eventually, in college, I heard the Christian equivalent of this dictum by Maimonides. Tertullian, one of the fathers of the Church, knew that the doctrine of the incarnation was philosophically indefensible, but he accepted it as a test of faith: *credo quia absurdum est*. As I went from elementary school to college, it was ever clearer that obeying the seemingly unimportant rituals was the real test of faith—but that was the test that I chose to fail at the age of ten. I long suspected that the handkerchief in my pocket was my revenge for not having been permitted to go to the movies on Saturday afternoon in

Youngstown when I was six. I had wanted to be like everybody else, and my father had not let me.

Five or six years later, in East Baltimore, I was no longer the only child who was being raised in the strict Orthodoxy, but I knew that we were few. The Jews who had moved into the area of "second settlement," in and around Park Heights Avenue, were more successful than those who remained in East Baltimore, and they were much more lax in their observance of religion. Occasionally, for a treat, my Uncle Itche, my father's only brother, would take the family out for a drive on a Sunday afternoon to enjoy the air of the prettier and more spacious neighborhoods. As we drove through Roland Park, where there were wide lawns around each of the houses, the row house in East Baltimore to which we would soon return seemed particularly miserable. I knew that Roland Park was not available, because you had to be rich and Gentile to live in that neighborhood, but Pikesville, where the wealthier "German Jews" lived, was equally lush. On those rides, I made a connection between being well-off in America and not being bound by all the rituals of Judaism. Many years later, I was not surprised at the results of a study that was done in the 1930s, which proved that observant Jews, who did not work on the Sabbath, were markedly less well-off than those who did. The evidence from statistics confirmed what I knew as I looked around me when I was a child.

The Sabbath day when I did not take the handkerchief out of my pocket and tie it around my wrist should have been the moment when I discovered that God would not strike me down with thunderbolts because I did not obey a ritual command. I should have gone on to reenact in my own life the clichéd story of the Jewish immigrant novels: the believing youngster frees himself of the restrictions of the faith and strives for success. Whether he remains poor or becomes rich, the hero of such novels can never free himself of his longing for the simpler world of his childhood, but he remains convinced that he was right to break out of the immigrant ghetto. This did not happen to me because I never identified my own particular part of the ghetto with backwardness. The ritual commandments were confining, to be sure, but the believers whom I knew were not cowering before an angry God. Many of them seemed to me to be people of great courage, and the rituals that they performed gave them joy. I followed after them and remained faithful to almost all the do's and don'ts of the tradition, even as I declared my independence by keeping the handkerchief in my pocket on the Sabbath.

Why did I cling to this secret act of defiance? I did not understand myself at the time, but I think, now, that I was angry with God because of the death of my grandmother. She died when I was nine, and the justice of God became an issue in my life. I had nightmares for at least a year. I remember not saying my daily prayers that year, and I broke several other taboos. I knew that she was a righteous woman who could not possibly have been guilty of any sin that deserved an early death. Such individual sorrows tend to fade as the years go by. Adults accept the pain as part of the human condition, but a child has no such defenses.

The people I remember best from my childhood all insisted on being themselves, even though many of them were defeated in the New World. The most tragic figures were those who knew that they were the last of their kind. Across the street from us there lived one of the important figures of our small community, Moshe Flaum. He was the most powerful layman in the most respected synagogue, Shomrei Mishmeres Hakodesh (the "keepers of the holy watch"). Mr. Flaum was so pious in his orthodoxy that he once threw out of his house a very renowned rabbi from Poland, who had come to raise money for his school of Talmudic studies. The fault that Moshe Flaum found in this distinguished visitor was that he was cutting his nails on Friday in preparation for the Sabbath, and not on Thursday as custom required. The explanation by this holy man—that he had been too busy doing God's work on Thursday, keeping some appointments to muster support for his academy of higher rabbinic learning—did not save the visiting rabbi from Moshe Flaum's wrath. But his anger was not rooted entirely in defense of the minutiae of the faith. Flaum was confronted every day by the drugstore next to his house. It was run by his eldest son. The store was open seven days a week, and it was even rumored that the elder Mr. Flaum owned the real estate and had a share in the profits of the business. Perhaps he thought that God would forgive him if his personal conduct was undeviatingly correct. As a child, I feared him, because he used to yell at the young when we were playful in the synagogue. As a teenager, I was annoyed with him, but soon I felt very sorry for him.

Next door to Moshe Flaum there lived a more obvious tragedy, Hyam Berger. He was a young man in his early forties, at most, but he was dying of consumption, as tuberculosis was called then. As long as he was able, Mr. Berger (that was how his students spoke of him) had taught in the Hebrew Parochial School, but he had to leave the job as his illness got worse. Mr. Berger was nearing the end in the year that I was to become Bar Mitzvah, but he insisted that he would teach me how to chant my part in the service of that Sabbath. He taught in a dark room. The atmosphere was all the more foreboding because he kept suppressing a cough. I did not want him as a teacher, but he was a friend of the family and I had no choice. Every time I went to Mr. Berger's house, I was afraid for myself. Berger was the age of my father. I sat with him, and I knew, at the age of twelve, that even pious parents are mortal. I wish I had not known this so early.

The most striking figures were my own parents. They lived by their own standards. Baltimore was a completely segregated city, and no one objected, in the 1930s. But my parents did. In the early days of the struggle for equality for Blacks, Martin Luther King Jr. asked me why, as the rabbi, then, of a comfortable congregation in Nashville, I cared enough to join the fight. I knew that he expected me to answer with rhetoric about the indivisibility of freedom in America. I told him that the source of my convictions was not in the Constitution of the United States, which had rewarded the slave owners with seats in Congress based on three-fifths of the number of their slaves. I was not even overwhelmed by the ringing opening lines of the Declaration of Independence, which had been written by a slave owner, Thomas Jefferson. "All men are created equal" seemed to mean those whom "enlightened" thinkers would accept as fully human. I told King that I had learned about equality for all from my parents, in the winter of 1931. One Friday we came to synagogue for the evening service to find that an imposing black man wearing a very high yarmulke was there. He introduced himself as Rabbi Matthews and added that he was also a cantor. To prove his self-description, the visitor produced documents from a very respected rabbi in Toronto who attested to the fact that he had officiated at the conversion of Rabbi Matthews, in order to remove any doubt of his Jewishness (Matthews had claimed that he was a Falasha, a Jew from Abyssinia [Ethiopia]), and that further training as cantor

had been imparted to Matthews in Toronto. What all this meant was
that the visitor had the right, in well-established Jewish practice, to
claim the reading desk so that he might lead in the chanting of the service—and, ultimately, claim a donation for his sustenance.

My father looked at the certificate and said very quietly (when he
was quiet, I knew he was at his angriest) that he was the rabbi of this
synagogue and it was his duty and prerogative to decide questions of
religious practice. The congregants refused. They pretended that they
did not believe that the visitor was indeed a Jew, and they barred the
way of this Black cantor to the reading desk. My father put his arm
around this man, whom he had met just ten minutes before, and headed
for the door. He stopped and said, very quietly, that he would never
come through that door again, because they had insulted a human
being made in the image of God. We said prayers at home that Sabbath. My father had thrown his job away over a principle, and he did
not find another for many months. I expected my mother to berate him,
but she did not say one word, that day or later.

Not long after this incident in synagogue, a calamity befell my family. A young man began to hang around the synagogue to which my
father had moved, and he soon became a frequent visitor to our house.
He was single—so he said—and my parents thought about an unmarried cousin in Youngstown. They brought the two together, and the
couple soon married. Within a year or so, they became the parents of a
son. Suddenly, a woman appeared and then another, each with proof
that this man was married to her. He was tried and convicted of bigamy,
and he was sentenced to jail in Baltimore. My parents were, of course,
upset and ashamed that they had brought this mess to the wider family,
but they visited the bigamist in jail and brought him kosher food. A
year or so later, when he got out of jail, he stayed some days with us. He
was sent on his way with a few dollars that my parents somehow found
to give him.

On my father's table, a book was always open. Whatever he did, even
when he talked with members of his family, he seemed to be on loan
from learning. But even he was not the most striking example of devotion to study whom I knew as a child. Right before my Bar Mitzvah, my
father took me to be examined by a Talmudist who lived in the neighborhood, Rabbi Michael Forschlager. I was proud of the amount of

Talmud that I had already studied, but the examination did not go well. By his elevated standards, I was not a child prodigy of Talmudic learning. My father tried to recoup the situation by telling Rabbi Forschlager that I was a good student in "English"—that is, in the secular school. The rabbi responded with good-humored scorn, "What is the big deal about being a good student in 'English'? In the United States the cat chases the rat in English."

This was not my last visit to Rabbi Forschlager. Even though I feared his questions, I knew that his being willing to spend some time with me was a rare privilege. He lived a few blocks away in a row house, like ours. Every morning before dawn, he would get on a trolley and travel uptown to one of the elegant synagogues, where he taught Talmud every weekday before the morning service. He eked out a living, but his real life was in what he did the rest of the day. The rabbi almost never left a small room on the second floor. The walls were lined with holy books, leaving little space for a small table and a chair. Rabbi Forschlager sat there, writing in an almost illegible hand a massive commentary on the Talmud. By the time he died in his early eighties, the rabbi had written over twenty thousand pages, but he had not completed the task. When his wife had something important to say to her husband, she would often communicate through my father, asking him to slip her complaints into their discussions of the Talmud. As I watched them, I thought of the legends that I was learning about the ancient rabbis who had gone into caves to study God's word with that devotion. Later, in the course in medieval history in high school, I heard about secluded monasteries. I knew that these stories were not fables because a small man with a gray-white beard was spending his life in such a cave, in my own neighborhood.

I heard about Don Quixote when we read Cervantes in high school, but he was not new to me. I had already met many such figures, who got back on their horses after they had been thrown by windmills. My father was one. He kept picking up his lance to defend his Lady Dulcinea, the culture of a rabbinic hildago from Eastern Europe. Even as a child of ten, I knew that his attempt, in 1931, to start a Yiddish weekly in Baltimore, which would be a proponent of the Orthodox faith, was bound to fail. I saw around me that only the immigrants—and not their children—still read Yiddish, and that their numbers were decreasing. I had seen that when Yiddish theater came to Baltimore, the audience was pathetically small. But my father persisted. He somehow persuaded a printer to take a chance with him. After many months of preparation, they published the first issue of the paper, but there was never a second. The printer would extend no more credit. The masses had not risen up to buy subscriptions, and the advertisers preferred to put their notices in the Baltimore *Jewish Times*, the local weekly in English. This failure was upsetting, but my father was soon planning the creation of a small Hasidic synagogue. After several false starts, he actually succeeded, and he remained the rabbi and leader of this congregation until his death in 1971. More than thirty years later, the synagogue is still universally known as "Herzberg's schul." They know that Don Quixote, in any language, is irreplaceable—and so they continue to repeat what they learned from listening to him and from the models of behavior that they remember from watching him.

We were never alone for a meal, not even for breakfast. The police in East Baltimore soon knew that if they found a Jew wandering in the street, looking for help, he was to be brought to our house. I often resented this open house, even after I had learned in the Bible that Abraham's greatest virtue was his hospitality to strangers. I sometimes wanted a more "American" home in which parents and siblings sat together at meals and enjoyed a family life of their own. I did receive an extraordinary amount of individual attention from my father, but I was ambivalent about this blessing. My father did not regard the education that I was getting in the Hebrew Parochial School as adequate. When I was ten or eleven, he began to study Talmud with me for an hour or so early in the morning, before I went to school, and all day, every day, during the summer vacation from public school, and he continued doing that through my high school and college years. My father insisted that I learn classic Hebrew texts by his standards. One day he was waiting for me to return from school in the afternoon to complete a lesson with him, but I had tarried on the ball field, hoping to be chosen by the other children as a player in a game of softball. I was not athletic, and neither side would have me on its team, but I came home a half hour late. My father, who somehow knew what had happened, was waiting for me at the door. With considerable heat, he told me that I was on the way to growing up to be an "American bum." I would have been even worse off if I had succeeded in joining the game, because I would have come home much later, to face greater anger.

This was, of course, not the only confrontation between my father and me. In junior high school, I tried another approach to becoming "American": I became a football fan. I read the sports pages avidly and began to remember the running and passing statistics of the great college players. One Friday I had even figured out the way to get to the football field where the University of Maryland would be playing one of its traditional opponents. The game was being held on Saturday, the Jewish Sabbath, but it would take place in the afternoon after synagogue and one of my classmates had offered to walk the two miles to the stadium with me and to carry my ticket. Having solved all the ritual problems, I approached my parents, triumphantly, and told them that I was going to the game. They quickly forbade it, repeating the formula that I had first heard several years before from my grandmother, when I had wanted to make off with an apple from a pushcart: "A Jew doesn't do such things." My father added that Sabbath afternoons should be spent in studying sacred texts or, if I insisted, in relaxing with a serious book, but not at a ball game.

But the Sabbath was not simply a set of restrictions. On the way home from synagogue, we always stopped at the homes of two or three friends, where we were served some food to help make the day enjoyable. This walk home often consumed several hours. We did not arrive for lunch until two or so in the afternoon, and my mother complained that lunch had been ruined in the oven. There were very few children on the Sabbath walk, for all of the adults were half a generation older than my father. The conversation very often consisted of stories that the walkers remembered about great Hasidic masters, some of whom they had known in their youth in Europe. On Sunday I read accounts about the glories of Notre Dame's backfield, whom the sportswriters had named the Four Horsemen of the Apocalypse, but I knew as I read about these American idols that I had an insignificant share in them. The heroes that I heard about on the Sabbath walk were mine. I wanted to be like everybody else, but I was different.

As they have told in countless memoirs, many of my contemporaries found the immigrant ghetto confining, and they hastened to escape into the wider world of American culture. My own experience was the opposite. I refused to accept the notion that my father and his friends were narrow and benighted and that culture was to be found elsewhere. I could not believe that the Talmud, the kabbalistic books, and the writings of the Hasidim were of little worth compared to the *Iliad* and the *Odyssey,* or to Dante's *Inferno.* I simply could not understand why knowing Hebrew and Aramaic was inferior to being able to read Greek and Latin. Several of my high school teachers could quote freely from several Western literatures, but I knew that this was no greater feat than being at home with the thousands of volumes of commentaries on the Talmud. Even as I became eclectic in the observance of some of the rituals, I did not use my "heresy" as the excuse to prefer the majority culture to my own. My allegiance shifted from undeviating obedience to every jot and tittle of the Law to a profound respect for the learning, and the moral character, of many of the people with whom I went to synagogue.

All of the clashing themes of my childhood came together when my Bar Mitzvah was celebrated in the late spring of 1934. Because I had skipped two grades in elementary school, I was, by that point, a ninth grader, and I had made friends with some older boys from uptown who were classmates. Several came to the party, but they seemed out of place. In the middle of the evening, the parents of one of these boys came to pick up their son to take him home. They had been attending a wedding. The boy's mother wore an evening gown, and his father was dressed in a tuxedo. When they arrived, I was in the middle of a long disquisition in Yiddish—it took an hour and a quarter—to demonstrate how much Talmud I had been taught. I stopped talking for a moment, and I envied my friend his "American" parents.

The tension between my two worlds had been evident at the very beginning of the celebration of my Bar Mitzvah. The fundamental meaning of the ritual is that at thirteen a Jewish boy becomes responsible as an adult to observe all of the prescribed rituals of the tradition, especially the commandment of daily prayer. To the end of his days, the now-adult Jewish male is enjoined to don the tefillin—two small boxes that contain four passages from the Bible, headed by the Shema: Hear, O Israel, the Lord Thy God, the Lord is One. The tefillin are worn on the head and on the left arm near the heart every weekday morning to symbolize that, with mind and heart, the worshiper is devoted to God. On the weekday morning that I actually turned thirteen (the Sabbath observation was two days later), when I was supposed to begin to put on the tefillin, my father did not merely take me to the early service at the synagogue. He did with me what his father had done with him. He first took me to the *mikveh*, the ritual bath, to purify my body. This ritual was all the more important because I was going to start my daily prayers with no ordinary set of tefillin. My mother's father in Lemberg had arranged that the scribe of the rebbe of Belz would write the Biblical passages on parchment for my tefillin. They had arrived in time, and I knew that they were very special.

I still put on these tefillin to say my daily prayers. They have become even more special and much holier through the years because they are the only tangible link that I have with my grandfather; he was murdered, together with all of my mother's siblings and their families, during the Holocaust. I had accepted that I needed to be purified in the *mikveh* on the morning when I first used these tefillin, but there was no way of my getting to school on time that day. I needed to write an excuse for my lateness for my mother to sign, but how do you explain such ritual to the truant officer of a high school in Baltimore in 1934? I composed a note in which my mother pretended that I had needed to keep a doctor's appointment.

A few days later, the Bar Mitzvah was formally celebrated on the first Sabbath when I could share in the conduct of the service as an adult. Our small synagogue was crowded, not only with family and friends from Baltimore but also with visitors from New York. In those days, no major hereditary Hasidic rebbe had yet moved to the United States. That was to happen in the next decade, after the Second World War began, when Jewish life was no longer possible in Eastern and Central Europe. In 1934, the Hasidic rebbes in the United States were, without exception, cousins or brothers of the leaders in Europe—that is, princes and dukes, but not kings or grand dukes. Most of these figures lived in New York, but they would regularly visit in other major cities to bond with their adherents and, not incidentally, to be helped with donations. Their favorite stopping point had become Baltimore because they could stay with my parents, with no doubt that my mother was absolutely exacting in her adherence to the rules of keeping kosher, and they knew that they had much to learn from my father, whose memory of Hasidic lore was unparalleled.

For the Sabbath of my Bar Mitzvah, a number of these New York rebbes came to Baltimore. One of them had a beautiful voice, and he was a composer of new melodies for various parts of the service. He was then a young man of about forty, short and with a long, very black beard. For the Sabbath he dressed in a shining, long black coat made of silk, and his hat was fur; this was the "uniform" of a Hasidic rebbe. His chanting at the reading desk, to grace my Bar Mitzvah, was a rare honor. It was even rarer that he and his colleagues from New York had come to listen to me expound the Talmud. My father had written me two texts, one for that Sabbath morning and another for the party the next day. He had made them sufficiently uncomplicated so that I understood them both, and I had even been able to contribute a bit to each. It took some weeks to memorize both talks, but I did. On Sabbath morning I held forth for about half an hour, but the major interest that day was the visiting cantor and the food after the service.

On Sunday, the party took place in a hall that was across the street from the home of the acknowledged leader of the Orthodox community in Baltimore, the aged Rabbi Chaim Nachman Schwartz. He was very ill. The party for my Bar Mitzvah was given as near to his home as possible, so that he might be able to attend, at least for a short while. Rabbi Schwartz was too weak to come that day, and so, before the party began, I went to his house and recited, at his bedside, the essence of the talk that I had memorized for that evening. He was very pleased. The scene was full of symbolism, because I knew about the story at the end of the Book of Genesis, of Joseph bringing his sons to be blessed by his father, Jacob, on his deathbed. But I was soon back to reality, to the gray inevitabilities of attaining the age of Bar Mitzvah in the midst of poverty. Many of the presents that were given me at the party were money, in small envelopes. By the end of the evening, my pockets were stuffed, and I thought that I was rich. When we got home, I handed the money to my mother. I was soon told that I had been given enough in presents to pay for the party, and for the new suit and shoes that my parents had bought for me, on credit. I could keep only the couple of dozen rabbinic texts that had been inscribed to me by various friends. I still have them. Sometimes I look at these inscriptions, in rabbinic Hebrew, and I wonder whether those who gave me the volumes would be pleased that I still study them, or whether they would be upset if they knew that, even as a child of thirteen, I was not a literal believer.

My father already knew. The last act of the drama of my Bar Mitz-vah, which had begun with my being taken to the *mikveh*, took place on the morning after the party. I was both too elated and too exhausted to go to school that Monday, so I was allowed to sleep late. After I had said my prayers in my new tefillin and eaten some breakfast, my father called me into the room where he kept his books. I knew it well, because I slept there on a folding cot. I was accustomed to the sight of all the walls covered with rows of rabbinic texts. He reached behind one of the rows and brought out some volumes that I did not know were there. They were translations into Yiddish of selections from Darwin, Spinoza, and Marx, along with four volumes of the collected essays in Hebrew of the agnostic founder of Cultural Zionism, Asher Ginzberg, who had written under the pseudonym Ahad Ha'am. My father handed me these volumes and said, "I know you are on the way to heresy. Read these books so that you might at least become an intelligent heretic." He then opened a volume of the Talmud: "Now that the party is over, let's go back to studying seriously." I was astonished; I did not know what to make of what he had done. He looked at me very sharply and explained, "I cannot make you believe, but you must know. You must learn the Hebrew texts. They will be your anchor."

The central experience of my generation was fear. With few exceptions, those who were growing up in America in the 1930s, during the Great Depression, were afraid that they would remain poor, and that they would never acquire the power to help themselves. Anti-Semitism was increasing year by year everywhere—in America, and, more violently, in Europe. The sight of refugees like Albert Einstein arriving in the United States did not cheer me up. When I saw him on the newsreels coming down the gangplank from the ship that brought him to New York, I was chilled by the thought that not even he was safe in Germany. I was all the more frightened because I was writing letters to the State Department in those days, acting as the secretary for my Yiddish-speaking parents, to try to get a visa to the United States for my mother's father in Lemberg and for her brothers and sisters. Only one of these letters was ever answered. The State Department informed us in 1938 that the quota for immigrants from Poland was oversubscribed for fifteen years. Perhaps my grandfather would want to reapply at the Consulate in Warsaw in 1951.

I read that letter not in tears but in bitterness. At the age of sixteen, I knew that Jews had to have some power in their own hands, so I became a Zionist. No port in the world was then under Jewish control. Everywhere, officials stood at the shore to say that the quota was oversubscribed; you must go elsewhere, or nowhere, but don't land here. These sights did not lead me to believe, even as an angry and frightened teenager, that there was no goodwill in the world. With one exception, a teacher of German who was an avowed member of the American Nazi Party, my high school teachers took great pains to help me. In the spring of 1937, I was interviewed for a scholarship to Johns Hopkins by Johannes Mattern, a German Gentile who had emigrated some years before because he could not stand the Nazis. I got the scholarship. I knew that Dr. Mattern was predisposed toward the son of a rabbi from East Baltimore because he wanted me to know—as he told me some years later—that some Germans belonged to the liberal tradition of the Revolution of 1848. And yet, I did not feel safe even in America. I seemed to be in the middle of dangers that I thought I had left behind. I had been born in Poland during a pogrom. My birth was never registered, because it was too dangerous to get to the town hall at the Ukrainian end of Lubaczow. Now, in my teens, Father Charles Coughlin was ranting against the Jews on American radio, and no one could stop him. The German-American Bund was holding rallies in Baltimore and New York to incite pogroms. My generation was suffering, even in America, from the continuing, centuries-old disease of powerlessness.

Everywhere the anti-Semites insisted that Jews deserved persecution because of their bad character, which flowed from their inherited tradition. I knew that this charge was false. There were scoundrels among Jews, even among the formally pious, but the Jewish religion continued to be the breeding ground, even in the poor ghetto in East Baltimore, of an extraordinary amount of virtue. Essentially, the battle against anti-Semitism and for an equal place in the world for Jews had to deal with its very root, the contempt for Judaism.

The most hurtful attacks came from many liberals and "advanced" thinkers. They seemed to agree that Judaism was a narrow, unworthy ancient culture—a "fossil," the scholar Arnold Toynbee called it in his *A Study of History*, which began to appear, to great acclaim, in 1934. The next year, as a junior in high school in Baltimore, I was required to take a course in medieval history. I heard in that class that many in Europe had believed that Jews had been taught by the Talmud to poison the wells and that the Black Death had been brought to Europe by "Talmud Jews." I learned that it was firmly believed in the Middle Ages that the Talmud instructed Jews to use the blood of Christians in the ritual of making matzoh, the unleavened Passover bread, and so the manuscripts of the Talmud were often burned by princes on advice of the church. A year later, in the required course in literature, we were studying *The Merchant of Venice*. The "enlightened" teacher made a point of telling us that Shylock's crassness and anger were not innate characteristics of Jews but the unfortunate cast that centuries of obedi- ence to the Talmud had given their character. This seemed to be the judgment of the mainstream of Western culture on Jews and Judaism. The liberals did believe that Jews could become better, but only if they remade themselves and ceased being Jews.

I had no doubt that what I was hearing at school was wrong and hurtful. My problem was, why had "they" been saying such things for so long? The obvious source of this contempt for Judaism was the Chris- tian theological bias, which is deeply ingrained in Western culture. But people of obvious goodwill, like my teachers in high school, were not devout Christians, and yet they shrugged off all of Jewish teaching and experience after the Bible. I tried to persuade my teachers of literature and history that they were wrong. Both said that they had no access to the literature in Hebrew and Aramaic, and they could not accept my obviously partisan account of its worth. In 1936 in Baltimore, there was very little in English that I could give them. The Talmud remained, for them, a vast literature that was locked as a mystery in ancient languages. But I knew that my teachers were wrong. The next year, as a freshman at Johns Hopkins, I felt better. I heard William Foxwell Albright, the greatest Semitic scholar of that generation, and the son of Protestant missionaries in Chile, denounce Toynbee's contempt for medieval and modern Judaism.

This "enlightened" idea—that the Judaism based on the Talmud was intellectually and morally inferior—had even appeared among Jews. Most socialists, many Zionists, and almost all Reform Jews be- lieved, until only a generation ago, that the Jewish spirit was hobbled by the legalisms of the rabbinic tradition. In the course of the years I have met people who are living in Israel because they had to flee from the place of their birth, but who would otherwise have preferred to be entirely alien to their Jewishness. There is a strand in Zionism itself of black hatred of the Jewish past. There are Zionist judgments as negative as those of the anti-Semites on the confined and cringing life of the ghetto, in which no redeeming inner dignity is perceived. Such Zionism expresses a fierce desire finally to achieve for the Jewish nation that which has always eluded the Jewish individual, full assimilation. Jews would at last become a nation among nations, "just like everybody else." Something of this spirit lives on even in the least warlike of Jews who take special pride in the reputation of the arms of Israel. This is not merely a rejoicing in the fact that the State has the force with which to remain alive in an unfriendly region; it is a way of transcending the memories of all the pogroms.

This tension was present in my own youthful Zionism. I was moved by its assertion of Jewish dignity but repelled by the pronounced element of contempt for the Jewish past. My father, the rabbi, tolerated my Zionism only because I was young and did not yet understand the basic meaning of the religion and experience of the Jews. He invoked the ancient response to our tragedies: we are a people once exiled by God as punishment for our sins; the exile will cease when He decides to redeem us; human effort to change the destiny of the Jews, to "bring the messiah," was a sin. But even on activism, I could quote my father against himself. He could say what he wished to denigrate the Zionists (he said that he held to the age-old wisdom that it was best for Jews to hide until the pogrom passed over), but his own stories of heading the Jewish self-defense in Lubaczow in 1919 against the pogrom makers denied his theories. He had gritted his teeth too often when he told of ambushing the pogrom makers on a Friday night, when these marauders were sure that all the Jews would be in synagogue or having Sabbath dinner at home.

Following my father's example of resistance, I could allow myself to think—and say defiantly in a classroom at high school—that Shylock was infinitely superior as a human being both to his daughter and to Antonio. The dignity that I found in Shylock was precisely that he did not cringe, that with unyielding foolhardiness he insisted on his pound of flesh; he would make no "Jewish" compromise with the swells of Venice. I knew that we Jews were weak, that the Nazis were strong, and that we depended on the largely absent goodwill of others. Yet the mammoth protest meetings that were organized in the United States, the boycott of Nazi goods, and the armed resistance in those days to the Arabs in Palestine moved me far more than any reasonings. Herzl had written in his diary during the days of the First Zionist Congress in August 1897 that he had created Jewish politics; he had taught Jews to act in the world as modern men were supposed to behave. Growing up in the 1930s, I could not help but subscribe to that desire.

And yet, on first reading, even in those days of pain and anger, I thought that Herzl was fatuous and silly in insisting at the beginning of his Zionist career that Jewish dueling clubs had to be formed in the Central European universities. I thought, why should Jewish students demand and receive "satisfaction" from anti-Semitic dueling societies on the "field of honor"? But I was transformed in the 1930s into the kind of person who found moral value in hitting back.

But a people can overuse power, especially when it is newly won after many centuries of weakness. In the summer of 1949 I became fearful of what having power might do to Jews, when I rode through Jaffa as a passenger in an Israeli military jeep—and watched the Arabs cringe. In the years since that day, I have thought often, with increasing pain, about the maxim in the Talmud that it is better to be one of the shamed than to belong to those who do the shaming. I have been on both sides: as a child, I ran from other children who wanted to beat me up for being a Jew; as a young adult, I toured the conquered and dispirited Arab areas of the new state of Israel. I spent much of my time that summer visiting the camps that had been set up for tens of thousands who were arriving every day to the new state of Israel. I saw hope, but the defeated Arab faces haunted me. I was uneasy at the sight of the swagger of some of Israel's soldiers. But, in the late 1930s, and through the years of the Second World War, being Jewish meant to not have power and to feel that you were under unrelenting attack.

Even in those bad days, in the mid-1930s, I was becoming a patriot, and not because I was imagining an ideal America that did not exist. I knew that many careers were closed to Jews and that social anti-Semitism was taken for granted. I had even been the target of some physical abuse as a child. The path from my home in East Baltimore to the Hebrew Parochial School led past Wolfe Street. At that corner the children of the Catholic parochial school waited to call me names and sometimes to chase me. This lasted only a few months, until the principal of the Catholic school became aware of what was happening and put a stop to it. Nevertheless, these experiences did not define my feelings about the American majority. I firmly believed—I knew—that America was different. In my teens, I was reading the letters, full of fear and foreboding, that my grandfather and my uncles and aunts were sending. The gauntlet that I ran at the corner of Wolfe Street and East Baltimore Street was a pleasant outing in comparison to what we were being told about the rocks that were thrown every day in Lemberg at Jews in Hasidic garb. In the Yiddish press, I saw repeated tales of beatings of Jewish university students in Poland who refused to sit on the benches for "Jews only." And in Germany, the Nazis were burning synagogues and murdering Jews. Our lot in America, even in bad times, was not the worst. American Jew-haters were raucous, but they were less threatening than Jew-haters in Poland or Germany. I had hope.

But I was plagued by the pervasive disrespect for Judaism. I attributed this attitude entirely to the influence of Christianity (I would change my mind twenty years later, when I studied the anti-Semitism of some of the gods of the Enlightenment), and so I kept thinking about the faith that pronounced Judaism to be a terrible error. I had learned very little about the religion of the vast majority of Americans as a student in the Hebrew Parochial School. On the contrary, the calendar of the school was consciously arranged to exclude Christian influence. There were classes on the twenty-fifth of December and all of the week that followed. The school would not compromise with the holidays at the end of December by regarding these days as expressions of a secularized, civic culture in which Jews could share. We were taught to know that this was a Christian festival and that we were to keep every possible distance from it. My bearings changed when I entered public school in the eighth grade. When December came in that year of Depression (it was 1932), the principal announced a "Christmas basket" campaign to collect food to give to the needy. I was moved by this concern, but I was soon in a dilemma. My teacher chose me to represent my class in the committee that organized the effort. I went to my father and asked him whether I could work at collecting and delivering Christmas baskets. He answered, "How can you not help poor people?" He then sat me down and talked very seriously, even solemnly, about

Christianity. He wanted me to know, and to remember, that the central affirmation of Christianity was not that the Jews were Christ killers. It was about the life and death of Jesus as one with the poor and the outcasts.

This talk with my father, the rabbi, made me think about the central story of Christianity, the crucifixion of Jesus. He chose this terrible and degrading death to say to all the weak of mankind that they are not alone. Therefore, ordinary Christian believers gave Christmas baskets to the poor. More august Christians knew that Jesus had commanded them to be humble. Every year before Easter, I saw pictures in the newspapers of the Pope washing the feet of twelve poor people. Yet, I could not believe that the Christians meant it. It was contradicted by what was happening to Jews—and not only to Jews—when I was growing up. Some leaders of Christianity, both in the United States and abroad, were standing against the Nazis, but most were silent, and some were open anti-Semites. The Christians whom I knew were mostly complacent racists. Baltimore in the 1930s was a completely segregated city, with separate and very inferior schools for Black children. The churches did not seem to care. In fact, Christianity, too, was segregated, in White and Black churches. But the scene was not totally dismal. At home in Baltimore, a few of the preachers were Christian Socialists; they believed in the Social Gospel, and they defended the workers against the capitalists. In England, Archbishop William Temple denounced what the Nazis were doing to Jews with unmistakable Christian passion. I was sustained by such Christians, but they were in the minority.

The louder voices were telling me that Jews had been condemned to suffering because they had refused to accept the religion of the Christians. Their troubles were part of the divine plan. Such people often added that Christianity was the religion of love; it was superior to Judaism, which they depicted as the religion of the angry God of the Old Testament who demanded "an eye for an eye." I could not understand how the God of love could condemn the Jews to interminable centuries of suffering because of their supposed lack of faith in Him. I was even more upset by the pretension of some Christian believers that they could affirm their faith in Christ's love of all men by hating Jews. My father, the rabbi, a lineal heir of the Pharisees who had been defamed by the Christians for many centuries, had taught me as a child of twelve that all the poor were my concern. What right had any Christian to stand aside, in good conscience, while Jews were beaten or murdered and Blacks were demeaned or lynched?

My Jewish reaction to Christianity was, I soon learned, not new. In the Middle Ages Jews had, occasionally, been forced into formal religious debates with Christians. Usually, the rabbis on the Jewish side did not dare show any disrespect for the doctrine of the incarnation, or question the meaning of the trinity, lest they be charged with blasphemy. In the most famous of these debates, which took place in 1263, in Barcelona, Rabbi Moses ben Nachman had built his defense against the demand that the Jews convert by asking Christians to look at the world as it is: Christianity had announced that it was bringing peace and new life to the world, but there is no peace; the Christians have been instigators of wars of religion. The Christian debaters gave two answers: peace means the inner serenity that each individual believer can attain in his own life; the peace of society as a whole would, indeed, come at the end of days, when the Messiah would return. Rabbi Moses ben Nachman had, of course, implied that Christian peace did not include Jews. I had reached the same conclusion when I was very young. When I read an account of the debate in Barcelona, I felt less alone. I knew that I stood where my ancestors had stood: they, too, had wanted Christianity to live up to its own ideals. I soon found that this thought was shared by the most eminent of contemporary dramatists, George Bernard Shaw. He was quoted in an English literature class, at college: "The trouble with Christianity is that it hasn't been tried yet." This remark was so telling that I even started to wonder that day whether this was not true of Judaism as well.

My problems with Christianity were all the more intense because the mid-1930s was a time of increasing Jewish interest in the figure of Jesus and his disciples. One of the giants of Yiddish literature, Sholem Asch, published two novels, one about Jesus and the other about Mary. A distinguished novelist in modern Hebrew, A. A. Kabak, wrote his own novel about Jesus. Joseph Klausner, a professor at the Hebrew University in Jerusalem and a leading Zionist ideologue, first published a study in 1920 of the life of Jesus, to which he added a book about the time after the crucifixion, until St. Paul appeared and defined the new religion.

I read these works as they appeared in the United States. At the time, I could not understand why the earliest history of Christianity had suddenly become an important concern for Jewish writers and scholars. I thought, then, as did many others, that some Jews were flirting with Jesus in the hope that lessening the distance between Judaism and Christianity would help protect them against the anger of the anti-Semites. There was no doubt some truth in this explanation, but it was not the essence of the matter. In the 1930s, those who hated the Jews were trying them for crimes they had not committed. In the 1940s, the Jews of Europe were murdered. The story of Jesus, from his trial to his crucifixion, was being reenacted, but the victim was the Jewish people, and the executioners had once been baptized in Jesus' name. It is no wonder that, as the tragedy began, Asch, Kabak, and Klausner were reaching for the suffering and sometimes defiant Jesus, the Jew. They wanted to take him back from those who were preparing to send his extended family to a new Calvary.

Within the Jewish community, these books about Jesus aroused angry debates. Sholem Asch had been one of the crown jewels of the leading daily in Yiddish, the *Jewish Daily Forward*, where he had been publishing his novels in installments. Abraham Cahan, the famous and crusty editor of the *Forward*, refused to print Asch's novel about Jesus. Cahan accused Asch of preaching conversion to Christianity. A furious debate erupted, in which Asch insisted that he was writing about the Jewish Jesus and Cahan countered that what Jesus may have been in his life on earth was irrelevant. The problem of the Jews was not with Jesus but with Christianity.

The deep anti-Semitism that seemed to suffuse the culture of the West became more and more upsetting as I read and studied some of the leading modern writers in my last years in high school. Jews had been presuming that their enemies were unenlightened Gentiles, who still harbored medieval prejudices, and that enlightened ones were their friends. But only Jews were fleeing Nazi Germany, in large numbers. True, the famous novelist Thomas Mann had left for Switzerland, and other opponents of the regime immigrated to various countries in Europe and to the United States, but the overwhelming bulk of the German intelligentsia did not leave, and many worked willingly, even eagerly, with the Nazi regime. In classes in literature, I came to know, with shock, that some major contemporary writers, such as Ernest Hemingway, Ezra Pound, and T. S. Eliot, were anti-Semites. I was particularly upset when I read the autobiography of a great figure of the previous generation, Henry Adams, who turned venomous whenever he mentioned Jews. I kept returning to their contempt for Jews because I wrote about some of their books in the high school paper. Intellect seemed to be divorced from compassion. I was sure that Jews did not need moral instruction from these great gods of Western culture.

Almost without exception, the Jewish children who were growing up in the 1920s and the 1930s were forced to learn to cope with anti-Semitism. My generation could no more forget anti-Semitism than Blacks could ignore racism. The burden of being the victim could be endured so long as one remained in the "island within," in the protective and supporting circle of the extended family. I could not have been more than eight or nine when I learned to sing the ditty in Yiddish that Jew-haters are drunks and that there are so many of them because drunkenness is pervasive among the Gentiles. I could have believed this chant so long as I was a student at the Hebrew Parochial School, even though I never saw hordes of drunks loitering in the streets and shouting anti-Jewish invective. The moment I entered public school, in the eighth grade, the easy defenses had crumbled, and my problem had gotten worse. No one tried to beat me up, physically, in junior high school and high school, but the assault on Judaism was unrelenting. I was being taught a version of Western culture to which Jews and Judaism were invisible and irrelevant or wrong and obnoxious.

Very early in my life, I learned a bitter lesson about power. The Christians had been sitting in judgment on the religion of the Jews not because the Christian faith was superior, but because they had power and Jews did not. Modern thinkers had long been proclaiming the superiority of secularized Western civilization to all others, because the West had power. The Europeans had become more inventive and more warlike, in recent centuries, than any other human element. But did the wit to make machine guns prove the worth of a civilization? I did not think so.

To be sure, my views did change in the 1960s as Christianity changed. The Roman Catholic church and many of the major Protestant denominations began to abandon their claims to religious and moral superiority over the Jews. Pope John XXIII was clearly a holy man who was working to end the hatred of Jews that had long been built into Catholic liturgy and teaching. But I remain one of those who has not yet erased from his mind and heart the memory of the Holocaust. I honor the Christians, in the many, many thousands, who risked their lives to save Jews, but I cannot forget the large numbers who collaborated with the murderers, and the churches that, with several notable exceptions, remained silent. Jews and Christians yet have miles to go in the quest for an untroubled sleep.

4

On the morning when I left home for my first class at college, my father waited at the door. He told me that he knew I would not be associating with Jews (he meant, of course, people like himself and Rabbi Forschlager) at Johns Hopkins, but he asked me to promise that I would seek out the company of intelligent Gentiles. He seemed to be saying that he had worked hard, together with his friends, to teach me the basics of Jewish learning. At college, he wanted me to find an equally serious circle of Western intellectuals.

I looked for such company. The obvious first stop in the charged year, 1937, was in the political circles on campus. In the late 1930s, there were less than five hundred students in the undergraduate college at Johns Hopkins. We knew the professors, and they knew us. Even the few large lecture courses were divided, at least once a week, into discussion sessions of less than thirty. This small community was, nonetheless, split along the fault lines of the major political and ideological quarrels of the time. Even before the Second World War broke out in September 1939, there was little doubt anywhere that, without the Americans, Hitler could not be contained. No one on campus was an avowed Nazi or Fascist, but there were some isolationists who

wanted to keep America out of the quarrels of Europe. Whether intended or not, the isolationists were announcing that they cared little
about the fate of the Jews of Europe, the people who were most endangered by the Nazis. I could not join those who seemed not to care
about my relatives.

College is not the same for everybody. I was sixteen and I lived at
home, commuting by trolley car every day, so I never knew the social
life on campus. I was also under great pressure to do well as a student,
because the scholarship, without which I could not have stayed in
school, would be continued only if I maintained a very high grade average. The only diversion that was possible was an occasional flier into
politics, not so much campus politics as taking stands on the larger
issues of the world. This was especially attractive because it took me out
of the ghetto in which I had been raised and into the larger world. I was
very soon a supporter of the republican side in the Spanish Civil War,
and I even stood on street corners collecting money for the cause. I
joined a Zionist group to help fight the restrictions that the British,
who then held the mandate of the League of Nations to rule Palestine,
had put on Jewish immigration into that country. I was an ardent supporter of the popular front because it was working to unite all the forces
that were resisting the Fascists and the Nazis. I was becoming very contemporary and very much involved in the liberal causes of the day, even
as I found one or two contemporaries at college who, like me, were
bringing kosher sandwiches from home. We usually ate lunch together
in the seminar room of William Foxworth Albright, the Orientalist
who headed the program in Semitic studies. I thought that my conduct
was a bit complicated until I discovered that one of my contemporaries
in that small circle, who was at that point even more vehemently
Orthodox in his religious behavior than I, was a deeply convinced and
even passionate follower of Leon Trotsky.

I remember dragging my father one day in the late 1930s to a then
famous play of social protest, *Waiting for Lefty*, by Clifford Odets. The
young dramatist, a child of immigrants, was beating the drums for a
Communist America. As we left the theater, I asked my father how he
liked the play. He replied that this drama was not about love or death,
or faith, or moral choices; it was about money. With a wry smile, he
added that if someone had given the angry hero of the play a check for

five thousand dollars before the curtain rose, there would have been no drama. My father's observation was prophetic. Clifford Odets himself left the revolution for a career as a Hollywood writer, and many young revolutionaries in his audience moved on after the Second World War to succeed in business or the professions. Some of them turned to conservative or even reactionary politics, and others became patrons of liberal causes; a few remained at the barricades.

I became a good bit of a Western intellectual, literate in a half dozen languages, but I was angry with much of what I read. I kept finding not merely contempt for the Jewish tradition but pervasive disregard for its assertions and its particular values. I kept being plagued by the fact that knowledge of classic literature in Latin and Greek was a source of pride, and that understanding Dante and Shakespeare was proof of possessing culture, but that knowing the Talmud in Hebrew and Aramaic was an irrelevance. I simply could not accept these judgments, and not merely because I had spent too many days and months learning the Talmud. I would not bow to the cultural provincialism and the arrogance of the Western tradition.

When I entered college, the popular front was the place for a worried young Jew with no fixed political ideology. I joined the chapter of the American Students Union. Its president that year, his last at college, was Murray Kempton, who would have, later, a remarkable career as journalist and pundit. The members included many, probably even most, of the obviously bright people at school. In their company, I felt that I was carrying out my father's charge to me, but this paradise rejected me. I had little trouble figuring out that the group was the public face of a Communist cell, and I soon knew that I was almost the only person in the American Students Union who was not secretly a member of the Young Communist League. I was urged to join the Communist Party, but I hesitated. My greatest personal concern was the question of religion: if the revolution came to America, would the Communist Party nationalize the church and synagogue buildings and use most of them as centers of antireligious propaganda? Would the clergy be declared to be the purveyors of opiate for the masses—as Karl Marx had defined religion—and would they be persecuted as "enemies of the people"? No one would deny that this had happened in the Soviet Union. Many institutions of Jewish culture in Yiddish existed in the

Communist state, but these were dominated by the Yevsektsia, the Jewish division of the Communist Party. The Jewish religion, the Hebrew
language, and Zionism were all attacked and defamed, in Yiddish, by
these servants of the Communist Party. The news had reached the
United States that the few rabbis who had survived the purges and mass
arrests were finding jobs that would allow them to observe the Sabbath
and holidays; the rabbi in Moscow was a night watchman. I could
imagine, with fear, that if the revolution came to America, this would
happen to my parents. I told the recruiter of the Young Communist
League that he was asking me to assent to parricide. After this chat, I
knew that I was an outsider in the American Students Union, and I
dropped out.

This early break did not end my quarrel with the Communists. Some
of them were very good students, who were at or near the top of the
class. We were together in various courses, and we kept rubbing up
against each other because we were in intense competition to hold on to
free tuition scholarships. These were granted year by year on the basis
of grades. The half-dozen serious competitors often lunched together,
and we usually studied together for exams, because we would not let
each other out of sight. No one could be allowed to acquire an edge by
saying something original in a final examination that he had not somehow, by ill luck or persuasion, told the others. At these close quarters,
the political debate inevitably continued.

My freshman year coincided with the treason trials in the Soviet
Union. Joseph Stalin accused some of the oldest Communist leaders,
among the very founders of the Revolution, and many of the generals of
the army, including the chief of staff, Marshal Tukhashevski, of being
in league with the Nazis and of having conspired to overthrow the
Communist regime. In show trials, these leaders "confessed" to their
crimes, and they were soon shot. Many tens of thousands were sent to
prison in Siberia. These charges were clearly absurd. Jews had special
reason to know that the charges were lies, because Jan Gamarnik, one
of the generals who was accused and executed, was a brother-in-law of
the famous Hebrew poet Haim Nachman Bialik. A Jewish military
man of such family connections might indeed be soft on Zionism, but
it was inconceivable that he had joined a conspiracy to turn the Soviet
Union over to allies of Adolf Hitler.

Stalin's treason trials were denounced by Leon Trotsky, from his exile in Mexico, and the worldwide disbelief spread quickly among Socialists and liberals who were neither Stalinists nor Trotskyites. The leading figure among the doubters in the United States was the famous philosopher John Dewey. He was the chairman of a committee in the United States that held hearings to disprove Stalin's charges. At the age of seventeen, I did not know enough about the history of the Soviet Union to debate this issue with my Communist contemporaries, but the Yiddish newspapers in New York seemed to be well informed. With the exception of a Communist Daily, the *Morgen Freiheit*, which thundered against the vermin that Stalin was sweeping out of the pure home of Communism, the Yiddish papers had no doubt that Stalin was conducting a purge, to make him into the sole dictator of the Soviet Union. This was also the view of the leading newspaper in Baltimore, the *Sun*. I kept equating the Jews in America who supported Stalin with his Yevsektsia in the Soviet Union. I was certain that the future of the United States could not be entrusted to the Communists, and not even to the Trotskyites, who were then Stalin's most vocal opponents. Leon Trotsky, when he had been at the center of power in the Soviet Union, had helped create its antireligious policy. I did not want my family to wind up in some gulag, perhaps in Idaho, at the orders of one of the Communist factions.

The battle with the campus Communists did not lead to a personal break until the beginning of my last year at college (I finished my first degree in three years), in the fall of 1939. Until then, the dominant political slogan had remained the need for a popular front against the Nazis and the Fascists. This seemed all the more necessary because England and France had abandoned Czechoslovakia to Hitler at the end of September 1938. The prime minister of England, Neville Chamberlain, had taken the lead in giving Hitler the German-speaking region of Czechoslovakia, the Sudetenland, and he had come off an airplane from Germany waving a piece of paper and claiming that he had achieved "peace in our time." Six months earlier, Hitler had marched into Vienna to the cheers of millions of Austrians, announcing the *Anschluss*, the joining of Austria to his German *Reich* in March 1938. The Jews in both Austria and Czechoslovakia were immediately desperate to leave. In Germany itself, almost all the synagogues were

burned and destroyed on the night of November 9–10, 1938.
Through all these frightening events, I kept listening to Hitler on the
shortwave radio. I understood German well, both because I was
studying the language at college and because its basic vocabulary is
the same as my native Yiddish. I heard, over and over again, that "the
Jews are our misfortune" and that the Aryan race had to defend itself
by attacking Jews. My family had relatives in all the countries in
which Jews were now in danger. We were getting terrified letters begging for help to get them out. Much as I disliked the Communists,
and especially those whom I knew, I would have remained with Satan
himself in the popular front. Even the quarrel over the treason trials
did not, therefore, end my connection with the Communists on campus. Whatever the sins of the Soviet Union, it was the only power
that opposed Hitler.

The inevitable break happened a day or two after the shock of the
Stalin-Hitler pact in August 1939. When the picture of Molotov and
Ribbentrop signing the pact, in Moscow, appeared on every front page,
the Stalinists immediately left the popular front. They said that they
would have nothing further to do with the inevitable "imperialist" war
between the Nazis and Fascists and the Western powers. I vividly
remember the Saturday night of that week. About thirty or forty young
people were invited to a party at the home of one of the Communist
believers. We sat on the floor listening to a broadcast of Beethoven's
Ninth Symphony, thus demonstrating that we were young men and
women of advanced culture. The Communists at the party—they were
the large majority—wanted all of us to listen to the music in quiet.
Their real purpose was clear: they had not yet gotten the "line" from
Party headquarters, and they wanted respect for the music to squelch
discussion. But not even Toscanini and his orchestra could shut me up
that night. I insisted on denouncing this betrayal. I even asked why
Stalin had shot Marshal Tukhashevski for supposedly conspiring with
the Nazis, when this was exactly what Stalin himself was doing two
years later. As the shouting match became more vehement, I noticed
that I was the only person in the room who had space around him. The
others who were sitting on the floor with me had been moving away,
even though that meant they were squashing together. I left the party
early and went home alone, on the trolley to East Baltimore. I was

hoarse and I was shivering. Hitler now had a free hand in Europe, and I was afraid for my grandfather in Lemberg.

This scene completed my alienation from most of the political intelligentsia at Johns Hopkins. A decade later, Senator Joseph McCarthy went after several of the people in the circle. I kept silent. Contact had been broken in 1939, and I had no idea a decade later, after many of these contemporaries had served in the American army, what their convictions had become. Mine had not changed essentially in the years since college, but I knew that many others had gone on long journeys in a very few years. By the late 1940s I had come to know some contemporaries, Communists in their college days, who had become fierce anti-Communists and were on their way to defining the future doctrines of the neoconservatives. I did not know then whether any of my college contemporaries had taken the same journey. I stayed out of the battle, neither attacking nor defending these classmates, but I never did accept the defense that American Communists were guilty only of having constitutionally permitted minority opinions. I knew that at least some of my Communist friends had surrendered their right to opinions of their own to the dictates of the Party. I remembered heated conversations with them in the late 1930s when they had maintained that "enemies of the people" should be shot. There was some distinction between the Communists and the Nazis: the Communists would purge you for belonging to the wrong class or ideology; the Nazis would kill you for belonging to the wrong race. I knew that I was in great danger from both the Nazis and the Communists: I was a Jew, a descendant of rabbis, and a bourgeois intellectual. Several kinds of ideologues were eager to kill me, in good conscience, for the sake of their supposedly higher principles. I simply could not understand how my Communist classmates could talk so glibly and self-righteously of purges.

Not finding a home in the American Students Union, I looked toward the Jewish activity on campus. I knew immediately that I could not join what there was of social life. At least 20 percent of the students were Jews; most of us lived at home. Two Jewish fraternities existed, because Jews were not being admitted to any of the others. In these Jewish houses the "brothers" drank beer and ate crab cakes just as the Gentiles did in their fraternities. I was too young and too poor to think of joining one of the fraternities, but the option had been closed completely by my mother a week before school began. A delegation came to our house to look me over and to persuade me, if they found me suitable, to pledge their house. I was very interested in the conversation, because they seemed to be opening the door to my becoming an "American" adult. I forgot that my mother was in the kitchen baking challah for the Sabbath. As the delegation listed the enchantments of the fraternity, including its possessing the largest list of available young women with few inhibitions, my mother burst forth from the kitchen, brandishing her broom, to sweep these "bums and loafers" out of her house. Thus ended my brief moment of association with the bon vivants of Johns Hopkins.

My Jewish associations on campus were, therefore, limited to those who studied hard and took their Jewishness seriously. Some were Zionists. Occasionally they went off for weekends of regional or national meetings of Avukah (the "torch"), the intercollegiate Zionist group. Even among this handful, there were ideological quarrels between the supporters of the kibbutzim, the collective farms, in Palestine, and the "general Zionists," who denied that the national homeland had to be fashioned according to a Socialist model. I joined the Zionist group, but I had no great passion for its activities. I could not afford the cost of the occasional weekend meetings out of town, and the ideological debates seemed to me to be irrelevant. The Jewish settlers in Palestine would make of their community whatever they wished, without the advice of a handful of college students in faraway Baltimore. Moreover, I knew that the real problem of the Jews, then, was not how to found one more kibbutz in Palestine but how to save one more Jewish family from the Nazis.

My "home" on campus became the only professor who was a scholar of the Bible and who respected rabbinic learning, William Foxwell Albright. As a very young man, in the 1920s, he had directed the American School of Oriental Research in Jerusalem, where he had made a point of learning modern Hebrew. He was the one major figure on the faculty who was connected with the Jewish scholars in his field, both in Palestine and in America. The rules were sufficiently loose in those days that Albright permitted a couple of undergraduates who knew biblical Hebrew to attend his doctoral seminar. I was comfortable in his presence, more at home in his classroom and office than anywhere else at college.

The "documentary hypothesis"—that the Five Books of Moses had been written by many hands and that the existing text had been created by an editor—was, and remains, the basic premise of modern biblical scholarship. Albright shared this thesis, with variations of his own. The "proof" of this theory was in the many conflicts that supposedly exist in the text of the Five Books of Moses. To quote the first of many examples, the story of the creation of Adam and Eve is told twice in the book of Genesis. We are told once that God put Adam into a deep sleep and fashioned Eve from his rib. Some verses later, the text states flatly that God created man and woman together. To the biblical critics, this is a contradiction, to be explained as representing two different sources of the biblical text. The ancient rabbis had harmonized the two versions by suggesting that God had originally created one creature, a Siamese twin of Adam and Eve. They were joined at the back, and were separated when God put these twins into a deep sleep. "Adam's rib" really meant Adam's side. In Albright's seminar, I did not simply have to choose between such diverse explanations of this and other texts. The issue was far deeper: did men write the Bible, or had Moses written the text at God's dictation? I could no longer restrict myself to doubting whether God cared that I carried a handkerchief in my pocket on the Sabbath. I was faced with nothing less fundamental than the question of who created Judaism: God or the Jews?

There was no one at Johns Hopkins with whom I could raise this question. Albright was a Christian. In the classroom we saw only the secular historian, though we knew that he was a believer. He was, in fact, writing a book then, *From the Stone Age to Christianity,* in which he described the Hebrew Bible as the record of man's preliminary encounters with God, culminating in the perfect revelation in Jesus. From what Albright kept saying, in and out of class, I understood that he was essentially a disciple of the Protestant biblical scholars of the nineteenth century. They had delighted in proving that the most sublime, universal teachings of the Hebrew Bible had come very late. They insisted that many psalms and prophetic texts had been composed as late as three or two centuries before the beginning of Christianity. Albright vehemently disputed the most radical assertion of these biblical critics: that monotheism had appeared among the Jews only in the teachings of the prophets and that Moses himself had been a henotheist—that is, a believer in the notion that each people had its own god. Nonetheless, Albright's account of the biblical text shook my Jewish faith. The Judaism in which I had been raised rested on the premise that the commandments in the Bible were the word of God.

When the question of faith became severe for me, in Albright's seminar, I could find no help in any of the other courses. So I looked for help in Jewish writings. Within Judaism, I knew that the theologians had been influenced by the Greek philosophers, and especially by Aristotle, for I had read somewhere a triumphant essay in praise of Maimonides because he had overcome Aristotle: he had proved that the world was not eternal, as Aristotle had maintained; it had been created out of nothingness by the will of God. But this proof was not something that I had been given to study by my father. The philosophical books that had been written in the Middle Ages, even though their authors were revered as great and holy men, were essentially forbidden. Philosophical theology was a dangerous field. The attempt to defend the faith against heresy meant giving heresy and disbelief a hearing, if only to refute them. It was better that the issues not be raised so the believers might concentrate on living a pious and righteous life. The rules of conduct were relevant and important, but metaphysics was much more problematic. Had not the Talmud itself declared, in a well-known passage, that the Holy Bible began in Hebrew with the letter beth, the second letter of the alphabet, because this Hebrew sign was closed on three sides and open only on the left? The lesson was that one should not speculate about what was either above or below, or even think much of what is behind: the past. The only proper concern is the future, and the way to embrace it is by living a life obedient to the commandments in the Bible, as read by the rabbis.

All the emphasis on correct conduct could not completely repress my curiosity about all the many things unseen. In the Talmud itself, one heard of heavenly voices that sometimes intervened in human affairs, even though the rabbis preferred that they be disregarded. There were even hobgoblins who troubled men and women in very curious ways, and Satan and his helpers often tempted people or did them harm. All of these tales reflected some reality, but it was never clear what that reality might be; it was best not to speculate. But I was curious.

The most intriguing questions of faith were raised not by philosophy or folklore but by the Kabbalah. One heard that there were great and troubled souls who used secret knowledge to bend even God Himself to their will. This was the "practical Kabbalah," which taught how man might acquire superhuman powers. The story of such power that was told most often had as its hero the great Rabbi Loew, the leader of the Jews of Prague in the sixteenth century. To defend his community against attacks, Rabbi Loew had created the golem, a living creature that moved because its maker had put into the hollow where its heart should have been a piece of parchment that contained the name of God. So, in the right hands, the practical Kabbalah could produce great good for the embattled and endangered Jewish people. The practical Kabbalah could also be used to right the wrongs of individuals. In my mid-teens, probably in my freshman year at college, I saw the play *The Dybbuk* on the Yiddish stage. The theme of the story is the insistence on justice of a dybbuk, a soul that had not come to rest but had entered the body of a young woman who had been promised to him when they were both born. Chanan, the dybbuk, had died from longing when the girl's father had refused to keep the promise. A court is convened. The claims of the dybbuk are heard, but they are denied. The Hasidic rebbe, who is the head of the court, uses his kabbalistic powers to drive the dybbuk out, but the girl dies. The two souls are at last united in death. I saw this play in awe and trembling. I knew that such stories were a world apart from the real life of being a Jew—and they did not prove the existence of God—but such Hasidic tales gave me hope. In many variations they taught one recurrent lesson: that man has the power to rise beyond himself.

In my early teens, I had heard many Hasidic stories from my father and his friends. In my years at college, I became more interested in these tales than I had ever been. I now turned to the literature about Hasidism that had been created by modern writers. I was not yet critical enough to know that Martin Buber's *Tales of the Hasidim* did not describe the Hasidic masters as they actually were. Buber had remade them to be a Jewish version of Oriental sages, and he had detached them from the day-to-day life of piety and of obedience to religious practice. His Hasidic masters sounded much more like Buddhist sages than like the rebbes about whom I heard in the family, and yet my first encounter with Martin Buber's work was uplifting and even exhilarating. The existence, and the fame, of his two volumes assured me that my study of the Hasidim, and my pride in being descended from one of the founders of the movement, Elimelech of Lizhansk, was a proper pursuit, even for that part of myself that was the American college student. The new encounter with Hasidism thus made me feel better about my origins, but it did not solve the problem of faith that Albright had provoked.

I became more confused as I read about the Hasidim in contemporary Hebrew and Yiddish literature. The writer in Yiddish who was most in love with Hasidic themes, I. L. Peretz, had identified his heroes as social revolutionaries. In one of Peretz's most memorable stories, a scoffing rationalist does not believe that the rebbe of Nemirov disappears every night to heaven to be with God. The scoffer follows the rebbe one night and finds that the rebbe does not go to heaven at all, but rather to a forsaken hut where he provides a poor widow with wood for her fireplace. The scoffer returns from this journey to tell the adherents of the rebbe that he has become a believer: he has seen the holy man ascend even higher than to heaven. I was attracted to the basic idea of the story: that holiness and godliness are in good deeds and not in mystical union with God; who knows what self-serving lessons men might derive from their mystical transports? But Peretz's rebbe of Nemirov, as the scoffer saw him, had become all too secular. Hasidic rebbes had not been engaged in the politics of good deeds to create some utopia in this world, or even to make society a bit better. They had been building bridges, deed by deed, to God.

I was much more sympathetic, because it spoke to my own condition, to another story by Peretz, in which he mocked the very rationalist scoffer who had been his hero in the earlier tale. The rationalist now appears as a young man from a Hasidic family whose wealthy father sent him to school at Leipzig to be educated in the ways of modern business. After some months, the young man returns for the holidays as a "Westerner." On Sabbath morning he does not rise early to go to synagogue, but chooses to sleep late. The father comes to wake him, but the son will not go to the morning service. He insists on delivering a philosophical critique of the very idea of prayer. He says to the father, You are a decent man. If you knew that down the street there was a poor family in need, would you wait to be reminded or would you go instantly to help? The father answers, indignantly, that he would not wait a moment to send help to the needy. The son then asks, If so, why do you attribute to God an inferior morality? Why does He, who knows everything, need to be reminded of our wants? The father is stumped, but he soon replies that there is another side to prayer, the expression of our reverence for God. The son is unrelenting. He asks, You, Father, are a successful businessman. How would you feel if a delegation came several times a day and stood in front of you chanting, "Great businessman, magnificent businessman, unique businessman, greatest businessman in all the world"? The father of course answers that he would be embarrassed and that he would try to stop such carryings-on. The son persists and asks, Why, then, must we embarrass God by repeating such praises to Him? The confrontation, however, does not end at this point, with a victorious son lying in his bed to contemplate his devastating logic. The father has the last word. He pulls the cover off his son and says, Nonetheless, one must pray.

But why must one say prayers? Why must one be part of the synagogue? The easy answer, which believing fathers had given their doubting sons at the end of such encounters, was that in synagogue they would be one with other Jews. By their presence, they would affirm and strengthen their belonging to the community of all Jews, past and present. But why must one wish to belong to that community? One of the essential meanings of freedom, in its modern version, is that each individual is free to fashion his own identity and to choose his own community. I did not yet know, when I first began to think about these matters, that you really cannot abandon your earliest identity and reinvent a community, at little cost and with much benefit. I did know that community for the sake of community is a form of idolatry. The most raucous proponents of community, in the 1930s, were the Fascists and the Nazis. The question could not be avoided: community in the name of what? to what end? Jewish community is certainly not exempt from this question. Even a teenager's acquaintance with Jewish texts left me with the certainty that the Jewish community had not created itself. It had been put together by an idea, the faith in one God, and that God commanded mankind to behave morally. One did not go to synagogue just to affirm one's ethnic roots.

Early on, I knew that I could not finesse the question of faith by accepting one of the modern, humanist interpretations of Jewish history. Almost without exception, they had been fashioned under the influence of nationalism, which was the dominant political and cultural movement of the nineteenth century. The Jews were described as a people who had imagined God as the representation of their own highest ideals. The Hebrew writer that I liked most, the turn-of-the-century essayist Ahad Ha'am (Asher Ginzberg), had written a famous and remarkably passionate essay about Moses, in which he argued that it was of no consequence whether Moses ever actually existed as a historical figure. Into the image of Moses, which included even his rages and his despair, the Jews had poured their vision of the highest form of human life. Moses, whether fact or fable, had set the standard of human nobility. It was obvious, even to a teenager, that Ahad Ha'am's essay was really not about Moses; it was about God Himself. Ahad Ha'am was telling the reader that it did not matter whether God existed, but the Jewish vision of Him, as He was described in the Bible, expressed the essential genius of the Jewish people.

I had trouble with this notion of Ahad Ha'am's, not only because I was trying hard to be a believer, but because one of my professors had given me Voltaire's novel *Candide* to read. I remember the shock with which I read the assertion that if horses were theologians, their image of God would be that of a glorious white horse. If God was man's invention, then man might decide to find more convenient values. I was soon reading Nietzsche, who had pronounced, "If God is dead, all things are permitted"—and I looked at the newsreels of Nazis beating Jews, which seemed to prove Nietzsche's point. Ahad Ha'am had taught that the history of the Jews was the continuing story of a people that behaved like a biological entity, responding to its environment by changing coloration, and even physical makeup, to defend its survival. But could the Jews bet their future on their capacity to adapt? What would happen if their enemies had no conscience? As the power of the Nazis grew, I heard Hitler thunder on the radio, and I kept looking at the newsreels of the huge rallies in which he whipped himself and his followers into frenzies of hatred. I knew that Jews could not acquire enough power to be secure. Our only hope for survival was in a world that was governed morally, and such conscience could not be left to human convenience.

The only hope that I had in the 1930s for my relatives in Poland was in unbreakable moral law. And so I found myself not believing the modern writers, both Jewish and Christian, who had faith in man. I was much more at home with what the Talmud taught about the nature of man. In one passage, the question was raised of whether a Jew could be allowed to go on a long journey in the desert in a caravan of Gentiles, who might rob and kill him. The Talmud answered that such a trip was permitted if the others in the caravan believed in God, and especially in the teaching that evil deeds are punished by Him. The anger that has never left me at the memory of the murder of more than 6 million Jews by the Nazis is not directed at the evil men and women who perpetrated the crime; many, perhaps even most, knew no better. But the churches did know better, and they did not excommunicate the Nazis to tell them that they were acting against the law of God.

At college, I came to know that I could not prove that morality is ordained by God. I had enough insight into myself to be aware that I had refused to let go of this faith, when I was young, because I thought it was my only defense against the Nazis. I was positing a moral God for the very reason that had moved Ahad Ha'am to describe a mythic Moses: a weak people needed to assure itself that God was on its side. I clung to this faith in a divinely ordained morality, even as I was taught at college that anthropologists had found many human societies that lived by widely differing values. These relativists scared me, but I was even more frightened by some of the believers. In the America in which I was growing up, some of the Christian clergy, such as Father Charles Coughlin and the Reverend Gerald L. K. Smith, were rabid anti-Semites. Each insisted that he was speaking for God. How could I, therefore, hold on to the idea of some nonnegotiable core to a God-given morality? I had no answer to this question, but I had to believe in moral absolutes.

My discomfort with moral relativism came to a climax at the very end of my days in college, in June 1940. France had fallen to the Nazis, and England was in mortal danger. On the very day that France capitulated I was a guest at a graduation party that was given by Col. and Mrs. Thompson Lawrence in honor of their son, John Biddle Lawrence, who was in the same class at Johns Hopkins in which I was graduating. John Biddle and I had been writing columns for the past year or so in the student newspaper, in which he wrote as the "house Republican" and I wrote as the "house Democrat," but we had become friends. His mother, a woman of great charm and verve, was very proud of that friendship because her father was a German Jew, a physician in New York, who had converted to the Catholic faith of his wife. When she came to visit, Mary Lawrence delighted in walking through the campus, accompanied by her son and me, proclaiming at the top of her voice that her son and I were the two smartest Jews at Johns Hopkins. It was perfectly in character for her to invite me, the only younger person aside from her children, to the graduation party for John Biddle at their house on the grounds of the War College in Washington. Among the older guests at that occasion were Lt. Col. Omar Bradley and several other officers who were serving on the general staff. The military men were very gloomy about the prospects of Great Britain's survival, and they had no doubt that afterward the United States would be attacked by the Germans. Some of the officers at that gathering feared that the United States could not withstand such an attack. I listened; I did not dare to take part in this conversation, but I shivered.

In those very days I was on the farewell rounds, to express gratitude to my various teachers for what I had learned from them. Inevitably, the fear of the Nazis arose in these conversations. One of the younger professors confronted, very directly, what was on my mind. He guessed that I was asking myself whether, if the Nazis came to Baltimore, he would hide me from them. My professor said to me without any hesitation, You are a Jew, and, therefore, you have no choice, because the Nazis have singled you out. I am not a Jew, and I will have choices. I have decided that if the Nazis ever take over the university, I will continue to teach here. Please do not come to my door to ask to hide in my cellar, for I will not endanger myself and my family.

When this conversation was over, I said nothing, but I walked out of that room chilled, frightened, and alone. What kept ringing in my head was the verse in the Book of Psalms: "Do not trust in princes or in the children of men who offer no salvation" (Ps. 146:31). I walked away from this teacher shaking in anger at his moral relativism. I went from his office to the library and reread a book that had become famous some years before, Julien Benda's *The Treason of the Intellectuals,* in which he had denounced the intellectual leaders of the secular West for abdicating moral responsibility. I was sure that prudence was not enough—it would never be enough—and that mankind could live only by the courage of those whose faith commanded them, at any cost, to be defiant.

5

I had come to college in search of community. I had rejected the Communists because I was too much of a Jew. All that was left for me was to study, which I had to do in any event in order to stay at school. But I began to read voraciously in the hope of finding a place for myself in the culture of the West. I was at college because Jews had been the most prominent and most passionate believers in Western education during the past century and a half. It had become an article of faith of those Jews who were intent on entering the modern world that the avenue was through education. Jews who shared the attainments of the Gentile intelligentsia in literature, philosophy, music, and art—and, of course, the sciences—would be accepted as peers and would find allies in their quest for equality. The enemies of the Jews were the Christian anti-Semites and political reactionaries of several varieties.

The trouble with this thesis was that, as I was learning to know and to understand the history and traditions of the West, it was clearly not true. Here I was, a student in an institution that was one of the beacons of learning in America, and I was surrounded by intellectuals who were anti-Semites. The president, then, was Isaiah Bowman. He did not even disguise his distaste for Jews, even as the world was burning around them. As decent people were expected to have special sympathy for Jews, the prime victims of the Nazis, Bowman inveighed in public that they had no particular claim on the human conscience; he was proud that he had advised President Woodrow Wilson, as a young aide during the Peace Conference of 1919, not to support the Zionists' ambitions in Palestine. There were very few Jews on the faculty and not a single avowed Jew who held a tenured professorship in any of the humanities. There were a few professors who were friendly but a larger minority that was distinctly hostile. It was a given that in America in the late 1930s the academic world as a whole was largely closed to Jews. One of the major lessons that I learned in the years I spent at Johns Hopkins was that those who controlled academe had decided to provide very little room at their inns for the likes of me.

When I entered college at Johns Hopkins in 1937, one of the intellectuals' gathering places in Baltimore was in the Peabody Bookstore on the edge of downtown, near Baltimore's monument of George Washington. In the back room of the store, there was a beer parlor in which H. L. Mencken, the most famous journalist of his time, frequently held court. The people who gathered around his table were in awe of the man who had used his accounts of the Scopes trial a few years before to skewer William Jennings Bryan, the protagonist, there, of literal faith in the Bible. Mencken had long been the editor of a quirky magazine, the *American Mercury*, which was the premier, and most irritating, journal, then, of literature and politics. In the mid-1930s, Mencken, always the master of finding ways to outrage the "booboisie," had turned to finding good words to say about Hitler and to deploring the Jewish influence on American culture, even as this famous gadfly continued personal friendships and working relationships with several Jews. Standing at the edge of the crowd on my first visit to the Peabody Bookstore, I was shocked to hear him voice these opinions, in an establishment that was owned by a Jew and to a group at his table that was at least half Jewish. I was even more upset that no one challenged him. I could have done so myself, but, at the age of sixteen, I did not have the courage to take on so famous, and so cutting, a controversialist as Henry Mencken. But I could not forgive the silence of the several older people at the table. Were they afraid of Mencken's sharp tongue, or were they avoiding the label "too Jewish"? I felt helpless and demeaned, and I knew that I could not trade silence for the illusion, or even the reality, of social acceptance. I was not going to grow up to be Mencken's "White Jew."

I knew almost from the beginning that I was too much of a Jew to fit easily into any of the molds at college. I could not join the Communists or the secular disbelievers, for I was restrained, always, by loyalty to the rabbinic tradition in which I had been raised. And yet, I could not pretend to myself that I could return home easily every afternoon. I took the Jew to college with me every day; I brought home the doubter. I was bringing home doubts about religion and problems with my personal identity, which were making me into an internal émigré in East Baltimore. One Sabbath afternoon as I drifted between studying the Talmud and reading an essay by Bertrand Russell, I suddenly knew with striking clarity that no bridge could be built between those texts. That afternoon I faced the truth: I could not keep the two worlds to which I belonged separate. I could not be a Western intellectual only at college and a believer and student of the Talmud only at home. But how could I escape this schizophrenia? I went looking for company.

In East Baltimore there were some young people who seemed to share my situation. The young men I knew best at the Hebrew Parochial School had almost all continued their education at the Yeshiva College in New York, the Orthodox institution that combined Jewish and secular studies. I tried to maintain the connection, but I failed. They were being schooled to live with schizophrenia, not to bring heretical questions with them to their studies in rabbinic literature. My seethings and ambivalences made my childhood friends uncomfortable.

Sometimes I thought that I would find company among Yiddish writers. I continued to write in Yiddish occasionally, during my college years. In addition to composing one or two callow essays, I was earning my personal expenses by acting as secretary for one of the synagogues in the neighborhood, writing in Yiddish the minutes of its meetings. Occasionally, I even earned a few dollars by contributing to the column called "The Week in Baltimore" in the Orthodox Yiddish daily, the *Morgen Journal*. But I soon knew that my identification with the Yiddish literati was a delusion. The "temple" of the Yiddish intelligentsia in the late 1930s was Café Royale in New York, on the corner of Second Avenue and Twelfth Street. The reporters and columnists of the

Yiddish dailies, and some of the actors in the Yiddish theaters, congregated there, especially late at night when the morning papers had been locked up for print and the shows had finished on the various stages on the avenue. I soon caught on to the gossip of the café, and even to the fierce intellectual and personal feuds that made each table into a territory at war with all the others, but I never became part of the scene. Almost everyone at Café Royale had come to the United States as an adult. Café Royale was the domain that they had created in the image of a literary café in Vienna or Warsaw. Almost without exception, the writers and actors were secular Jews who might, on occasion, write sentimentally about the deep piety of the shtetl from which many of them came, but literature had become their substitute for religion. A few of those whom I got to know at Café Royale even admitted to me that they would have preferred to write in English. They longed for a much wider audience and, not incidentally, for the money that came with a best-seller. They were surprised that I might want to identify with them, for they felt trapped in their foreignness.

The main subject matter of these writers was the life in Eastern Europe, which the next generation, to which I belonged, knew only from hearsay. The more I became part of the scene at Café Royale, and even the mascot at one or two of its tables, the more sure I was that I was a visitor in a place that was dying. I remember how I felt at Café Royale more than fifty years ago every time I drive by the corner of Second Avenue and Twelfth Street, even as I grieve at the sight of a Japanese restaurant (it was preceded by a cleaning store) on premises that still house these Yiddish ghosts.

I was deeply upset by a personal crisis at the end of my first year in college. For the following year, only three full-tuition scholarships were going to be awarded, to the three students who had received the highest grades as freshmen. I was not one of them, having placed either fourth or fifth. The college offered me two hundred dollars toward the annual tuition of four hundred fifty dollars. My parents hoped—they even presumed—that a rich relative would give me the difference, but he shocked them by brusquely refusing. His answer was, "Let him go to work in my shop." I was rescued by people who did not belong to the larger family, or even to East Baltimore. Dr. Louis Kaplan, the president of the Baltimore Hebrew College, took an interest in me, even though I was not his student or disciple. He opened the door to the Jewish Scholarship Fund, which helped poor young people with their college tuition. Their committee on grants wanted to refuse my application, because they knew I was related to a prominent, wealthy family, but Dr. Kaplan explained to them that I was out in the cold. I was soon invited to meet with the executive director of the fund, an older woman, Mrs. Laura Guttmacher, who was the widow of a Reform rabbi. I came into her office feeling nervous and very nearly frightened. I was there to plead for help from a "German Jew" from uptown, and I did not expect her to have any particular sympathy for a youngster from East Baltimore, from an ultra-Orthodox rabbinic family. She was so gracious and so warm that I melted immediately. She made me feel like a young scholar in need and not a poor beggar from the other side of town. I soon got a letter from her on behalf of the fund, lending me the money in the expectation that I would return it, and more besides, when I was able.

The kindness of Dr. Kaplan and Mrs. Guttmacher jolted me out of some prejudices. Throughout my childhood and into my teens I had been sure that the poor in East Baltimore worried about each other, but that the people uptown had no such concrete sympathy. Yes, I knew they contributed to charities that did help the poor, but I thought they were insulated by bureaucrats and social workers from any direct contact with those in need. There was more than a tinge of religious prejudice in my attitude. How could those who did not believe that God had commanded them to be kind to others really care? Yet, when I was begging for money to continue in college, a heretical Jewish intellectual and the widow of a Reform rabbi were the two people who were concerned. Both were extraordinarily careful not to demean me. On the contrary, they suggested that the day would soon come when I would join them in helping others. I soon burst out at my father. I insisted that the kindnesses of Dr. Kaplan and Mrs. Guttmacher had a deep religious quality, so how could we continue to deplore their "heresy"?

I expected my father to be flustered and to offer a clever evasion of the question, but he did not. He spoke with remarkable appreciation of those who had founded Reform Judaism in the middle of the nineteenth century. My father said that they had been wrong in throwing over so much of the tradition, but they were facing real problems, in a new age. The changes they had made, even as they abandoned many Jewish practices, reflected serious concerns about living as a Jew not in the ghetto but in the open society. The founders of Reform Judaism had chosen to turn from most of the prescribed rituals as needlessly separatist, but they had held fast to the moral teachings of the Bible. My father argued that ritual and concrete laws regulating conduct, even more than abstract ideas, defined Judaism, but he agreed that these were important issues about which serious people could differ. Unfortunately, many Jews had chosen Reform not on principle but because they wanted a more convenient, less demanding Judaism. In America of the 1930s many East European Jews and their children were joining Reform congregations because they thought this would advance their social prestige. This unlovely scene should not diminish respect for the moral seriousness of the early Reformers, to whom Mrs. Guttmacher clearly belonged. My father then added a comparable appreciation of Dr. Kaplan: he was much too radical, but he had a talent for decency.

Knowing that I could not find a home at Café Royale, or even with Dr. Kaplan or Mrs. Guttmacher, I thought of avoiding the problem of identity and community by becoming an academic. In the course of my college years, I transferred a good bit of the passion for the Talmud and its commentaries to the study of history and literature. I did well in almost all the courses. I was grubbing for grades in order to keep a scholarship and stay in college, but I actually liked to study. I even tried to learn both Greek and Arabic, but the task of memorizing grammar exhausted my patience. I quickly drifted toward those subjects that required large amounts of reading, and the desire to argue about the meaning of the texts. I was most comfortable with the intellectuals among my fellow students and with those professors who seemed to like the young rebels who asked challenging questions. These teachers seemed to keep hoping that we would grow beyond being smart into becoming serious. I began to believe that I could spend my life as a scholar and teacher. But this dream was unreal. I looked around at the faculty of the college to find that there were almost no Jews in any of the departments. I remember one in the English department who was kept at low rank until long after I left the school, and another in political science who eventually resigned to take a job with the Associated Jewish Charities in Baltimore because he lost hope of advancement at Johns

Hopkins. To be sure, the physics department had hired a refugee from Germany who had already won the Nobel Prize. There was even a scattering of professors of Jewish origin in other disciplines, but they were very nearly Marranos who hid their Jewish origins. Everyone knew that the situation at other schools was the same. I might go on to graduate school, but I would have little chance at a faculty appointment anywhere in America.

The question came to a head in my senior year at college. I was offered a scholarship to study for the doctorate in Semitic studies at Harvard. When I proudly showed the letter to William Foxwell Albright, he insisted very firmly that I must decline the honor. He had no doubt that I would write a decent, perhaps even brilliant, dissertation, but I would then find that Jews were not being hired anywhere to teach Semitics. Jews were especially unwelcome in this field because they were suspect of being biased in favor of the Hebrew Bible as the prime source of monotheism. Christians, who tended to believe that monotheism was perfected only in the New Testament, could, of course, be trusted to be objective. The only faculties that hired Jews were at the rabbinic seminary of Reform Judaism, the Hebrew Union College, in Cincinnati; and at the comparable school of the Conservative movement, the Jewish Theological Seminary, in New York. These schools were turning out rabbis, but some of the students were choosing not to work in congregations but to become scholars. Almost all the elder figures in both faculties were Europeans, but a few younger people who had been trained in America had recently been given junior appointments. Albright seemed to think that I could be one of them. He knew that I would not go to the Hebrew Union College. The ideological issues did not even need to be discussed, for the kitchen of their student dormitory was not kosher and I would, therefore, have nothing to eat. Albright pointed out that I had no real choice but to apply to the Jewish Theological Seminary.

When Albright finished, I was silent—and sad. In the course of the conversation, Albright had mentioned that he knew that I could not afford to go to graduate school without reasonable hope of a job at the end of my schooling. Only the rich might gamble, because they could support themselves while waiting for a break. At that moment, during a conversation that I knew was a turning point in my life, Albright was quickly aware of my despair. I had been put in a box of academic anti-

Semitism and poverty. Acting as a mentor and friend, Albright had just finished telling me that in the eyes of America I was an unwanted Jew. I was again the four-year-old child who had run away from the main square in Lubaczow when a bunch of Polish kids were calling him a *parshive zhid*. I had run then toward the safety of my mother's arms. Albright sensed that I needed immediate reassurance. He had to find me a refuge, so he picked up the telephone and called his friend Louis Finkelstein, who was then assuming the presidency of the Jewish Theological Seminary. In my presence, he told Dr. Finkelstein that he had a bright young student who was proficient in Talmud, who might become a scholar. Albright got off the telephone to tell me that Finkelstein would be expecting my application to the seminary.

I was churning as I walked out of Albright's office. He had told me the truth, but I felt betrayed. He had put me at ease from the very beginning of our relationship. As a sophomore, he had not only allowed me to attend his doctoral seminar; he had even permitted me to argue with him in class. The sharpest incident had been a debate between the two of us over the meaning in the Bible of the word *Ezrah*. Albright had maintained that the word always means the Jewish inhabitants who had conquered, and populated, the land of Canaan. I countered that, though I could remember no immediate proof texts, there were passages in the Bible in which the word meant the aboriginal inhabitants whom the Jews had displaced. After class I went immediately to the library and found at least three passages in the Hebrew Bible that seemed to support my argument. The next day, I brought these references to Albright's office and he promised to look at them. A few days later, at the opening of the next seminar, he began the discussion by quoting the passages that I had found and agreeing that I was probably right. I was overwhelmed by the honor and moved by his capacity to admit that he might have erred. Several years later, in 1942, he published a book called *Archeology and the Religion of Israel*. I was elated to find that he thanked me in a footnote (it was the first time that I was mentioned in a work of scholarship) for the argument that I had made in class and the evidence that I had marshaled in support. From Albright, therefore, I expected protection and support—and not the cold truth that my choices were limited because I was a Jew.

His call to Dr. Finkelstein again brought the religious question to the surface. I had been thrashing about, but mostly within myself. Overtly, I had remained observant of the rituals and I had arranged to take only those courses that did not require attendance on Saturday morning. At home, I lived the life of my family. My parents knew, of course, when I took a required course in geology in which the earth was described as many hundreds of millions years older than the fifty-seven hundred plus of the Jewish calendar. My father and I never argued about the theories of the biblical critics or about the findings of anthropology that Jewish rituals were not unique. So long as I behaved as an Orthodox Jew, the questions of faith were ignored. If I enrolled at the Jewish Theological Seminary, I would be attending a school in which one of the teachers, Mordecai Menahem Kaplan, was known to insist that the Jews had written the Bible as an expression of their own highest ideals, and that God existed only as a term that various traditions used to denote the values they had decided to revere. To be sure, some of the professors at the Jewish Theological Seminary were undeviatingly Orthodox, and others, whose absolute piety was in doubt, were towering scholars whom even the Orthodox respected. No one at the seminary would force me to change my religious practices or to define myself as a religious liberal, but I would be becoming a member of another camp. This did not upset me personally, but I knew that it would create difficulties for my parents.

But the seminary was attractive to me. Everybody on its faculty was a university graduate, but almost all had remained traditionalists in religion. I was struggling with the many rubs between secular Western culture and Judaism, but I presumed that Louis Ginzberg, the star of the seminary faculty, had dealt with an even more intense version of this conflict. He was an acknowledged genius of rabbinic learning, and he had written his dissertation at the University of Heidelberg on the uses of the Talmud by the fathers of the Church. The much younger Louis Finkelstein had been educated at City College and Columbia University, but he was reputed to be one of the most Orthodox members of the seminary faculty. Both the older and the younger scholar had published works in the 1930s that explained some of the conflicts of opinion in the Talmud as representing views that reflected class interests. These scholars, so I presumed, had found a way to resolve the conflicts between cultures that were troubling me. I hoped to find some answers in their classrooms.

When I told my father of Albright's call to Finkelstein, I was more than a little surprised to find that he was not opposed. The next day he wrote a letter in rabbinic Hebrew to Louis Finkelstein to describe what his son knew of the Talmud and to suggest, with polite circumspection, his fear that I might go astray in the seminary, turning away from classic Jewish learning toward newfangled ideas. Dr. Finkelstein replied almost immediately in excellent rabbinic Hebrew. He said that, if I was indeed as rooted in the Talmud as my father had suggested, Louis Ginzberg would be pleased to have me as a student. I would be arriving at the seminary knowing enough to learn much from that great master and from the rest of the faculty. Finkelstein's answer was encouraging, not only for what he wrote, but especially because Dr. Finkelstein had "passed" my father's examination of him in rabbinic Hebrew.

My parents soon agreed that I should apply to the seminary. They knew that I wanted to become an academic, and they agreed with Albright that the seminary was my only real choice. My father had no problem with its level of learning, and my mother, who did most of the worrying about money, was pleased to hear that the school offered full scholarships to those whom it admitted. Neither my father nor I thought for a moment that I would become a rabbi in a Conservative congregation. My father had no patience with congregations because his contemporaries, of the immigrant generation, had treated him badly in the several small synagogues of which he had been the rabbi. The more affluent immigrants, and their children, had founded Conservative synagogues in the major cities, in the areas of "second settlement" to which they had moved from the Jewish ghettos. Their members were more "American," but they were not different. They seemed to want rabbis who would edify or entertain them from the pulpit, officiate at life-cycle ceremonies, and cheer them up when they felt bad, but not rabbis who would be keepers of their conscience.

There were, indeed, some famous exceptions. Stephen Wise, a Reform rabbi, had become the most prominent Jewish figure in America by defying the German-Jewish oligarchy who controlled the major Jewish institutions. He kept fighting for his liberal and Zionist convictions. None of the Conservative rabbis had attained equal fame, but several had joined Wise in the leadership of the Zionist movement in America. After Hitler came to power in 1933, Stephen Wise and his associates had organized an economic boycott of Nazi Germany. The bulk of the Jewish high bourgeoisie was vehemently opposed to this tactic, but Wise insisted that Jews had to fight back. It seemed far-fetched to me, at the age of nineteen, that I might follow after these men, to become a public figure. They were few, and they were larger than life, but the rabbis whom I knew in Baltimore, whether downtown or uptown, seemed to be engaged in getting on with their congregations. The only rabbi who was at war with his laymen, again and again, over matters of principle was my father, and I did not want to repeat his heartaches in my own life. At nineteen, I hoped to spend my life arguing with Rabbi Akiva and with Maimonides, on the margins of great tomes, and not with the board members of synagogues. I did not yet know anything about the bitter politics of academe, and so I harbored the illusion that academic preferment was based entirely on intellectual merit. I was eager to take my chances. The more I thought about it, the more attractive the seminary became.

I was all the more eager to study at the seminary because my inner ambivalences were becoming more painful in my last months at college. It was no longer the tension between Western and Jewish culture; I was at war with God. The age-old question, Why do the righteous suffer? had ceased being an abstract question to be studied in the Book of Job or in the recurring discussions in the Talmud. The worsening situation for the Jews of Europe was not remote. We had relatives in Germany—Polish Jews who had moved there after the end of the First World War—and some in Vienna. After *Kristallnacht* in November 1938, when the Nazis destroyed almost all the synagogues in Germany, our relatives wrote asking for affidavits, the promises of support in the United States without which no one could apply for an immigrant visa. We were too poor to be able to help in our own name, but we scurried around asking well-off people whom we knew to write affidavits. Some did. The letters from Poland, where the bulk of our family lived, were just as frightening. Anti-Semitism was rising among the Poles. My mother's siblings wrote us about being pushed out of jobs and about their fear that the Nazis would soon march into Poland. Had they not just taken over Czechoslovakia and Austria, with no opposition?

I had been raised in the unquestioned certainty that the Jews of Europe were the very best of our people. The countries of Central and Eastern Europe were the principal home of Jewish learning and of Jewish piety. In the 1930s, Jewish culture and learning in the United States, and even in Palestine, were essentially satellites of Polish and Lithuanian Jewry. I simply could not understand how a benevolent and merciful God could inflict the Nazis on the very heart of Judaism.

This problem became all the more acute as refugees began to show up at our home in Baltimore. Each was desperate to find help for the rest of his family. My father and mother kept running around to raise money to help them get settled and to find affidavits for those still trapped in Europe. It had become very nearly their full-time preoccupation. I did not hear all of the stories because I was at school most of the day, but I knew ever more painfully that the enemies of the Jews could destroy your life even if you had lived a life of shining virtue. The refugees who came through our house were more deeply Jewish, more pious, than most of the Jews whom I knew. They came from a more vibrant Jewish life. Why should these communities be the most endangered?

War broke out in Europe in September 1939, at the beginning of my last year at college. Warsaw was bombed and half obliterated by the German air force. By the end of the month the Germans were in control of Poland, to the line of demarcation between them and the eastern part of Poland, which the Soviets had annexed. My mother's immediate family was mostly in Lemberg, under Soviet control, but the majority of the Jews in Poland were in German-held territory. The news of brutality and murder began to seep out that winter, but these acts were regarded as sporadic pogroms. Organized mass murder had not yet begun, but no one could avoid knowing that the Jews were very much worse off than the rest of the population. I heard it at home, and it was soon confirmed for me at college. Several months after the Nazi conquest of Poland, an American journalist came home with film that he had made in Warsaw, as bombs were falling. He was invited to Johns Hopkins to show us the newsreels and to describe what he had seen. At the end of the evening, I asked him where the Germans had concentrated their bombing. Without hesitation, he answered, "In the Jewish quarter."

The bombs falling on Warsaw that I saw that night terrified me. I had very nearly been there myself. At the beginning of 1939, my father had written to Professor Moses Schorr, the rector of the Institute for Jewish Studies, in Warsaw, to suggest that I might come to study there after graduating from college. The immediate plan was that I get a cheap ticket on the Polish-American Line to spend a couple of months that summer in the land of my birth. I would visit my grandfather and the rest of the family in Lemberg and Lubaczow, and then go on to Warsaw to meet Schorr. The answer soon came. Elegantly, but sadly, Schorr suggested that this was not the right time for a youngster from America to come to Poland. Too many dark clouds were very low in the sky. I did not make the trip. I am left with a few memories of Poland, as I lived in it as a very young child. Perhaps the grief that this world is gone is less intense because I never saw it as an adult, but I doubt it. As I was getting ready to leave my parents' home for school in New York, I held fast to every connection with Polish Jewry. After the war began, I was suddenly much more attentive to the many East European rabbis who had always taken turns staying with us. I talked with them, because I could not talk with my grandfather.

In the first year of the war, I had not yet lost all hope that my grandfather might still be alive, but the fear that I would never see him again became greater and more painful every day. I do not remember exactly when I started to know that the ultra-pious Hasidim of Poland were almost all dead, but I certainly did know it by the spring of 1943, when the last survivors of the ghetto in Warsaw revolted during Passover week and were destroyed by the Nazis. I knew by then that the Jews of Poland were gone forever and that all I could do for my grandfather was to carry on for him, as he had implored me without words when I was five, when he ran beside the train that was taking me to Antwerp to board ship for the United States. And I finally understood, in 1943, that he had not been running then just to catch a last glimpse of me. He had wanted me to see him as he was, to remember the deep and strong Jewish traditions that he represented. I was not tempted, in 1943 or at any later time, to do something theatrical such as donning the black caftan and growing the beard of my forebears. And yet, I always know that his caftan envelops me.

6

The move to New York in the fall of 1940 gave me more space than I had ever enjoyed. The apartment in which we lived in East Baltimore, on the third floor of a row house, was not large enough for me to have a room of my own, and the college library in which I studied between classes was usually crowded. At the Jewish Theological Seminary in New York, I was assigned a living room and a bedroom to myself. As I got to know the other students, I found out that I was not the only one whose standard of living had risen. The bulk of my contemporaries came from urban "east sides," and their families, too, lived in cramped homes.

The school knew who we were, and it proposed to socialize us. The quarters in which we were housed were a striking symbol of the message that the seminary seemed to want to convey: it was preparing rabbis to live in the style of the respectable, middle-class congregations in which they would serve. Part of our education was to attend occasional teas and receptions, to prepare us to behave properly at the many such functions in our future careers. The grandest event was a dinner in the spring. This affair celebrated the joyous festival of Purim, which commemorates the story in the Book of Esther of the victory of the Jews of

Persia over the wicked anti-Semite Haman. The seminary's student body had been organizing this party each year; it was a formal affair that everyone, faculty and students, attended. The faculty brought their wives, and the students came with their dates—and everyone dressed in formal clothes. I do not know if any of the other freshmen had ever worn a dinner jacket before, but I had not. A black tie seemed to me as much a uniform as a black caftan. I preferred the neutrality of conventional, everyday clothes. I was sullen at the party, but the clothes I had to rent were not the cause of my discomfort. When this celebration took place, in the spring of 1941, Europe had been at war for a year and a half. At the very beginning, Germany had conquered Poland. We soon knew that the Nazis were killing Jews. I thought that the leaders of the seminary should have canceled the party and that its total cost should have been given to help those who were suffering in Europe. America was still neutral, and we could still get money and food packages even into Poland. I have never destroyed my copy of the group picture that was taken at that dinner. I look at this photograph every few years to remember with shame that I did not have the courage that spring to refuse to attend the party.

Training for middle-class life in America was imparted not only through formal functions. Everyone was required to take a course in elocution; it was the one discipline that was taught by a non-Jew, who had once been an actor on the stage. This department had been larger and more important in earlier decades, when the students themselves were recent immigrants who spoke English with an accent. By 1940, almost everyone entering the seminary was native born, but the lilt of Yiddish could still be heard in the speech of many. These lessons in elocution were necessary to help achieve the objective that Solomon Schechter had announced in 1902 when he arrived in the United States from Cambridge, England, to assume the presidency of the revitalized Jewish Theological Seminary. He had been asked by reporters, as he was debarking from the ocean liner that brought him to New York, what he intended to achieve in America. He answered, "I have come here to make traditional Judaism fashionable." The class in elocution was supposed to make us preachers in the manner of Stephen Wise or Abba Hillel Silver, the two premier orators of the Reform rabbinate. If we could speak English as well as they, the Conservative movement, which was peopled by immigrants and their children, could hope to achieve equality with the Reform Jews, who had been in the United States two generations longer.

Most of the students regarded the hour or so each week that we spent in elocution as an annoyance. The dormitory was not a quiet place, and one could hear the sounds from the other suites down the long corridor. I never heard anyone practicing the vowels that we were assigned to accustom our throats and mouths to sound them properly. For me, the ultimate value of these exercises was that they prepared me to understand the wit of George Bernard Shaw when I saw *Pygmalion*, even though I could not really think of myself as the equivalent of Eliza Doolittle, the flower girl whom Professor Henry Higgins taught to sound like a duchess. The root of my resistance to the process was, however, different from Eliza's motivation in *Pygmalion*. (She complained that Higgins had taught her to speak and behave as a member of the upper class. She could not go back to being a flower girl in London's Covent Garden, but he had made no place for her among the swells.) I knew that I had chosen not to return to East Baltimore, but I would not accept the role that the Seminary promised. I refused to make myself over as a posh clergyman. My ancestors had never accepted the idea that they existed as rabbis to please their congregations, and my father was still fighting bitterly for his independence. I had not come to the seminary to forget what had been bred into me.

I had come to the seminary to learn from its faculty, which included some of the greatest scholars of Judaica in the first half of the twentieth century. I found out, immediately, that the stars deserved their reputations. The professor of Talmud, Louis Ginzberg, gave the entrance examination orally in his office. He was universally revered by everyone in the Jewish world, with the exception of some of the ultra-Orthodox who resented his moderate religious liberalism. At a very famous event in international scholarship, in 1935, when Harvard University celebrated its tercentenary by awarding several dozen honorary degrees to the preeminent figures in all fields of learning, Ginzberg was the one chosen to represent learning in Judaism. On Morningside Heights in Manhattan, everybody knew him by sight, especially the members of the faculty of Union Theological Seminary, the Protestant divinity school, which was across the street from the

Jewish Theological Seminary. Its most famous faculty member was Reinhold Niebuhr, who once said of Ginzberg, who was five feet tall and yet seemed to tower as he walked down the street, his head back and his cane in hand, "There but for the grace of God, goes God."

He asked me which part of the Talmud I had studied, so I mustered all my courage and told him that I had studied six tractates, an almost unheard number of texts for an applicant for admission. Ginzberg was imperturbable. He asked a further question: in which tractate would I prefer the examination? With rising courage, I chose the volume Nedarim, on the taking of vows and their nullification, which has always been considered one of the most difficult of all the tractates in the Talmud. Ginzberg reached behind him and handed me that volume of the Talmud. I waited for him to find an extra copy, but he simply said, "Open the text wherever you please, read, and interpret." I did and very soon found some difficulty in the text, about which I made a suggestion as to its possible meaning. Dr. Ginzberg nodded that my suggestion was possible, and then he proved very rapidly that the true meaning of the text was not what I had supposed it to be. I kept looking at him in awe because I had the text in front of me and he was, from memory, into all of the intricacies of a text that I had chosen at random from all of the Talmud. My pride in the amount of Talmud that I had studied was gone very quickly. Ginzberg was using parallel passages from the whole of rabbinic literature, and information from Hellenistic and Christian texts and from the discoveries of archeologists, to explain the passage in the Talmud that I thought I had mastered. Ginzberg was kind enough not to demolish me completely that day; he did agree that one of the questions that I raised in that discussion was worth considering. He indicated with some warmth that I had done well and that he would not stand in the way of my being permitted to enter the seminary. I walked out of his room humbled and even a bit humiliated. I did not know that he had decided that he would be not only a teacher but a mentor and even a friend. Some weeks later, I heard that he had admitted me, upon arrival as a freshman, into his senior class in Talmud. He half-adopted me, often inviting me to Friday-night dinner in his home and letting me carry his books after class. I tried hard in my years at the seminary to become a Talmudist in his image, but he was a genius. His students could admire him, and a few could even claim to be his friends. I knew from the very first moment, at the entrance examination, that I would never know Talmud by his standards.

Hillel Bavli, a poet who taught Hebrew language and literature, befriended me in my first weeks at the seminary. Bavli had come from Lithuania to the United States in his teens. He was particularly upset with me because I was not at home in modern Hebrew. He called me aside soon after I arrived to tell me that I had not done well in the entrance examination in the Hebrew language; this result was in sharp contrast to my high grades in Bible and Talmud. Bavli did not persuade me to read belles lettres, but I did study the many essays and books in contemporary Hebrew in which the break between the inherited Jewish tradition and modernity was debated. This tension was the very issue that I had brought with me to the seminary. I was looking to the faculty for a solution, but I soon knew that no one had answers that I could accept. I had deep affection for Hillel Bavli, but he was clearly at war with himself because he was not in Tel-Aviv, the proper home of a poet in Hebrew. Bavli's poems spoke of the pain of his alienation both from the shtetl in which he had been born in Lithuania and from the Zionist culture in Palestine amidst which he did not live. He might have taken me with him had he chosen to move to Jewish Palestine, but he did not. He seemed to want to live in New York and long for Tel-Aviv. I could not imagine spending the rest of my life among the handful of Hebraists whom I met in Bavli's apartment.

Very early I turned toward the two members of the faculty who were directly involved in defining themselves as Jews in America, Louis Finkelstein and Mordecai M. Kaplan. Finkelstein had been born in America, and Kaplan had arrived in his childhood. Both were, like me, the sons of immigrant rabbis. They had already traveled the journey on which I had embarked, and, therefore, I looked to them to help me. Finkelstein had just assumed the presidency of the seminary, but he had not yet developed the remoteness that came with the office. He used to lunch almost every day in the cafeteria of the school, and I was often invited to sit with him. I soon discovered that, in his personal life, Finkelstein was undeviatingly Orthodox, to the last seemingly insignificant detail of religious observance, but he made few demands on the Conservative synagogues around the country. He wanted their support for the seminary, and he seemed to have need of their admiration.

The board of the seminary was dominated, then, by non-Zionists. Finkelstein was the only member of the faculty who shared their views. I could not help suspecting that he wanted the good opinion of these powerful laymen, mostly "German Jews" who were important in American society. As I got to know Finkelstein better, I realized that he cleared his account with God by the way he lived as an individual. That freed him to preside over much that I found repugnant. I must have been asking him too many pointed questions, or perhaps he got tired of my brashness. After a few months, I was no longer his frequent luncheon partner. I had fallen permanently out of favor. At the time, and for years thereafter, I thought that the fault was mine: Finkelstein had found me wanting in piety and scholarship. I did not realize until the 1960s, after I had grown up and made my own way, that the early and decisive rift between us had been caused by my lack of tact. I had been pulling off the bandages with which he had plastered over some of the discontinuities in his own life.

I had the reverse experience with Mordecai M. Kaplan. I fought him for three years, from the very first hour in his class, but we became friends. Kaplan was then the dominant influence on the students, but he was a lone wolf in the faculty. In his adult years, after serving for two decades in Orthodox synagogues in New York, Kaplan had become an avowed, and even pugnacious, religious radical. He was different from all the other members of the faculty. Most of them had become somewhat less exacting in their obedience to some of the rituals, and no one seemed to believe that the Five Books of Moses were, literally, the word of God, but they were traditionalists. God existed, and the Jews were his "chosen people." It was possible that God might not have pronounced this at Sinai, as the literalists believe, but the special glories and particularly intense woes of Jewish history through the ages proved that the descendants of Abraham, Isaac, and Jacob were His best beloved. In practice, the liberalism of the seminary consisted of the absence of a divider between men and women at religious services and the freedom not to cover heads except at study and prayer. Mordecai Kaplan roared that such a version of Judaism was an intellectual sham and that it was irrelevant in America. The majority of the students in the 1930s and 1940s applauded him and became his disciples.

Kaplan had become a follower of pragmatism, the philosophy that dominated in America in the first decades of the twentieth century. He no longer believed in God of the theologians, in any version. Kaplan defined God as the name that people give to their highest values. God is a force, even a tool, which men and women use to help them make the society for which they long. As Spinoza had said three centuries earlier, no community dare claim special possession of truths that are available to human aspiration and reason everywhere and always. The moral values that the God-idea (in Kaplan's rhetoric) represents are universal. Any claim to chosenness is thus an affront to philosophy. In America, the doctrine that the Jews remained a chosen people was an even greater affront: it contradicted the very democracy that was giving all immigrants the chance to be equal. But Kaplan was not an assimilationist. He made a sharp distinction between morality and culture. Each of the many ethnic communities in the world had fashioned its own way of life, through specific customs and, in most cases, its own language. Many of these ethnic groups were now represented, in substantial numbers, in America. Kaplan was one of the first to deny that America was, and should be, a melting pot—a society in which all these ethnicities would disappear and perhaps add color to the only legitimate entity, American society as a whole. Kaplan helped devise the counterimage of American society as the home of cultural pluralism. All immigrants did, indeed, need to learn English and their children should attend public school together to learn to be Americans, but the members of each ethnic group should also live within their own communities. They should not be swept away into rootlessness and anonymity. These ethnic communities should remain the extended families for all varieties of Americans. Kaplan added that the Jews in America had a particular need for the warmth of their own community. They suffered the unique pain of anti-Semitism, and, even though Kaplan denied that they were God's chosen people, Jews had an ancient and continuing passion for a just society.

Kaplan's views have been known, and debated, for years, but the controversies became vehement when he defined his position in 1934 in a book that he called *Judaism as a Civilization*. A decade earlier, he had founded a synagogue on the Upper West Side of New York, in which he had eliminated every affirmation in the liturgy that the Jews were a chosen people. He now proclaimed, through his book, that he was "reconstructing" all of American Judaism. The essential content of this reconstructed religion was a love of Jewish ethnic culture, but Jews now had the freedom to recast or eliminate any belief or custom that was not acceptable to the "modern" mind. Kaplan insisted that this was the only way in which appreciable Jewish loyalties could survive in the New World. Kaplan had made it possible—so it seemed to many children of immigrants—to be, at once, a modern man, an American, and a Jew. The younger generation could leave the Orthodoxy of their parents in good conscience.

The faculty and administration of the seminary wanted to get rid of Mordecai Kaplan, but they did not dare. They regarded him as a heretic, but he was too popular, and they knew that he would not go quietly. They chose to curb his influence, hoping that he might became angry enough to leave. When I arrived in the fall of 1940, the first salvo in the battle had been fired, by limiting the courses that Kaplan could teach and by putting his classes together in one morning a week. The presumption seemed to be that the students would then spend the rest of the week having the effect of his lectures diluted in all the many other classes. Kaplan never spoke in class, or even informally, about the attacks on him by his colleagues, but the atmosphere seemed to make him even more short-tempered than he was known to be. He had always preached democracy in a very imperious manner, and that habit became ever more pronounced.

I arrived in his class with a mixture of respect for his courage and sympathy for his travail, but I did not expect him to be a teacher I could follow. My temperament was an obstacle to becoming his uncritical disciple. I was too much a loner to join, easily, the many other students who were his adherents. There was also, I soon discovered, an impassable chasm between the Orthodoxy in which he had been raised and the one in which I had been educated. Kaplan demanded that religion be reasonable and orderly. He was the son of a father who had been nurtured in the legalism of the Lithuanian Talmud academies. I had been born into the culture of the Hasidim, the mystical pietists of central and southern Poland and the Ukraine. Kaplan, the legalist, insisted that liturgical texts had to be intellectually coherent and acceptable. I had grown up among believers whose Judaism was much more emotional. They looked to religious experience not for logic but for transcendence. In this spirit, I found it possible for me not to believe the literal meaning of some of the prayers and yet be moved by them to feeling near to God. In the very first week of class with Kaplan, I raised my hand not to ask a question but to burst out with an objection. I said to him that the prayer book was like the libretto of an opera; it did not always have to make philosophical sense; its music, the mix of melody and words, could move us beyond ourselves. Some weeks later, I argued that rewriting the prayer book was an act of vandalism, like removing the gargoyles from an ancient cathedral to make room for very visible lightning rods.

So it went during my freshman year, and the years thereafter. Once a week, Kaplan would deliver his lecture—it was always an exposition of his thought, no matter what the announced subject of the course might be—and I would soon raise my hand. He invariably let me have my say, and then he roared back. One day, I went beyond the bounds of dissent. I challenged his reading of some Talmudic passages that he had quoted to support a point he was making. This was a low blow, because Kaplan's critics on the faculty kept deriding his rabbinic learning and I was known to be a disciple of the leading Talmudist, Louis Ginzberg. Kaplan governed his temper, with visible effort. He said that we would discuss this matter further in the next class, after he had looked again at the texts. The next week I was in bed with the flu. He commanded two of the students to go to my room and fetch me, so that he could demolish my scholarship and chastise my impertinence. I continued to fight with him to the very last class, but he became a profound influence on my life. We were friends to the very end of his long life. In 1982, when his magnum opus was republished in honor of his hundredth birthday (he lived one more year), I gladly accepted the honor of writing an introduction for the book with which I had first disagreed when I had read it soon after it was published more than fifty years ago.

What did I learn from Mordecai Kaplan? I did not know it at the time, but his major gift to me was his personal example. He was irascible, opinionated, confrontational, and unafraid. He stood up to harassment at the seminary and to being excommunicated publicly in a ceremony that some Orthodox rabbis staged at a New York hotel in

1941. He refused to compromise, ever, with the members of the congregation that he had founded. Reports used to circulate frequently that
he had again offered to resign rather than to bend any of his principles,
and he always prevailed. No matter how much I disagreed with Kaplan's
thought, I admired his character. My father had the same temperament, but he had remained the rabbi of an out-of-the-way Orthodox
congregation of immigrants. Kaplan had proved that, with talent and
guts, you could be your own man even in mainstream America. I ver-
balized none of this when I was a student, but I knew it, then, in very
deep levels of my soul. Even as I argued with Kaplan, he became a role
model. He was the assurance that I would get away with being myself.

The encounter with Kaplan was, also, intellectually decisive. In almost every paragraph that he wrote, or uttered, Kaplan repeated his
insistence that the conditions of Jewish life had changed radically in the
past two centuries: Jews were no longer confined to the ghetto and they
were no longer constrained by an absolute religious faith. Like all other
contemporary men and women, individual Jews were now able to define
their identities to suit themselves. I soon knew that he was right. The
difference between the United States and czarist Russia, from which
most American Jews had come a few decades before, was clear: in
America no one was forced to be a Jew. In Kaplan's class, I tried to
resist, and to believe that he was describing too sharp a break between
past and present, but I could not.

After my first semester at the Jewish Theological Seminary, I was
given permission to take some courses in history at Columbia. I was
eager to study with Salo Baron, who then occupied the only chair in
Jewish history at any American university. The post existed because the
university had accepted an endowment for that specific purpose. Baron
had been chosen because he was universally regarded as the most
broadly learned Jewish historian of his generation. When I became
Baron's student, during my first year at the seminary, he was in the final
stages of work on a study, published in 1942, entitled *The Jewish Community*. Baron's central point was that for many centuries, the Jewish
community had possessed the power of coercion over individual Jews,
but this had ended in the modern era. Jews could now choose who they
wished to be. Baron had proposed this distinction as a category of historical analysis; Kaplan used it, with unrelenting passion, to insist that

Judaism—and, for that matter, all other cultural and religious identities in America—would exist in the future only if they were redefined and reconstructed. Everything that I have written in the past half century—the historical monographs, and the books and essays about the future of the Jews—has rested on the premise that I learned from Kaplan and Baron. Kaplan, even more than Baron, convinced me that the Jews were being separated from their past by the chasm of modernity. Even as I resisted Kaplan's answers, I knew that he had the courage to ask the basic questions.

On the surface, Louis Finkelstein seemed to be the most "American" figure on the faculty. He was very visibly involved in interfaith activities, and he soon founded a new organization based on the seminary: the Conference on Science, Philosophy, and Religion. This body was host to lectures and a luncheon every Tuesday, at which such figures as Robert Maynard Hutchins, of "Great Books" fame, and the physicist Arthur Compton spoke. On those Tuesdays, the students were exiled from the cafeteria to pick up some sandwiches in a hallway. We invariably mocked these gatherings as Finkelstein's "Gentile business." We were unfair, because serious issues were being discussed, but we were not completely wrong. The element of public relations and institutional advantage put us off. The atmosphere of these meetings was correct and respectable. No one was asked to get his hands dirty with the bitter social conflicts of that era. This organization had been created as the calling card of the new seminary administration. It announced that the Conservative movement was vying for place with the more established institutions of Reform Judaism, to become the Jewish partner in dialogue with Christian America. Some of us knew that Mordecai Kaplan, who was not particularly welcome at these gatherings, was much more seriously involved in refashioning America than the seminary's new president. Finkelstein was suspected of being a Republican, and we knew that Kaplan was an avowed New Deal Democrat.

Kaplan made much, in class and in his writings, of Thanksgiving and the Fourth of July as sacral events that bound all Americans together in spiritual fellowship. In one of his books he even suggested the main outlines of an American civil religion. He wrote prayers for the synagogue to encourage support for labor in its battles with the capitalist owners of American business and industry. In 1942, the secretaries and staff of the seminary wanted to join a labor union. Finkelstein resisted, and he succeeded in keeping the student body from declaring its support for the workers. During the quarrel, the faculty had been divided: some sided with Finkelstein; others muttered about the need for higher salaries for the secretaries and for the professors; a few insisted that they were pure scholars, too remote from the dirty business of the world to take sides. Mordecai Kaplan was the only member of the faculty to speak out for labor.

I spent most of my time at the seminary imitating Louis Ginzberg. I studied Talmud not only in his class but also as his special student, with a monthly appointment to report to him at home on my studies. (When the questions that he asked became difficult, his wife would invariably call a halt by bringing in a tray with tea and cake.) I took courses at Columbia University in ancient history, so that I should understand his references to Greek and Latin authors. I thought that I was trying to become a worthy disciple of Ginzberg. I did not know that I was really adopting Kaplan as a role model. He seemed to know, long before I did, how much I identified with him. The climax came toward the end of my student years, when I was required to prepare a sermon under his aegis. I was sure that he would not give me an easy time, so I wrote a text that was based entirely on what he himself had said on the subject. On the Thursday before I was to give it in class, I took my sermon to Kaplan for criticism. He nodded in agreement—but later, in class, he totally demolished all that I said. I countered in considerable outrage that what I was saying was, verbatim, a set of quotes from him. Kaplan was waiting for me; he smiled benignly and said, "But, Arthur, I have grown since Thursday." A few days later, he invited me to his house for coffee and asked me to write for *The Reconstructionist*, the periodical that he had created to disseminate his views. He knew that I did not agree with him, but he was sure—so he said—that I would know better as I grew older.

Kaplan was only half right. I could not go back to living in the ghetto, and I would not dismiss and forget the heresies of Spinoza and the biblical critics, but I could not follow Kaplan. He was a fighter by temperament and a political liberal by conviction, but his theories proposed to make me into a well-adjusted, normal American. In the New World, the prime function of the faith of the ancestors was to provide positive, joyous experiences to make you feel better. I could not read the inherited religious traditions that way. The prophets and the rabbis, from the very beginning of the Jewish experience in the days of Abraham and Moses, had not been well-adjusted, comfortable people. They had not taught the techniques of getting along in the world. Abraham had broken the idols of his father, and Moses had spent his years in repeated confrontations with the people he led. I was just as hostile to Kaplan's distemper with the doctrine of the chosen people. Even in America, the Christians themselves were holding fast to the belief that they were the true bearers of the faith in God. They were asserting the chosenness of the Church. No one had ever demanded that American Christians abandon this central tenet of their faith in the name of democracy. The civil order could require people to treat each other as equals, but every American could believe what he wished. So long as no religious group coerced another, each could strive to be a special "light unto the nations." Why, therefore, should the doctrine of chosenness be forbidden to Jews in America? Without some mystical sense of their specialness, why should Jews want to remain within the fold?

Kaplan asserted that individuals needed to belong to some community. The logic of this assertion was not compelling. Would it not be more sensible for Jews, who were the particular targets of anti-Semitism, to move to some safer community? I once insisted, in a heated exchange in class, that Kaplan was assuming that Jews would have a substantial feeling of guilt at leaving Judaism, which his theories about community could not justify. By his principles, what wrong did an individual do by leaving the community of his birth for some other in which he felt more comfortable or more realized?

I had even less patience with Kaplan's description of God. God was portrayed as a limited being who encouraged us toward the good but had no responsibility for the evils and the sorrows of the world. This theology seemed to me to be a thinly disguised humanism. When I first heard Kaplan expound this doctrine, I remembered that some months before, in my senior year in college, I had been required to read an essay by Bertrand Russell entitled "A Free Man's Worship." Russell was an avowed atheist. He insisted that the universe made no sense; it was a cosmic wilderness. Man had made a clearing in this forest, which he lit by the fire of his intelligence. This fire kept the wolves at bay, but they would ultimately overwhelm the clearing. When the fire was gone, no memory or meaning would remain. Russell knew very clearly that this vision of human life was contrary to the fundamental premise of the biblical faith, that there is God-given purpose to the world and that He remembers what we do and what we are. The biblical believer is sustained in tragedy by the faith that even his pain has meaning in the mind of God. His redeemer lives. Kaplan had dispensed with this supernatural God in the name of theological naturalism. I was in his class during the war years, when God's love and mercy seemed to be absent, but I could not absolve Him of the death camps by proclaiming His impotence. How could evil be outside His sphere? Kaplan's "limited God" was a respectable and proper gentleman who cheered us on to do good. The biblical God was mysterious and unknowable, but man could wrestle with Him and call Him to account. He is the father who makes us suffer and loves us. It is not easy to make peace with the biblical God, but He—and not Kaplan's "power that makes for salvation"—must be taken seriously.

In my years at the seminary, I never found a set of answers to the religious questions that preoccupied me. As the months went by, I got to thinking that these issues were not as important as I had believed at the beginning. Europe had already been at war for a year when I arrived at the seminary in the fall of 1940, and I was less and less able to shut myself off in abstract thought. One day when the lights went on again, I would wrestle with the angel of faith, and the demon of disbelief, but I could not do that in the years of war. The world was too much with us.

On the train to New York in September 1940, I had imagined that the Jewish Theological Seminary was a haven, or even a sanctuary. When I wished, I could leave this fortress and take the subway to Times Square, to a theater or to a jazz club, or to hear the leftist agitators in Union Square, but I would be a temporary observer, on loan from the Jewish monastery on Morningside Heights. Instead, those were years of emotional and intellectual turmoil. The seminary was battling with itself over how to be Jewish in America. Meanwhile, my family in Poland was being murdered. Confronted with the fact that we were unable to help them, I became an activist as a Zionist.

My vision of the seminary as a monastic retreat was an impossible dream. Satan can never be banished, even from monasteries. Even there, only a few are touched by holiness. Most men and women continue to love and to hate, to seek status for themselves and to want to deny it to others, even when they are all wearing hair shirts to mortify the flesh. In my early months at the seminary I found some friends among the students, and some mentors in the faculty, but I was soon certain that there were no saints in the building. Perhaps I was wrong.

The Talmud teaches that the world survives by the merit of thirty-six holy men and women, who are present in each generation but whose virtue is hidden. Perhaps one or two of the thirty-six were living in disguise at the seminary in 1940, and I was not sensitive enough to suspect such a presence. In a few weeks, I realized that the Jewish Theological Seminary was not the Garden of Eden; it was the world after the fall of Adam. People were jostling each other for position. I could not join the game, for I knew that I had little talent for politics.

I was so upset by the struggles at the seminary that, after a few months, I packed my bags one Sunday, to quit. On the way to the front gate, I stopped to tell one of the older students that I was leaving for good. He did what I obviously wanted him to do: he persuaded me that running away was a foolish, self-defeating gesture. Only the maladjusted fled. I should stay and learn to survive. I stayed, but I did not adjust. The very person who had talked me out of leaving tried—so I thought—to help me become more sociable. He soon invited me to a secret poker game in which the lions of student society played. It was an honor, so I was told, to be admitted to this august circle even for one evening. I went to the game, and within several hours I lost the forty dollars that my mother had scraped together to give me when I left the house. I had been reeled in by those who knew that, underneath a surface of intellectual bravado, I was an innocent. The people who had taken my money were not completely wicked. The next morning, one of them came to ask me to take over a small teaching position for which, he said, he no longer had time. I took the job, and I was grateful for the concern that had prompted the offer. The loss of face, and money, at the poker game did not prompt me to think again of running away. I had caught on that I would only find other wolves, who would have even less compassion than the ones I already knew. I withdrew more into myself and spent most of my time at the library. I could not beat these sharks at poker, but I could argue with Maimonides on the margins of his books.

Everything changed on December 7, 1941. I was in my room that Sunday afternoon, reading with a radio tuned to a concert by the NBC Orchestra under Toscanini's direction, when an announcer interrupted with the news flash that the Japanese were bombing Pearl Harbor. The next day, after Congress had declared war, the students at the rabbinical school held an emergency meeting. We voted to ask for leaves of absence and to volunteer for the army. I was one of the most vehement proponents of leaving school and enlisting in the war. This was not a theatrical gesture on the part of the students. We meant it that day, and we should have acted on that impulse, but we did not. Within a few hours, Louis Finkelstein called us together. He told us that the military would need chaplains. Our studies would be accelerated by at least a year; all of us would soon graduate and we would enter the armed services as rabbis in uniform. He told us that each of us was, of course, free to resign from the student body and become a foot soldier, but we would be wasting our training and our knowledge. The combination of carrot—our accelerated graduation into the chaplaincy—and the stick—the suggestion that those who enlisted would have to resign from the school because he would not give anyone a leave of absence— worked. Finkelstein achieved his goal, to keep the seminary functioning as a school. We went back to our classes.

Most of us were more than a little ashamed in the next months, as our contemporaries enlisted or were drafted, that, as divinity students, we were exempt from the draft. I had become something of a recluse the year before, but I could not just go back to study and to wait to graduate. I had to do something now, immediately, to fight my bit of the war. I still believed that the world could not survive without learning and piety, but I could never believe that anyone has the right to detach himself from society. My mantras became a statement in the prayer book that man is commanded "to learn, to teach, to obey God's laws, and to act," and an injunction in the Talmud that "you are not commanded to complete the task, but you have no right to avoid it." I stayed in school, but, contrary to my innate temperament, I became an activist.

I had been moving in that direction for many months. Every time I had gone home to Baltimore, my parents had shown me a few postcards they had gotten from the family in German-occupied Poland. On the surface, the messages, written in Yiddish, seemed cheerful; they told that all was well with them, but we knew that this was not true. We received a coded message from my grandfather. He wrote that Uncle Unesaneh Tokef had come to live with him and the rest of the family in Lemberg. Unesaneh Tokef is a central, solemn prayer in the liturgy of the High Holidays that describes the scene in heaven when, before God

Himself, on that day, the angelic tribunal with God presiding decides "who shall live and who shall die." My grandfather had used these words as the name of a mythical uncle. He took the risk that the censors of the German occupiers, some of whom read Yiddish, would not catch this allusion. Thus we knew that the situation of the Jews in Poland had become dire and disastrous. We heard from stories that had reached other families, and from the newspapers, that Jews were being rounded up and murdered in many villages and that there were random killings in the cities.

We were especially concerned about some cousins who were the wives and children of American citizens. Several Hasidic leaders had been spending much of their time in the United States to tend to their adherents and to collect some money, but they had kept their families in Poland. They wanted their children to grow up in the piety of the shtetl and not be tempted by the pleasures, and the heresies, that were so easily available on the streets of New York. After Poland was occupied by the Nazis, these cousins were desperate to save their families. Some of the wives and children actually had American visas. The United States still had an embassy in Berlin and even had some access to occupied Poland. Repeated appeals were made to the State Department to ask our representatives in Germany to intercede for these families, but we were told that nothing could be done.

Every time I came home, I found that my mother looked more somber and that my father was ever angrier. Both my parents felt—and so did I—that the United States government was indifferent to the fate of the Jews of Europe. One day, my father told me a story that was circulating among these husbands and fathers who were trying to save their families. One of these men was in London rather than in New York in September 1939, when the war broke out. His family had spent some years in the United States, and his wife and children held American citizenship. The head of the family went for help to the American Embassy in London, to be told that it was "out of their hands." He was so upset that he badgered everyone who walked out of the doors of the embassy building until he got an appointment with Ambassador Joseph Kennedy, who was known to have warm personal relations with some of the leading Nazis in Berlin. Kennedy received him coldly and told him to stop being a pest. The rabbi was so disheartened, and so outraged, that he uttered a curse: May God have as much compassion for your children as you have for mine. The story of this incident was quickly repeated in the Hasidic circle in the United States to which my family belonged.

In my own life, these worries reached a crescendo in the fall of 1941. My father was the rabbi, again, of a small synagogue of Yiddish-speaking immigrants. Among his congregants, some families were older than we were, and they had been in the United States longer. Their children had finished their education, only to find that it was very hard for young Jewish lawyers or social workers to get jobs, especially during the depression. Roosevelt's New Deal opened the door for thousands of these recent graduates. There were jobs to be had, without discrimination, in the new government agencies that the New Deal had spawned. The overwhelming majority of American Jews, including my father's congregants, were deeply, and even passionately, devoted to Franklin Delano Roosevelt. He had given their children work, and he had even appointed Felix Frankfurter to the Supreme Court. My father did not share this feeling. He had been railing against Roosevelt for years, because the president was doing too little to save the Jews from Nazi persecution. In May 1939, before the war broke out in Europe, the American government had not allowed the German ship *Saint Louis* to land its many hundreds of Jewish passengers who were fleeing the Nazis. The *Saint Louis* was forced to return to Hamburg, and almost all of its passengers were murdered in the Nazi death camps during the war. When the *Saint Louis* was turned away from Miami, my father screamed that, if the passengers on this ship had been Dutch or English, the American authorities would have found a way of letting them come ashore.

In the fall of 1941, my father could no longer contain his worry and his anger in public. On the afternoon of Yom Kippur, right before the solemn ending of the Fast, he told the congregation about the horrors that were already being inflicted on the Jews in Eastern Europe. He began to weep uncontrollably, and then he gasped out that only the president of the United States had the power to protest and make the Germans fear the consequences of what they were doing to Jews. My father asked his congregants to take the short journey to Washington, on the very next morning, to picket the White House. He added that he knew that he was making his congregants uncomfortable, but how could they do nothing while their brothers and sisters were being murdered?

We were exhausted when we came back home from synagogue because we had been fasting and because our insides had been churned by my father's speech before the last moments of the Yom Kippur service. As we were finishing the meal, we heard a rustle outside. The elder of my two sisters went to see what was happening. She found a letter that had been pushed under the door. The board of the synagogue had held an emergency meeting immediately after the Yom Kippur service. It decided that my father had committed lèse-majesté: he had insulted the beloved president of the United States. Without even the ceremony of addressing my father as rabbi, the board informed him that he was fired. That night, when my father received the letter of dismissal, we were all stunned. My father turned white. Soon, he rallied and said that he needed to talk with his closest friends among the laymen, Max Zemel and Max Beigel, to ask them to join him in creating a synagogue in his own home where there would be no board of directors. Those people who would want to come and worship with him could come freely, but they would own nothing of the synagogue. If they felt like contributing, they could, and if, at any point, they felt like leaving, they would be free to go.

My father fought back on that night of humiliation by reenacting his Hasidic origins. The adherents of a Hasidic master belong to no organization, and they have no control whatsoever over the actions of their rebbe. They are free to abandon him. Their belonging to him is an act of assent to what he represents in his person and in his teaching. My father decided on that night of crisis that he would never again try to be an American rabbi—that is, the employee of a congregation. He was going to be a rebbe for the rest of his life. Together with his friends, he created his own Hasidic court—and he came into his own. He created "Herzberg's shul," which became a unique power in Baltimore and, ultimately, throughout the Jewish world.

That night I listened to my father as long as I could, but, after a while, I had to excuse myself. I went upstairs to cry. Here was a holy man, a man of profound principle, being cast aside precisely because he cared for the tortured Jewish people more than he cared for the immediate convenience of his congregants. That night I heard again the mob lynching a prophet and shouting, "The man of the spirit is insane." But my father was not insane. He was God's angry man, and I was his son and his disciple. I wept for him that night—but also for myself. How would I survive in a world that did not want to hear the truth? Here I was in my second year at the Jewish Theological Seminary, where the tide was moving to carry me into some congregation where the board would want me "to behave myself" and "to not make waves." But my father had taught me that a rabbi serves God by taking personal risks, even wild ones, to tell uncomfortable truths. He had taught me that Moses had never been popular, that the Jews were always itching to vote him out, but Moses had remained their leader, despite them, because he spoke the word of God. I was not Moses, and even my father was not Moses, but he could speak his piece and live his life only on his own terms. That night I knew that I, too, could do no other, but how could I possibly manage it as a rabbi in America? Or perhaps I could find a way of avoiding this destiny.

Thus, I knew from the very beginning that the Nazis were murdering Jews in ever greater numbers, and I also knew that the Jews of America were essentially unwilling to get into a public fight with Roosevelt over the issues of immigration and rescue. In the fall of 1941 few had attacked Roosevelt in public. We knew that we had to send help, but soon that became a problem. When America entered the war, all citizens were immediately forbidden from trading with the enemy. My family disobeyed the law. We sent money to occupied Poland through Switzerland. We had little assurance that any of the money was reaching the Jews in Poland, but we had to try. I had no money to give, but I could, at least, write letters and lick stamps. I started to hang around the office of the American Federation of Polish Jews, which was deeply split between those who were sending some money to Europe and those who insisted that the law of the land had to be obeyed. In these circles I found that two elements of the American Jewish community were using any means, including those which the law forbade, to try to help the Jews of Poland: Orthodox Jews, and the Socialists in the Jewish labor unions. Both groups consisted, largely, of more recent immigrants, whose language had remained Yiddish. Their primary loyalty was to the Jewish people. They were grateful for America, but they had not become Americanized. In contrast, the atmosphere at the Jewish

Theological Seminary, where I was at school, was much more Americanized. No one dared call into question the law that forbade us to try to send help into enemy-occupied territory or to use money to try to bribe Nazis to get some people out.

In 1942, I spoke English almost all the time, and not Yiddish, but, instinctively, I was on the side of my parents and their friends, and not of the law-abiding Jewish Americans. I became more confirmed in that opinion in the summer of 1942, when the American government allowed some ships to carry food through the blockade in the Mediterranean to Greece, where hundreds of thousands were starving under German occupation. If the United States was willing to make this exception for Greeks, why were Jews forbidden to help their families in occupied Poland? At that time, I did not rationalize these feelings further, but a few years later, as I watched the Nuremberg trials, I was confirmed in my conviction that the state cannot overrule my moral conscience. If the Nazis in the dock at Nuremberg were guilty of mass murder, and had no right to claim innocence because they had obeyed their government, had I been wrong in 1942 when I disobeyed the law to try to save Jews from the Nazis?

I did not base this conclusion on some bowwow assumptions about abstract, universal justice or even on some theory of an American national identity that could allow, or at least ignore, unlawful acts in the name of justice. I did remember what I had found in Spinoza several years before. Spinoza had asserted in his *Theological-Political Tractate* that the individual had the right to rebel, on principle, against the state, but that he had to accept the right of the state to punish him if the rebellion failed. I knew in 1942 that we who were sending money to Switzerland might be found out and that we would probably be punished by being sent to jail. I was willing to accept the risk. The thought that I might go to jail—it lived with me straight through the war—evoked other memories. I recalled the exchange between Henry Thoreau and Ralph Waldo Emerson. When Thoreau was jailed for civil disobedience, Emerson came to visit him and asked him, "Henry, why are you in jail?" Thoreau answered, "Why are you not?" Spinoza and Thoreau thus cheered me up, and gave me rhetoric that I might use in the dock in some court, but I knew that they had not inspired my defiance. These were external, socially acceptable stories. I was breaking the law because I was a Jew. My extended family was being murdered, and I was required by the Bible not to stand idly by while their blood was being shed. For many, many centuries, redeeming the captives had been a Jewish commandment of the highest importance. In 1942, my religion was in conflict with my political loyalties, and it was no contest: the Jew won.

Once I had joined those who were trying to help the Jews of Europe, I was drawn into thinking about their future after the war. These issues were not being discussed at the seminary, but Salo Baron talked about them after class at Columbia University. When I had first met him, in the winter of 1940–41, Baron was still hopeful about the results of the war. He thought that the Nazis might make more pogroms like the one on *Kristallnacht*, the night of November 9–10, 1938, when they had burned almost all the synagogues of Germany, but Baron was convinced that most Jews would emerge from the war to rebuild their former lives. Baron clung to this hope even as the news became more somber. I soon knew why. His parents were in Galicia, where they had been very wealthy, and Baron wanted desperately to believe that they would survive and that they would return to lead a still-functioning community. When Baron published the first version, in two volumes, of his *Social and Religious History of the Jews* (in 1942; he later redid this work as his magnum opus, to be thirty volumes, of which he lived to complete eighteen), I found, with shock, that Baron had remained an optimist. He had not changed a fairly cheerful forecast for the future, which he had written in manuscript in the early days of the war. I was very much in awe of Baron, and flattered by his personal kindness to me, but I could not agree with him. How could so brilliant a mind be so wrong?

A few years before, in college, I had played at being a Zionist, but now, in 1942, I became one in earnest. I had become convinced that the Jews of Europe would not be able to go back to the homes that they had fled or from which they had been dragged. I had little hope that the doors of America would be wide open after the war. The only alternative was Palestine. It was clear, beyond any doubt, that the Arabs would fight against the arrival of large numbers of Jews and that the British, who still governed Palestine, would continue to yield to Arab pressure. The doors of the Jewish homeland could be opened only by a Jewish state.

I heard this argument for the first time in Louis Ginzberg's home, where I met Rabbi Stephen Wise. I was surprised to find him there. Ginzberg was a towering scholar, and Wise was not particularly learned or intellectual. He had made his reputation as an orator, a Reform rabbi who observed very little of the inherited tradition, and as a Zionist leader. Nonetheless, there was obvious warmth between Ginzberg and Wise. Louis Ginzberg, the semirecluse who avoided communal issues, admired Wise and held him in affection because Ginzberg approved of the side that Wise took in many battles. I paid attention to what Wise was saying at that tea in Ginzberg's house. He was already upset at Franklin Delano Roosevelt for promising him, or seeming to promise, much more than he ever did for the Jews in Europe, but he still hoped that his good friend Franklin would speak out and act much more decisively. Wise insisted that the real hope for the future was a Jewish state. It had to be created right after the war to raise the morale of the battered people and to provide a refuge for many hundreds of thousands who would have no other place to go. In Ginzberg's study that afternoon, I was listening not to the orator and occasional poseur but to a deeply worried, pained Jew who was pouring out his fears to the somewhat older man whom he seemed to regard as his rabbi. I conceived an affection for Wise that lasted to the end of his life and beyond. That day, in the elevator going down from Ginzberg's eleventh-floor apartment, I asked Wise to let me help the Zionist effort. He said that he would, and he soon kept his promise.

When I met Stephen Wise, the major topic on the public agenda of American Zionists was the effort to organize an inclusive meeting to make plans for the future. This meeting was held at the Biltmore Hotel in New York in early May 1942. Even though it had been called as an American gathering, the conference was, in fact, an international event. Chaim Weizmann, the preeminent figure among the Zionists, who was then living in New York, and David Ben-Gurion, the leader of the Labor Zionists and the predominant figure in Palestine, both spoke at this conference. After impassioned debates among the various factions, the conference agreed that the creation of a Jewish state in Palestine had to be the centerpiece of a postwar program of American Jews and, indeed, of all the Jews of the world. Stephen Wise had arranged for me to be one of the ushers at the meeting. I was in the large ballroom of the Biltmore Hotel for some of the debates, and especially for the climactic scene, and I had circulated for two days before in the corridors, which were seething with factional arguments and angers. These people, I thought, were in the real world. They were debating and fighting over questions of fundamental importance for the future of the Jewish people. I had been given the chance to join them, if only as a beginner who helped guard doors against those who wanted to enter the hall without credentials. The turmoil, and the passions, at the Biltmore Hotel seemed so much more alive than the forced gentility at the seminary. I even looked back at East Baltimore and thought that this meeting at the Biltmore Hotel was a far greater stage than the ghetto in which I had been raised. I even felt that I could forgive myself for not being in the army, because I had enlisted in the service of the Jewish people.

Alas, the "high" of those few days at the Biltmore Hotel soon ended. I saw that the brave demands for a Jewish state were making no difference in Europe, where Jews kept being slaughtered. The next year, when the Zionists won a famous battle in August 1943, I did not share their pride and passion. This fight took place at the other great Jewish meeting of the war years, the American Jewish Conference, which almost all of the Jewish organizations in the United States agreed to attend. The Zionists fought for the creation of a Jewish state. They were opposed by a minority led by Joseph Proskauer, the president of the American Jewish Committee. Several attempts were made to compromise, but these efforts failed and the Zionists won an open, dramatic vote of 494 to 4. The American Jewish Committee refused to bow to the result. Proskauer stood on the platform waving his delegate's card in the negative and then he walked out.

The great victories for Zionist maximalism at the Biltmore Hotel in 1942 and at the American Jewish Conference in 1943 were dramatic, but these Jewish demonstrations did not have the slightest influence on the Nazis. Great Britain and the United States did not offer to take the Jews of Europe to some neutral place, to keep them alive until the war was over. The two meetings had simply tied hundreds of people into knots over a program that could not be realized until after the war, and in 1942, and even in 1943, the Germans were still winning—and my relatives were dying.

I was soon attracted to a group that was demanding the rescue of the Jews of Europe. The organizers were several young men who had come from Palestine to the United States, to represent the Irgun Zvai Leumi, the armed offshoot in Palestine of the most nationalist of Jewish factions, Jabotinsky's Revisionists. The leader of this small delegation from Palestine used the name Peter Bergson as his alias in the United States. (His real name was Hillel Kook, but he used the name Peter Bergson in America, so as not to embarrass the memory of his uncle, the late chief rabbi of the Jews in Palestine, Abraham Isaac Kook.) While the Jewish establishment argued about war aims, and still did not want to confront Roosevelt, Bergson and his associates attracted many members of Congress and a strange combination of both highly assimilated and very Orthodox Jews. Bergson was overt and confrontationist. His various front organizations put large ads in the newspapers and held rallies and protest marches to urge the United States to ransom Jews. They demanded that the United States force Britain, in return for American help in the war, to open Palestine for Jewish refugees or at least to place them in temporary places of refuge until the war would end. I had never been attracted to the style of Jabotinsky's Revisionists. Their youth groups wore paramilitary uniforms in the style of Mussolini's Blackshirts. I could not imagine joining the Irgun Zvai Leumi, which had been shooting at the British. Nonetheless, the defiant activism in America of Peter Bergson and his group attracted me. Here were Jews who were not afraid of what the Gentiles might say. They made no concessions to American Jewish fears. The Jewish people were hurting, and they were reacting by screaming in public. Their behavior was uncouth, but they were right. The respectable American Jews who wanted people to think that they were concerned about "human rights," and not about something so parochial and personal as the murder of their relatives in Europe, were wrong.

At first, I did not quite have the courage to join Bergson publicly, but the pull on me toward him was becoming all the stronger because the Bergson people were the only group who had made Jews of the old school, with beards and even black caftans, into their allies and spokesmen. Every other element in the Jewish community in the early 1940s wanted to be represented in public life by Jews who spoke English without accent. The leaders of the American Jewish Committee prided themselves on the semi-truth, and semi-illusion, that they were part of the American establishment; some had been to college at Harvard or Princeton. Even the Zionists, most of whom were immigrants who spoke Yiddish as their first language, preferred to be represented by leaders, such as Stephen Wise, whose manners and diction were very American. By common consent, the Jews of America could not be represented by rabbis who were clearly old world. Such men would simply be regarded as a bunch of aliens, who were trying to bring their parochial concerns to America. I could not swallow this line. I had bowed to this idol of assimilation a few years earlier, in December 1937, when out of embarrassment I had buried an invitation for my conspicuously Jewish and Orthodox parents from the dean of Johns Hopkins, but the memory of this act continued to upset me. Bergson and his colleagues offered me a chance to repent. They had rabbis of the old school on the platform and in the front rows of their rallies. When I met Bergson for a cup of coffee in New York, I was surprised to find that this man, who had managed to overturn the settled order of American Jewish life in a very few years, was not much older than I was. We talked easily, because both of us came from rabbinic families and were rooted in classic Jewish education. I asked him where he found the courage, and the brass, to confront both the Gentile world and the Jews. His answer did not dwell on his certainty that he was right. He said, very quietly, that he was not afraid to be attacked and vilified.

He let slip that some of the major figures of the very Jewish establishment that he was attacking had been quietly encouraging him and even giving him money. He singled out Rabbi Abba Hillel Silver, who had just assumed the leadership of the mainstream Zionist movement in America, as the one who was most sympathetic and most helpful. Rabbi Silver's thesis was that Bergson, the extremist, was helping the Zionist cause because he was pushing the American government harder than anyone else dared. From that day forward, Bergson and I were friends. I found him some money, and I thought of him more and more as a role model. In his life and by his actions, Peter Bergson/ Hillel Kook was confirming for me something I had once heard from my father: "What is there to be afraid of in America? They might fire you from your job, but you won't really starve because you can always sell shoes."

In October 1942, before Yom Kippur, Peter Bergson and his associates organized a march on Washington of hundreds of old-world,
Orthodox rabbis from all over the United States. Rabbi Eliezer Silver,
the towering figure in this community, led special prayers in a fast day
that was observed in one of the large synagogues in East Baltimore, on
the way to the demonstration in Washington the next day. My father
helped to arrange this service. Rabbi Silver broke down, and so did my
father, when they chanted the passage "answer us on this fast day, for
our strength is exhausted"—and I wept with them. The next day I
watched these rabbis march in front of the White House. I saw the official who came out to tell them that President Roosevelt was too busy to
see a representative delegation from among the rabbis. He agreed to
take a written petition from their hands through the gate.

I wondered that day whether the president would have been too busy
to see the leaders of Amish from Pennsylvania, or American Indians, or
hundreds of priests and nuns marching in habit before the White House
to beg help for their communities in a time of trouble. Perhaps the president would have avoided all of these groups because they were not mainline Americans, but these minorities, and especially the Jews, were his
bedrock constituency. They looked to him as the one American leader
who included them in his affection. I even knew that day, as I watched
the gates of the White House remain closed to the rabbis on the sidewalk
outside, that Roosevelt did not want to give his enemies any opportunity
to call the war against the Nazis a war to defend the Jews. It hurt that
"defending the Jews" was a slur to be avoided; it hurt even more that the
president would not allow some rabbis to come to his office and to cry, in
broken English, about what was happening to their people.

It became public years later, in memoirs and other accounts of the
Roosevelt era, that Jewish advisors had told the president that Bergson
was a troublemaker and that these rabbis were not the real representatives of American Jews. We were being told that the White House was
closed to Jews who had not made themselves over into proper Americans. I was furious. I remembered being shut out that day nearly thirty
years later, in September 1971, when I was invited to a state dinner at
the White House for the first time. Walking up the stairs toward the
dining room, I found myself speaking in Yiddish to Leonard Garment,
who only half understood the language. Born to Jewish parents in

Brooklyn, he had been counsel to the president under Richard Nixon and he remained with Gerald Ford. My wife turned around (as protocol demanded, she was ahead of me, on the arm of a young Marine officer) with a look of surprise. I told her later that, as we were ascending the stairs to the formal dining room, I had suddenly remembered the scene thirty years earlier when Rabbi Eliezer Silver, and some others including my father, had not been admitted to the White House. But this incident in 1971 did not really help the grief that I remembered. In 1942, when it mattered, a Yiddish-speaking Jew was not acceptable in the White House.

Throughout 1942, and into 1943, my life was divided into three parts that seemed to live in different universes. At home in Baltimore, and through the news that came from my parents in letters and phone calls, I was living in Yiddish with the emotions of a recent refugee who was watching his relatives bleed to death without being able to reach them or to help them. I did not question or even wonder, at the time, at the habit of speech that my parents had adopted. Even as they heard that the Jews in the towns from which we came had been uprooted and sent away to unknown destinations, my parents continued to speak of Lubaczow, Dinov, Sanz, and Yavorov in the present tense. They never said, "*in Sanz hat men gezogt*" ("they used to say in Sanz"); it was always, "*in Sanz zogt men*" ("they say in Sanz"). My parents would never abandon this locution, not even after the war, when they knew for certain that all these Jewish communities were gone forever. They kept these towns alive by evoking them, in all their details, as a present reality. My parents were not sentimental about these Jews whom they remembered, but they also did not dwell on the sinners in these towns. In the 1960s I was annoyed by both Abraham Joshua Heschel, who painted the Jews of Eastern Europe as otherworldly pietists, and at Isaac Bashevis Singer, who highlighted the weird and sexually intriguing side of the East European shtetl. I had occasion to tell each of them, bluntly, that both their accounts were denied by my parents, who had continued to keep this world alive for me by describing it as an intense, often brawling, and complicated society. My parents had kept these communities alive, in all their details—rabbis, heretics, crooks, businessmen, prostitutes, and the simple people who stopped at synagogue to pray and read psalms on the way to work. My father had a formidable, probably unparalleled, memory for family relationships. He knew which holy men were related to each other, which magnates had improved their social positions by arranging for their children to marry into rabbinic families, and which socialist leaders were the grandchildren of famous scholars of the Talmud.

But I was spending most of my time, in the first year after America entered the war, at the seminary, where life went on with very little change from what I had found when I arrived as a freshman in the fall of 1940. To be sure, the spring dinner dance to celebrate Purim was canceled in 1942 and not given again. We even stayed at school for part of the summer to carry out the acceleration of our studies so that we could enter the military chaplaincy sooner. Nonetheless, the school continued on its established course. Individuals among the faculty and students did take part in the efforts of rescue and in the political debates, but almost no echo of these concerns were heard in the program of the school. There was one exception, the renewed Zionist energies after the Biltmore Conference in 1942. My class, which was to graduate in June 1943, suggested to the administration that the Zionist hymn "Hatikvah" ("The Hope"—that is, the hope of establishing a Jewish state) be sung at the graduation ceremony. The president, Dr. Louis Finkelstein, refused, because, in his view, this was a political statement in which all Jews did not share and our ordination as rabbis was a religious act. On this issue, even though I had become a fervent Zionist, I was not one of the firebrands, because I thought that a case could be made for the separation between Jewish religion and any version of Jewish political ideology. Nonetheless, this controversy added to my sense that the seminary was a place that was trying to make me into an American of the Jewish persuasion, whose real difference from the Reform Jews was that I would be more observant of the rituals and more learned in the ancient texts. Its conscious intent was to take me away from Eastern Europe, to change my identity.

I began to pay attention to a story that was still being told about Cyrus Adler, the president of the seminary who had died in the spring of 1940, a few months before I arrived at school. He had, supposedly, asked applicants for entry into the school whether they held to an "Occidental" or an "Oriental" view of Judaism; he wanted to find out whether they wanted to become proper American gentlemen or whether they were still attached to East European Jewish culture. It was no accident that in my years at the school, I seldom heard any of my teachers utter a word in the native language of most of them, Yiddish, not even in response to my use of a Yiddish phrase or sentence when I spoke with them. I did that less and less from year to year; I found myself learning the lesson that Yiddish was a bit uncouth, reminiscent of the ghetto. I resented myself for complying, but, even more, I lost respect for those who were ashamed of their origins.

As my years at the seminary were coming to an end in the spring of 1943, I sadly admitted to myself that I had found no role model at the school. My admiration for the learning of several of its towering scholars had grown rather than decreased during three years of sitting in their classes, but I soon knew that they were no closer to answering the question of how to be a Jew in contemporary America than I was. The man I most admired, Louis Ginzberg, was always intellectually dazzling, and he was an aristocrat, but I could discern no clear line in his religious outlook and practice. He was an eclectic traditionalist who seemed to have withdrawn, at least in part, from active involvement in the community because he could thus avoid explaining his own life to others. Everyone knew that Ginzberg could not tolerate Kaplan's pragmatic Americanized version of Judaism and Jewish identity, but he preferred to ignore Kaplan or to make oblique digs at Kaplan's scholarship. We also knew that Ginzberg was upset when someone in the Orthodox community wrote him a letter of bitter reproach that this great master of the Talmud had deviated from the faith and practice of his parents and ancestors. He had chosen to be a professor, a historian of rabbinic Judaism, and not an impassioned exponent of its rules from which Jews dare not deviate. In answer to Kaplan, and to the Orthodox, Ginzberg offered his students no coherent account of his religiosity. Eventually, I understood that Ginzberg was even more alien to the United States than my father was. He seemed to have put up a wall to protect himself and to keep America out. Inside his study, he communed with his peers: twenty centuries of rabbinic scholars. This continuing dialogue with his intellectual predecessors was really what sustained him. He did not seem to need the society around him, or perhaps he did but he could not cope with it.

The most recent addition to the faculty, Saul Lieberman, was even more vehement and overt in his sniping at Mordecai Kaplan. Lieberman was proudly, and even pugnaciously, Orthodox. He convinced almost everyone at the seminary of his Orthodoxy, but I did not really believe him. I kept wondering why someone of his convictions would join in ordaining rabbis for a branch of Judaism that had moved away from Orthodoxy. I found it all the more difficult to reach toward Lieberman because he was impatient and often cutting. He would let me come to him to ask for an explanation of a difficult passage in a Talmudic text, but I could not get him to talk about his beliefs. I suspected, from my first encounter with Lieberman as his student, that he was far too worldly to believe, literally, that God had sat on Mount Sinai and dictated the first five books of the Bible to Moses, who acted as His scribe—but I could not discern what he really thought. From the very beginning Lieberman made no attempt to integrate himself personally in America. Even more than Ginzberg, he was buried in his study, without any bridges to the surrounding society.

The one figure at school who devoted himself to the question of how Jews were to orient themselves in America was Mordecai Kaplan. I had known very early that I could not follow his religious views, but I was attracted to Kaplan's definition of American society. He rejected the nativist doctrine that a proper American was a Protestant of Anglo-Saxon ancestry and that everyone else had to remake himself to conform to WASP culture and values. Kaplan fought even harder against the proponents of the newer notion of the melting pot. They imagined an America that continued to change as it kept absorbing elements from the cultures of newer waves of immigration and adding them to the life of all Americans. Kaplan argued, correctly, that both these doctrines expected minorities to disappear. Kaplan convinced his students that the difference between the nativists and the proponents of the melting pot is that the nativists insisted that new immigrants should simply abandon every trace of their ancestral traditions; the theorists of the melting pot would allow minority cultures a more graceful and more honorable death. Kaplan was among the first to define a new theory, cultural pluralism. He proposed that all Americans should, indeed, share in the political and civic culture of the United States. They should communicate with each other in the English language, and they should behave as equals within the democratic political system. However, each minority could also live, at least part of the time, by its own traditions.

These ethnic minorities would be expected to redefine their cultures, so that each would fit into the American way of life.

At first blush, Kaplan's cultural pluralism made me feel better: I was entitled to be a good, even a fervent, American, and yet I had the right to cultivate my own Jewishness. I was soon disenchanted. Kaplan seemed to me to be too American; he was conceding too much. The test case was his attitude toward parochial education. Kaplan was unalterably opposed to Jewish parochial schools. He insisted that Jewish children, and those of all other minorities, had to attend public school to be rooted in American democratic culture. I could not agree. The Roman Catholics were then educating the bulk of their children in their own parochial schools. To attempt to deny them that right, or to denigrate their use of that right as un-American, was to accept the proposition that one had to behave like the Protestants to be a good American. Moreover, even the Protestants, were not unequivocally committed to public education. Franklin Delano Roosevelt had been educated at Groton, a private boarding school that was markedly, and parochially, Episcopalian. The American aristocrats could raise their children in separatist, avowedly Protestant, schools, but it was not acceptable, so Kaplan seemed to be saying, for others, and especially for Jews, to try to do the same with their children.

I rejected Kaplan's cultural pluralism. I wanted a society in which everyone would be free to be himself, so long as they did not break the law. I simply could not accept the thesis that a boarding school headed by an Episcopalian priest, in which the Book of Common Prayer was read every day at compulsory morning services, was acceptably American, but a Jewish parochial school run by rabbis, in which morning prayers were said in Hebrew, was a hopelessly foreign ghetto. I was caught in a dilemma. I knew that the public school was a binding force of a democratic society, but I had been commanded to repeat in my prayers twice a day the biblical injunction to teach the Jewish tradition diligently to the young. What they could learn in voluntary classes that children were attending for a few hours in the afternoon or on Sunday morning was inherently shallow. Thirty centuries of texts and tradition were inevitably reduced to a few rituals and some nostalgia. But the public school was the one institution in America that had always been open to Jews. This dilemma would trouble me, and remain unresolved, for many years.

A lthough I was a "rabbi, teacher, and preacher," I tried to find a way of remaining a student. The seminary was pushing us to work in congregations, to replace the rabbis who had taken leaves of absence to become military chaplains. We were available to cover civilian needs, for, as new graduates, we had to wait two years, to acquire practical experience, before we could join the military.

The seminary administration announced one exception: it would choose one of the members of my class to be registrar of the school. This news gave me the courage to ask to stay on as a postgraduate student in a self-created post of instructor. I had already passed most of the examinations in Talmud toward the highest form of rabbinic ordination, and I was halfway through the graduate courses at Columbia toward a doctorate in Jewish history. I wanted to serve out the two years of waiting to enter the service by completing my graduate studies at both schools. With Louis Ginzberg's agreement and support, I cleverly offered to act as an instructor in Talmud, in return for my keep. All that I needed was one hundred dollars a month to pay my incidental expenses, and the right to live in the dormitory. Louis Finkelstein would have none of this. He told me, bluntly, that my scholarly plans were my own affair; the seminary was concerned with its own institutional interests and with the needs of the congregations in the field. He implied that he had no sympathy with my veiled attempt to become a very junior adjunct to the faculty. I walked out of that interview knowing that I was being cast out. I was determined that I would not be manipulated as a pawn in his chess game and that I would find my own way to an academic environment. If I had to find a job, I wanted to work at some college. As the colleges were being emptied by the military draft, no junior faculty appointments were available, but I could become a rabbi to the Jewish students on some campus. I did not show up for interviews that the seminary had arranged with committees from synagogues in middle-sized towns in Pennsylvania and upstate New York. Instead, I applied to the national director of the Hillel Foundation, Abram Leon Sachar. This organization staffed and supported the work among Jewish students in many of the colleges and universities throughout the country.

In a few days I was invited to meet in New York with a small committee that chose rabbis for the jobs in Hillel. I walked into the meeting imagining that I would have to sell myself, and I was afraid that I would not succeed. I should not have been nervous. Many of the Hillel rabbis serving on campus had gone off to the war. The foundation was having even greater problems than the congregations in finding replacements. Not long after the interview began, one of the members of the committee let slip that he had telephoned Louis Ginzberg, who had indicated that I was not totally stupid or illiterate. I was offered the job of director of the Hillel Foundation in southern Massachusetts. I would work out of rented quarters in Amherst, leading religious services and other programs for the Jewish students at the several colleges in the neighborhood. The two nearest schools, Amherst College and Massachusetts State College, had very few students, for most young men were already in the armed forces, but some of their facilities were being used to train soldiers for intelligence duties or to serve in the American military governments that would soon be set up in Germany and Japan. The intact schools in the area were two famous women's colleges, Smith and Mount Holyoke. Very few of their students had joined the Wacs or the Waves, but both student bodies were not as serene as they seemed on the surface. There was little social life and much tension because their boyfriends were on the fighting front and some were being killed.

In the weeks before school began, I begged for cast-off chairs and couches with which to furnish the building that had been rented in Amherst, and I tried to arrange for the High Holiday celebration in late September. The local advisory committee did find some furniture for the Hillel House; I would not have to ask the students to sit on the floor at religious services and group meetings. But I failed to organize the High Holiday services. Most of the students, and the military personnel in the training programs, were from the Northeast, and the rest had relatives in the area. All had arranged to go home for these solemn holidays.

Since I would not have anything to do at any of the colleges, I agreed to preach in Youngstown, at the High Holiday observances in the synagogue that my relatives attended. Their rabbi had entered the army, and the congregation had not yet found a replacement. I looked forward to returning to Youngstown. I thought that, now that I was all grown up and a rabbi, I would impress and please my cousins. I could not have been more wrong.

In my first sermon on Rosh Hashanah, I criticized Roosevelt for not trying hard enough to save the Jews of Europe. By the fall of 1943, the death camps were producing tens of thousands of dead each day, and the reports of these atrocities had come from too many sources to be disregarded or denied. My remarks from the pulpit were not as sharp as my father's outcry in Baltimore two years before, but what I said outraged the congregation in Youngstown. My relatives were embarrassed, as members of the congregation grimly asserted, to my face, that my words were unpatriotic and even treasonable. I had no doubt that I had spoken the truth, but it was clear that the people in this mainstream synagogue did not want to be upset by hearing uncomfortable truths. I was asked to soften my remarks for my sermon on the second day of Rosh Hashanah at Youngstown, but I refused. I did not know whether I was impelled by temperament or by principle, but I could not back down.

I was elated when I returned to Amherst from Youngstown. There I was my own boss. The members of the advisory committee were helpful, but they did not think of themselves as a board of overseers to whom I had to report. They were investing time and concern but not money from their own funds or that they were soliciting from others. The bills were paid by the national office of Hillel. I did write regular reports on what I was doing, and, on occasion, I asked for advice, but no supervisor ever came to help me or to bedevil me. I was on my own. At the age of twenty-two, I was no older than the students whom I was serving. We could be frank with each other because we knew that we had been thrown together only for a while. The students would soon graduate, and the soldiers in the specialized training programs would soon finish their training. None of us needed to tone down his sharpest opinions. We were a temporary community that was held together only by our Jewish feelings. Most were conventional, young men and women from middle-class families, but there were a few striking exceptions. In the first weeks after I began my job, I found an ultra-Orthodox young man in the army program at Amherst College, who was struggling to keep kosher and to find a quiet corner every morning before reveille to put on his prayer shawl and tefillin. At Smith College I encountered a great-granddaughter of Isaac Meyer Wise, the founding figure of Reform Judaism in America. This student was singing in the choir of the Protestant chapel; she agreed to help with the Jewish Friday-night services. One of the sophomores at Smith had come to America from Vienna just before the war began in Europe. She was especially concerned with what was happening to the Jews in Europe. She had left behind friends from early childhood, and she had not heard from them after 1940.

There were very few Jewish students at Smith College and even fewer at Holyoke. No one talked about quotas even though they existed in some form. Instead they used euphemisms about "geographical distribution" and "national representation" in the student bodies. The proportion of Jews among the students in both schools was perhaps 5 percent. The prevailing atmosphere was such that many of the Jewish students preferred to become semi-Marranos; they did nothing that would set them apart from the vast majority. Five or six young women attended the first Friday-night service that fall at Smith College, and the number did not grow. There were two stalwarts, both sophomores, Reline and Zelda, who had resisted the tide of assimilation from their very first days on campus. One of them had even turned vegetarian in order to eat only kosher food. In the course of the winter, I met others who told me they belonged to strongly committed Jewish families and that, after graduation, they intended to continue in the traditions in which they had been raised, but as long as they were at Smith, it was simply easier for them to play down their identity as Jews. I did not sympathize with these young women until the day in December when I was a guest in a class in religion. The inevitable subject was the trial and death of Jesus. The consensus of the discussion was that the Jews remained responsible for the death of Jesus and that Christians could not help feeling some distance from this eerie and wrongheaded people.

This was the very first time that I was confronted with this painful question, in discussion with Christians, and I was at a loss. I knew the arguments that had been advanced by Jewish scholars that the Sanhedrin could not have tried Jesus. No Jewish court could sit at night, because these tribunals were commanded to make judgments that were "as clear as the sun." At that time, Judea was under Roman occupation, and the Jewish courts no longer had the power to try capital cases. I did not use these arguments that day. Most of the students had been brought up to believe that everything in the New Testament, including its historical accounts, was true. They were not likely to be convinced by a young rabbi fresh out of school. I was even more upset by the not so hidden premise that Jews bore corporate, continuing guilt for the death of Jesus. I felt that I could argue against this idea, because it was less intimately connected to the story of the trial and death of Jesus, and so I did. The class was surprised to hear me ask, What if a Jewish court had, indeed, condemned Jesus to death? Was the guilt of one judicial murder, nineteen centuries ago, a crime that forever condemned the descendants and relatives of those ancient judges? If this were true, then what of the murders of countless Jews by crusaders, inquisitors, and pogrom makers? Should Jews insist that all Christians continue to bear eternal guilt?

The students seemed surprised by what I said, but they were not convinced. Several distinguished between the crucifixion of Jesus and all other deaths. In the Jesus story, men had dared to condemn God incarnate in human form; this was a far more heinous crime than the murder of ordinary human beings. At that point in the discussion, I lost control. With some heat I asked the class whether they really believed in the doctrine of the incarnation. Before anyone could answer, I added that there are only two possibilities: either the carpenter from Galilee was God Incarnate or he was a man, an itinerant Jewish preacher. If he was "the word made flesh," then mere men could not crucify him. He had to will his death as part of a cosmic drama in which Jews and Romans played the parts for which they had been cast by God. In that case, those who judged Jesus and crucified him, whoever they might have been, were not guilty of anything more than carrying out the will of God. Hangmen carry out the decisions of the courts. Are the descendants of ancient hangmen guilty of anything? But what if Jesus was a man like other men? What right had Christians to harp on the guilt that they imputed to Jews for his death?

At the end of this scene the class was quiet and clearly unhappy. Almost on cue, the bell rang and the session ended. The several Jews in the class seemed especially upset with me. Later that day two of them found me and invited me to a cup of coffee away from campus, in the diner near the railroad station. After some hesitation, they got to the point. My job, so they said, was to make life easier for the small Jewish minority at Smith, and I had done the opposite by challenging some of the fundamentals of Christianity. They had expected me to come into class and talk of Jesus as a great Jewish prophet, to praise the moral values that Jews and Christians share, and to extol brotherhood. They admitted they knew that the epithet "Christ-killers" was alive even at Smith College, but why had I confronted it?

I listened with sympathy. These young women wanted to live at peace by obscuring differences, and they hoped that their niceness would buy them acceptance. The two students at coffee suggested that I was an extremist; I did not care that I was straining their connections with Christian friends. I tried to explain and defend myself, but the students and I were talking past each other. They were asking me to help smooth off any Jewish angularities that might irritate the Gentiles. I was making trouble for them, because I had not accepted the notion that Jews should talk about Christianity and Christians only in ways that would create a surface of goodwill. I tried to tell them that Jews have their own perspective on the early history of Christianity and on its theology; we could reach understanding, and equality with others, only if they would hear what we had to say in our real accents. As the discussion kept going—it lasted nearly two hours—I could not stop myself from saying that in the United States of the day there were three major religions: Catholics, whose highest principle was obedience to the hierarchy of their church; Protestants, who believed that their congregations were a reenactment of the early church; and Jews, who were less committed to Judaism than to interfaith.

When that conversation came to an end, I knew that I was fighting on two fronts—with my generation of Jews, and with the culture of the Gentile majority. For many of my immediate contemporaries, their Jewish identity was defined in opposition to anti-Semitism; many were "proud to be Jews," but their pride was based on the "Jewish contribution to civilization," which they measured by the strikingly large proportion of Jews who had won the Nobel Prize. Similarly, everyone seemed to know that Marx, Freud, and Einstein were Jews, and the more learned knew that Spinoza could be added to this list, but almost no one spoke of Maimonides or of such eighteenth-century figures as the Talmudist Elijah of Vilna or the founder of Hasidism, the Baal Shem Tov. This Jewish pride was outer directed; it existed to establish that Jews were, and could be, useful to the larger society. Talented individuals were knocking at the door and saying that, if they were given half a chance, more Einsteins and Freuds would appear from among them. The questions that concerned me—to keep Jewish learning alive and to define the values of Judaism in contemporary terms—were simply irrelevant. To the degree to which anyone thought about these matters, Judaism was described as an inconvenient set of ritual restrictions and atavistic memories; this Jewishness was a burden, and a barrier to the success of individual Jews, in the larger society.

I had argued with the two Smith students with considerable heat that day, but I soon cooled down and telephoned my apologies. Walking home from the diner, I had seen the obvious. These students were not self-created; they were the product of the world in which they had been raised. They were children of parents who were well-off enough during the depression of the 1930s to send their daughters to college. These young women had been educated as Jews in the Sunday schools of middle-class congregations. The Jewish books they had seen on coffee tables at home had one recurring theme: Jews were proving that they were true-blue Americans, from the very beginning. The authors of

these volumes asserted that Christopher Columbus himself had probably been a crypto-Jew, and that one of his principal assistants was
known to be a very recent convert; Jews had made an outsized contribution to George Washington's army and to both the Union and Confederate forces during the Civil War; Jews were among the founders of
Western science and philosophy. The "Jewish" novels of the 1930s
harped on the clash between the immigrant parents, who were trying to
keep their families within the stifling boundaries of the Jewish ghetto,
and their children, who fought bitterly for the freedom to leave the past
behind. In the novels, the young almost always won their battles, but
they were often left with some guilt toward their parents. An act of
expiation might free them to live as new men and women. The quintessence of this tale had been told in the script, in 1927, of the first talking movie, *The Jazz Singer*. The hero of the story, played by Al Jolson,
had been raised by his father, who was cantor in an immigrant synagogue, but the "American" son had fled to become a jazz singer. At the
end of the film, the young man comes home, in the year of his father's
death, to chant the service in the synagogue on the Day of Atonement,
but it is clear that he would leave in a few hours to return to his life as
an entertainer on the American stage.

How could I blame two sophomores for being the kind of Jews that
they had been raised to be? My quarrel was not with them. Years later,
I would come to know that it was not even with the books of the 1930s.
Far greater men than the novelists of the 1930s had invented the argument that Jews could claim equality in the West because they were
cofounders of the very culture that was excluding them. Leopold Zunz,
a founding father of modern learning in the history of Judaism, had
made this very point in the 1820s. I did not yet know enough history in
the fall of 1943 to trace this self-abasement to its source, but I was convinced even then that the Jewish community—and every other minority, for that matter—had a right to equal treatment. The right to one's
own identity did not belong only to those who could prove their worth.
No one should be forced to behave by the norms of the majority.
Acceptability and conformity to someone else's standards could not be
the test for equality and even for survival.

I witnessed the pressure of anti-Semitism on a mass public occasion.
The then young Yehudi Menuhin came to Northampton that spring of

1944 to give a concert at Smith College. He was accompanied by Moshe Menuhin, his father, who was then acting as his manager. I bought a ticket for the concert with great pride that this Jewish artist would be a guest on campus, and I felt particularly honored to be invited to a reception for the violinist after the concert. At that party I happened to be standing nearby when the elder Menuhin was asked the question, Where does your name come from? He understood the meaning—that he was being asked whether he was a Jew—and he quickly replied that the name and the family origin were Armenian. The son, Yehudi, heard this answer, and grimaced, but he did not say a word. I had no choice but to let it go, even as I thought that Moshe Menuhin was making a ridiculous and unwarranted concession to anti-Semitism. Had he not just met a young rabbi who had been invited to the party on the clear assumption that the Menuhin family had much more to do with rabbis than with Armenian priests? Clearly, Moshe Menuhin was spreading this fable around because he thought it would make it easier for his son to be accepted by the top echelons of Gentile society.

While I felt let down with some of the Jews with whom I was working, I was even more perturbed by the Gentiles. I did encounter friendly people, but I soon understood that some of them regarded me as a half-alien exotic. Bill Easton, a Protestant minister who was the chaplain at Massachusetts State College, was the warmest. He simply wanted to make the Jewish students comfortable, and he was pleased that the Hillel center for the area was on the edge of his campus. Ralph Harlow, who was professor of religion at Smith, reached out to me because he believed in the Social Gospel. His concern for the weak and poor extended to Jews under attack from the Nazis and from homegrown American anti-Semites. I found no comparable friend at Amherst College, but I did get to know Jesse Trotter, the minister in charge of the oldest church in town. He often took me to lunch at the famous Lord Jeffrey Amherst Inn. Trotter's congregation contained the Amherst establishment. The house in which Emily Dickinson had lived was just a few yards away, and her father had been the pastor of this congregation. I thought for months that Trotter was conscious, as he befriended me, that he was being gracious, en grand seigneur, but I kept telling myself that I was a supersensitive Jew. This was probably true, but it was even more true that I could not depend on my new friend to have the tact not to upset me. At one of our lunches, Jesse Trotter told me that there were about twenty Jewish families in his congregation. I was both shocked and incredulous, because there were almost no Jewish residents in Amherst, and I was sure that the mass conversion of so many Jews would have come to some public notice. Trotter replied that he was talking about one Jew who had come to Amherst near its beginnings late in the seventeenth century and had remained to marry one of the young women of the town. The descendants of this couple, nearly three hundred years later and without the addition of any other Jewish ancestors, were still talked about as the Jewish members of the church. He did not seem to be asking me to reclaim these families for the synagogue. He was telling me that, even after ten generations, Jewishness is ineradicable and that it remains alien, even in the church. I guessed that he had told me of these families to suggest, perhaps without fully realizing what he was saying, that avowed Jews like me would always be regarded as outsiders—as the other—in America. As I walked away from our lunch that day, I looked around at the buildings on the green in Amherst. This was picture-postcard America. I had been told that I was, at best, a guest here—but I did not want to spend the rest of my life in a land in which I lived on sufferance under the judgment of those who presumed that they were the real masters of the country.

I was thus learning, in my very first months in southern New England, that the establishments at Smith and Amherst were not stretching to include me. The few Gentiles who paid any heed to my work with the Jewish students were almost all liberals of one kind or another who were themselves regarded as disturbers of the peace. The dean of Smith then was a woman, Hallie Flanagan, who had worked in one of the agencies of Roosevelt's New Deal. Flanagan was soon in hot water with the trustees and the alumnae because she shared the liberal outlook of her great friend Eleanor Roosevelt. Hallie Flanagan invited me to tea soon after I arrived, and she was friendly and gracious at other occasional encounters. I knew that this was an expression of the persona that was getting her into trouble with the mainstream at Smith.

Among the other colleges, the warmest welcome had come from Massachusetts State College. I soon understood that this was not merely an expression of the personality of the school's chaplain, Bill

Easton. Massachusetts State College was funded by the taxpayers, and Jews were second only to the Irish as a distinct, recognizable power in the politics of the state. Even a twenty-two-year-old rabbi on campus, whose personal roots were in Baltimore and New York, was proud to have behind him a hundred thousand Jews in Boston and, much closer by, perhaps ten thousand in Springfield. I was listed at both Massachusetts State and Smith as chaplain to the Jewish students. At the end of the academic year, the existence of Hillel was emphasized in the yearbook of Mass State and ignored in the Smith annual.

The experiences with the military groups in the neighborhood were much more positive. An average of about seven hundred men in the specialized training programs of the army were housed in the dormitories of Amherst College. They were taught not by a few members of the Amherst faculty but mostly by instructors in uniform. The group was too small to have its own military chaplain, so the command was glad to have me take care of the Jewish soldiers. This was also true for the Wave officer candidate's school, which was housed at Smith. These young women were more posh than the young men in the army at Amherst. The Waves were a volunteer body that clearly preferred officers who had graduated from the elite women's colleges. Nonetheless, the Wave command was a military establishment of the government at war. I was welcomed every time I showed up at the office. The Wave commanders obeyed the doctrine that the war could be pursued and won only by the combined efforts of all Americans.

In my first job, I had no feel, yet, for power relations on the larger stage of American society. The first glimmerings of understanding came to me that winter of 1943–44, as I wondered why I was being made more comfortable in a public college and in military offices than in the more polite and gracious parlors of several elite colleges. I began to know that, contrary to Shakespeare, the fault was not in ourselves but in our stars. I was the same Jew everywhere, but the environments were different: I was the least accepted where Jews had the least power. America at war needed the energy and talent of all its citizens; the elite colleges, with most of America's young men away, had no need, yet, to change their long-standing attitude that Jews were to be admitted in small numbers, and on approval. These experiences were evidence, if only subconsciously, for a premise from which I would never waver for the rest of my life. Jews, and other minorities, cannot bet their future on changing the hearts and minds of the majority. They will find their place in society by using their power in the public arena to force change.

No such complexities bedeviled me as I made my way into the Jewish community in the area. The only avowed Jew on any of the faculties, Charles Goldberg, taught English at Mass State. He had been the part-time counselor to Jewish students before my job was created, and he had even been paid a little for his work. That ended with my arrival, and I expected him to be a bit cold to me. He was not. He and his wife made a point of befriending me lest I become lonely and despondent. In Northampton there had long been a small Jewish community, of less than a hundred families, with a synagogue of its own. One of the older women, a widow who kept a kosher kitchen, fed me quite regularly. That task was taken over in midyear by Rabbi Eric Lowenthal and his wife, recent refugees from Germany who were the rabbinic couple at the local synagogue. The rabbi was not being paid very much, and he had wanted to be the Hillel director, part-time, to add to his income, but he was too much of a gentleman ever to complain. Lowenthal had received good scholarly training in Europe, and I looked forward to talking with him at lunch or dinner several times a week.

The large and vibrant Jewish community of Springfield was less than twenty miles away, so I went there often to purchase "Jewish soul food," the bagels and the smoked fish that were mandatory fare for the brunches on Sundays that I arranged for the students. I was made welcome like a visiting cousin. Herman Abramson, the cantor of the leading Orthodox synagogue in town, and his wife took me into their family. I could come and go at almost any hour. When I left for my apartment in Northampton, they gave me food packages to take along to the small-town desert, where there was no hot pastrami and no chicken soup. I was comfortable in Springfield because I found people there with whom I shared my Jewish feelings. Quite a number had been born in Eastern Europe; some knew Yiddish, and a few had studied the Talmud.

As I felt the hurts in Amherst and Northampton, the clear temptation was to run back to the sustaining and protecting ghetto. That path was available, for many jobs were open in synagogues all over America, but I would not give in. I had gone to Johns Hopkins, and not to a yeshiva, and to the Jewish Theological Seminary, and not to one of the

Orthodox rabbinical schools, because I had decided in my early teens to move into America, beyond the transplanted shtetl in East Baltimore in which I was raised. If I could not come to terms with the America of the "intelligent Gentiles," my alternative would not be the lifestyle of the American Jewish bourgeoisie; it would be the Zionist settlement in Palestine.

The Gentiles in Amherst and Northampton, and the Jews in Springfield, were teaching me some lessons about America, and about myself, but the most intense and revealing journey of discovery was in my work with the Jewish students and the Jews in the military. I was the same age as they, but I did not think or feel like them. They were optimists, but I had brought some sadness with me. By 1940, when I left Baltimore for New York, my neighborhood was shrinking. The synagogues were no longer packed when virtuoso cantors came visiting to chant the Sabbath or holiday liturgy. Some of those who used to come to hear them had died, and others had moved out to the areas of second settlement, to Park Heights or Forest Park. The Hebrew Parochial School was shutting down and moving to a new building in Park Heights. The children who came to class were having difficulty understanding the Yiddish of their teachers, so the language of instruction in Bible and Talmud was shifting to English.

In New York, in the early 1940s, the theaters on Second Avenue were closing one by one. The last time I saw *The Dybbuk*, in repertory at the Yiddish Art Theater, was in 1942 or 1943. The cast was extraordinary. The star, Lazar Fried, played the young Hasidic hero of perhaps twenty so believably that I went backstage to meet him and congratulate him. I was astounded to find a thin, obviously ill, old man taking off his makeup. Fried was very sad. There had been perhaps twenty people in the audience, and he did not brighten up later at Café Royale, because the room was nearly empty and very subdued.

I had brought with me to my first job the sadness and sorrow of watching the end of an era, but almost none of the college students in Amherst and Northampton had such concerns. They were thinking about their future. The Great Depression was behind them, and anti-Semitism had been driven underground, at least in part, by the entry of the United States into the war. Unlike me, they had been born in America and they had been raised in the mentality of the second generation. They were becoming more confident that there would be a place for them in its postwar society. I was sad, because I saw myself as the last of the Mohicans; they were glad, because they looked forward to an America in which careers would be open to talent. I was saddest on Saturday afternoons, when the students were busy with the weekend bustle at college. I stayed home to study the Talmud, as part of the observance of the Sabbath, but no one joined me.

It would be wrong to suggest that I was totally alone in the college environment. Now that I had a few dollars in my pocket, I bought a record player and started to collect records of Yiddish songs and of selections from the Hebrew liturgy. The incidental music of *The Dybbuk* had been recorded. Sidor Belarsky, a bass baritone, who specialized in the songs of the Zionist movement, was at the height of his career. I was very much his fan, and I even tried to bring him to southern New England. A time convenient to his schedule could not be found, so, instead, I bought all of his records. Six or seven students from the various schools came to my apartment every other week to hear the music. We did not listen in silence, because I explained the texts, with the avowed intention of bringing my guests closer to their spirit. During Hanukkah that December, dozens turned up to join in lighting candles every night at the Hillel House in Amherst and at the services in the college chapel at Smith. Some students came whom I had never seen before. In the early spring, the Hillel House was overflowing for the reading of the biblical Book of Esther, in celebration of the festival of Purim. However, I did not need to organize a public celebration of Passover, because all who cared went home to celebrate the Seder on the first two days, and almost no one even approached me for help to find the unleavened bread that is prescribed for the holiday. Several years before, Dr. Louis Kaplan had said to me that the next generation of American Jews would hold on to those holidays, which provided them with joy, but would abandon the kosher rules, which restricted their diet, and the commandments that limited their activities on the Sabbath. Working with students in southern New England, I found that Kaplan was a well-informed prophet. I was happy in the company of those who came to the holiday celebrations, for without them I would have been alone, but I was not at ease. I kept saying to myself that a religious tradition or an ethnic culture—and Jewish identity is a compound of both elements—defines itself by what it rejects, or will not do, even more than by what it affirms and does.

My most exciting Jewish and intellectual experience at Smith was a growing acquaintance with Hans Kohn. He had come from City College of New York to teach the history of modern Europe. Kohn was a refugee from Germany who was widely regarded as a leading authority on the Nazis. He was an entertaining lecturer who had brought with him a vast stock of learning rooted in Central European culture. The WASPs at Smith were intrigued by him—not least, I suspected, because he was a Jew who was obviously foreign. They did not need to regard him as the harbinger of the arrival of other Jews who spoke English without his accent, who would break the WASP monopoly of the faculty. Kohn was, by then, very secular, and he had even abandoned his youthful Zionism. He participated in nothing Jewish at Smith or at Hillel, even though he had belonged to the circle of Martin Buber in the 1920s and he had even spent some years working for the World Zionist Organization in Palestine. I sought Kohn out. He received me graciously, letting me join him often in the long walks that he liked to take. Kohn was, by temperament, an optimist. When I raised the question of the fate of the Jews in Europe, Kohn expressed his well-known contempt for the Nazis, but he did not believe the accounts that the worst was happening. In any event, he added that we could do very little directly to help the Jews in Europe. Kohn was much more interested in persuading me that the Zionists had not done enough to come to terms with the Arabs. He rejected my argument that, even if the Zionists had behaved from the beginning as saints and angels, violent Arab opposition to the building of a national Jewish home in Palestine was inevitable. Kohn tried to educate me by giving me a copy of a book that he had published in 1929 in German about Martin Buber and his humanistic Zionism. He did succeed in moving me beyond simplistic, Jewish self-righteousness. He made me understand that the Jewish-Arab conflict is a clash of two rights: the Jews could not be condemned for wanting to become again the majority people in their ancient homeland, and the Arabs were not monsters for wanting to hold on to Palestine as their land.

The encounter with Kohn did more than make me think about political ambiguities. He was the first Jewish intellectual whom I had ever encountered, up close, who had moved away, totally, from the Jewish religion. Everyone else whom I had known either was a believer or was experiencing some kind of doubt and ambivalence. Kohn had moved away both from the liberal Judaism of his childhood and from the Zionism that had filled his life in the 1920s. He was not angry at his past, for he talked about his earlier beliefs amiably, as a stage in his life that he had outgrown. He had become someone who was no longer bound by one religio-ethnic tradition; he was concerned with universal human values. Kohn was a challenge to a young rabbi, and Zionist, at the beginning of his career.

Kohn was charming, and sometimes even dazzling, but he did not sweep me away. I refused to accept his basic contention: that he had risen beyond his Jewishness to belong to universal culture. He was obviously and unmistakably a Central European intellectual. He had come to abhor nationalism because he was affirming the universalism of the eighteenth-century Enlightenment against the nationalism of the next century. But I had begun to think a few years earlier, in college, that the universalism of the Enlightenment was itself suspect. The model of universal man that the Enlightenment extolled, the philosophe, represented the culture of White Europeans. Others could join if they made themselves over in that image. I had found the Talmud's view of universalism more believable: that mankind would belong to one universal culture only in the messianic era. In the here and now, after the separation at the Tower of Babel, when God had divided mankind into many languages and many tribes, universalism could only mean the teachings, present in almost all cultures, that enjoined decency toward all of God's beings. After my initial enchantment with Hans Kohn, I concluded that he was as much a tribalist as the Hasidim in East Baltimore, with one exception: they had remained in the tribe into which they had been born, but he had chosen to move into another, newer, tribe—the Central European intelligentsia.

The more subtle challenge to my sense of my Jewish identity came from Harry Austryn Wolfson. He was professor of Jewish thought at Harvard. Northampton was only ninety miles from Boston, and the train connections were adequate, so I traveled to Harvard once a week to attend his seminar on the philosophy of Maimonides. Wolfson, a bachelor, was an undersized, odd-looking man who spoke English with the accent of the Lithuanian yeshiva student that he had been in his youth. He was so strange that he was beyond even a Harvard eccentric, but he was held in awe at the university. He quoted from Greek philosophy, the Church fathers, and Islam as freely as from medieval Jewish philosophers and the Talmud. In the lore of Cambridge, he was the one about whom it was said that he knew everything. Wolfson never had a meal at home, so the Harvard Faculty Club was opened for breakfast to accommodate him. He lived in the library and went back to his apartment only to sleep. I walked him home once because he wanted to give me a reprint of a scholarly article. Wolfson could not find this text until he opened the refrigerator, which he used for its shelves. It could not even be called a filing cabinet, because parts of manuscript, letters, and offprints were piled in no order.

Wolfson was as learned, in his own way, as Ginzberg, but he did not live within any of the bounds of Judaism. When challenged about his own beliefs, Wolfson invariably answered with a bon mot: "I am a nonobservant Orthodox Jew." In the spring, during the week of Passover, this paradox came home to me in a very personal way. I walked with him after class, as he headed toward the faculty club. At the door, Wolfson said to me that he would like to invite me to lunch but he knew that I was observing the ritual restriction against leaven on Passover and that I would not eat there. He then added that he did not want me to think ill of him, because he was being careful to eat only crackers in the dining room of the club, because "they looked like matzoh."

In my two semesters with Wolfson, I learned much from his explication of Maimonides, but Wolfson was much more important to me as a Jew than as a professor. He cared about the Jewish community, and he had many personal connections with other Jewish scholars, but this towering scholar of Judaism was living, personally, outside the tradition. Knowing and admiring Wolfson made me ask the question, Can Jewish learning be value-free? As I kept thinking about Wolfson, I realized that my dilemma was simplistic. His life's work was very Jewish, and even chauvinistic. When I was his student, he was in the middle of a series of studies in which he would try to prove that both Christian and Muslim philosophy and theology, in all their varieties, were based on premises that had first been stated by Philo, the Jewish thinker in the first century in Alexandria, who had invented a way to mediate between philosophy and biblical religion. Wolfson was not eating matzoh on Passover, but he was using his intellectual power to describe Christian and Islamic thinking, before the modern era, as variations on themes that they had learned from Philo, the Jew. Wolfson was turning on its head the attitude toward Western culture of Judah Monis, the first Jew to teach at Harvard. Monis had been hired in the 1720s to teach Hebrew, and had inaugurated his career by converting to Christianity in Harvard Hall. On that occasion Monis gave a public lecture in which he insisted that biblical Judaism had long been superseded by Christianity and that the separate existence of the Jews was, therefore, an affront to the truth. Two centuries later, Wolfson was turning the tables by insisting that the culture of the West, and that of the Near East, were footnotes to the Bible and to Hellenistic Judaism.

I did not know enough, when I was a student, to dare have an opinion on his bold thesis, but I was in awe of his Jewish passion and pride. I learned from Wolfson that being Jewish among the Gentiles did not simply mean to resist assimilation and to cling, obdurately, to the inherited ways. From Wolfson, I learned to think about Jews and Judaism as an integral part of the history of mankind. He took me beyond apologetics, beyond the rhetoric of the "Jewish contribution to civilization." Wolfson was not trying to convince the Gentiles that Columbus crossed the Atlantic because he used astronomical tables that had been prepared twenty years before by Joseph ibn Zacut. The hermit of Widener Library at Harvard was engaged in something much more radical: a Jewish critique of Christian and Muslim culture.

That year I was not consciously aware of how much I was learning from Wolfson, but I did know that in his presence I was breathing different air. I did not follow after him in exchanging crackers for matzohs, but I began to see him, this hunchbacked gnome, as a Jewish Prometheus, and once or twice I even thought about him as the snake in the Garden of Eden. He was bringing fire into the world, and he was opening my eyes. When the war ended less than two years later, and the death camps were opened, I could not simply blame the Nazis. Wolfson had prepared me to ask some terrifying questions: is hatred of the other endemic in Western culture and, for that matter, in other traditions? Was the Holocaust a unique expression of that hatred, or was it a pogrom, or a Crusade, carried out with modern tools? I could not even avoid the most frightening question of all: did such hatred derive from the ancient Greek contempt for the unlike whom they called barbarians, or did it also have roots in the element of ethnic fierceness in the Hebrew Bible? After my year with Wolfson, I could no longer think of myself as a Jew who was maintaining and defending his tradition against the majority culture. We all belong to the same forest, both the green trees that let the sunlight through and the dead ones that make us afraid. I would never understand any one of the trees unless I thought of all of them together.

I left Harvard at the end of that academic year, and so I did not remain a student of Wolfson, but I did maintain connection with him for many years. Wolfson continued his monastic life, spending most of his time in a small office deep in the bowels of Harvard's Widener Library. He continued to write books that were widely praised as masterpieces. By the time he died, Wolfson had succeeded in making it impossible to study Western theology and philosophy without paying attention and great respect to the work of Jewish scholars through the ages. He had fought a heroic battle for Jewish dignity.

After a few months as Hillel director, I was sufficiently interested and sufficiently intrigued by my job as the "official Jew" among the New England WASPs to want to stay another year until I was old enough to be admitted as a chaplain in the armed forces. But it was not to be. Abram Leon Sachar, the national director of Hillel, had decided that I should go to Montreal, to McGill University. I objected, but he was adamant. He made an official announcement that I would soon be on my way to Canada. I could either accept his order or quit my job at Hillel. So I quit.

Having resigned, I had to find another job, and I could no longer be finicky. The office of the Rabbinical Assembly, the national organization of Conservative rabbis, told me that it would be easiest to place me in some congregation. It did not seem to matter where I would spend the next year, because at the end of it I would be entering the army. The only limit that I put was that I wanted a job in or near New York so that I could return to Columbia University on my day off, to continue working toward a doctorate in Jewish history. A small synagogue in North Philadelphia, Ahavath Israel, agreed that it would accept a young beginner. The congregation served a neighborhood of row houses, in the northern end of town, to which immigrants and their children moved when they started to rise into the middle class. Except for mixed seating—the women sat with their husbands and were not relegated to a separate section or to a gallery—all of the ritual was Orthodox although the synagogue was officially Conservative. The trustees of the congregation told me that I would, of course, preach in English, but an occasional talk in Yiddish would be very welcome. They agreed that I could take a day off in the middle of the week to go to New York to pursue my graduate studies. I accepted the job without hesitation. I would be spending the next year among people who were like those whom I knew in Baltimore. The congregation treated me with great kindness and forgave my mistakes as if they were my extended family. I was wrong only about my length of stay in Philadelphia: the war ended near the end of my first year at Ahavath Torah. I was being processed into the army, but my orders to report were canceled. I remained the rabbi of the synagogue for nearly three years, until I finished my graduate courses at Columbia.

Soon after I arrived at my new job, the board of the synagogue decided that it wanted to install me as their rabbi at a formal occasion. I was pleased, because this was the first time in my life that such public notice was being taken of my career. No one of substantial prominence agreed to speak at the occasion, but I was realistic enough to know that the new, very young rabbi of a small synagogue was of little consequence to dignitaries. At the function I was welcomed, officially, by the leaders of the congregation. The main address was given by my father, in Yiddish, and no one who heard it ever forgot it. He spoke with great emotion about entrusting his son to this community. He asked the congregation to welcome me, to sustain me, and to protect me against my own bad habits. He then turned to defining the role of the rabbi. My father used a parable. In Eastern Europe, in the small town from which most of our families had come, people were poor, and very few could afford pocket watches. Everyone told time by looking toward the clock tower, usually placed on top of city hall, which could be seen from every part of town. In the United States, people are better off, and everyone is able to own a watch. In Europe, everyone had the same time; in America, the time varies, from person to person. What is the difference? In America, each of us twiddles with his own watch, to suit himself; in

Europe, people look toward the clock tower, which they cannot control or maneuver. A rabbi, so my father concluded, should not be a pocket watch, in anyone's hands; he should be a clock tower giving everyone the same, principled answer. That evening I was especially moved by my father's wit and brilliance. I did not share his Orthodox certainties, but I could accept his metaphor. I was sure that I would never be a pocket watch to be wound up, or wound down, in someone else's pocket. My errors would be my own.

One of my bad habits to which my father had alluded was the tendency toward indiscipline—to do whatever struck me as necessary at that moment. As a student, and in my year as a Hillel director, I had essentially continued to make my own schedule. In the new job, I was required to conduct and preach at the Sabbath and holiday services and to direct and teach in the religious school. I had to live by a routine, for I was now, for the first time, responsible for a list of regular, recurring duties. I found myself scrambling to keep up, especially since I soon became involved in public life. I really did not learn to live comfortably with a set, exact schedule. But having to behave like an organized bureaucrat was a minor irritation.

The important change was in the content of my life. The war now became real. During the year that I had worked at the colleges in Amherst and Northampton, the bloody battles in Europe and the Pacific had seemed remote. I could tell myself that I was doing all that I could by acting as the chaplain to the several military programs in the area, and that I would soon be in uniform myself. I even imagined that I would get into the army in time to be a part of the brigades that would rescue the Jews from the Nazis. Organizing a meeting to protest the passivity of the American government and its allies at the ongoing murders was out of the question. The Jewish community in Northampton was small, and essentially dormant, and the students at the colleges certainly did not want to draw attention to themselves. In Philadelphia, however, I had returned to a familiar world, of a large Jewish community numbering nearly a quarter of a million souls. The leading Yiddish newspaper, the *Forward,* still published a Philadelphia edition every day, and all of the parties and factions in Jewish life were actively represented in the city. Important national leaders of Zionism lived in the city. The anti-Zionist American Council for Judaism had established its headquarters in Philadelphia in 1943. This organization was headed by Lessing Rosenwald, one of the heirs to the Sears Roebuck fortune; he lived in Jenkintown, a suburb not far from my synagogue. I soon became a heated participant in this quarrel. The very first time that I was on the radio I was debating the much older Lessing Rosenwald on a local talk show. I was an actor in a great Jewish debate, and I had joined the fight for a Jewish state.

I could have made other choices then, as a young rabbi in his first congregation. There were at least thirty Conservative synagogues in Philadelphia. Most of their rabbis were beyond the age for the army, even if they had wished to volunteer as chaplains. Almost without exception, these men spent their time working within their congregations. They visited the sick and presided over all the occasions in the life cycle of their congregants, from birth to death. Their memberships were growing, because most of the adult children of the immigrants were affiliating, then, with Conservative synagogues. They were sufficiently traditional (hats and prayer shawls were worn in the synagogue by the men, as they had been for centuries) so that Orthodox parents could come to the Bar Mitzvahs of their grandchildren without embarrassment, but the Conservative synagogues had enough "American" decorum so that those who attended could feel that they had moved beyond the immigrant ghetto of their childhood. Almost everywhere, rabbis and lay leaders were making plans to expand, or even to move, their synagogues to roomier and more prestigious sites after the war, preferably in the suburbs. The programs, too, were fashionable. The most talked about of my rabbinic neighbors packed the social hall of his "temple" once a month by giving reviews of the best-selling books of the day. These occasions, which took place on weekday mornings, drew hundreds of women from all over the city. My own small congregation pushed me to emulate, and even compete with, my neighbor. I gave in, but I could not bring myself to speak about any of the various popular and saucy novels of the day. Instead I gave my audiences summaries of new history books. After these increasingly poorly attended sessions, my literary mornings was mercifully canceled.

After a few months, my life again became divided into three parts. I worked at the synagogue, and I took courses at Columbia, but my most intense energies were devoted to Zionism. I did not realize at the time that I had essentially chosen to live in three different, and even distinct, communities. My friends in the synagogue were doctors, or lawyers, or the owners of small businesses. The wealthier Jews lived less than a mile away, on the other side of Broad Avenue, where row houses did not dominate the landscape. My congregants went to work every morning knowing that they were not the bosses, and they did not come home at night to command. I thought at the time that I was delivering worthy lessons by alluding to Hegel, Marx, Buber, and Maimonides in the same ten minutes. I was really showing off. Most of the regulars at the Sabbath morning service were older men and women who had not gone to college, or even finished high school, but they indulged me, with little complaint. I did get my deserved comeuppance at the very end of my stay, at a reception to mark my departure. One of the older men walked over to me and said, in Yiddish, that he had listened to me preach every Sabbath for nearly three years; he was sure that I must have been a wonderful rabbi, because he had understood very little of what I had been saying!

There was no connection between my friends in the synagogue and the scholars and teachers with whom I associated in New York. My most intense relationship was with Professor Baron's circle. He had admitted me to the program that led to a doctorate. In addition to his lectures, I was expected to attend the seminar in which people presented first drafts of parts of their dissertations. The group was expected to comment; at the end of the discussion, Baron reacted to our remarks and made his own suggestions. Baron maintained great personal reserve in class, and he spent most of the rest of his time secluded in the stacks of the library, but the students did get to see something of him in his office. I established even more personal connections, perhaps because we had both been born in southeastern Poland, in the province of Galicia. We talked often about the growing fears that each of us had for our relatives. Sometimes I walked him home, and his wife, Jeanette, would invite me in for a cup of coffee. They had met in one of his classes when she was a graduate student in economics at Columbia. She soon gave me an open invitation to their apartment and even encouraged me to telephone and visit whenever she and her husband were available. The conversation was seldom about scholarly issues. It was, most often, an exercise in "character analysis."

In my seminary years, studying with Ginzberg and Lieberman, I had become interested in the interplay between rabbinic and Hellenistic cultures, so I thought that I might write my doctoral dissertation in history with Baron at Columbia on the uses of Roman and Jewish law in Judea before the destruction of the Second Temple. To prepare for such a task, I needed to learn about Roman imperial practice from Professor William Westerman, a respected authority on the Hellenistic period. I soon abandoned that thesis because it became clear to me that I could do such a study only if I spent a few years doing nothing else. Unfortunately, the graduate scholarships that were available paid little beyond tuition. Nonetheless, I took my studies with Westerman seriously, and I was surprised that he took a personal interest in me. He asked me once to see him in his office. Of course, I agreed to come, and I soon found out why he wanted to see me. He invited me to lunch at the faculty club, which professors almost never did in those days, to tell me that he had been an expert on the staff of President Woodrow Wilson during the peace conference at Versailles in 1919. He knew the Near East well, because he had traveled widely in the area, had worked in archeological digs in Turkey, and had taught at the American College in Istanbul. Westerman told me that he had advised President Wilson against agreeing to the aims of the Zionists, because the prime interest of the West in the region was to increase its influence with the Arabs and to protect access to the oil resources of the Near East. In any event, Westerman thought that the Jews would best make their future by assimilating into the majorities in all the lands in which they lived. Jews should not be moving backward in history, to reestablish their national identity. Westerman added that his opinions had not changed. He continued to identify with Reform Jews who were anti-Zionists. The effort to create a Jewish state in Palestine had led to ever greater trouble between Jews and Arabs. Right now, in the midst of the Second World War, the Nazis had been able to find allies among the Arabs, such as the Grand Mufti of Jerusalem, because the Allies had supported the Zionist settlement in Palestine.

I struggled, quietly, to find a way of replying to Westerman. For one moment, I thought of staying out of trouble by pretending that I had wanted to reflect on what he had said, but I could not let myself avoid the issue. I replied that I could understand why he liked the Reformed anti-Zionists, but I could not be one of them. My Jewishness was not a set of universal moral principles to which anyone, of any persuasion, could agree; I was not an American of the Mosaic faith. I had been born in Eastern Europe among Jews who lived in two languages of their own, Hebrew and Yiddish. The home of this culture was being destroyed even as we talked, and the major hope for its survival was in creating a new base for this tradition. Part of the answer would be found in America, but here Jews were living in a society dominated by the symbols of Protestant Christianity. If Jews were to express their true selves, some of them needed to establish a community in which their culture predominated. Westerman was not convinced, so I played my last card. I reminded him that he had been among the very American types who had campaigned, while America was still neutral, for "Bundles for Britain." Their rationalization was that the American spirit descended from the Anglo-Saxon tradition and that the United States would be impoverished if Britain became a Nazi province. I asked Westerman what difference there was between the particular concern of the American Protestant elite for Englishness and the connection of American Jews to their Jewishness. Westerman repeated that the English were a nation and that the Jews were a religion, but he knew that I would not be convinced by such an argument.

Columbia had its fair share of Jewish refugees from Nazi-dominated Europe. Some of the people whom I had come to know were no longer religious believers, but they had remained involved in the concerns of the Jewish community. Not even Hans Kohn, whom I had encountered at Smith the year before, had suggested that he was completely detached from his Jewishness. At Columbia I met a refugee who seemed to be uninvolved. I enrolled in a course in the Greek papyri under Professor Isaac Taubenschlag, a scholar from the University of Krakow, who was the acknowledged authority in the field. He had found his way to Columbia after fleeing from Poland just ahead of the Nazis. I presumed that I would find in Taubenschlag not only the sorrow of an exile but also the warmth of a Jew from the very region in which I had been born, and in which my family had lived for generations, but I did not. Taubenschlag belonged to the element among the Jews of Poland who had made an ideology of assimilating into Polish culture. He did not seem to know any Yiddish or Hebrew, or perhaps he did, but he chose not to respond to my occasional use of a word in either language. I was increasingly awed by his enormous learning, and by his courage to go on with his work, but I could not connect with him as a person.

The most important Jewish refugee scholar at Columbia that year was Ernst Cassirer, who had fled from Germany before the outbreak of the war to come to Yale University. Cassirer was internationally famous, both as a historian of philosophy and as a philosopher in his own right. He had come to Columbia as visiting professor, and it was regarded as a privilege to be allowed into his class. I somehow managed to wangle a place in the course that he gave during the spring semester on the philosophy of Kant. Cassirer taught by having the class read a few lines at each session. The students were asked to explain the meaning of the text, and Cassirer then corrected our interpretations and gave his own extensive comments. We moved slowly, covering not quite ten pages in the course of the term. One day, as class was ending, I felt impish enough to approach him and say that he was teaching Kant as if it were a page of the Talmud. He was exploring every implication, or hidden contradiction, to produce a large commentary. Cassirer lifted his head—he looked the part of a scholar, with a thin, angular face framed by white hair—and smiled at me ruefully. He agreed that he saw the connection.

My impertinence had the effect that I hoped, because Cassirer began to let me walk with him after class. The conversations always began with some question of interpretation of the text of Kant that we had not quite finished discussing in class, but Cassirer almost always changed the subject to talk about the war. When the semester had begun in late January, the last German offensive on the Western front, the Battle of the Bulge, had been defeated. The newspapers and the radio broadcasts were full of pride at the American victory in battle. Everyone was repeating the brave and jaunty response of General Anthony Mc-Auliffe, the commander in Bastogne, to the German demand that he surrender: "Nuts." The cost of the battle, twenty thousand killed and one hundred thousand wounded, was still a military secret, but everyone was aware that the fight had very nearly been lost. Even after the attack in the Ardennes, Hitler was still blustering about turning the tide through new weapons. This did not seem entirely far-fetched, because buzz bombs powered by jet engines were falling on London. On our walks, Cassirer spoke of these new worries with more fear than anyone else I knew. He had been the rector of the University of Hamburg before the Nazis forced him to emigrate. Even though his own work was in philosophy, he knew much about the capacities of German scientists and engineers. I had supposed, in youthful optimism and innocence, that the best scientists and technicians had left Germany after the Nazis came to power, or, at the very least, that they were not cooperating with this murderous regime. Cassirer disabused me of this illusion. He told me that, of the great phalanx of Germans who were Nobel Prize winners in the sciences, only the "non-Aryans" had left. The great majority had remained, and Cassirer presumed that, almost without exception, they were working for the government. He feared the surprises that they might yet produce. Cassirer's account of German science and its immorality scared me.

Cassirer had created a more personal problem for me. Despite some of my disappointments at college, where I had encountered several teachers who were either avowed anti-Semites or indifferent to the troubles of Jews, I had hung on to the belief that the intelligentsia were the bulwark of Jewish rights. Jew-hatred was, supposedly, left over from benighted times; it would eventually evaporate as modernity spread and education triumphed. This was belied by Cassirer's account of the German academics whom he knew. In the first third of the twentieth century, these scientists and intellectuals had been the leaders and the cutting edge of modernity. They were the bearers of the *Kultur,* which was widely regarded as the vanguard of contemporary creativity. Cassirer was telling me that this very class was essentially indifferent to the fate of the Jews. Some, such as Martin Heidegger, the only philosopher in Germany whose reputation had been as great as Cassirer's, had become Nazis. Many lesser figures had joined the party out of conviction or to protect their careers. Some had let former friends and colleagues know that patriotism kept them from standing against the regime in power. The scientists and humanists whom Cassirer was deploring were only names to me, but I was learning that Hitler's minister of propaganda, Joseph Goebbels, who had a doctorate from Heidelberg, was not an isolated aberration. During that term Cassirer did not make me into a scholar of Kant, but I learned a lesson that he did not perhaps intend to teach me. On the day that I had left for my first class in college, my father had instructed me to associate only with "intelligent non-Jews." One of the century's greatest intellectuals, Ernst Cassirer, was convincing me that intellectuals were no likelier to be moral and decent than anyone else.

I was too much in awe of Cassirer to dare ask any questions about his own Jewish feelings, but he raised the matter himself. I did not think, then or later, that I was hearing "confession," but he seemed to take some pleasure in having a young rabbi, who obviously admired him, among his students. He told me that he had not cut himself off from Jewish concerns during his academic career in Germany, for he had served on the board, in Berlin, of the graduate school for the scholarly study of Judaism, and he had worked in the 1920s as one of the editors of the anniversary edition of the complete works of Moses Mendelssohn. Nonetheless, he told me frankly, and even with some pain, that he regretted not having been more involved. He was even self-critical about knowing Greek and Latin, and the major modern languages, but not Hebrew. I wondered for a moment whether he was telling me what I wanted to hear, but I banished that idea almost as quickly as it came to mind. Cassirer was an honest man; he would not pretend. He was telling himself, in my hearing, that his deepest root was Jewish; he had come to admire the classic Jewish texts and to regret that he did not know them firsthand; he had not been turned into a Jew because Hitler had made him one of the victims. Walking with Cassirer, I asked him to meet my father. I thought that the philosopher from Berlin and the Hasid from Lubaczow would reach out to each other. Cassirer agreed, but they did not meet. A few days after our conversation, Professor James Gutman, his closest associate in the philosophy department, called to tell me that Cassirer had died of a heart attack while walking on campus. He asked me to take part in the funeral service.

Cassirer's funeral was held in the auditorium of Earl Hall, the non-denominational building that was used by all the religious groups at Columbia, and not in St. Paul's Chapel, the campus church, which was restricted to state occasions at the university. Several eulogies were given, including one in German by a young scholar who had studied with Cassirer in Hamburg. The choir sung a favorite piece by Mozart, and I read two psalms in Hebrew. After the service Cassirer's body was taken to a crematorium. I did not join the cortege because cremation is contrary to accepted Jewish practice. When I called on his widow the next day, she told me that they had obeyed the wish he had expressed in a will written some years before. She thought that, had he rewritten his will more recently, he would have asked to be buried in a Jewish cemetery. Mrs. Cassirer added that having a young rabbi as a student had touched her husband. I left her apartment much sadder than I thought I would be. On the stairs I thought of Odysseus at the end of his long journey. Cassirer had made the journey through the oceans and the storms of Western culture. In his last days, I had heard some hints of his journey back to his Jewish origins. His wife had just confirmed that I had understood him correctly, but I would never hear him describe the shape of the Jewishness toward which he was moving near the end of his life. And yet, as I encountered intellectuals of Jewish origin who took pride in their indifference to the tradition into which they had been born, I would always remember what Cassirer had told me about his life.

When I returned to Philadelphia from the university, I confronted a different set of issues. At the synagogue, I kept trying to suggest that this generation, even as it fought its enemies, must remember that Jewish identity had been defined not by troubles but by religious texts. Even at a terrible moment for Jews, in the winter of 1944–45, I insisted that the synagogue had not been created to be a cheering section in the battle against anti-Semitism or to urge on the effort to create a Jewish state. These tasks needed to be done, and I was committed to them with great passion, but these purposes belonged to the secular organizations. As a rabbi, I kept asserting the conviction from which I had not ever wavered: that the Jews existed not because they have suffered uniquely but because they have created a unique and towering religious tradition.

This question was not a new one, for I had been asking it of myself during the war years. It is simply not true that we in America did not know what was happening in Europe. We did. Even the readers of the general press had enough information to know that the Nazis had decreed and were carrying out the total destruction of the Jews in the lands that they controlled. Those of us who read the press in Yiddish knew even more precisely what was going on. I could not reject the accounts of the horrors as unbelievable, because I had read Hitler's

Mein Kampf before the war. I had believed that he would carry out the assault on the Jews as prescribed in his book.

The last year of the war was not a time to make a neighborhood synagogue into a realm of learning and serenity. Some of the young men from the congregation were soldiers on the western front. Letters were beginning to arrive telling the stories that they had heard about the deportation and murder of most of the Jews of France by the Nazis, with the help of the Vichy regime. The Russians, advancing on the eastern front, drove the Nazis from Auschwitz in January of 1945. The reports of the death factories could no longer be denied, especially after the Allied armies captured Bergen-Belsen in western Germany that spring, a few weeks before the war ended. The news had kept reaching the West throughout the war that the Nazis were murdering millions of Jews, but now we saw it before our eyes. I was, of course, frightened by these pictures, because I was certain that some of my relatives were among the piles of dead bodies, but the dominant emotion was rage. I kept going to the movies to see the newsreels that showed the corpses, the emaciated survivors, their stunned liberators, and the German civilians who kept saying that they did not know what their government had been doing. I left the theater swearing again and again that I owed it to my grandfather, if he were still alive, to build him a new, better home.

The spring of 1945 was the beginning of the most difficult time in all my life. Everywhere in America people were dancing with joy at the news of the German defeat and surrender, but I was in mourning. The Allies had destroyed Hitler, but not before he had murdered most of the Jews of Europe. My sorrow was all the more intense because I knew that as late as 1939 Central and Eastern Europe had been the creative heart of Jewish religion and culture. New York and even Tel Aviv were recent, and even shallow, Jewish communities by comparison to Warsaw, Vilna, Prague, and Krakow. I had been raised to think of this region as home. I would go there to find a Jewish authenticity of which even the most intense immigrant life in America was only an echo. Even as I heard the bad news that was seeping out of Europe during the war, I would not let myself imagine that all would be gone. I would soon have to face that truth after the end of the war, but in the winter of 1944–45 I tried to hold on to some hope.

It has become the fashion in recent years to talk of guilt. American Jews have been attacked for having been too passive during the war, for not putting more powerful pressure on the Roosevelt administration to help save Jews. This criticism is not newly invented. I had read the pained and angry essay by Hayim Greenberg, in 1942, in which he demanded that the Jews of America say kaddish, the memorial prayer for the dead, for themselves, because they were going on with their own lives and had not broken down in mass lament for their brothers and sisters in Europe. I had shuddered when I read Greenberg, but I did not really believe the charge. The generation that he was denouncing was still too foreign, and too weak, to have much influence in American politics. American Jews were not silent during the war years, and the government in Washington knew what was happening in Europe, even in the death camps. The administration chose to do nothing, and it could not be budged until early 1944, when it established the War Refugee Board to try to rescue some of the Jews who were still alive. Even at the end of the war, I felt ashamed. I was alive, and almost all of our relatives in Europe were dead. I would never know my uncles and aunts in Lemberg and their children. Why were they ashes while I was safe?

But even these feelings were not my most intense reaction to the ruin of the Jews of Europe. Feeling pain at the loss of my relatives, feeling guilty that I had survived in safety, and being angry with God to the point of defiance—intense though they were, these responses did not surprise me. They had been brewing within me in the last two years of the war, as the news of the destruction of the Jews in Europe kept seeping out. I had thought all this, quite consciously, in April 1943 when the Jews who were still alive in the ghetto in Warsaw revolted and held out for more than two weeks against the German army, until the dreadful announcement came that the ghetto had been conquered and no longer existed. The revolt of the Warsaw Ghetto had evoked mixed reactions in America. These fighters were mourned, but there was a flash of pride at their heroism. Jews, in particular, seemed to feel that this burning ghetto was a Jewish Stalingrad, in which a surrounded population fought steadfastly against the enemy. I did not share that pride, for I could imagine what most of the Jews in that ghetto were likely to have thought and felt. I knew that Jews under persecution had long survived by accommodating, bribing, or making themselves as inconspicuous as possible—not by fighting. The revolt in the Warsaw Ghetto was not a sign that Jews were able to fight back. On the contrary, the decision to start a hopeless battle proved that the Jews in Warsaw had given up all hope of surviving. They could only decide how to die.

When the war ended two years later, I had to face my Jewish horror: I had no power. While the ghetto in Warsaw had burned, no one had helped its people. The Poles on the other side of the wall, even those in the underground who were loyal to the government-in-exile, had not joined the fight. In the next two years, while the death camps were efficiently transforming millions of living Jews into ashes and smoke, we who lived in freedom in the United States, and the Zionists in Palestine, had been in no position to organize rescue efforts. We had turned to the Allied governments, but our begging, cajoling, and protesting had not moved the United States and Great Britain to give us anything more than a few words of sympathy. In the summer of 1945, I stopped believing in goodwill. The Jews of Europe had hoped that there was enough decency in the majority culture to save them, but they had been wrong. The Jews in America had wanted to believe that the leaders of this democracy would be moved by conscience to make some special effort to save Jews from their special tragedy, but such action never came. I learned the bitter lesson, that summer, in the shadow of Auschwitz, that a people without power is a prime candidate for murder.

This angry truth made me take a radical new look at what had already happened in my own life. When I was a child, and then a teenager, in the 1930s, my family had had no money. My parents had not been able to write affidavits of support for any of my mother's siblings, without which they could not apply for a visa to the United States. By the time my father and mother could persuade some moderately well-off friends to provide such a guarantee, it had been too late. In high school and in college, I had been made uncomfortable by the prevailing certainty that Jewish culture and experience were beyond the pale. Every time I spoke up for the Hebrew texts that I was studying, I was told that Jewish values and ideas might be accepted only if they were judged worthy by those who spoke for the prevailing culture. In the summer of 1945, I realized that exclusion and contempt were the lot of the weak, who could only beg for money and respect from the powerful. In the summer of 1945 I knew that I could not live, ever again, within this box. I would spend the rest of my life to gain some power of my own, as a Jew in America. The battle would not be short or easy. American society would have to change, fundamentally, and not only for the benefit of Jews. All of the excluded, and not only Jews, would be demanding some share of power and some new respect. But even as I thought about the future of America, the image before my eyes was the millions who had had no way of resisting in Europe, or who could only choose to die in some hopeless revolt. I would not be part of some second act in this tragedy.

In the summer of 1945, my mother ran every morning to meet the postman, hoping to find a letter from her father or from her sisters and brothers, but none came. My father wrote, over and over again, to every Jewish agency that was caring for the survivors, and I was enlisted to write to the International Red Cross in Geneva. We got no information about our family, but we learned from accounts appearing in the Yiddish press that the Hasidim were the earliest to be slaughtered and that their destruction was even more total than that of the rest of Polish Jewry. The men wore beards and were dressed in black caftans, and the married women were distinctive in the wigs or cloth caps with which they covered their heads to make themselves as little tempting as possible. In such families almost no one spoke Polish, and those who did had a Yiddish accent. The children of such families were being educated in ultra-Orthodox schools; they could not pass as Aryans. It was not until the 1960s that we found a survivor who had grown up with my grandfather's children, who told us that the Jewish community made substantial effort to keep my grandfather safe, together with several of the rabbis. My grandfather was a high official of the Jewish religious community of Lwów—he had been head of the supply of kosher meat.

These men survived in an underground bunker longer than almost all the Jews of Lwów, but the Germans, eventually, gassed every hiding place. My grandfather and his companions were among the last to die, in July 1942.

The mail kept arriving in Baltimore, bringing nothing. None of the names that I sent to the Red Cross had appeared on any list of survivors. On Yom Kippur of 1946, my mother lit thirty-six candles (one each for the souls of those who had been alive in September 1939) for her father, her siblings, and their children. I did not see that sight because I was in Philadelphia with my congregation, but I heard about it the next night when I phoned my parents. I did not dare ask her how she had felt when she lit the candles, but I have never been able to imagine this scene without weeping. It took three years—after Israel had declared its independence and thousands of survivors had come to the new Jewish state—for my parents to receive a personal account of the last days of the family in Lwów. A letter came from Tel Aviv in which the writer, Haim Mardor, identified himself as having married my mother's youngest sister in the ghetto during the war. He and his wife were soon deported to Auschwitz and torn apart. He had survived, but his wife had perished. This uncle by marriage (whom I met for the first time in Israel in the summer of 1949) was the only survivor of the entire family.

I knew that those horrors and my doubts were not new. In the first century, in the year 70, the Roman army had destroyed the Temple in Jerusalem. The conquerors had slaughtered thousands upon thousands, and they had sent many of the living to Europe as slaves. Less than a hundred years later, between 131 and 135, the Romans had suppressed a major Jewish revolt, in bitter fighting, and they forbade the teaching and practice of the Jewish religion. The rabbis defied the ban, so they were tortured and executed. The story of these martyrs is repeated every year in the liturgy of Yom Kippur. The account in the ritual includes the terrible question that was asked at the time: "Is this the proper reward for undeviating obedience to God's law?" A heavenly voice answered, "Be silent, or I will turn the world into chaos"—but not everyone obeyed. One of the most eloquent of all the rabbis, Huzpit, "the interpreter," had his tongue cut out by Roman soldiers and thrown to the dogs. At the sight of this horror, another of the rabbis, Elisha ben Abuyah, blamed God Himself, Who had let this happen, so Elisha left the faith. Henceforth, he was known in Talmudic literature as "Acher," "the other." I kept suppressing the image of Acher as I saw the pictures of hundreds of corpses thrown into ditches, of mounds of human hair that had been shaved from the heads of victims just before they were driven into the gas chambers, and of rooms full of eyeglasses that had been taken from those who were about to die, but Elisha ben Abuyah would not go away.

But I could not follow Acher. Elisha ben Abuyah had left the Jews when they were being persecuted, to live the life of a pagan, Hellenistic intellectual. Such conduct was being repeated in the mid-1940s. Some concentration-camp survivors were choosing to disappear into the Gentile majority so that such a horror might never again happen to them. One of them told me that he had no reason to be a Jew, to face the horrors that might yet come, because he no longer believed in Judaism, in any form. Even in my lowest moments, I felt that such conduct was dishonorable and even despicable. Those who were leaving were diminishing the numbers, and the energies, of those who remained. For Jews, even for those who had trouble believing in the Jewish God, no Shangri-la, no society that was free of man's wicked past, was waiting. What did exist was Western society, which was still the home of anti-Semitism. Overt anti-Semitism was not going out of fashion in the aftermath of the Holocaust. Many survivors who tried to reclaim their homes were unwelcome, and some were murdered. In one town in Poland, Kielce, there was a pogrom in 1946 in which forty-two returning Jews were killed. Even in the United States, ancient, biblical Judaism was still depicted as a narrow, angry, tribalist preamble to Christianity, and the Jews were still described as an odd footnote to Western history. Society was quickly forgiving itself for its sins against the Jews, and as a French-Jewish survivor, Jules Isaac, would write some years later, the "teaching of contempt" remained. I kept thinking about Elisha ben Abuyah and wondering how, even in the midst of his disenchantment with the God Who had allowed the Romans to throw Rabbi Huzpit's tongue to the dogs, he could have left the Jews to join the Romans.

My distaste for those who would abandon their Jewishness to join the supposedly wider society kept increasing as I watched the myth of the Resistance being invented immediately after the war. Many of the

French, the Dutch, and the Belgians, and even the Poles and the Austrians, were asserting that they had been part of the clandestine war against the Nazis; they insisted that the collaborators had been a small, unworthy minority. Even then, in the euphoria of victory, I could not believe it. Six million Jews had been murdered in Europe, while the churches and the intelligentsia had remained largely silent; some, even many, had joined the Nazis. Anti-Semitism and anti-Judaism were still pervasive, even among the victors. In the United States—despite a succession of wartime films in which southern rednecks, Blacks, Italian Americans, and Jews became comrades under fire—Blacks were returning to segregated lives, and Jews were socially acceptable, sometimes, but only if they had eradicated every trace of their own character and temperament and behaved like respectable Gentiles. That was the message of a novel about anti-Semitism that was widely read, and admired, in those days, Laura C. Hobson's *Gentlemen's Agreement.* The hero of the story pretends to be a Jew in order to test the prejudices of an upper-middle-class town in Connecticut. No fault can be found in his manners or culture (in the movie version, the protagonist was Gregory Peck), but his Jewishness is unforgivable. At the time, the novel and the movie were applauded as courageous attacks on anti-Semitism. No one questioned the underlying premise that a Jew had to become, at very least, an "amateur Gentile" to become acceptable. I asked the inevitable question, Is this the purpose of modern Jewish life? Is this what emancipation means, that a prejudiced Yankee town in Connecticut would agree to tolerate a Jew, but only if he hides his origins?

In these months of doubt and pain, I asked myself what it was that Jews had to do to win the basic respect that would allow them quite simply to live as Jews. Near the beginning of the nineteenth century, Jews had begun to say to the Western world that they were a worthy people because they had made superior contributions to human culture and they should be respected. The clear implication was that those who had been persecuting Jews for many centuries were unaware of what Jews had given the world or, worse still, that they did know about the Jewish contributions to civilization but they were ungrateful. Not only had this argument not worked; the anti-Semites had distorted it into claiming that the Jews were overly prominent and, so, overly dominant. Ultimately, the debate was futile. What if the Jews had not invented monotheism? or had not been the first to proclaim that the essence of God was not power but morality? What if the Jews had not produced a remarkable proportion of scholars and scientists in the modern era? Would their lack of achievement diminish their claim to life and to decent treatment? In those days of doubt and inner turmoil, I even thought that the claim of Jews to being special, for whatever reason they might choose to give—chosenness or contribution to civilization—was a root cause of anti-Semitism.

I was not alone with these thoughts. Perhaps the greatest Yiddish poet of the day, Yacov Glatstein, published a cycle of poems in 1946, in memory of the dead. Glatstein had been born in the Polish city of Lublin, so he made the burning of his hometown the symbol of the destruction of all the Jews of Poland. The death of its children was the burning of the Torah, the divine word, itself.

> *We received the Torah at Sinai,*
> *and in Lublin we gave it back.*
> *The dead do not praise God,*
> *the Torah was given to life.*
> *And as we together, all of us together,*
> *stood at the giving of the Torah*
> *so we all together died at Lublin.*

Even my father, whose faith had always seemed profound and unshakable, also went to war with God. In response to the unique suffering of the Jews, my father proposed that we send a delegation to Mount Sinai to demand that God choose some other people for the glory and pain of bearing His teaching.

Along with the doubts about God came a burst of shame. It appeared that the overwhelming majority of the Jews in Europe had gone passively to the slaughter. We argued with ourselves that it was not their fault. In a lecture at my synagogue in Philadelphia that winter, only a few months after the end of the war, I argued that if Hitler had come to America, the Jews would not have done better. The police station in our neighborhood would have been controlled by Nazis, and almost all the Gentiles in the area would have been, at best, too frightened to help. Where could we have found an apartment building, or a piece of land, as the base for making a heroic last stand? I added that the historic experience of the Jews in the Diaspora had been to lie low at a time of trouble, to survive by hiding and bribing. At Masada in the year 73, where the last battle of the war with the Romans was fought, the Jewish defenders, and their families, had chosen to die fighting to the end rather than surrender. I even added that we, the living Jews of this day, were not grandchildren of the heroes who had died at Masada. Our ancestors were those who saved their lives by running away, to hide in caves. The Holocaust evoked sorrow, but it was not a source of pride. Those who heard me speak that day were not happy. They would have very much preferred that I had emphasized the heroism of the hopeless revolt of the Warsaw Ghetto rather than pointing out that under the Nazis—indeed, under any attack of mass anti-Semitism—Jews were essentially helpless. Our safety was tied inextricably to the economic and moral health of the societies among which we were scattered.

The feeling of shame was a sign of the distance the Jews had traveled toward adopting the conventional attitudes of the majority society. In the Middle Ages, the highest Jewish virtue had been to die "for the sanctification of God's name": to accept martyrdom. Intellectually, such passivity had gone out of fashion in recent centuries as Jews had begun to long for the power to fight back. In 1896, in his pamphlet "The Jewish State," Theodor Herzl had urged Jewish students to "demand satisfaction" in duels from Gentiles who insulted them. In 1903, after a murderous pogrom in Kishinev, the Hebrew poet Chaim Nachman Bialik had written a long poem, "The City of Death," not to console the victims but to denounce them for not fighting back. Jewish self-defense agencies soon arose, both in czarist Russia and in the new Zionist communities in Palestine, to make sure that no one could attack Jews with impunity. When the major memorial for the victims of the Holocaust was established in Jerusalem, the Knesset ordained an annual day of mourning and remembrance. It was called the Day of the Holocaust and of the Heroic Resistance. Every attempt at shooting back was remembered, because Jews were ashamed to think of themselves as helpless victims.

Our private shame that the victims had not fought back was not allowed to rise to the surface publicly among the American Jews in the immediate aftermath of the Holocaust. How could those who had not suffered be critical of the victims? The pictures of gas chambers and of huge piles of emaciated bodies were evoking wide sympathy among American Gentiles for the tragedy that had befallen the Jews. This pity for the Jews would be lessened by any criticism of the dead. Most important, after the end of the war, American Jews were convinced that they were on the way to full equality in American society—that storming the barriers that shunted their talents was a matter of time. They took pride not only in the tens of thousands of their young who had served with valor as ordinary soldiers, but especially in the strikingly large numbers of Jewish scientists and managers among those who had produced the munitions that made victory possible. Even in the midst of tears for the 6 million who had died, and of gratitude for Gentile sympathy, some distance was put between the victims in Europe and the Jews in America. We wanted to be thought of as part of brave, undaunted, victorious America. We were saying Kaddish as Jews, and we were glad for the condolences from the rest of America, but we wanted our neighbors to think of us as wrapped, together with them, in an American flag, preferably with the slogan Don't Tread on Me written over it.

Not only did the destruction of the Jewish communities of Europe fill us with shame and guilt; it redefined what it meant to be a Jew. Until the mid-1940s, American Jewry was a province on the edge of the Jewish world. Jewishness was preserved by relatives in the old country, while the immigrants to America, and their children, went about the business of trying to succeed in America. After the Holocaust this was no longer possible. The Jews of the old country, the "authentic" Jews, were either dead or homeless. American Jews were now the main community; passing what was left was up to us. Passing what was left meant helping the embattled Jews of Palestine. Few American Jews wanted to leave for Palestine, an underdeveloped Middle Eastern place in which room had first to be found for the refugees who desperately needed a new home. The heady, and available, new content of the American Jewish life was to help the survivors and to fight for a Jewish state. Commitment to these tasks finessed the question that was barely considered: how to create an equivalent in America or Palestine of the Jewish culture that had been destroyed in Europe. Some of the few who were concerned reassured themselves that Jewish culture was safe in

Palestine, as it had been in Europe before 1939. In the mid-1940s, being Jewish in America ceased being revolutionary, as the socialists had once maintained; or being nice, as the "German Jews" still insisted; or being learned, as a small minority like my father kept preaching. Its central meaning became: to be active in Jewish causes.

Despite my inner reservations, I was carried along by the great wave that was lifting American Jews into passionate and proud activism and muffling their sense of shame. I would study another day, but this was not the time in which I could write a doctorate or prepare to pass the examination for a higher level of rabbinic ordination. I could not think of removing myself from the actions and passions of the day. This modesty was not, however, the main reason for my refusing to become a reclusive scholar. The activists were compelling. Before the eyes of the world, they were performing the miracle of resurrecting the half-dead survivors of the Holocaust. I longed to be one of these miracle makers. The American-Jewish Joint Distribution Committee, the major voluntary agency that was helping displaced Jews, was recruiting staff. I applied for a job, but I was turned down. I knew the necessary languages—Yiddish, Hebrew, and German—but I had no training in social work, and there were more than enough American rabbis in Europe. The *brecha*, the underground immigration to Palestine, depended on rabbis who were still in uniform as chaplains. A civilian with no military connections would be of little value. I had no choice but to stick to the unglamorous task of helping to buy guns that others would shoot or a ship that others would sail. These activities were not dramatic or memorable, but they were my small contribution.

Many of us identified with the few hundred thousand Jews in Palestine. They were vastly outnumbered by the Arabs and outgunned by the British, but they were fighting with fabled bravery. Emissaries from the *Yishuv* (the Zionist settlement in Palestine) were all over Europe. Thousands of survivors of the Holocaust were being brought by underground routes to ports on the Mediterranean. Cast-off ships were being hired, or bought, to be used to run the British blockade and deposit their passengers, by night, on the coast of Palestine. Some of these emissaries from Jewish Palestine were in the United States, and not only to raise money. American Jews were enlisted to help buy "army surplus," such as machine guns and rifles that were being sold as scrap metal. Such scrap was shipped to Jewish settlements in Palestine, with documents that declared the loads to contain farming implements. The disguised headquarters of this network was in New York, but the large military presence in Philadelphia made it an important center. An army arsenal on the outskirts of the city was selling machine guns like candy. One of my congregants was the civilian bureaucrat in charge of disposing of this scrap metal. I introduced him to a young man from Palestine, and my friend was soon selling army surplus to junk dealers. There were American citizens (not all Jews) who fronted for the network. In the winter of 1946 a handful of activists in Philadelphia even found a Chesapeake Bay excursion boat, the *President Garfield*, rusting in the harbor. It was decidedly not seaworthy, but a committee in Philadelphia bought it anyway, supposedly as scrap, and staffed it with volunteers. The ship was renamed *Exodus 47*. It staggered across the Atlantic, took on a large load of refugees, and entered Zionist mythology when British sailors stopped it in the eastern Mediterranean and forced the 4,500 refugees aboard to return to the French port near Marseilles. The French authorities refused them entry, and so the ship was directed to Hamburg in the British zone of Occupied Germany, where the passengers were forced to land.

The battle to bring the refugees to Palestine, and to create a Jewish state in the ancient homeland, was changing, forever, the relationship of American Jews to the American government and to their own Jewish heritage. For nearly two centuries, from the very beginning of the Republic, Jews in America had always petitioned the government for help in times of trouble; they had appealed for goodwill, and they had couched their requests in the rhetoric of faithfulness to democratic principles. Confrontation with authority was beyond the limit for a small minority. To be sure, some Jews had fought the state in the earlier decades of the twentieth century, but they had acted as socialist revolutionaries and not as spokesmen for American Jews. During the Second World War some individuals, and a few organizations, had slipped money into Nazi-occupied Europe in efforts to help Jews, but these illegal activities were few and highly secret. The public efforts of the organized community had all been aimed at evoking humanitarian concern from the Allied governments. This ended in 1946 when Jews campaigned against, and defeated, a congressional candidate in a Bronx district because he was not sufficiently pro-Zionist. Jews would continue to say, for many years, that they were voting as individuals, "just like all other Americans," but the Jewish community was not hiding its use of political pressure to support Zionist aims. Jews were no longer supplicants. They were willing, "just like all other Americans," to punish their enemies and reward their friends.

Unhappy at being relatively underemployed, I fell back on quoting the Talmud at myself. The Talmud teaches the lessons that we do not choose our form of service and that we can have no accurate sense of its importance. God judges us by the devotion with which we perform our seemingly unimportant duties. These maxims helped some, but the lessons did not become real until I encountered a tired, ill, and visibly aging Rabbi Stephen Wise at a small Zionist dinner in Philadelphia one night in 1946. He was no longer the central figure of Zionism in America; he had been pushed aside two years before by a younger and more imperious figure, Rabbi Abba Hillel Silver. Wise had come to Philadelphia to speak at a dinner of such minor importance that no local dignitary was in attendance. Instead I was assigned to be in the chair. The occasion ran late, so that Rabbi Wise missed the train that would have brought him home to New York before midnight. I had driven him to the station, and I sat with him in a deserted coffee shop as we waited nearly two hours for the last train. He told me that his wife had begged him to spare his energies, but he insisted on accepting all such invitations. I asked him why he tired himself in these tasks. Wise answered without any self-pity, "I am a foot soldier now, and I will do what I am asked." I soon helped him up the stairs to the train, and I waited until I saw him find a seat in the railroad car. I walked down those stairs almost sure that I would never see him again. He died in January 1949, soldiering as he wanted up to the end.

There were many larger-than-life figures in those hectic years. Among the emissaries from Palestine, Teddy Kollek was the most striking. He bellowed at those who did not produce quick results, and then he lowered his voice and whispered a list of the supplies (mostly guns) that he needed for the Haganah, the armed force of the Israelis, in Palestine. He was then a junior official; he had come to the United States to make sure that the *yishuv* in Palestine would have the means with which to defend itself in its war with the Arabs. In the years to come Teddy Kollek changed from a chauvinistic figure into an Israeli diplomat, the fabled mayor of Jerusalem who rebuilt the city and who, ultimately, became the admired elder statesman of the Jewish people.

Helping the gunrunners and the *brecha* was moving and dramatic, but these activities occupied only a small portion of my time. Most of my time was taken up by my duties at the synagogue. I had no trouble teaching teenagers in afternoon classes at the synagogue who came after public school. Those who chose to attend wanted to learn some Talmud, and I enjoyed teaching them some easier passages from texts that I loved. I was not under much greater strain on weekends, when I preached twice at the Sabbath services, on Friday night and Saturday morning. I could talk about the issues of the day with passionate conviction, for it was easy to denounce the British for blockading Palestine to keep Jews out or to urge the congregation to put pressure on Washington to support the Zionist agenda.

My deepest trouble came when I had to deal with the sorrow and grief of individuals. I was too young to be a consoling father figure, and I could not glibly repeat to those who were mourning the death of children, or of young husbands or wives, the formula that God's love would sustain them or the assurance that they would be reunited in heaven with those whom they had lost. In my first weeks at the synagogue, I read the service at the burial of a young woman who had died in childbirth, and I wept uncontrollably, much more than her husband or her parents. I was, of course, upset by the tragedy, but that day I was also weeping for myself. Her death reminded me of the loss of my younger brother when we were both children in Poland and I asked the question, Why him and not me? I also cried for my cousins who had all been murdered in Poland, while I was safe in America.

The black wall at which I kept staring became blacker a few months later. One of my friends, an older man who had come from Poland before the First World War, asked me to read the service at the wedding of a niece who had just come to Philadelphia from a displaced-persons camp in Germany. She was marrying a young man with whom she had "kept company" before they were both deported by the Germans. After I accepted, the bride-to-be telephoned and asked to see me. In my office, she rolled up her sleeve to show me the number that had been tattooed on her forearm. I had seen such numbers on the wrists of other survivors, but I was shaken by the line that had been tattooed below the number. She had been indelibly identified as a *Feldhur,* as a woman from one of the brothels near the front that serviced the soldiers of the *Wehrmacht.* The bride-to-be asked me whether her years as a prostitute had any effect on the ritual of the wedding—or did she even have the right to be married? I told her that Jewish women had been raped or forced into prostitution throughout the centuries. Rabbinic authorities had decided, long ago, that such women lost none of their rights. The bride-to-be then told me about her fiancé. He was one of the very few survivors of the *Sonderkommando* in Auschwitz. These were the young men who had taken the dead bodies from the gas chambers and disposed of them in the crematoria. The bride-to-be drew no conclusions from both their lives. She did not ask me why she had remained alive or why she had been condemned to be married, almost alone, in a foreign city. She told me that she knew the tradition that a memorial prayer for dead parents is to be said at a wedding, but she suggested that I should not chant these somber lines. The memory of her father and mother would be with her, always, but she was getting married to begin her life over again.

This woman had opened a door in my black wall. Suddenly, I knew that I had been seeking an answer in the wrong part of the biblical Book of Job. The center of that tale is that Job, a righteous man, suffers unimaginable and unmerited woe. He demands to know why he deserves this fate. Job's friends come to console him, and they try to explain away his pain, but he rejects their reasons. Job wants an answer from God, but He is silent. Finally, at the end of the book, God appears out of a whirl-wind to assert that His plans are beyond our understanding; what man experiences as suffering has another meaning in the mind of God. I had tried, over and over again, to accept this answer, but I could not. Why had His plans and His purposes required the horrors of Auschwitz? "Where were you when I founded the world?" is not a solution to the problem of evil; it is a cop-out, by waving God's majesty at a powerless, tormented man. I realized that whatever hope could be found in the Book of Job is actually at the end of the story. In simple prose we learn that Job survived his woes and that he rebuilt his life. Job married again, had children again, and became again the master of flocks and herds. These flat sentences do not mention his continuing pain at the memory of the wife and children whom he had lost, but Job could not have forgotten. He had chosen, like this young woman, to seal off the heartache in some private chamber of his soul and to build a life again.

I knew, of course, that Jews have no monopoly on courage. Other peoples have lived near volcanoes but kept refusing to leave and kept rebuilding their homes after each eruption. But Jews had rebuilt their shattered selves and their destroyed communities more often than anyone else—and this young woman and the man she would soon be marrying were doing it again. It no longer mattered to me that day, and thereafter, whether a personal God had commanded the Jews at Sinai to be his special people or whether they had devised their self-image. What mattered was that Jews were again finding within themselves the courage to rebuild.

Her wedding took place toward the end of the summer of 1946. I was surprised that the bride and groom could dance, but they did, and so did the guests. There were even toasts. At the end the groom responded, in Yiddish; he thanked his wife's uncle for bringing them to the United States and for being the host at the wedding, and he was grateful to all of us who were acting as his family. He then added that he and his bride knew that they had to live their lives for themselves— and for their families that had been destroyed. Some weeks later I asked the young man whether he hated the Germans. He answered that it would not resurrect his parents, and his brothers and sisters, if he were to become, again, part of a *Sonderkommando*, but in a camp in which Germans were the victims. He would never forgive those who had sent him to Auschwitz, and he wanted them to be caught and punished, but he could not spend the rest of his life trying to get even. He could only hope that what had happened to him would never happen to anyone else. I was staggered by the refusal of this survivor of the *Sonderkommando* to respond with hatred or to demand vengeance. At the end of that conversation I knew that I had stopped caring whether God or man makes morality. What mattered was that, even in the most harrowing part of Auschwitz, this young man had remembered what he had learned from his murdered family: that the backbone of Judaism is decency. I had listened to him in utter silence, but I responded at the end not with words of mine but with a quotation from the Talmud, "He who has no mercy within him does not belong to the seed of Abraham." And we both wept for the dead.

I was so much obsessed in 1945 and 1946 with the problems of the Palestinian Jews that I took little notice of the founding of the United Nations at a conference in San Francisco in 1945. I could not believe that a better and safer world was being born with a secure place for Jews; we all knew we had to create our own country. I remembered other times when false hopes were raised. After the First World War, the rhetoric of the founders of the League of Nations had been as grandiloquent as the words from San Francisco. In the "Palace of the Nations" in Geneva, the diplomats had talked for years of collective security, but their governments had not rallied together to stop Mussolini in Ethiopia in 1936 or Hitler in Czechoslovakia in 1938. The founding documents of the League of Nations had even included guarantees for the rights of minorities such as Jews in the new countries that had emerged in Eastern Europe, but these promises had not been honored. The Jews of Eastern Europe had found no protection in the League of Nations from the anti-Semites in their countries. The prognosis for the United Nations was supposed to be different, but I could not make myself believe that a new age was being born. My immediate experience denied that hope. American immigration laws had not been changed; they kept out all but a few of the survivors of the death camps who wanted to come to the United States. Jews everywhere—in Palestine, in Europe, in the camps of the survivors, and in the United States—were at war with the British, because they were rigidly enforcing their ban against Jewish immigration into Palestine. I remembered then that a half century earlier, Moshe Leib Lilienblum, writing in Hebrew in czarist Russia, had suggested that even in the most hopeful times for all mankind, the Jews might yet be left behind in their particular misery.

The immense suffering of the Jews evoked popular sympathy but official irritation. America offered very generous help to its allies, and even to its recent dictator-led enemies, in rebuilding their countries. Yet the Jewish survivors in Europe had to scream for attention. The most respected voices in American public life were speaking of solving world problems, but some were visibly impatient with what was derided as Jewish "special pleading." I began to suspect that our country's intellectuals, politicians, and policy makers were mostly convinced that Jews were an irritant who made trouble and not a partner in making the new society. The least that I owed to my dead relatives, and to the distant

cousins who had survived the murder of the Jews of Europe, was to join
the troublemakers.

I could not stop asking the question, How could they have committed these crimes? This question was not new. Some of the earliest rabbis had been disturbed by the account of the conquest of the land of
Canaan. These rabbis had elaborated in the Talmud on the biblical
explanation that the Canaanites, and all the other aboriginal tribes
whom the Jews found in the land, were idolaters who sacrificed children
to their idols. If they remained alive, their heinous practices might con-
taminate God's people. (But, I kept asking myself, had not the Nazis
made comparable accusations against the Jews: that their culture and
values subverted civilization?) The rabbis had taken further refuge in
the argument that God had created all of the land and that it is His prerogative to give any piece of it to any people that He chooses. (But did
He have to do it by commissioning the conquerors to wipe out those of
His creatures who were in their way?) The rabbis seemed to know that
these explanations were not enough. They walled off these bloody tales
by ruling that whatever had happened during the campaign of conquest, which Joshua had begun at Jericho, had set no precedents. Such
conduct could never be permitted again. The ancient rabbis could not
help acknowledging that these cruelties had happened, because they
could not disavow any part of the Bible, but they had found a way of
editing the text, by interpretation, to bring it in line with their moral
conscience. In this spirit, they used exegesis, and allegory, to explain
away other cruelties in the Bible. In the Book of Deuteronomy
21:18–21, the fifth of the Five Books of Moses, the father is granted the
right to ask the judges to condemn a rebellious son to death. One opinion in the Talmud read this text not as a blueprint for action but as a
parable to terrify the young so that they would honor and obey their
parents. The Bible prescribed the death penalty for a long list of crimes,
but Rabbi Akiba, in the Talmud, had tightened the laws of evidence to
make it impossible for the court to ever sentence anyone to be executed.
Rabbi Akiba added that a Sanhedrin that would send even one person
to his death in the course of an entire generation was to be regarded as
a murderous court.

My wrestle with the biblical account of the conquest of the promised
land liberated me from any vestige of a belief in the literal truth of the

Bible, but I could not really take refuge in the Talmud. Some of the rabbis had softened the fierce passages in the Hebrew Bible, but they were contradicted in the Talmud by contrary opinion. It is a settled principle that only the Holy Land is pure; all the land of the Gentiles is by definition impure. There are many tales that describe the wisdom and kindness displayed by some Gentiles, but there are at least an equal number of stories full of suspicion and enmity. The oft-quoted ruling that the pious among the Gentiles are as entitled to a share in the world to come as the righteous did not obviate the angry outcry that even the best of the Gentiles remain mortal enemies. These ambivalences were rooted in the Bible itself. In the Five Books of Moses, the Jews had been commanded to be forever at war with Amalek, because that tribe had ambushed them on their way to the promised land. In contrast, the prophet Amos had insisted that God cared no more for the Jews than for their worst enemies, the Philistines. Amos had denounced ethnic fierceness, choosing compassion for all mankind. A thousand years later, Rabbi Akiba had brooked no cruelty to individuals even in the name of God. They had made choices. Amos and Rabbi Akiba had found the truth of the Bible in injunctions to love your neighbor as yourself (Lev. 19:18), to love the stranger and treat him fairly (Lev. 19:32), and to offer peace to enemies (Deut. 20:10). I was certain that such unlimited kindness was the main thrust of the biblical-rabbinic tradition, but I knew that the ancient texts did not speak with one voice. For the rest of my life, I would not ever be able simply to quote authority. I would have to keep questioning the texts and making choices.

I was aware then, in 1946, that I could never return to the Orthodox faith in God. I would not forgive Him for the Holocaust, and I would not absolve Him by agreeing that the death camps had existed in a realm that He could not control. I had no trust in man. I had learned that men and women can do the most terrible crimes in the name of their definition of virtue. The Nazis had just killed millions of Jews in good conscience to protect the purity of the Aryan race. In the Soviet Union the "enemies of the people" were still being murdered by the tens of thousands to help prepare the way for the victory of the proletariat. Communism and nationalism were "gods that failed," not because they failed to produce a new heaven on earth, but because all they promised was hell. What if they had succeeded? What if the

Germans had won the war and had established their Aryan society, realizing their poster images of a blond population not sullied by Jews, gypsies, homosexuals, or the feebleminded? I was haunted by the pictures of good-humored, self-satisfied soldiers herding children toward the trucks that would take them to their deaths. I could not forget the fear in the eyes of the children, but I was even more upset by the faces of the murderers, who were certain that, by these abominations, they were defending civilization. This was not new, because the inquisitors in Spain had sent heretics to be burned in the name of God, and revolutionaries in France had used the guillotine on those who were lacking in "civic virtue." In 1946 I learned that the greatest scourge of mankind is not a pirate or a highway robber, for these know that they are scoundrels. The lasting danger to humanity is the uncompromising defender of the faith—any faith.

A fter two years in Philadelphia, I became restless. My two younger brothers were growing up, and both were boarding students in yeshivot in New York. The family needed more money, and I did not have more to give. In the orderly processes of my denomination, I could not hope to be recommended for promotion. Along with millions of other soldiers, chaplains were being demobilized and some were looking for jobs. They had an undeniable first claim on preferment. One day, when I was feeling especially sorry for myself, I opened a letter from Nashville, Tennessee, in which the president of the Conservative synagogue there asked me whether I would consider becoming the rabbi of the congregation. This inquiry was followed by a telephone call. I asked the secretary of the congregation, Max Levine, who was on the other end of the telephone, how he had heard my name. He answered that an itinerant fund-raiser for pious causes had praised me and urged that the congregation invite me for an interview. This man was one of the many who stayed with my parents when they came to beg in Baltimore. I agreed to visit the congregation.

The encounter went well, and the match was quickly made. The leaders of the synagogue knew that they could have appointed an older, and safer, rabbi, but they preferred to take a chance on a seemingly bright near-beginner. Nonetheless, I hesitated. I would no longer be able to go to New York or Baltimore on impulse, and Vanderbilt University, in Nashville, was obviously not Columbia University, in New York. I told myself that I might stay there a few years, to learn what I could from this experience in the South. My decision became easier as I realized that Nashville was not just another country town. It was one of the first American cities to be established on the frontier beyond the Appalachians, and it had played an important role in the history of the country. In southern terms, Nashville was a moderate city. Businessmen and professionals, and their employees and staffs, dominated Nashville, and such people were not threatened by the handful of middle-class Negroes (the term that was then in use) who lived there. Crosses were not burned in Nashville, and no lynch mobs had been rampaging in the city in recent decades. Those poor Whites who based their status on the insistence that they were superior to Blacks lived in the smaller towns nearby. Nashville itself took pride in its gentility. An imitation of the Parthenon in Athens graced one of the parks. The sons and daughters of the best families often went north to school, to Princeton and Harvard, and Smith and Wellesley. Such people returned home to live according to the accepted rules of the South, for Nashville was completely segregated racially, but very few were embittered true believers. The aristocracy in Nashville certainly knew in their hearts that separate benches, in public places, could hardly be defended by men and women who had been brought up, and caressed, by Black maids and had been driven to school by Black butlers. It was, therefore, possible for a liberal newspaper, the *National Tennessean,* to be the major voice of opinion in the city. On the question of race, the *Tennessean* was not a flaming voice for desegregation, but its editorials kept insisting that progress had to be made toward racial equality. The churches of the rich middle class remained segregated, but their preachers were sufficiently embarrassed by the segregationist doctrine that God had created the Whites to be above the Blacks that they almost never mentioned this piece of theology. They avoided it by speaking of the responsibility of their congregants to be stewards of the poor. I would not be coming to a town full of active haters.

The Jewish community was small, less than three thousand souls, but several national leaders on both sides of the struggle over Zionism lived in town. After weeks of doubt, I persuaded myself to accept the job. I took up the appointment as rabbi of the Gay Street Synagogue in the spring of 1947. In this job, I was no longer a bright young man whose opinions did not really matter, as I had been in Philadelphia. I had become the rabbi of one of the three synagogues in town, and what I said and did was noticed. The honeymoon in Nashville was brief, because I said what I thought. I had not made a conscious decision to be a man of principle; I simply did not know how to be politic or circumspect. Such skills had not been taught me by my father.

The first tensions came from my being a "Yankee liberal." Despite the embarrassment of some of the ministry, no church had allowed even a few token congregants from the Black middle class to join, even though everyone knew, or knew of, the Black businessmen and professionals, mostly doctors, who served the Black community. The teachers on the faculties of Fisk University and the Meharry Medical College, the two Negro schools, were regarded by the Whites as below the academic standard of Vanderbilt University, but they did have higher academic degrees and middle-class manners. The Fisk Jubilee Singers, a choir made up of students, was famous in the United States and even abroad. I heard that, as an act of largess, some Blacks were permitted to attend an occasional service at one of the churches, but they always had to sit in a segregated section in the balcony. There were no Black Jews in Nashville, so the synagogues were not directly challenged by the immorality of racial segregation, but the Jews could not avoid the question. Many were in retail business, and some of their stores served a Black clientele. These storekeepers adhered to the southern custom that Blacks had to buy clothes without trying them on. Some of the owners explained to me that they had no choice. Jews were a small, tolerated minority in an essentially anti-Semitic region, and it was wisest, and safest, to keep one's head down. A few did break the prevailing speech code by addressing their Black customers as Mr. and Mrs. and not, patronizingly, by using their first names. A handful quietly gave money to the National Association for the Advancement of Colored People.

Max Levine, the secretary and sexton of my synagogue, never talked of principles; he simply helped anyone who came to him. He had once been in the grocery business in the Black part of town and had gone bankrupt extending credit to his customers. Max would not let poor people starve, so long as he still had something on his shelves to give them. These connections were not one-way streets; at difficult moments, they were of use to the congregation. Max Levine supervised the synagogue cemetery, and he never had any trouble finding grave diggers, even on Easter or Christmas: his old friends among the Blacks would help out. They remained his friends because he kept feeding hungry people in the kitchen of the synagogue and giving handouts to those who could not pay their electric bills. Some of the money came from his own pocket, and he raised the rest from members of the congregation and from others who owed him favors. When he died, many years after I left Nashville, I flew to town to read the service at his funeral. The synagogue was packed by a thousand people, Black and White alike.

My encounters with the Black leaders began soon after arriving in Nashville. I asked to see the president of Fisk University, Charles Johnson. He had been trained as a sociologist. I was astonished that he could talk about the misery of Blacks as analyst, keeping his bitterness under control. He described Nashville society by using the language of the refugee Jewish scholar Kurt Lewin, who had offered an explanation of the relationship between majorities and minorities as the inevitable conflict between in-groups and out-groups. The Blacks, so Charles Johnson explained to me, had been the lasting out-group in American society, as the Jews had been the lasting, pervasive out-group in Europe. Johnson urged that I read Gunnar and Eva Myrdal's massive study, *The Negro in America*, which had recently appeared; he wanted me to understand all the painful and terrible consequences of segregation. Johnson enlisted me in one of his concerns: to elevate the educational level of the Black clergy. Most of the Black preachers in Nashville had never finished high school, so Fisk organized an outreach course to add to their training. I volunteered to help teach the course. My job in that class was not to suggest what to preach, because I was obviously foreign to the religious sensibility of "twice-born" Black Christians, but to help them structure their sermons.

One day I insisted at great length, sometimes even pounding the table for emphasis, that these preachers had to think of a subject by Monday and then spend much time during the rest of the week refining and rehearsing their ideas so that by the next Sunday they would have a well-prepared sermon. From the back of the room, one older man raised his hand and said to me, "Brother Hertzberg, I can't do that." I asked him why, and he replied that if he prepared his sermon in advance, that "old devil," Satan, would know what he was going to say and be prepared for him. To outwit Satan, he had to get up, unprepared, each Sunday morning and preach from the "pure spirit." I had no answer. At the next session of the class, I invited the students to attend a Sabbath service at my synagogue. In my innocence, I thought that these preachers might adopt some of the polite and sedate tone of my congregation, but they knew better. They would not come, because what I was offering was foreign to their natures. Several of them countered by inviting me to their churches. One Sunday, not long thereafter, I was an honored visitor at a service in which the congregation sang with great enthusiasm, reaching ecstasy and shouting "Amen, brother" after every phrase that the preacher uttered. In the midst of this holy tumult, I saw that these Black Christians were really Black Hasidim. The scene at the church underlined how far the established, mainline, synagogues and churches in America, in all their varieties, had moved away from expressing religious emotion and religious passion. The next Sabbath I told my congregation that God seemed to be much more alive in the Black population in Nashville than among the bourgeois Whites, Jewish or Christian. Clearly, the Blacks needed Him more. The reaction was uncomfortable silence.

The next year Billy Graham, whose reputation as an honest and morally untainted evangelist was rising, came to Nashville to conduct a "Crusade for Christ." The expenses of the endeavor were underwritten by leaders of the local establishments. James Stahlman, the publisher of the conservative afternoon daily, the *Nashville Banner*, was a leading spirit in this group. He invited me to a luncheon that he gave in honor of Billy Graham. I did not attend, because I felt that I would be in a strange position at a gathering devoted to Christian evangelism, but I did arrange to have a brief meeting with Graham the next day. In that conversation I asked him where his "crusade" would take place. He answered that the meetings would be held in the football stadium of Vanderbilt University; it was the only place in town that could seat twenty thousand people. I wondered aloud what arrangements had been made for the Blacks who might come. Graham answered that they would be sitting in the end zone of the stadium, where Blacks conventionally sat at football games. Graham added that he had come to Nashville to save souls and that the segregated seating was a political question. He was not happy with this arrangement, but he had to comply. Most of the people who were paying for his work in Nashville would walk away if he announced that anyone could sit where he wished at his rallies, and most Whites would refuse to come "to give their souls to Christ" if they had to sit beside Blacks. Graham would lead no fight against segregation; he had to work within the established rules. It was clear that his conscience was troubled, for he certainly knew all the verses in the Bible that command equality for every one of God's children. We did not continue the uncomfortable discussion, for he was called away to an urgent meeting.

I burned my last bridges to the respectable, segregationist establishment when I joined the board of the Highlander Folk School. This institution was then the flagship of defiance in the South to the region's racist policies. Blacks and Whites ate together and slept in the same dormitories at the frequent conferences that the school convened. I received a letter from Eleanor Roosevelt, in 1950, speaking also for the theologian Reinhold Niebuhr and the former governor of New York, Herbert Lehman, who asked me to join the board of the Highlander Folk School. I was flattered beyond words that my name might be added to a letterhead together with such men and women. When I came down to earth, I read the description of the Highlander Folk School that Mrs. Roosevelt had enclosed. It was an adult camp and education center in the mountains of East Tennessee near Knoxville. Its director was Miles Horton, a Protestant minister in his mid-thirties who had been a favorite student of Niebuhr's. At the Highlander Folk School people worked and lived as if the South had already been redeemed from segregation. I called Miles Horton, and he told me, very candidly, that I was being invited because no member of his board lived in the South. As a rabbi in Nashville, I would be especially useful and uniquely exposed. I agreed to join. I never found out whether I made any real difference by joining that board, but I soon knew that Horton had been a true prophet when he predicted that I would be counterattacked by defenders of the status quo.

Some months later, one afternoon in the spring of 1950, my secretary brought me that day's edition of the *Nashville Banner*, and pointed to the announcement on the front page that Senator Joseph McCarthy would soon come to town to investigate the radicals in the area. This would be another of the public hearings that he was holding in many places to smoke out, so he said, the Communists and the "Comsymps," those who sympathized with Communism. My name was mentioned as one of those whom he intended to summon. The telephone was soon ringing with calls from congregants who were upset by the notoriety that I had brought the synagogue. I thought about it overnight with some fear, but, in the morning, I shook off my concern and telephoned Jimmy Stahlman. I had guessed, correctly, that he was the instigator of the visit to Nashville by the Senate's scourge of Communism. I told Stahlman "on the front end," in the southern dialect that I had begun to speak comfortably and fluently, that I would take the fight to Mc-Carthy. At the hearing, I would denounce segregation as morally reprehensible, and I would ask Senator McCarthy whether such views proved that I was a Communist. Fortunately, Senator McCarthy never came to Nashville. His office announced, a few days later, that the Senator could not find the time to hold this hearing.

The barrier between Blacks and Whites was the major tension in town, but Jews were also kept out of "society." The relationship between Jews and non-Jews existed during the business day, from nine to five, but not thereafter. This "rule" governed all the connections. Sam Hunt, a senior vice president of Nashville's major bank, was assigned to deal with its Jewish clients. He was freely available for lunch, but I knew no one who had ever been invited to his house for dinner. At the end of my years in Nashville, in 1956, when the White majority was being rocked by the Supreme Court's command two years earlier to integrate the schools "with all deliberate speed," I did receive an invitation to his daughter's wedding. I could not attend, but some of his other Jewish associates did go to the wedding. The social division was codified in the existence of two country clubs: the Belle Meade Club had never admitted a single Jewish member, and the Woodmont Country Club had never had a single application from a non-Jew. This was all the more pointed because in each of these two clubs the major activities were the same: golf and weekend parties. Once a year the barrier went down, and the best golfers in the two clubs competed in a tournament that was held alternately on each other's courses. I was never a member of the Woodmont team, so I do not remember whether this tournament culminated in a dinner, but, even if it did, such a social event had no consequences. These two middle-class communities lived apart.

The social division was so complete that it applied even to the charity endeavors that were organized by women. The classy Jewish women longed desperately for invitations to the Junior League, but they were never asked to join. These ladies created their own network of charitable endeavors; they worked especially hard to support a local facility for the older poor. The women who took the lead felt, rightly, that they were doing something as citizens of Nashville, and not for some parochial Jewish cause, because none of the clients of this charity were Jews. They were also keeping step with the good works of the Junior League. I respected this endeavor, but I once got into deep trouble at a dinner party by suggesting that there were three parallel societies in Nashville, each of which distributed titles and honors: the Gentile social set with its country club and its Junior League for the women; a Jewish society with its own country club and its local chapter of the National Council of Jewish Women; and a Black middle class in which such groups of their own as the Elks (Blacks were not allowed in the national organization of the Whites) offered aspiring members the chance to rise to the dignity of "grand exalted potentate." This analysis—that the excluded minorities aped the majority—did not seem illuminating or funny to my dinner partners. They preferred not to think of such issues.

The wall between Jews and Gentiles was not completely sealed. The politicians, of all varieties, cultivated connections with Jews, because they were a source of support. A few radicals in politics and culture, on the fringe of both groups, were friends. My strangest early encounter was with a middle-aged, hard-drinking, failed politician, the namesake of his grandfather, Edward Carmack. The grandfather had been a powerful and controversial United States senator who was shot to death on the grounds of the state capitol in the midst of a quarrel over prohibition. The senator had supported the edict against the "demon rum," but his assailant wanted the law to be repealed. The senator's statue had been erected on the spot where he had fallen; I saw it every time I walked toward the Gay Street Synagogue. After a few lunches, washed down with gin and Coca-Cola (he allowed me not to keep up with him), my new friend invited me one day to drive some thirty miles with him to the old family home in Murfreesboro. In hushed silence, swearing me to secrecy, he took me into a back room that had seemingly been locked for many years. On the wall opposite the door, there was a portrait of a man with a long nose, fierce eyes, and a short black beard. The subject was obviously, even exaggeratedly, Jewish. As I kept looking at the picture, with obvious surprise, my host told me that this was a portrait of a great-grandfather. He had come to Tennessee as a peddler before the Civil War and had stayed to marry one of the local young women. This ancestor was the guarded secret of the family.

The next day I asked Manuel Eskind, the president of the synagogue, a native of Nashville who knew much of the local lore, whether there was any truth to this story. Eskind had never heard it. Although he wondered whether this story was simply the raving of a drunk who was angry that he had not lived up to the family name, Eskind thought that the story of the Jewish great-grandfather was possible. He added that there were probably more portraits like this one, well hidden in the back rooms of some of the first families of Tennessee. My new friend seemed to need my company. He had become an outcast, who seemed to think, at least between drinks, that he might find a home among sympathetic Jews. The portrait of this ancestor, real or supposed, was his passport. We remained in touch for the next ten years, until I left Nashville to return to the Northeast. At the time I did not understand why I kept the connection. Years later, thinking back on my days in Nashville, I realized why I would not let go of him. He had ancestors. He was not a "new" man, traveling light; he was burdened by the grandfather he could not live up to, for he had failed in two attempts to be elected to the Senate, and by the Jewish great-grandfather whom he could not forget. He knew who his demons were; he had not gotten rid of them by inventing a new identity.

My happier early connection with southern life was with the small circle of avowed and defiant radicals in Nashville. Their leader was Jennings Perry. I sought him out almost immediately after arriving in town because I had long been reading his columns in *PM,* the left-wing daily, in New York. The local gossip about him was that he had been fired from the job of editor of the *Nashville Tennessean,* the morning paper that supported the "New Deal," because he had become either a Communist or a fellow traveler. This may have been true before I got to know him in the late 1940s, but the man with whom I spent innumerable hours, for the next ten years, was not a conspirator or card-carrying ideologue. On the contrary, he was open, and profane; he was most at ease with a drink in one hand and a cigarette in the other. Perry was a political radical for very southern reasons. He came from a different class than the plantation owners before the Civil War, who had needed slaves to farm cotton; he was not a son or grandson of the poor Whites who had flocked to the Ku Klux Klan, after the South had lost, to safeguard their status against the competition of the freed slaves. Perry had grown up on a farm near Jackson, Tennessee, where several generations of his forebears had raised corn and cattle. The work on the farm had been done by members of the family, so he told me, helped by hired hands of both races. Populism had begun among such farmers in the last years of the nineteenth century. Farmers were angry at the banks, which gave them no credit and took their property when they could not pay back their loans. They wanted easy credit so that they could survive. Their enemies were the financiers and captains of industry from the Northeast and Midwest, whose main concern was profits and fiscal stability. Some of these populists became anti-Semites, but the majority did not imagine that Wall Street was a Jewish affair; they remained angry with the "interests." Jennings Perry had inherited their outlook. It taught him to be, in his time, on the side of labor, the masses, against the capitalists, the rich elite. He did not need Karl Marx to teach him about class struggle; he had grown up with it. He had no doubt that the muckrakers at the turn of the century had been right in their assertion that at the root of every American fortune there was an act of larceny.

Jennings Perry was even more vehement on the subject of race, and I could not understand how he had come to such views. After some months, I challenged him. His passion for equality did not sound like the rhetoric that I heard in New York from radicals who wrote for the Communist weekly, the *New Masses*, or even like the speeches that I had heard Paul Robeson give a few years before. These advocates had insisted that the Negro would achieve equality only if there was a revolution to end capitalism in America. Perry did not propose revolution; he spoke of restoration. His parents had told him of a time after the

Civil War when some of the freed slaves had acquired education; they had held state and federal offices, and they behaved at least as well as the White racists who soon drove them out. Perry did not think that the end of the world would come, even in the South, if equality was restored. He kept insisting that the cure for racism was readily available: repeal the poll tax and the other restrictions that southern Whites were using to keep Negroes from voting. He knew, of course, that the local jurisdictions would do no such thing; only the national government could make such practices illegal under the Constitution, which had promised equal protection for all Americans.

I came often to the Perry household to talk politics with Jennings. These visits were my other life, my assertion of myself as an American radical. The visits were a refuge from the job that took most of my time and that presented me with my most immediate problems. I had imagined that I had been invited to Nashville because the congregation was troubled by the very questions with which I was wrestling: how can men and women who had grown up in America and took part in its culture retain their Jewish faith and their connection to the ways of their ancestors? I quickly found out that these issues were not the major concern of my congregants. They wanted their synagogue to shed its immigrant past and to become more "American." Such a transformation would increase their prestige in Nashville. In the minds of the Gentiles, the Conservative synagogue would join the Reform temple as one of the "Jewish churches," to be respected, even as the Jewish community as a whole was kept at some distance. The most immediate objective of the congregants of the Gay Street Synagogue was to improve their position in the Jewish society. The American-born children of immigrants from Eastern Europe wanted parity with the older settlers, the "German Jews," who dominated the Reform temple.

At the turn of the century, when the immigrants had arrived from Eastern Europe, they had built their synagogue on Gay Street, behind the state capitol, where they had found housing in the same neighborhood with freed slaves. The Blacks were working as servants in the homes of the rich, and the Jews sold the Blacks groceries and clothes. When I came to town in 1947, a few of the founding fathers of the Gay Street Synagogue were still alive, but the next generation was now in its middle years. They had opened dress shops, furniture stores, and other retail businesses in the center of town, and they had all moved to new homes in safer and more pleasant places. They were no longer in awe of the earlier wealth of the "German Jews." Some were buying or building homes with columns and porches in front, in the image of southern mansions in the center of the old cotton plantations. The pervading passion for the trappings of gentility reminded me of a Hasidic story that I had read in my teens. The rebbe of Talne once visited an adherent who had become rich. The host escorted the rebbe through his large and well-decorated house, and he then took him to the stables, where he showed the rebbe his coach and twelve matched horses. With glowing eyes, he waited for some comment from the visiting holy man. The rebbe of Talne quietly asked the question, What do you do to experience joy in this world? His host was astonished: hasn't the rebbe just seen my beautiful house and my coach? The rebbe of Talne replied, These are your "world to come," the pleasures that you take in your ultimate ideal, success. What are you doing to experience the simple pleasures of this world?

In 1947, no member of the synagogue still lived on Gay Street, or anywhere nearby. The area had deteriorated, and some of the houses in the neighborhood were in use as brothels. That was not the only reason for the desire to move away. The synagogue building was a relic from an earlier time: it was a reminder that the founders had been poor and foreign. The exterior of this Jewish tabernacle was adorned with cupolas, like a Russian church; the only difference was that Stars of David, and not crosses, had been placed on top. A few hints of modernity had crept into the interior of the synagogue. The Orthodox practice of separating the sexes at prayer had long been abolished, but otherwise the ritual and atmosphere of the synagogue at Gay Street were unchanged from its beginnings. The main sanctuary had been modernized further, by removing the reading desk from the center of the floor; in respectable American fashion, the congregation now looked toward the platform from which the service was conducted. But the basement had been left untouched. It was furnished with wooden tables and long benches that seemed to have been there from the very beginnings of the synagogue. Copies of dusty Talmudic texts were scattered about. The sacred books had once been studied there regularly, but they had not been touched for years. No one remembered how to put them back in proper order on the shelves.

The service in the Gay Street Synagogue had remained Orthodox. It was still chanted entirely in Hebrew, in the minor, essentially somber key that had been defined through the centuries by cantors who had stood at their reading desks in the old country in fear and trembling, in awe of God. A handful did come to the Sabbath morning service; they were the few who knew the old ways and cared about them. The large majority were American-born, and they had been taught, as children, just enough of the Hebrew of the Sabbath service to perform the Bar Mitzvah rituals but not enough to understand the meaning of the sacred texts. They attended synagogue on the High Holidays, enduring the many hours of the Hebrew service out of duty but feeling more resentment than respect.

I had been hired by the American-born majority to make them more comfortable. I would be the first rabbi in their history who spoke English without an accent. They knew that I had grown up among very Orthodox Jews and that I was fluent in Yiddish, but I had recently graduated from a rather liberal and contemporary rabbinical school. My old-world training would be, they thought, a useful tool to help ease the transition to the new neighborhood, uptown, and to a more modern, "American" style of worship. They thought I could keep a few old people quiet, in Yiddish, while we moved from Gay Street to West End Avenue, the street that already contained some of the city's "best" churches. The leaders of the synagogue trusted me because I seemed to have expressed my own desire to move from the Jewish immigrant ghetto by choosing to study in New York at the posh Jewish Theological Seminary. I was, therefore, a suitable rabbi to preside over their new era. They would be leapfrogging over the Vine Street Temple, the Reform synagogue of the "German Jews," which was still downtown, a couple of hundred yards away from the abandoned Nashville Opera House. The opera house had come back into use as the "Grand Old Opry," the home of country music. There, every weekend, farmers' children twanged on banjos and guitars and sang plaintively about love, loss, and betrayal. Late on Saturday nights, where the carriages had once come to take the elite of Nashville home from performances by touring companies featuring Caruso and Gigli, whiskey bottles now littered the street. What a triumph it would be for the Gay Street Synagogue to become the first Jewish congregation to move uptown.

These hopes were overbold, but they were not entirely unreasonable. Some of the East European Jews had been rich for two generations, and a few had even intermarried with the "German Jews." A handful of the members of the Gay Street Synagogue had been admitted to membership in the Woodmont Country Club, the social bastion of the older Jewish settlers. The leading families in the Gay Street Synagogue could, therefore, imagine that they were moving toward social equality with the "German Jews;" and that building their new synagogue would hasten the process. I was caught up in this maneuver, because I knew that we had to move from Gay Street, but I soon became uncomfortable with the effort to build a new synagogue. I had not moved away from my Orthodox origins because I hankered to dine and play golf with rich people. I did not need a sleek American synagogue. I preferred the old building with its cupolas and the musty smell in its basement. I could be modern and contemporary anywhere; the synagogue was my link to my parents and to all of my ancestors. The very structure, in its foreignness, seemed to invite the souls of past generations to pray in these familiar surroundings. I could not help asking the question, over and over again, Why did their children remember so little? With variations, they all told the same story, of immigrant poverty and of the struggles of their families to achieve some wealth, but almost no one knew anything about the earlier generations of their families in Europe. Had their parents told them nothing about the past—or had they preferred not to listen?

I worked hard for the next two years to help raise the money for the move from Gay Street, and I even found the architect for the new building, Percival Goodman, but the discomfort never left me. In my first year in Nashville, the congregation still worshiped in the building on Gay Street. I became attached to the ghosts in the basement. I spent hours paging through the old books, and I was particularly moved when I found a learned comment handwritten in Hebrew on the margin by someone who had brought with him to Nashville some learning in the Talmud, which he had acquired in Jewish schools in Poland or Lithuania. These aliens in a southern town, which was dominated by the memory of Andrew Jackson and the Civil War, had huddled together to study the texts that they had learned in their youth. I was in their company when I touched the pages. All were dead, or dying, by 1947, except for David Kahn, a man well over eighty who had been the

Shochet, the religious official who slaughtered meat according to Jewish ritual. When I met him, he was nearly blind, and he had long given up his office. Nonetheless, he still chanted the first hour or so of the High Holiday service, from memory. I heard him for the first time that fall, in the building on Gay Street, where the High Holiday service was being given for the last time. He sobbed as he chanted the ancient prayers for mercy, forgiveness, and long life. I knew that David Kahn was surrounded by the men with whom he had studied Talmud in this building fifty years before.

For the next two years the High Holiday services were held in a movie theater that was rented for those occasions. This was not a pleasant alternative, but the old building had been locked up and sold to the state (which was razing the neighborhood to extend the park surrounding the state capitol), and the new synagogue building was still under construction. During these years in the wilderness of the Belle Meade Theater, David Kahn did not take part in the services because no one lived nearby to offer him lodging for the sacred days, and he would not transgress the Orthodox dictum that one is forbidden to travel on Sabbath and holidays even to the synagogue. Finally, in 1950, the bright, very modern new building was opened, and David Kahn again chanted the first part of the service. He had been asked to give up this honor, because he was very old and sick, but he refused. Mr. Kahn had to be led to the reading desk, and he trembled until he began to chant, but then the tremors stopped. He could not see the prayer book, so he sang the complicated liturgy from memory. I prayed with him. He was defying the very American new building, to take himself back to the Old World—but I knew that many of my congregants wished that he would go away. They were waiting for me to conduct the service, to lead some readings in English, and to take them, step-by-step, through the rest of the ritual. It was only earlier, in an almost empty synagogue, that I had stood beside Mr. Kahn before the God of my ancestors. During the next two hours, when the younger cantor and I led the service, we seemed assured and competent, but I kept asking myself, Are we helping anyone to stand before God? Are we evoking for them the memory of their ancestors?

The countersymbol to David Kahn was Manuel Eskind. His father and his father-in-law had been the early leaders of the congregation. As a young man Manuel and his two brothers had acquired control of the department store that anchored the business district downtown. The venture had failed, in the depression years, and the bankruptcy had clouded the family's reputation. After the repeal of Prohibition, Manuel and his older brother, Herbert, recovered from this disaster by acquiring a franchise to sell liquor, but the whispers about the past never quite died down. The Jews of Nashville were both southerners and Jews: they belonged to two inbred societies that never forgot anything, especially if it was scandalous or disreputable, but Manuel Eskind was too formidable to confront directly. He was short, squat, and fierce; he seemed immovable. His enemies in the synagogue nibbled away at him as an incongruous leader of the congregation, for he had almost no Jewish learning and he rarely attended synagogue services. He expressed his piety in large donations to Jewish charities and, especially, in leading the effort to move the synagogue. He was at home with the "German Jews" in Nashville, and he had even become a leading member of their social set, but some barrier remained. He would seize leadership in the entire community by transforming the old immigrant congregation of his parents into the West End Synagogue.

From the first moment that I met him, Manuel Eskind devoted much of his energy to guiding me through the quicksands of Nashville society and to defending me in the midst of its frequent intrigues. I would not have survived very long without his friendship and support. He stopped two serious attempts to oust me, but he never asked me to mute my opinions or to change my conduct in order to mollify the critics. Manuel remained president of the congregation for all of my ten years in Nashville without ever admitting to me that he kept the post that long in order to protect me. He put limits on me only once, at the very beginning. Soon after I arrived, Manuel asked me to promise that I, a "damn Yankee liberal," would say nothing about the racial customs of the South until I had spent at least six months in town. He wanted me, so he said, to have some feel for the local scene before I stirred up trouble for myself. I agreed, but I asked him whether my well-being was his only worry. He replied by changing the subject. I heard this lecture as a warning that I should not endanger the community by making speeches against segregation. I said exactly this to Manuel, but he waved me off. He did not try to defend the ways of the South, or even to insist that I might cause trouble for the Jews. It was just as likely that I would be shrugged off as a transplant from the North who really did not understand southern society. Nonetheless, Manuel Eskind advised that it would be best for me to take some time before I became a public firebrand. What I might do in six months or so was my affair.

That day, Manuel Eskind became my friend—sometimes my critic, sometimes my teacher, and always absolutely loyal and absolutely unselfish. I would leave Nashville ten years later, some months after he had become tired of being the perennial president of the synagogue. I could not stay with a conventional synagogue president who would try to hem me in rather than be my friend and elder brother. Some fifteen years later, Manuel died and I flew back to Nashville to read the service and preach the eulogy at his funeral. I still remember how I began the eulogy. I quoted the verse in the Bible that was the opening line of King David's lament for Abner, the son of Ner, the field marshal of King Saul: "A prince and a great man has fallen this day in Israel" (2 Sam. 3:38).

I was so astonished at Eskind's generosity that I asked one of his cousins, a poor relative who had quickly become a close friend, why Manuel was so involved in the Jewish community and in the synagogue of the "Russian Jews." This cousin explained to me that the Nashville Jewish community was divided into clans—that is, extended families, several of which fought each other with ferocity that approached that of the Montagues and the Capulets. Manuel was the head of the Levy-Eskind clan (his wife's family and his own, which had long been linked by marriages and business connections). I was the rabbi who had been brought to Nashville when this clan was in the ascendancy, so its loyalty to me was assured; it was part of their own dignity. For the two other clans that wanted to wrest primacy from Manuel and his family, it really did not matter what I said or did. I would be attacked even if I recited the Ten Commandments, for Manuel's enemies could best embarrass and weaken him by proving that he had chosen a troublesome rabbi. This explanation frightened me. I would always be embattled, because I was the available target in a clan war. The only cheerful thing I heard that day was the emphatic assurance, by the cousin, that Manuel sincerely liked me and that he kept saying, in private, that he would not let my enemies, even those I had earned on my own account, break my neck. Manuel Eskind was concerned that a defeat in Nashville, early in my career, might make me lose heart.

Because of his support, I felt secure in my job even on the occasions when I was attacked. My confidence kept rising as the prestige of the synagogue increased because we were the first Jewish institution in town to succeed in moving to the new neighborhood, but I soon realized that this coup did not really change the local pecking order. The smallest of the three synagogues (it had remained undeviatingly Orthodox), and the Jewish community center, which housed some charitable and recreational activities, both soon moved to new premises in the West End neighborhood. A few years later, the Reform temple finally abandoned the downtown and built a new building in a wooded area beyond the city limits. It did make some difference that the rabbi of the Vine Street Reform Temple, Julius Mark, left Nashville in 1949 because he was elected to the premier job in the Reform rabbinate, the pulpit of Temple Emanuel in New York City. Rabbi Mark had dominated the Jewish community for most of his twenty years in Nashville, to the degree that the Conservative synagogue felt so honored when he came to visit that, as a matter of course, he displaced their own rabbi and gave the sermon. His departure to the fabled post in New York added to the luster of the temple in Nashville that had nurtured a figure of such importance. Nonetheless, his successor, William Silverman, arrived with no such prestige. On the contrary, he was soon losing respect. The turning point came when he and his wife entered the annual competition for the prize that was given to the home that was best decorated for the midwinter holidays. That meant, in practice, Christmas decorations, and the contest was universally known as the Christmas contest. The Silvermans took an ecumenical view, so they decorated their home for the Jewish festival of Hanukkah, inventing unheard-of displays for this holiday, which is normally celebrated simply, with the lighting of candles for eight days. It was predictable that the Silvermans would win, for it made quite a splash in this town of churches that a rabbinic couple had the best "Christmas" decorations.

But, despite such lapses in judgment by the rabbi, the primacy of the Reform temple as an institution was not diminished. The Jewish community in Nashville retained its own style. The "German Jews" remained its leaders. Elsewhere they were becoming too few, and too tired, in the 1940s to continue to dominate the Jewish communities. Many were using their money for their pleasures, or they had become notable supporters of writers and artists. In Nashville most of the "German Jews" still cared; they had not abandoned the organized Jewish community to the "Russian Jews." On the contrary, the "German Jews" in Nashville were still the largest donors to Jewish charities; they even helped finance good works in Palestine, though most were vehement anti-Zionists, who kept insisting that they were Americans of the Jewish religious persuasion. The fight in Nashville over Zionism was, thus, not about money. It was about public support in American politics for those who were creating the state of Israel. This was the critical boundary between the two parts of the Jewish community. To be sure, several "German Jews" had broken ranks to support the Zionist effort, but the large majority of the local Zionists were people who had grown up in the old Gay Street Synagogue. Attachment to their own group was, in fact, their dominant Jewish emotion. This feeling was especially intense because almost every family among "Russian Jews" had been in some connection with living relatives until the war had begun in 1939.

Letters had begun to arrive from cousins who had survived the death camps; they were asking for help in finding a new home in Israel or in the United States. The letters were usually in Yiddish, which their American cousins could no longer read, so they were brought to me for translation. I often had trouble containing myself, for the letters that I was reading told of the murder of parents and siblings before their eyes in the public square of their village or in the synagogue, which was set afire after all the Jews whom the Nazis could find had been forced inside. One letter gave me a shock of another kind. It had been written by an obviously well-educated man in his middle years to a father in Nashville with whom he had lost touch many years before. The address was forty years out of date, but the post office had delivered the letter to people of the same family name. They had brought it to me on the presumption that they were hearing from long-lost cousins. On first reading I knew that I would have to dissemble. The refugee in Eastern Europe was a son who had been abandoned, long ago, together with his younger brother and their mother, by the father whom he was trying to find. This man was the father, now dead, of my congregant. The father had come to Nashville many years ago as a "bachelor." He had married into a good family, and his two American-born children were now my congregants, sitting in my room. I could not tell them the truth that had now appeared in this letter, that their father had abandoned his first family, had sent them some money for a few years, and had then broken the connection. I "translated" the letter to say that these were cousins who needed help and that they could be written to only in Yiddish. I offered to conduct the correspondence. For the next several years, I transmitted some thousands of dollars to these "cousins" to help them survive and find their way to Israel. After a while, the correspondence petered out. I do not know whether these relatives ever encountered each other.

In all of the letters that were brought to my office, the Europeans referred to common grandparents or great-grandparents, whose names were barely remembered in Nashville, but these letters did evoke deep, long-dormant feelings of identity. The connection of language and culture had evaporated, but the biological ties had not been forgotten. The Jews in Nashville were affirming their ancestors in the only way they knew: by helping their cousins. Betrayal of this folk feeling was unthinkable; it would be the unforgivable act of apostasy. Family loyalty required even more than the money that was being sent to a displaced-persons camp. The members of my congregation, who were almost all children of emigrants from Eastern Europe, had no doubt that they had to help make a home in Palestine for these survivors.

I was a fierce partisan in this battle with the anti-Zionists, but my motives were not quite as simple and as praiseworthy as I wanted to believe. So far in my life, I had been plagued over and over again with the feeling of powerlessness. As a child I had been a "free" student at the Hebrew Parochial School, because my parents could not pay any of the small fees, and I had gone through college because my tuition was covered by scholarships. I had been looking at myself with anger (I would learn years later that this was a sign of depression) because I had been forced to survive by my wits and on the goodwill of others. This was an unpleasant, "Jewish" life; it was the way that Jews had survived for many centuries in the Diaspora. I was irresistibly attracted to the Zionists because they were making a historic bid for power in Jewish hands. This demand was all the more moving because I remembered that if my mother's father had persuaded her to remain in Lemberg in 1926, I would, at best, be one of the survivors in the displaced-persons camps in Germany. I would be waiting for some door to open, with the knowledge that the only place to which I might soon be admitted would be a recognized Jewish state.

These were motives that I could defend in public, but I also knew that the Zionist cause was deepening the gulf between my congregants and the "German Jews" to whom many of them aspired. I went to the Woodmont Country Club almost every Saturday night to argue with Bernard and Albert Werthan, who were the leaders of the anti-Zionists. They were the grandchildren and heirs of the founder of the Werthan Bag Company, the most important Jewish-owned manufacturing company. The two brothers were quite different: Bernard tended to be quiet and reserved, whereas Albert was argumentative and sociable. Albert used to sit me down at the bar almost as soon as I walked in the door, to try to persuade me that the Zionists were guilty of "dual loyalty": they had greater passion for a Jewish state than was seemly for patriotic Americans. I answered back that he did not care enough about other Jews. Within moments of our resuming this debate, we were invariably surrounded by partisans of both views. We did not succeed in convincing each other, perhaps because we were both wrong. His premise, that patriotism is an absolute loyalty, was being rejected, in those very days, by the courts that were sentencing Nazis. These tribunals were denying the excuse that the Nazis had followed orders; they should have refused to carry out some commands, because conscience is the final judge of conduct. I was wrong to accuse Albert Werthan of not caring enough for Jews in trouble. The Werthan family had remained the leaders of the local campaign for Jewish charity, even though an ever larger proportion of the money was being allocated to the embattled Jewish community in Palestine. Once or twice, at impassioned moments in the political quarrel over Zionism, the Werthans threatened to withhold part, or even all, of their annual gift, but they never did. Such actions were taken elsewhere by a few embittered anti-Zionists, but in Nashville the Jewish community was united by noblesse oblige, the virtue of helping other Jews in trouble.

And yet my congregants, who had been in the United States for less than two generations, knew so little about the pasts of their families in

Europe; they seemed so intent on forgetting the ways of their parents. They had abandoned memory and were defining their identities through success. I would soon read David Reisman's *The Lonely Crowd*, in which he distinguished between the outer-directed man and the inner-directed man: the outer-directed person looks to others to define his identity; the inner-directed person makes his life by his own values. The most famous new American drama, then, was Arthur Miller's *Death of a Salesman*, in which the father, Willy Loman, who has spent his life as a drummer on the road, keeps insisting to his son, Biff, that he must become "well liked." I read Reisman and Miller with the feeling that they were talking about people whom I knew, but I kept thinking that both had missed, or avoided, a central issue. Outer-directed people had no ancestors, for they had made themselves over to be socially acceptable. Even the inner-directed person seemed to be defining himself by choosing among immediately available, largely contemporary values, or slogans. No one seemed to have a past to affirm, or even to fight against.

I was well on the way to convincing myself of the importance of ancestors until I met Jake Markel. He was one of the few adults to be the grandson, and not the son, of East European immigrants, and he even took pride in the rabbinic learning of his late grandfather. That worthy had not even tried to make a living as peddler or petty shopkeeper when he arrived in Nashville; he had held the job of sexton of the synagogue from the day the congregation was organized, and he was still remembered as a man of learning and piety. The family tradition had been strong enough, even into the third generation, so that the young Jake Markel had been given an unusually intensive education in Judaism. Though he almost never came to synagogue, Markel could still read the Hebrew of the service with substantial understanding of its meaning. He had done well at college, and he had even acquired a degree in law. Markel did not last long in legal practice because he had cut some corners very early in his career, and he was disbarred. When I encountered him, Jake Markel was florid and a bit dissipated, pale and flabby like the night person that he had become, and expensively dressed with a diamond stickpin in his tie and a diamond ring on one of his fingers. He did not bother pretending, even to the new young rabbi, that he was an ordinary businessman. Markel was making a lot of money running a gambling joint on the outskirts of Nashville. His clients came in large numbers because the county police were well paid to protect him, so that there was no fear of a raid. "Everybody"—Gentiles and Jews alike—knew Jake; he was the local Arnold Rothstein, an underworld figure with good manners who gave some money back to those who had ruined themselves at his gambling tables.

We barely talked to each other even on the rare occasions when we were in the same room, but Jake Markel troubled me. His life contradicted any easy conclusion about the importance of ancestors. People delighted in telling stories about Jake Markel, but these tales about his raffish life did not explain his transformation from the disciple of his grandfather that he had once been to the disbarred lawyer and gambler that he had become. Inevitably, I realized that there are no absolutes. Jake Markel was not the first Jew of good family who had turned to crime. I even knew that Lepke Buchalter, the infamous head of "Murder, Inc.," in New York, who was then on his way to the electric chair, was the half-brother of a well-known rabbi. Nonetheless, I continued to believe that such criminals were exceptions. The rule was incarnate in my grandmother—or, for that matter, in Jennings Perry's grandmother—who had handed on to their grandchildren the moral values of past generations.

What disturbed me most about Jake Markel was the fact that his establishment had become a local fad; it was chic to be seen there. Teenagers were not admitted to Jake's place, and young adults could not gamble on their parents' account, but this gambling joint had a serious effect on some of the young people in town. The parents who were spending much time and money on the pleasures of the new rich were bribing their children with expensive presents. Many teenagers were being given cars of their own the moment that they turned sixteen. The young seemed to be defining their social pecking order by comparing the size of the gifts and the cost of the cars. "Sweet sixteen" parties were ferociously competitive. I took to wondering out loud, in sermons that were largely resented, whether the parents who were defining themselves through money, and were using it to buy connection with their children, were heading toward the ruin of their families. What I said made little difference. The adults had been poor as children in the

Gay Street neighborhood; they were trying to erase the memory of their deprivations, and they even felt virtuous about heaping more money on their children than they knew how to use. Jake Markel was not the enemy. He was merely providing an outlet for people who hoped to feel better by behaving conspicuously, even outrageously, as rich people.

The houses kept becoming bigger, the new automobiles were ever longer, and the social affairs were becoming bigger and plusher. One night in my early days in Nashville, while I was still a bachelor, I attended one such party. The couple who gave the reception, Harry and Esther Klein, had been kind to me, so I went willingly to help celebrate their wedding anniversary. In every room of their large house, and outside on the lawn, the tables were heaped high with food, and there was a bar in every corner. Six hundred people came that night. Esther and Harry circulated among their guests, embracing and kissing their friends, and they kept repeating the local salutations "honey" and "dear." They seemed to be rejoicing in their wide network of friends; they were celebrating the triumph of giving—and being able to afford— the largest party that anyone had ever seen. The last of the other guests did not leave until two in the morning, but I stayed on for another half hour. I wanted to hear how they felt at this high moment. Harry would not talk until Esther excused herself and went up to bed. Sitting in the living room, in the midst of the debris of this great party, Harry poured us both drinks from the inevitable bottle of bourbon.

I expected him to express pride in the success of the party, and in his own rise to wealth, which this lavish spread announced as effectively as a flourish on drums and trumpets, but he did not. Instead, he leaned forward and said to me in the most serious voice that I ever heard him use, "Rab, you think that all of these people are my friends. I know that they aren't. My real friends are the people who would come around the day after they sold this house at auction to pay some of my debts. Maybe there were two or three of them in the mob that just left, but I'm not sure who they are." I did not argue with him. Though he had never read that text, Harry had just offered his own variation on a statement in the Talmud: "The poor man is treated as if he does not exist." I drank up in silence and left. As I drove home, I kept wondering whether the gaiety and bonhomie at the party masked widespread fear. The American economy and American power then dominated the world, and millions of people all over America were becoming richer and more confident. How many of them were still terribly afraid that, on the way up, they might fall down? How many longed for the simpler time when poverty did not make anyone into a pariah? I did not know the answers to these questions, but the early-morning chat with Harry Klein took the edge away from my anger at the new rich, and the not quite rich, who were so busy pushing to raise their social status. Harry Klein had told me that they were afraid: they had bet their lives on success, but each of them knew that he might lose the bet. But I knew that I did not have the power to take them away from the gamble. I was afraid for them and very sad.

During my years in Nashville, I was thrice an alien: I did not belong among the southern Gentiles, I was not part of the Black community, and, even as I served as one of their rabbis, I lived my inner life at some distance from the Jews. I could not respect the culture of the South, because it had been fashioned by slaveholders, and, even in Nashville, the atmosphere was still pervaded by sorrow that the South had lost the Civil War. I had chosen the side of the Blacks against those who belonged to the cult of Confederate "Blue and Gray," but I never had any illusion that I had found the community to which I could belong. No matter how much I opposed segregation, I went home to my apartment in a White, middle-class neighborhood. I was a sympathizer and a supporter, but I could not become a "White Negro."

The entrenched social anti-Semitism that I encountered in Nashville made it all the more certain that I would live my life, there, only among other Jews. I was in a "gilded ghetto," despite the freedom to take part in civic functions or to attend concerts; even on such occasions, Jews usually had their coffee at intermissions in the company of other Jews. I found much warmth and friendship. During my first three years in town I was unmarried, so a number of families, and not all of them from my own congregation, invited me to come to dinner whenever I wanted. Nonetheless, I was nearly alone; I was in a Jewish pale that had lost most of its Jewish culture. For too many of the people whom I knew, success had become the measure of all things. Few would admit, flatly and openly, that they were angry with their parents and their grandparents. On the contrary, I kept hearing about the profound respect that many had for their immigrant forebears; they had had the courage to come to the United States, to start a new life in a new country; they had given their children the chance to do well in the "land of opportunity." But these words of praise were often a cover for resentment. Parents who had been poor had left it to their children to fight their battles for success. This feeling was sometimes expressed in the form of a question: if my father and grandfather, who had studied the sacred texts in Poland or Lithuania, were so good or so smart, how come they were so poor?

I kept rereading a book that I had savored in college, Thorstein Veblen's *Theory of the Leisure Class*. Fifty years earlier, he had mocked the gilded age: it was a time, so he said, when social status was achieved by "conspicuous wealth" and "conspicuous consumption." This assessment seemed to describe my time, when, in the immediate aftermath of the Second World War, America was at the beginning of a new gilded age. I should have been rejoicing that many Jews who had been poor in the 1930s had now vaulted into affluence and were demanding and, if necessary, buying respect. The Jews were not alone; they were only a small part of what was happening throughout American society. But, I could not abide the new culture of self-indulgence.

12

The local Zionists took part in the struggle for the partition of Palestine by lobbying the senators and congressmen from Tennessee, to help firm up American support in the debates in the United Nations. We heard snatches on the radio of the debates in the General Assembly at Lake Success, near New York City, but that only emphasized how far away we really were. Being so remote was particularly hard for me because the leaky boat that I had helped buy in Philadelphia at the beginning of 1947 had actually sailed into the Mediterranean that summer, under the name *Exodus 47*, carrying 4,500 survivors of the death camps toward Palestine. The ship was stopped and boarded by the Royal Navy. It was towed into the harbor in Haifa, but its passengers were not allowed to land. They were all forced to return to Europe. The radio sounds of the hopeless fight to repel the British sailors, in which several passengers had been killed, and the newsreels of the arrival of the ship in Haifa were all played in Nashville. I could not sit still; I had to take part in the struggle.

That summer I went to New York. I was clearly not entitled to a vacation, since I had arrived only a few months earlier, in mid-April,

but the officers of the synagogue knew that I was restless. They dele-
gated me to go to New York to find an architect for the new building,
and they gave me additional time to spend with my family in Baltimore.
I did look around for an architect, but I could find no one to recom-
mend. I decided to postpone the search until the next summer, so I
could spend my days in New York as I wished. I did some work in the
libraries toward my doctorate, but I spent most of my time on the fringe
of the Zionist effort. The headquarters of the battle was in two brown-
stones next door to each other on East 65th Street. I was going to be in
New York for only six weeks, so I did not dare ask anyone for a defined
job, but I was allowed to hang around. Sometimes I was asked to carry
some documents from the offices to one of the hotels where Moshe
Shertok (later Sharrett), the "foreign secretary" of the Jewish Agency, or
some lesser member of the delegation from Palestine was staying.
Occasionally I sat in when one of the Zionist leaders from abroad was
interviewed by American journalists, because many of the visitors spoke
English haltingly and needed to be helped to make themselves intelligible. I felt more relevant to the central Jewish drama of the day—the
struggle for a Jewish state.

The strangest moment of my activism in the summer of 1947 came
when I was called into a meeting in one of the Zionist offices in New
York. A leading Zionist figure carefully closed the door and asked me
to perform a very delicate task. The well-known gangster Bugsy Siegel
had suddenly discovered his Jewish roots, and he had passed a message
to the leaders of Zionism in America that he would arrange for Ernest
Bevin, the British foreign secretary, who was widely described as an
enemy of Jewish aspirations in Palestine, to be bumped off when he
next arrived in New York. Obviously, if this happened, it would not be
the service to the Jewish people that Bugsy imagined it to be. I was
asked to fly out to Los Angeles to thank him for his profound Jewish
emotions, but to persuade him that this was not the way to express
them. I had no choice but to undertake the task, and in a very brief
meeting with Mr. Siegel he accepted the request that this should not
be done.

I soon had to go back to Nashville. I was in my office at the synagogue that fall during the final vote of the United Nations to partition
Palestine on November 29, 1947. I heard David Ben-Gurion, on short-

wave radio, proclaiming the new state of Israel in Tel Aviv on May 14, 1948. People were dancing in the streets both in Tel Aviv and in New York on both occasions, but the elation was much more muted in Nashville. We were seeing this history with pride, but it seemed to be happening to someone else. We were delighted onlookers, but from afar, from some other life.

When the state was declared, the Jewish defenders did not have enough soldiers to protect it against the local Arabs and from the armies of all the states on the borders. Many hundreds of American and Canadian Jews, and even a few non-Jews, volunteered. The crucial battles in Israel's war of independence were fought early, in the first weeks of hostilities, before most of the volunteers arrived, but those who chose to go were instant heroes both in Israel and in America. They were freely putting their lives on the line to help defend the new Jewish state. I was torn between an inner compulsion to volunteer and the unpleasant truth that I could go fight in Israel only if I hurt my family, which could not manage without help from me, and if I broke with the congregation, which refused to grant me a leave of absence. I could go off to war only if I resigned my job and left my parents without the money that they needed for my siblings. I decided that I could not go, but that only made me more unhappy.

By the next summer, of 1949, the hostilities on Israel's borders had stopped after a series of armistices, but there was still some sporadic shooting. Regular air connections did not yet exist. The commercial airlines that flew the Atlantic would not extend their schedules to this war zone, and Israel itself was just organizing its own airline, El Al, which had not yet acquired any long-range planes. El Al was bringing in cargo from Europe in a collection of cast-off aircraft that it had bought from the surplus of several national air forces. I got to Israel by taking a charter flight to Paris and then picking up another charter some days later from Geneva to Tel Aviv. The trip was even more difficult than it seemed because the first plane lost an engine over Newfoundland. We had to wait almost three days in a Quonset hut in Gander for a new engine to be brought from New York. Our group missed the connection to Israel, so we were forced to stay in Paris for five days until the next charter came along from Geneva. From the airport, I had telephoned a friend, Rabbi Emanuel Laderman, to help me find a hotel room in the overcrowded city. He was the director of one of the organizations that were helping the survivors of the Nazi death camps. Laderman assigned his assistant, Phyllis Cannon, an attractive and very intelligent young Englishwoman, to fend for me. She had been invited from London to work in the Paris office because she knew the necessary languages: French, German, and Yiddish. Nine months later, on March 19, 1950, she and I were married in London. This encounter did not, however, keep me from completing the trip to Israel. I had not been there at the very beginning of the state, but I would be part of its second year.

I landed in Israel with no preconceptions, at least none of which I was aware. I was, of course, not an objective observer; I was a partisan of the new state of Israel. I did not come to find fault with the treatment of the refugees from Europe, many of whom were being housed in tent cities, or to decry the new state's behavior toward the defeated Arabs. I had already heard such talk in New York, especially in the editorial offices of *Commentary*, which was the leading Jewish monthly of those days. The first reports from Israel to appear in that journal had been carping and ungenerous. This was not surprising, because *Commentary* was then edited by Elliot Cohen, an ex-Communist, who had become an American nationalist, aided by two assistants, Irving Kristol and Nathan Glaser, who had abandoned their left-wing views in college but who had not become Zionists. These editors were comfortable with the publishers of their magazine, the American Jewish Committee, which had not yet made its own peace with the existence of a Jewish state. Nonetheless, *Commentary* was especially attractive to me because it was the only journal that concerned itself equally with the concerns of society as a whole and with the particular interests of Jews. It was especially attractive because its style was self-consciously intellectual.

On my way to Israel, I went to see Elliot Cohen to offer to write for him about the new state. I was surprised that, without committing himself to print what I sent him, he agreed. Cohen wrote a letter to introduce me as a special correspondent for his magazine. I thought that I knew why he was hospitable to me: *Commentary* was being attacked for its coolness to Israel; an essay or two from a Zionist would help mute the criticism. It would allow him to claim that, as an editor, he was being fair and open to clashing points of view. I would find out that winter that he was not quite as fair as I believed. Some months later, while editing the two articles that I wrote from Israel, he emphasized every critical observation that I made, and he played down the praise. A year or two later, I would learn that he was a leading figure in an anti-Communist organization of intellectuals, the Committee on the Present Danger. He and his young disciples had become "cold warriors" at the very time of the founding of Israel. In its first two years, the new state had not yet decided to side with the United States. There was even some fear that it might play the permanent neutral between the superpowers. Cohen, the fierce newly anti-Communist, told me none of this in 1949. He talked of his concern for the rights of Arabs and admitted that he was uncomfortable with Jewish nationalism. Nonetheless, I was delighted with Cohen's letter of introduction, because I would be arriving in Israel as a writer for a journal of substantial reputation. His letter would open doors to the leaders of the new state.

My senses were overwhelmed from the very moment that I stepped off the airplane on the runway near Lod, outside of Tel Aviv. This field had been a British air-force base, and it was now in use as Israel's international airport (it is now renamed Ben-Gurion Airport). My passport was stamped by a young woman in Israeli uniform. In another corner of the customs shed a line of new immigrants, each of them carrying or dragging large bundles, was being processed. I had asked the immigration officer who was dealing with the American visitors where the immigrants would go. She told me that they would live in tents in transit centers, until they got jobs and housing could be found for them. She did not seem pleased when I said that I would like to visit such a facility. Once I cleared her desk, I was in Israel but without a place to stay or even transportation into Tel Aviv. I found a government liaison officer at the airport and told him that I was a correspondent for an American magazine. He offered me a ride into the city in an old Ford that belonged to the foreign ministry, and he instructed the driver to take me to the hut by the seashore that housed the offices—and the bar—of the military officials who rode herd on the foreign correspondents. The road from the airport was very narrow. Suddenly the driver jammed the brakes and stopped just short of a frontal collision with an equally ancient, but larger, Chrysler. The driver of this magnificence leaned out of his window, identified himself as the chauffeur of the president of

Israel, and began to yell at the driver of the Ford for daring to be on the same road with him. The anger began at high pitch, and it kept escalating. The driver of the Ford did not crumble. He brought his face as close as he could to the face of the president's chauffeur and spat out the first epithet that I would hear in Hebrew in Israel. He dared call the president's driver *mamzer ben chazir*—that is, "bastard son of a pig." The nascent Israeli society was clearly egalitarian.

At the press office, I was received warmly. The officers in charge were Lieutenant Colonel Moshe Perlman, a native of England, and Major Lionel Paytan (he had just hebraized his last name from Feitelson), who was a recent arrival from South Africa. My "passport" was that I spoke Hebrew and was obviously elated to be in Israel. Perlman and Paytan told me very openly that they had not been happy with what had been appearing in *Commentary* and that they were sure that I would do better. They soon added that the foreign correspondents in the country, especially those from England and America, were mostly biased against Israel. They were glad to find a "friend" to take along on press tours. Perlman and Paytan had one of their assistants fetch the list of available housing. I was assigned a room in an apartment no more than a hundred yards away. The owners of the apartment, a widow and her daughter, were renting out a bedroom. They could offer me no food, not even breakfast, because Israel was then under severe rationing, but that was not a problem. I could have morning coffee in the press club. Within a few hours of arriving in Israel, I had a place to sleep and the promise from Perlman and Paytan that they would help me roam all over the country. I knew that I was being romanced. Perlman and Paytan were doing their job: to suggest, and not even very indirectly, that I was a member of the family; unlike the correspondents from the international press, I would write with love of Israel. Even before I had written the first word, Elliot Cohen had suggested in New York that I should not abandon my critical faculties, and Perlman and Paytan in Tel Aviv now hoped that I would keep myself from seeing even the slightest speck on the new state. I could not follow either suggestion alone; I would have to see Israel for myself—but with love.

I went as correspondent to write about the birth pangs of the new state, but soon after my arrival, I was asked by Perlman to do some things for him. Not all the foreign correspondents were friendly to

Israel, and he wanted to know what they were saying over drinks at the bar. He was particularly concerned with the correspondent of the *Times* of London. The request that I report on what I heard put me in a quandary. I did not want to be a snitch, but the image of Israel in the world press was a matter of profound importance, for its greatest asset was the good opinion of the world. My resolution was that I would give Perlman an assessment of what was being said, but without naming names. He agreed that he really did not need names. What he needed to know was whether opinion was growing among the foreign correspondents as a whole that Israel was not behaving well in its policy toward the Arabs. The main issue was the question of the flight of the Arabs from the territory in Israeli control: had they been and were they still being forced out at the point of a gun, or were they fleeing of their own free will? I knew then that Israel had taken a far more active role in expelling Arabs than the government of Israel was willing to admit, but I also knew that many of the Palestinian Arabs had left their homes to stay out of harm's way in the war. Some had believed the assurances of their leaders, and of the generals who commanded the troops from the neighboring Arab states, that they would sweep the Jews into the sea.

In recent years there has been large and growing controversy over who caused the Palestinian refugees to leave, but everyone who was on the ground in Israel in the first year or two of its statehood knew the truth. There was blame on both sides. Each side was telling the story in such fashion that its version would bolster the national myth. The nascent state of Israel had to insist that all of its actions were pure because Israel had to appear to itself as if some messianic aura was surrounding it. The Palestinians, even though they had begun the war with the Jews, needed to maintain that they had been wronged and that they had been the victims of a great disaster.

Even after nearly fifty years, I remember many striking images and incidents, many more than I can recall from all the innumerable visits to Israel in the years thereafter. The state and its society were just barely born, and I was seeing this world for the first time. I was not prepared for most of what I saw. Zionist clichés wore thin, and the issue of the unity of the Jewish people raised its head as soon as the state of Israel was born.

David Landwehr, who worked for Perlman and Paytan, took me along with some other journalists to visit a tent city that housed recent arrivals from the camps in Europe. I thought that these immigrants would be eager to talk, but they were not. The atmosphere was icy. They looked at us, saying with their eyes, What right have you to your privileges? Why are you the ones who will drive off to normal lives? I have never been able to forget what I heard that day. I know that American Jews, when they think about Israel or go for a visit, repeat the favorite slogan, "We are one." But we who lived through the war in America are not the same as those who fled the Nazis. We who did not go to Israel on a boatload of refugees are not one with those who survived Auschwitz and became soldiers on the day they arrived in Israel. We who have not lived hour by hour with radio broadcasts, hoping to be reassured that our children had not fallen in battle, are not one with Israelis who have hardly ever known a day of peace. We can sympathize; we can help—but we are not one.

Back in 1948 the leaders of the new state, men and women in their middle years, were overwhelmingly children of the East European ghettos—and so were the leaders and the majority of their followers who made up the American Jewish community. Even for those in Israel whose contempt for Yiddish was a matter of ideological principle, this was the language and the culture they shared with the European and American Diasporas. It was still the lingua franca of most of the Jewish world. But what would happen in thirty, forty, or fifty years, when the next generation in Israel and the Diaspora took over? What would the English-speaking young Jews of America and the speakers of modern Hebrew in Israel have in common? This question, which I posed in 1949, was ignored at the time. I was indeed denounced in the Yiddish press by several of the Zionist columnists as a treasonable fellow, lacking in Zionist faith—but this question has remained the pained, and unavoidable, question of Jewish discussion worldwide.

The new Israeli intelligentsia was a serious, sensitive, even humorless, crowd. One evening, I sat in the Café Casit, the hangout of the local intelligentsia, in a circle of Hebrew writers. I left after two hours, even though they had not yet finished a vehement argument about the newest cultural fad in Israel, "progressive culture," which wanted to break with the Jewish past and use models from modern European literature as the source of new creativity in Hebrew. The next day I got on a crowded bus jammed with many people hanging from straps in the front while few went to the back. The driver yelled, in the faulty Hebrew of a very recent immigrant, "Please progress backward." The next night I went back to the Café Casit and told of this incident, but nobody laughed. No wonder some of the new immigrants used the term *Zionist* to mean anybody who preached to them. There was above all a certain contempt for the Jewish past.

The press office arranged an appointment for me with David Ben-Gurion, at his house nearby. I appeared at the hour that had been set. His wife, Paula, opened the door only to shut it in my face. I had been told that she was a "character," a trial to her husband, and she lived up to this description by shouting at me that I was unforgivably rude in daring to come see the prime minister without announcing myself first on the telephone: "We Jews have a state now, and we must learn the proper manners." She had expected me to call ahead to reconfirm the appointment with the prime minister. I answered that I had presumed that the office that had made the appointment would have reconfirmed it, but she stood her ground. She made me go to the telephone on the street and to call the office and be told, formally, that I might come ahead. Finally, I was in the presence of the prime minister. He did not have to put on any airs or act out any roles for a visitor to let me know that I was in the presence of greatness. He wanted to know what had impelled me to ask for an interview. I answered that I had been deeply troubled for years by the question, What will be the nature of the new Jewish culture that modern Zionism is creating? Ben-Gurion looked a bit startled that I would raise this question so sharply, but he took the challenge. He insisted that Zionism had come into the world to cure the Jews of the inferiority complexes that they had acquired in the Exile. A new Jewish life would have to choose what it could accept from the Jewish past and what it had to reject. He had no qualms with doing just that. I answered that I did not think he could ever succeed. The past could not be scuttled; it would have to be assimilated into the Jewishness of our future. He countered that this could not work because we Jews would be keeping alive the diseases of our past. He soon ushered me out. It was an argument that he clearly had held before, many times with many people, but he still remembered the incident with me twenty years later. By then he was out of power and living in retirement in a kibbutz on the edge of the Southern Desert (the Negev). Ben-Gurion came to address a conference that the Rabbinical Assembly held in July 1967 soon after the Six-Day War. He had come to say, most emphatically, that Israel would have no peace if it insisted on holding on to the newly conquered West Bank, and I had been asked to chair that meeting. He recognized me as he walked in. When he sat down at his place in the center of the speakers' table, he turned toward me and said, "You're still wrong."

On the road to Jerusalem in 1949 I sat beside a man in his thirties with a black beard and curls on the side of his head, who was dressed in the round black hat and long caftan of the Hasidim. Everyone else in that cab, in the mid-July heat, was bareheaded, in open shirts and shorts, but the atmosphere in the car was icy. The youngish Hasid was ignored; the secular Israelis were busy talking with each other, but he was excluded. I was quietly angry, so I stopped chatting in Hebrew with the man on my right and began a conversation in Yiddish with the Hasid on my other side. We talked together for the rest of the trip, but then no one else in the car would say another word to me. By helping the Hasid out of his isolation, I was choosing sides. I had moved out of modern Israel, the land of the "new Jews" who fought with guns; I had, in the eyes of Israelis in shorts, returned to the world of the old ghetto where Jews were unprotected and prayed to God to save them. Nonetheless, I kept on. I soon found out that this Hasid was part of my own history. He had studied before the war at the court of the rebbe of Belz, in southeastern Poland, together with my uncles, my mother's brothers. He told me that he had last seen them in 1942 in Bochnya, the Nazi concentration camp from which almost no one had escaped alive. The Zionists had just won a historic victory, and they were building a new reality that I admired and applauded, but I would not break the bond with the Hasid sitting beside me. My uncles had looked like him.

On occasion, however, the Zionist modernists got their comeuppance. In the summer of 1949, Israel had not yet moved any of the government agencies to Jerusalem. Its parliament, the Knesset, was housed in a requisitioned movie theater in the center of Tel Aviv. The day that I visited the Knesset was the occasion for a debate on the salaries and other allowances of the members of that body. The proposal before the Knesset was that salaries be augmented by an allowance for the wife, and for each of the children, of married members. One of the deputies was a Jew of Yemenite origin; this community was still permitted to follow its own ancient custom of polygamy, and he had four wives. The Yemenite gentleman took the floor to suggest that he was entitled to an allowance for each of his wives. This remark caused an uproar. Ada Maimon, one of the representatives of the Labor Party, denounced the request. She shouted that he and all the other Yemenites should be ashamed of their lack of culture. Her opponent was not intimidated; he shot back that Miss Maimon, who had never married, had no right to criticize him, because he was producing many children to help populate the land of Israel with Jewish citizens while she was doing nothing for the future of Israel except shout at him—but the Yemenite deputy was not yet finished. He insisted, with a broad smile, that the men of the Yemenite community were far more decent and upright in their sexual habits than the monogamous Jews from Europe. He sharply pointed out that many of the Jews of European origin were not really monogamous. They had affairs with other women but accepted no responsibility for their well-being. He had four wives, openly, keeping none of them hidden in some back room, and he was providing decently for each of them.

My first visit to Jerusalem forced me to confront the costs of Israel's struggle to survive. The first ten days of my visit to Israel were spent in Tel Aviv, and not only because it was the seat of the new government and the center of modern Israeli culture. I was having problems with the thought of going to Jerusalem. The Israeli army had lost the battle, a few months earlier, to capture the Old City, where the holiest shrine of the Jews, the remaining Western Wall of the Temple in Jerusalem, was located. Israel's army had fought bitterly to retain even the largely Jewish West Jerusalem. The city had been completely surrounded by Arab troops, and it cost many lives to open a new road. The Israeli government had decided to leave all the burned-out cars and trucks in place, on the shoulder of this "road of heroism," in memory of those who had died in the battles. They are there, to this day. I felt unworthy to travel that road, but after ten days in Tel Aviv, I simply had to go. I reserved a seat in a taxi, and we were soon driving by the burned-out cars. Some thirty minutes later we reached the top of the last hill, and, for the first time, I saw the outskirts of Jerusalem. The Talmud prescribes that he who has seen Jerusalem in its destruction must rend his garment in mourning, but I was arriving in West Jerusalem, which was not in ruins, and which was becoming the capital of Israel. Should I instead pronounce the exultant blessing of thanksgiving for that victory, or is that blessing appropriate only when the Temple Mount is in Jewish hands? I compromised: I said no prayers and I did not rend my garments; I simply cried. In a very few minutes we were at the terminal of the taxi-cab company in the center of the city. I got out and looked around downtown Jerusalem, expecting that I would see the prophet Isaiah or the prophet Jeremiah walking toward me, dressed in sandals and a tunic of rough woven cloth. What I actually saw was a sign on the movie theater across the street announcing the time for the evening performance of a Hollywood epic starring Clark Gable and Lana Turner. I went there that night to see the show. The film had been dubbed into French. At the bottom there was a running translation in Hebrew, and along the side the dialogue was printed in Arabic. I sat in the theater hearing Clark Gable saying to Lana Turner, "*Je t'aime beaucoup*," and reading the Hebrew and the Arabic versions of this deathless line. When I walked out at ten o'clock, I still could not find Isaiah or Jeremiah on that street.

In Jerusalem, the Jordanian snipers on top of the wall of the Old City did not pretend that they were not there. On the contrary, they seemed to have been ordered to make themselves visible, to instill fear in anybody who might try to sneak across no-man's-land. Nevertheless, the border was not completely sealed. There was a transit point, the Mandelbaum Gate (named after the family that had owned the last house on the Jewish side), through which officials of the United Nations, Christian clergy with parishes that extended through all of Jerusalem, and diplomats were permitted to pass. Under the armistice agreement between the two sides, which had only recently been signed in Rhodes, one Jewish convoy could pass through every two weeks, to Mount Scopus. That enclave contained the buildings of the Hebrew University and the Hadassah Hospital. During the war, the Jordanian army had not succeeded in capturing the area, so it had been agreed that the Israel caretakers would remain in the area and be resupplied periodically. I tried, and failed, to get permission to cross the border, but I kept returning to the Mandelbaum Gate. I thought something was likely to happen there. Perhaps there would be a clash between the Israeli and Jordanian soldiers at the opposite ends of the passage, or someone from the Vatican might come bearing proposals for permanent peace, or King Abdullah would cross from Amman to parley with David Ben-Gurion.

Nothing like this ever happened, but I did have one strange encounter on the street on the way to the bridge. A young man stopped me and introduced himself as the "foreign minister" of Neturei Karta, the bitterly anti-Zionist group of ultra-Orthodox Jews who had lived in that neighborhood for generations. His name was Leibel Weisfish. He spent much time near the Mandelbaum Gate, and he had been observing me for several days. He had found out, somehow, that I was writing for an American magazine, and he wanted me to include the opinions of his group in my account of Israel. I tried to cut him short by telling him that I knew about the Neturei Karta from my father. It was not news to me that the people of this neighborhood believed that the Zionist state was against God and that only He could reestablish the Jews in the Holy Land, through the miracles that he would perform "at the end of days." Weisfish answered that I did not really know what was happening now. He was often meeting Jordanians at night in the no-man's-land between the lines, to ask for Jordanian citizenship for the Neturei Karta. They did not want to live under the secular flag of the Zionist heretics. Until the end of days, it would be better if they lived under the government of non-Jews. Weisfish admitted that he was making the Jordanians a bit uncomfortable by his requests, but he assured me that he would persist. He even offered to take me with him that night into no-man's-land to hear him continue these conversations. I refused the invitation. I was not eager to be shot at from both sides or jailed in either West or East Jerusalem. A couple of days later, Weisfish showed up at my hotel bearing a gift, a pack of Jordanian cigarettes, which he told me had been given him the night before in no-man's-land. He wanted me to think of him as a hero of the Jewish resistance to the Zionist state; he was as heedless of danger as the soldiers who had fought to keep West Jerusalem in Jewish hands. Clearly Weisfish was not a coward. He did not fit into the Zionist stereotype that the ultra-Orthodox were totally passive. Perhaps Weisfish, despite himself, had learned from the Zionists whom he hated, upholding his views, in their manner, by risking his life.

Again and again, I was confronted with the high price in Jewish blood that had been paid for the new state. Before leaving for Israel, I had asked my teacher Hillel Bavli, the professor of Hebrew literature at the Jewish Theological Seminary, for some introductions. He gave me several names, but he spoke with particular warmth of his friend Reuven Grossman. He was a Hebrew poet, European born but educated in America, who had moved to Palestine in the 1930s. He supported his family by teaching English in the premier high school in Tel Aviv. A few days after my arrival in Tel Aviv, Grossman came to coffee at the press club. He was friendly, but very sad. The next day at lunch in his apartment, I saw pictures everywhere of a young man, perhaps eighteen or nineteen, in Israeli military uniform. Grossman and his wife told me that this was their eldest child, Noam, who had fallen in battle just a few months before. The father showed me letters that the son had written from the front and the poems that he had sent home from army camps. The Grossmans were shattered by Noam's death, and not only by their loss as a family. Noam was already a talented writer; he would have been among the creators of the new Hebraic culture of the Jewish state. The Grossmans kept inviting me back to their apartment; in their grief, they needed to express to younger people, of their son's generation, some part of the love that they had for him. One day I came to their apartment looking unkempt; I explained that my shaving machine had cracked, so Grossman went into the bathroom and brought me an electric razor. It had belonged to his son, and he was lending it to me. I brought it back to him a week later because I could not bring myself to use it. Grossman responded by telling me that he was changing the family name. Henceforth he would be known as Reuven Avi-Noam— that is, the father of his fallen son, Noam. He had begun to work on collecting and publishing his son's writings. I said nothing, but I knew that he would not be able to find a quick cure for his grief by erecting a literary monument for his son. The book finally appeared, but many years later.

In May 1949, the government decided to celebrate the first anniversary of Israel's independence, with a military parade through the center of Tel Aviv. This was the first time in more than twenty centuries, since the time of the Maccabbees, that a Jewish army would be marching in victory in a Jewish state. The parade would be an announcement to all the world that Israel was a nation among the nations. The hearts of Jews in Israel, and all over the world, would race with pride. In the event, the parade—Israel's first—proceeded with less than military precision. The people on the sidewalks stopped the marchers. Everyone seemed to insist on greeting his son, or cousin, in this line of heroes. The international press had, of course, covered this event, and the dispatches suggested that Israel's army was really a collection of irregulars who might just as well have been the home guard of some shtetl in the old ghettos in Eastern Europe. The Israeli government and its general staff wanted to erase this embarrassment. A few months later, in August, a new parade was held in a sports stadium, where the spectators could be contained. Lieutenant Colonel Moshe Perlman took me along in his jeep, and I sat with him on a bench right below the reviewing stand. The marching was still ragged, but the various formations did not bump into each other and the armored cars kept in line. Israel's army was proving that it could stage a respectable public performance. The journalists on the bench were suitably impressed, and Perlman beamed as he looked at their faces and caught snatches of their conversation with each other. I was not interested in the journalists or even in the parade. What difference would it make whether the Israelis knew how to stage a march? It was enough that they had won the war.

I kept turning around to pick out the faces in the reviewing stand. The entire cabinet was there, led by David Ben-Gurion. He looked pleased and even defiant. Near him was Chaim Weizmann, receiving the salute as president of Israel. Every time I looked, aides on either side of him had their hands under his elbows, to help him stand. He was nearly blind, so he did not really see the regimental flags that passed before him, but he stood there until the last formation had marched by. Perhaps he and Ben-Gurion exchanged some words that afternoon, but whenever I looked, they seemed to be in the same place but existing in different dimensions. Ben-Gurion was jaunty with victory. Weizmann was stooped and somber; he seemed to be carrying all of the pain of past generations and bending under the great contemporary sorrow of the murder of the Jews of Europe. After the parade, Perlman offered to take me along to the reception that Ben-Gurion was giving, but I begged off. I told him that I wanted to walk the streets to see how the people were rejoicing, but that was an excuse. I had that day overheard a fact so closely guarded that it was not made public for many years: Israel's victory had cost six thousand dead, 1 percent of its entire population. I had looked at Weizmann, who obviously knew this appalling fact, and I had thought of my dead relatives in Poland, and of Noam Grossman. I could not attend the gala.

The Israel that I encountered at the beginning of the second year of its existence was still so new and so small that nothing of any consequence was really hidden from sight. Its population had more than doubled in the fourteen months since the state was proclaimed, and many of the newcomers had gone straight to battle as soon as their ships reached port. Such people had already suffered much for Israel; they could not be excluded from the intense discussions about the future. Even a visitor from the United States, especially if he spoke Hebrew, was included: I got very little sleep that summer. Evening after evening, into the small hours of the morning, I sat in on fierce debates about the issues that then troubled Israel. The great questions that were being argued then are not yet resolved. I reread my notes, occasionally, to remember how they were first defined and to remind myself of what I thought then.

The angriest debates were about the issue of how Israel was using power, because, for the first time in twenty centuries, Jews were now ruling over others: the hundred thousand Arabs who had not run away. Everyone knew that the official story—that some seven hundred thousand Arabs had left their homes during the war because they had been promised by their leaders that they would come back in triumph after the Jews were pushed into the sea—was simply not true. Some such bluster had existed, but it was common knowledge that many thousands had been bluntly pushed out by Israel's army, or they had run away as people do in war or because they were scared at what they might suffer under Israeli rule. Some Arabs had been asked to stay, but no one pretended that much effort had been made to invite back the villagers who had fled. There was a reason for this toughness. Under the partition boundaries that had been defined by the United Nations, Jews would have been a bare majority. This might have worked had Israel been born in peace with Arab consent but not after a bitter war; a sullen near majority, bitter at its defeat, would have been the source of permanent unrest in the new state. The official narrative soon became, and remained, that Israel never expelled the Arabs: they did this to themselves. This account was challenged forty years later, in the 1980s, by revisionist historians. They asserted that less than half of the Arab refugees were actively pushed out in 1948 by the Israelis. The revisionists were immediately counterattacked as exaggerating the negatives and of taking perverse pleasure in putting Israel on the moral defensive.

I have no doubt that the revisionists are telling the truth, because I was there in the summer of 1949. Soldiers who had served in the battles told their families, and the press, that a few of the commanders had tried to reassure Arabs to keep them from fleeing, but most were glad to see them leave. That summer, the literary scandal of Israel was a short novel called *Sippur Khirbet Hizah*, by S. Yizhar, a writer from a distinguished Zionist family, who had served as a soldier in the War of Independence. Yizhar depicted an Arab village filled with terrified people, as they watched the Israeli conquerors swaggering through the streets waving their guns. Yizhar was asking for sympathy and compassion for the enemy. His book was much praised and much hated, but no one ignored it. Yizhar had put his finger on a new, and troubling, problem: what were the limits of power, especially in the hands of a people that had been powerless?

Yizhar's views were especially upsetting, in Israel and throughout the Jewish world, because he was tarnishing the pure and heroic image of Israel. Those who had just won Israel's War of Independence were being lionized and lionizing themselves as "new Jews." Israel's victory was being interpreted everywhere as the "answer" to the Holocaust. They were the heroic antithesis to the passive millions who had just been slaughtered in Europe, and, for that matter, to the "frightened Jews" in the United States who had not pushed their government hard enough to save Jews. To cast any doubt on the moral stature of the Israelis was an unforgivable heresy almost everywhere in the Jewish world. S. Yizhar was a disturber of the peace, and those who brought his views from Tel Aviv to New York were the agents of wickedness. One of the essays that I published that fall, upon my return to the United States, mentioned Yizhar's book and described the moral problems that came with the power of the new state. I was bitterly denounced in a series of articles in one of the Yiddish papers by a leading Zionist, Dr. Samuel Margoshes, for treason to the Jewish people.

Even deeper emotions than pride in Israel were involved in these quarrels. The meaning of Israel's victory could not be questioned because the leaders of the victorious state and army were insisting that all the centuries between the beginning of the exile in the year 70, after Jerusalem was captured by the Romans, and the creation of the state of Israel in 1948 were a historic mistake and a cultural nullity. The Zionist dismissal of the history of the *galut* (exile) served a practical political purpose. Jewish history had really resumed only with the first stirrings of modern Zionism in the middle of the nineteenth century, when a few Jews began the effort to reestablish sovereignty in the land of the ancestors. I heard this thesis from David Ben-Gurion himself, the second time I encountered him that summer. I had gone to Tiberias, on the shore of the Sea of Galilee, to visit some Jewish shrines in the area and to observe the solemn fast of the Ninth Day of Av, which commemorates, together with other disasters, the destruction of the Second Temple, in Jerusalem, by the Romans, and the beginning of the exile. I wanted to be that day in the Galilee, the one region where some Jews had been present without a break throughout all the centuries, and not in Jerusalem, where the Jordanians would not let anyone come to pray at the Western Wall of the Temple. That night, I found Ben-Gurion in the lobby of the hotel; by chance, I had found a room in one of his favorite vacation places, the Hotel Galei Kineret. He recognized me, so his aides let me approach him. Ben-Gurion offered me tea, and he was visibly surprised when I told him that I was fasting that night, in accordance with tradition. Ben-Gurion chided me for observing this fast; our ancestors fasted and prayed when they should have acted.

What Ben-Gurion had said was not new to me, for I had read many elaborations of this opinion by radical Zionist writers whom Hillel Bavli had put on the list of required reading for his classes in Hebrew literature at the Jewish Theological Seminary. Until I listened to Ben-Gurion in the lobby of the hotel in Tiberias, I had thought that such views were theoretical and exaggerated. To be sure, these writers wanted to straighten the backs of Jews who cringed before their enemies, but I really did not believe that they were as contemptuous of their ancestors as they said they were. Ben-Gurion had left me in no doubt that the break was real and profound. The Zionist revolt against the past contained a frightening amount of contempt for the parents and grandparents of the men and women who were making this brave new world. Some of the most bitter, nearly anti-Semitic essays were written in the first decade of the century by Josef Haim Brenner. The Zionist agricultural settlements in Palestine were then in their infancy, and Brenner was angry that so few pioneers were coming to the land; the millions of Jews, most of whom were living in misery in czarist Russia, were refusing to make a radical change in their lives:

> Certainly we wish to live, to survive in any way, even like ants or dogs. Certainly the live dog, following the rule of self-love, adaptation, and propitiation in order to survive in the world, is better off than the dead lion, whose self-love drives him to stand against all comers, so that he perishes from the earth. A "living" people whose members have no power but for moaning and hiding a while until the storm blows over, turning away from their poorer brethren to pile up their pennies in secret, to scratch around among the goyim, make a living from them, and complain all day long about their ill will—no, let us not pass judgment upon such a people, for indeed it is not worth it.

I had not believed that Brenner was as angry as he seemed, but I did not doubt what I had just heard from Ben-Gurion. He wanted to fashion the new Israel in defiance of the life, religion, and culture of his immediate ancestors.

In the course of the night, I got up my courage to continue the argument with Ben-Gurion, but in the morning he was gone, and I would not see him again that summer. I was even more troubled than I had been the night before, because Ben-Gurion seemed to be writing off more than the Jewish past. He had said, offhand, that the Jews outside of Israel were equally irrelevant, because they would be remaining in the exile. He was particularly caustic about those in the gilded exile of the United States. Ben-Gurion expected the Jews in New York and Kansas City to help Israel absorb the refugees who were streaming into the country. The victims of Hitler, and those who were fleeing from Arab lands, were a charge on the conscience of all the Jews of the world, but Israel owed no gratitude for this help. The Israelis were putting their lives on the line to remake Jewish history; the people in the Diaspora were merely giving money. Despite what I was hearing from Ben-Gurion (he would soon be expressing these sharp views in public), I had no doubt that the Jewish Diaspora would keep supporting Israel. It was not only an issue of conscience. The heroes in Israel had "reversed the shame" of centuries of passivity; they were forgiven—and even admired—for their arrogance.

But there was another, even deeper connection—hidden and never defined—between the new Israel and the postwar Jewish community in America. The Israelis were giving the Americans something even more precious than vicarious pride; they were offering forgiveness. Israel was proclaiming that the Jewish past had been a mistake; one could feel proud, and not guilty, of starting a new life in defiance of Jewish memory. In the deep subconscious of American Jews, in midcentury, this message resonated: they, too, had the right to fresh beginnings. In the new land they, too, had the right to fashion their own new lives, of success and well-being. Ben-Gurion was saying to them, in words, that they ought to come to Israel; by his very being, he was conveying another message: that Jews everywhere had a right to jettison the past to enter a new and healthier world.

Did Ben-Gurion really speak for the new country? I left Tiberias hoping that he did not, so I arranged to spend some time with segments of Israel's life that he did not control. To the left of him there were the kibbutzim, the collective farms, of Hashomer Hatzair (the "young guard"), which were pro-Soviet; Ben-Gurion was then moving toward a pro-American policy. There were other differences. The children born in the settlements of Hashomer Hatzair were raised together in children's homes, and they were not allowed to sleep in their parents' quarters; Ben-Gurion's more moderate labor movement believed that the family unit should be fostered even within collective farms. Another difference: did one have the right to one's own clothes, or did everyone choose garments in his size, when all the wash returned from the laundry? Such issues were passionately divisive, but the left-wing kibbutzim were not much more at war with the Jewish past than the mainstream Labor Zionists who followed Ben-Gurion.

I heard echoes of his views in Sasa, a settlement in the north of the country, where the members were still living in tents, and in an older, much more developed kibbutz, Merhavia, in the center of Israel. The young people in Sasa were especially attractive. They were a group of about fifty who had chosen, just a few months before, to establish a kibbutz on a hill in northern Israel, overlooking the border with Lebanon. So far, they had been lucky; they found tracks in the fields below almost every morning, but no infiltrator had dared come up the hill to shoot at them. No one complained of living in tents or of doing guard duty at night, because they were elated that, here, in this rocky, unsafe place, they were creating part of the future of the state of Israel. The Israelis in the group did not talk very much about such high purposes. One evening, I walked around on guard duty with someone who had just been demobilized from the army. He would not let me say anything in praise of his group: "We are no different from anyone else; this is what we were raised to do." I even overheard one of the Israelis saying to another that such talk is the language of a *shwitzer*—that is, of someone who is sweating to make an impression. It was cool never to use such language. The Americans at Sasa—there were some twenty of them—talked much more freely. They had "ascended" to Israel to become new people. They were seizing the chance to not live in a Jewish minority in the United States and to be rid of the aspirations of their parents that they become doctors or lawyers or businessmen. They had broken away to become secular citizens of the new state. One of the young women in the group sat me down for tea one afternoon and said, without any preamble, "I have come here because I want to be as far away as possible from the Jewish neighborhood in Brooklyn. Here, I am free to make my own choices." Suddenly, at that moment, I understood: she had not made *aliyah* ("ascended") to Israel because it was the ancient land of the Jews; she had come to an exciting frontier where she could invent herself. We were not sitting together in Sasa on one of the hills on which the Maccabees had fought the Syrian Greeks more than two thousands years ago; she had come to an outpost of the Wild West. Here, too, on the border of Lebanon, personal origins and history were irrelevant, because here, too, settlers had come to make their own new world.

I went from Sasa to Merhavia. This kibbutz had existed for thirty years, and much of the ideology of Hashomer Hatzair had been

fashioned by leading members of this collective. The educational material for the schools of these left-wing secular kibbutzim was created in
Merhavia. Everyone seemed to be very busy working, so the chore of
talking with me was left to the secretary, who was both the manager and
the "foreign secretary" of the kibbutz. The conversation turned, almost
immediately, to the question of education. I asked the kibbutz secretary
whether even Maimonides, the rabbi, philosopher, and physician who
had lived in the twelfth century, was ever mentioned. I was told that he
was ignored, even though he was one of the supreme intellectual figures
of the Middle Ages, because he could not be made intelligible to high
school students without explaining his defense of religion. In Merhavia
and in all the kibbutzim of its kind, Jewish religion was not taught in
any form, even as history. The parents were convinced, unbending, secular nationalists and socialists; they would not even describe the religious past, which they wanted to bury and transcend, because such
knowledge might complicate the lives of their children.

A few days later, I arranged to spend Sabbath in the south of the
country in one of the collective farms of the religious Zionists. The one
that invited me, Yavneh, was near the border with the Gaza Strip, from
which it was infiltrated almost every night by snipers who shot to kill.
In Yavneh the ancient religious forms were followed and the holy books
were studied, every day, but some adjustments to the new, national life
were inevitable. Protective surveillance required the use of searchlights
and cameras even on the Sabbath, in ways that were often at odds with
the Orthodox rules, but the need to preserve life took precedence.
Young men and women went, in turn, to the guard towers, sometimes
leaving a not-quite-finished Sabbath meal and returning in the middle
of a study session in the sacred texts. Here, Zionist modernity was
defined as incremental. These religious Zionists thought of themselves
as deeply rooted in the heritage of their ancestors, but they, too, had
passed negative judgment on the past. They had broken with its passivity. They revered Maimonides as a religious thinker, and as a supreme
authority on the laws of Judaism, but they were disappointed that he
had remained in Egypt and had never moved to the Holy Land.

I stayed at Yavneh a few days longer than I had expected because the
people in that kibbutz were especially compelling. Yet, I was soon
uncomfortable. These religious Zionists thought of themselves as actors

in a profound drama: they were hastening "the end of days." Their rabbis had just composed a new prayer that was to be recited in the synagogues every Sabbath and holiday: the state of Israel was defined as the flowering root of Redemption. I soon understood that the men and women in Yavneh shared a profound certainty with their ideological opponents, the vehement enemies of religion in Sasa and Merhavia. Both sides knew that they were on the side of the inevitable. Either God or History guaranteed their triumph. Such Zionists were not creating a new home for refugees or even a majority society in which Jews could cultivate and develop their culture and tradition.

The new state was the end value, the purpose of Jewish history. Such faith frightened me. Ideological certainties are usually sustained by fanatics, who almost never have any tolerance for nonbelievers. I found it hard to think so harshly of the people whom I met in Yavneh because, despite the tense days through which they were living, they had made me welcome. Joseph Unna, the leading figure in that community, went out of his way to talk with me. He told me that he had come from Germany as an adult after receiving a substantial education in both Western and Jewish culture. Unna was an intellectual who had chosen to be a farmer and an Orthodox Jew who had decided that the great religious commandment of this day was to fight for a Jewish state. His forebears had served God by studying the holy books, to learn how to obey the most minute prescription of God's law. Unna knew that God had commanded the Jews to reclaim the Holy Land now. His voice was quiet and not at all dramatic, but the words he spoke, as we walked from the dining hall to the guard tower and back, almost made me hear the wings of angels beating—but only almost. I could not believe that anyone—not even the admirable Zionist heroes whom I was meeting that summer—really knew what was on the mind of God, or His secular avatar, History. I preferred politics, even Jewish politics in the great age of a new beginning, to be less grandiose.

By the end of the summer of 1949, I was even more of a Zionist than I had been when I arrived seven weeks before. The determining and indelible moment had been at the beginning when I arrived at the airport, when an Israeli officer had inspected my passport and waved me through. Here, at last, for the first time in two millennia, a Jewish government controlled the ports of entry. I bore the pain of the thirties, when my parents could not get a visa to the United States for any one of our relatives in Poland, and of the war years, when we could not save them from being slaughtered. That day, and the many dozens of times since then when I have landed in Israel, I still approach the desk where my passport is examined with emotion. All my relatives who did not live to stand in this prosaic and harried line walk with me. Strange as this may sound, it is the holiest moment that I can experience in the Holy Land.

But this memory of my murdered relatives also made me love Israel less that summer. I was hearing a near consensus from Zionist believers of all the factions that they were ashamed of the Holocaust, because the millions who were slaughtered had not resisted their murder. Everyone agreed, of course, that the Nazis and their helpers, and those who had stood idly by, bore unforgivable guilt, but the new Jewish state could not punish them; it would have to leave that task to the powers that had won the war. But the new state could make an end of the shame of the Jews. Its fighters and citizens were a different breed from the masses who had been murdered in Europe. Both in Israel and America, accounts of the horrors of the Holocaust were an essentially forbidden subject. Everywhere, we wanted to hear about Jewish soldiers in battle, because these images raised Israel's morale and pride, and they gave heart to Jewish politicians and activists in the Diaspora. I could not share this euphoria. I was not ashamed of my murdered grandfather who had lived as a Hasid in Poland. His faith and culture had not been a waste, and his death was not ignoble. He had hidden from the Nazis in a bunker and had not faced them with a gun in his hand, but could anyone imagine that more Jews would have survived if they had fired at the Nazis from the windows of their apartments? At the end of the fabled uprising in the Warsaw Ghetto, the Jews had killed a few Nazis, but almost all of the inhabitants of the ghetto were dead. How dare we criticize people who had tried to survive in the worst of circumstances and say that they should have chosen to "die with honor"—to make us feel better?

One night in Tel Aviv I was part of an angry interchange with Avraham Shlonsky, who was then a leading left-wing figure in Hebrew letters. Shlonsky began by insisting that the passivity of the Jews during the Holocaust was proof of the moral decadence of the older Jewish culture. I challenged him to prove that the modern men and women, the nonbelievers, in Poland and Germany had really behaved any better. He invoked the small minority of Zionists, Socialists, and Communists who had joined the partisans, but he soon admitted that the guilt did not belong to the older culture alone. The Jews had long lived everywhere as a minority, depending for their very life on the decency of the majority. The Holocaust was the ultimate proof that all Jews must come to the new Jewish state. They would not be safe anywhere, not even in the United States.

I had heard Shlonsky's view before because it was the basic premise of Theodor Herzl's Zionism: the Jews are aliens everywhere; even the most liberal environment will eventually be poisoned by anti-Semitism. Shlonsky had insisted that the Holocaust had proved this Zionist axiom: the world of the Gentiles is hopelessly and forever anti-Jewish and it is capable of building Auschwitz again. I was not persuaded. America in the years of the Great Depression, when I was growing up, was not some never-never land without anti-Semitism, but I did not believe that being nasty to Jews, let alone killing them, was always at the center of the American Gentile agenda.

The more upsetting element in the argument with Shlonsky was his contempt for the Jewish past. I had come to the meeting accompanied by a friend from New York, Charles Shulman, who was then the rabbi of the Reform congregation in Riverdale. As soon as we were introduced, Shlonsky told us that he was pleased to meet two American rabbis who were not Orthodox; he deplored that we were still involved in the Jewish religion, but he hailed us as a stage on the right road, toward abandoning the old nonsense. Shlonsky hoped that we would go back to the United States to lead the Jewish community toward secularism. All of this was said with cockiness, which reflected his personal temperament, but also with undisguised triumphalism, which the people in that room, some twenty men and women of the progressive Tel Aviv intelligentsia, shared and applauded. Shulman and I took immediate exception: we insisted, with vehemence, that we were not stalking horses for left-wing secularism; we had our differences with the Orthodox—he more than I—only because we thought that the Jewish religion could not, and should not, be forced into the straitjacket of fundamentalism. The argument did not simply continue for the next three hours; it raged on, and both of us had to discover fluency in spoken Hebrew that neither of us really thought that he possessed. We left the "battle" after midnight, unconvinced by Shlonsky and his friends but sure that we had not made a dent on any of our hosts. The murder of the Jews of Europe and the victory of Israel had proved to these Tel Aviv intellectuals that they had always been right: the millions who had made the choice to remain in the Diaspora had paid with their lives for not coming to help create the *yishuv*, the Zionist community in Palestine; they had committed this suicidal error because the Jewish religion, in most of its forms, had taught political passivity. Shlonsky simply flicked off those who had died believing in assimilation or in socialism. It was self-evident, so he insisted, that only the Zionists had the correct ideology. What Shlonsky and his friends were celebrating that night was their "victory" over the Jewish religion of their parents and grandparents. The rabbis and the Hasidic rebbes were dead or discredited, and the Israelis in that room had no doubt that the few who remained would soon vanish. The men and women in that room that night were announcing themselves as the new secular priesthood.

I did not believe them. Earlier that very week I had been received by the Hasidic rebbe of Belz. The rebbe was a short man, and he was so thin that he seemed to be lost within his silk caftan. He had to be carried in on a chair, because he ate some solid food only on the Sabbath. The rest of the time he fasted, prayed, and studied holy books. Before the war, this man, Rabbi Aaron of Belz, had been the mentor of many tens of thousands of disciples, and the head of a large family of his own. Almost all of his adherents in Poland had been murdered. The rebbe had lost his wife and all of his children and grandchildren. The Nazis had tried to find him in the ghetto that they had established in Bochnya, but one of his adherents had dressed himself in the rebbe's clothes to fool the Nazis, who saw him on the street and murdered him. (After the rebbe's death, a memorial stone for this martyr was placed in the cemetery in Jerusalem near the grave of the man he had saved.) In 1944, the rebbe, and his brother, were spirited out of Poland disguised as Hungarian officers, having removed their beards in order to save their lives. They were supposed to pass certain checkpoints at exact times, when the guards would be the ones who had been bribed to let them through. On two occasions, the rebbe insisted that they should

stop to say prayers and miss the appointed time. The rabbi of Bilgoraj
was frantic, but his brother would not budge. When they reached the
two checkpoints, at the supposedly wrong times, they were waved
through. The guards on duty then were the ones who had been expecting them; the duty rosters had been changed while they were en route.
After a short time in Budapest, they made their way to Palestine. The
believers greeted them as miraculous survivors. Many of the secularists
attacked them for having been anti-Zionists before the war; some
added that these broken people and the remnants of their disciples
could not possibly revive their world.

That night in 1949, the court of the rebbe was small and his adherents seemed sad, but the rebbe was not broken. When I was allowed
into his room after more than an hour of waiting, he was bent over,
studying a passage of the Zohar, the "book of splendor," which is the
main text of the Kabbalah. He raised his head, without quite looking at
me, as if he were still on the way back from some other realm. I was
eager to see him because my family had a long personal connection with
him. He talked willingly of the grandfather whose name I bore, remembering that Avraham Herzberg (the correct version of our family
name—the *t* was inserted in the United States) had been his teacher
when he was young, but he was totally silent when I mentioned my
mother's father and her brothers, who had been his disciples until they
were murdered during the war. I was upset. This strange behavior was
later explained to me by his principal assistant: the rebbe had not once
said any of the prescribed prayers for his wife and children, because
those who had been killed by the Nazis for being Jews were of tran-
scendent holiness; they were beyond our comprehension. Any words
about them that we might utter were irrelevant and perhaps even a des-
ecration of their memory. The rebbe did talk about the school that he
had just begun to establish in Jerusalem, to teach young people the ways
of his sect; this task was self-evident, and the effort would succeed.

When I entered his room, the rebbe had taken my hand but he had
gone immediately to a cask of water behind him and opened the spigot
to wash his hands. He repeated this washing several times in the course
of my few minutes in his presence, and he was washing his hands again
as I walked out. I could not help thinking that these repeated washings
were a neurotic symptom, but I was far from sure. I remembered that

the priests in the ancient temple in Jerusalem washed their hands over and over again to keep them pure as they performed the various rituals. The rebbe belonged to the realm of faith, and it was impertinent to judge him by other standards. I walked out of the room with the certainly that he would never give up. He had suffered as much sorrow as the biblical Job, but he was different: he had not spoken even one word of complaint, and he had not demanded that God explain Himself. Several nights later, in the debate with Avraham Shlonsky, I kept seeing the Belzer rebbe before my eyes. I could not believe that Shlonsky would displace him. I returned to Nashville at the end of the summer with these two encounters as my sharpest memories and with an increasing connection to Phyllis Cannon in Paris.

My 1934 Bar Mitzvah picture sent to my grandfather in Lemberg (Lwów), Poland. My father is absent because he didn't want his father-in-law to see he no longer wore a caftan and had compromised with America by wearing a black suit. Arthur Hertzberg at thirteen; mother, Nechama Shifrah Herzberg; and two younger brothers, Isaiah on left, Joshua on right

The twenty-fifth anniversary of the World Wildlife Fund (1986), marching to St. Francis Basilica in Assisi. I got only as far as the door, where I sounded the shofar summoning people to this event. *L-R, first row:* Karan Singh, former Maharaj of Kashmir; HRH Prince Philip; Arthur. *2nd row:* The man on the right with Saudi headdress is His Excellency Dr. Abdullah Omar Nasseef, then the secretary general of the World Muslim League. *Claude Berger*

A Zionist rally (1967) in New York City when Golda Meir marched over to me and announced that I had done a lousy day's work ten years earlier as the U.N.'s messenger. She was still annoyed (see pp. 253–255). *L-R:* Abraham Schenker, Dr. Emanuel Newmann, Jacob Katzman, Golda Meir, Charlotte Jackson (president of Hadassah), Rabbi Israel Miller, Arthur.

Golda Meir and Henry Kissinger had strongly disagreed over his policies toward Israel. Through the years I had had my own differences with Golda and yet, toward the end of her life, when she was out of office and not in high spirits, I gave a dinner in her honor in 1977 in New York and Henry came to speak her praises. *L-R:* Arthur, Louis Kissinger, Golda Meir, Paula Kissinger, Henry Kissinger.

Bill Bradley launches his campaign for president in West Orange, New Jersey, in March 1999. I was asked to give the opening prayer and I chose instead to give a speech in praise of the high moral stature of Bill and Ernestine. *L-R:* Ernestine Bradley; Bill Bradley; Phil Jackson, then coach of the Chicago Bulls.

Reaffirming deepest roots, Jerusalem 1984. My connections and Israel Singer's to the dynasty of Hasidic leaders from Belz in southeastern Poland were very deep, generations old. We were visiting the rebbe in Jerusalem and had persuaded Edgar Bronfman to come with us, to make his acquaintance. The incumbent Hasidic rebbe of Belz, Isachar Dov Rokeach, the only nephew of his predecessor Aron Rokeach. Also pictured: Rabbi Israel Singer, executive director of the World Jewish Congress, and Edgar Bronfman, the president of the World Jewish Congress.

Secretary of State Henry Kissinger and his undersecretary of state for political affairs, Joseph Sisco, met with leaders of Jewish organizations prior to Kissinger's scheduled departure for the Middle East: 1975, Cabinet Room, White House. *Across table:* Arthur Hertzberg, Max Fisher, Joe Sisco, Henry Kissinger. *World Wide Photos*

The religious representatives at the World Wildlife Fund anniversary in 1986 were housed in the central monastery of the Franciscan order next to the Basilica. We held a separate meeting for two days on the religious imperatives for conservation. Walking with minister general of the Franciscan order, Father Lanfranco Serrini, and the Venerable Lungril Namgyal in the cloisters of the monastery.

Celebration at Temple Emanu-el (1960). Annual dinner, here also celebrating Arthur's appointment to life tenure as Rabbi. Fred and Florence Thomases; Mike and Helen Halpern; Harold and Frances Rosenberg; Arthur and Naomi Fisher; Dr. Harry and Shirley Passow; and Arthur and Phyllis Hertzberg.

Meeting in September 1987 at Zagorsk Monastery of the Russian Orthodox Church with the vice rector. Irina, a scholar at the Oriental Institute, is the interpreter. Arthur Hertzberg signed their guest book and added a paragraph in Hebrew about the need for peace for all peoples and religions.

My father and I at prayer together at the Western Wall after the death of my mother, summer 1970. *Irving Abramowitz*

Greeting the president of Israel, Professor Ephraim Katzir. At a reception at his official residence in Jerusalem, 1976. *Isaac Berez*

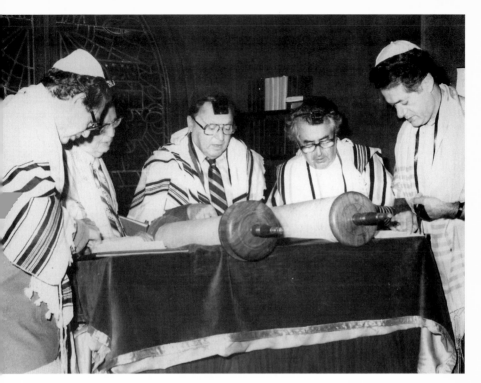

At weekday morning prayer in Englewood in the early 1970s. *L-R:* Leo Herson; Dr. Louis Greenwald; Arthur Hertzberg, reading the Torah; Sol Kaplan; and Gabe Schlisser.

My parents, late 1960s. Rabbi Zvi Elimelech Herzberg and Nechama Shifrah Herzberg.

My granddaughter Rachel's Bat-Mitzvah, August 25, 2001. Dr. David Merzel; Dr. Linda Hertzberg Merzel; Rachel Merzel, twelve and a half; Michael Merzel, nine.

Stephen Brody and Susan Hertzberg; Michelle Brody, twelve; and Derek Brody, six. October 2001.

Arthur and Phyllis Hertzberg, April 2002.

13

After Phyllis and I were married in London, where she had been born and raised, on March 19, 1950, we arrived in Nashville together, at the end of March. The congregation gave a reception to which "everybody," including even some of my anti-Zionist sparring partners, came. The party was popular, because this was the first time in anyone's memory that the Jews in Nashville could celebrate the marriage of a rabbi. Much goodwill and warmth were in evidence. Several people predicted that I would now be less critical and a little less irritating, because I would not be coming home to a bachelor apartment to brood alone. They certainly guessed right that I would be less contrary, but not because Phyllis would be sitting on me. Suddenly, this young woman, who had not yet passed her twenty-first birthday, was a public figure in a place for which she was totally unprepared. She could not adjust to the sultry, humid climate, and she had trouble coping with the fact she was "onstage" from the moment she walked out the door of our apartment. Phyllis soon discovered what I had found out when I first came to Nashville: anything that you said to anyone would be repeated back to you by someone else, often with unexpected embellishment, within a day or two. I was too busy giving her a crash course in Nashville society to have time to be the community scold. On the surface, we appeared to be relaxed, confident, and uncomplaining. The congregation got the impression that I had changed and, from their perspective, for the better.

The truth was that, within a few months, I was becoming angrier than I had ever been. The issue was no longer, as it had been, a clash of values. Phyllis and I, as a young married couple, were being sustained by much friendship and love, but we also were being harassed by ever more intrusive curiosity about every detail of our life. We could never go down the stairs from our apartment on the third floor without having one of the neighbors "accidentally" come to the door to greet us and ask the inevitable question about what we were doing that day.

I was on the way to making a stinging public defense of our right to privacy, when our situation changed radically. The United States had to defend Korea, so the armed forces were quickly expanding. Suddenly, the Pentagon was asking not only for fighting men but for personnel in the support services. Young doctors were being drafted; and priests, ministers, and rabbis, who could not be drafted, were being asked to volunteer. The Rabbinical Assembly, the organization of Conservative rabbis, decided to return to the procedure that it had used during the Second World War: it instituted a self-draft. The enforcement provision was that those who would refuse to "volunteer" would very likely be expelled from the organization. Those who had already served in the Second World War were exempt, but everyone else was subject to call, if needed. I had a high number, because when Japan had surrendered in 1945, in the very month when I was to report for military training, my orders had been canceled. Unmarried rabbis, and those among the married who had no children, were soon asked to take leaves of absence from their congregations and join the service. When the letter came telling me it would soon be my turn, I took it immediately to Manuel Eskind. Without any hesitation, he responded by telling me that I must, of course, go. He was clearly proud that his young rabbi would be seen in the community as doing his patriotic duty. In the South, a proper American was supposed to have been a soldier.

The news that I was on the way to becoming a chaplain did "play well" in town. Even James Stahlman, who did not approve of me because I was a "Yankee liberal," telephoned to suggest that I enter the navy, the service in which he was still a reserve captain. He offered to intervene with his friend, the admiral in command of the American fleet in the Mediterranean, to get him to ask for me for his staff as soon as I finished the preliminary training that was prescribed for navy chaplains. I thanked Stahlman very warmly, but I declined his offer, maintaining, with a degree of posturing, that I was going to do my military service straight, without the protection of any kind of influence.

In the event, I applied to the air force. The immediate vacancies for Jewish chaplains were in that branch of the service. The response came toward the end of 1950: I would be called for a physical examination in Nashville, and if I passed, I would be given orders to report for induction at the beginning of the summer. The physical examinations were given at a military facility but by civilian doctors. The physician who happened to be on duty the day of my physical was someone I knew. After taking my blood pressure and applying a stethoscope to the usual places on my chest, the examining physician closed the door and asked me, very seriously, whether I really wanted to join up. He offered to find a plausible reason, a hint of a heart murmur, to reject me. I refused the offer, adding that now that I was on the verge of putting on a military uniform, I had discovered some unexpected zest for this endeavor.

My orders to report for duty came in the spring; I was told to turn up for induction on the first of July at the air-force base on the outskirts of Montgomery, Alabama. In Montgomery, the heat was one hundred and six in the shade and the air-conditioning in the hotel where I stayed that night was not working. I did not sleep at all, and not only because the room was so stuffy. I was restless because I was afraid that I would not be able to cope with military life. I would be part of a culture where you took orders and replied with "Yes sir." Near dawn, I was almost ready to run away, even before I had been inducted. What saved me from this ignominy was pride. As dawn was breaking, I said to myself that bigger idiots than I had survived the military. The chances were that I too could function in this strange world. At six o'clock in the morning I took a cab to the front gate of Maxwell Air Force Base. Within a few hours, and after standing in several lines, I had a military number, dog tags on which my name and serial number were stamped, and a set of orders to report to chaplain school at Fort Slocum, New York, on an island near New Rochelle, in two weeks.

At Fort Slocum all the trainees were assigned beds in an open bar-
rack. Since we were officers, there was no compulsory "lights out."
Some of the people in the beds nearby read or talked until very late, and
a few kept a bridge game going in a corner until the early morning.
Things finally quieted down around 2 A.M. Two or three of the
Catholic priests soon arose, at about four, to sing mass. We showered
together in one large room with showerheads, and there was no privacy
even in the toilets. The military insisted that we should perform our
natural functions publicly, in full view. No partitions were allowed. I
soon began to wake up in fear that any troubles with my bowels would
become a matter for discussion. After a few days of this regime, I
decided to commute every day to the apartment on the Upper West
Side of Manhattan that Phyllis and I had rented so we could at least be
together on weekends. I got up every weekday morning before five to
make it to the base for the first training session at seven, and I left as
soon as the classes, and occasional drills, ended at five. I did not get to
know the other trainees because I saw them only at class and at a quick
lunch, but this was a price that I was willing to pay to avoid living in the
noise of the barracks at Fort Slocum.

In the six weeks there I made only one lasting relationship, with a
Baptist minister named Earl Grandstaff. He had served as an enlisted
man in the Asian theater during the Second World War. At the end of
the war, so he told me, he had parachuted into Manchuria to help free
the American prisoners who were held there by the Japanese. He told
me other stories that more than hinted at a continuing connection with
American intelligence, and he even suggested, obliquely, that in each
training class there was at least one person whose job it was to make
sure that no one among the new chaplains was a security risk or a spy
planted in the trustworthy role of chaplain.

In the training at Fort Slocum none of us ever learned to shoot a gun,
because chaplains were not supposed to carry weapons. We did not
learn how to march or salute with acceptable crispness. We did find out
what the duties of a chaplain were on a day-to-day basis: to be available
to counsel soldiers in difficulty. That was known in military parlance as
"punching the ticket"—that is, listening to problems. The standard
advice given to chaplains was to avoid fighting the cause of the soldier
against the military establishment and to limit themselves to organizing

and conducting religious services. Particular care was taken to teach us our duties when someone died in combat or in an accident. The chaplain needed to make sure that the body be prepared for shipping home according to the traditions and rituals of the faith to which the soldier belonged. One day, during a class on this sensitive matter, an especially unworldly Catholic priest, who had come to the military after years in a monastery, asked an insistent series of questions. The monk wanted to know how the chaplain determined the faith of the deceased. When the instructor answered that you look at his dog tags, which usually noted the bearer's religion, the monk asked what he should do if the dog tags had been blown away or lost. The instructor answered that you ask the comrades of the dead soldier, or, if they did not know, you tried to make an educated guess on the basis of his name: Corporal Goldstein was likely to be Jewish, and Sergeant O'Flaherty was likely to be Roman Catholic. The monk was not yet satisfied, so he began to ask one more question. The instructor exploded and told him to shut up.

This fit of anger led to immediate trouble. The commander of the training program was a Catholic priest of special authority, because he had been in the service long enough to reach the rank of colonel. The monk left the room and headed for the commander's office. The colonel came back to class to publicly dress down the instructor. After class I walked over to the instructor to commiserate with him. He told me that he was angrier than he had showed, for he remembered such an incident during his own training in the last year of the Second World War at the chaplain school, which was then at Harvard. The class on funerals was being taught by a Jewish chaplain, who had responded to such badgering with visible anger, saying, "Look in the pocket of the deceased and, if you find a bingo ticket, he's a Catholic." By morning this rabbi had been detached from the faculty and sent to a unit on the line in the Philippines. Our teacher had gotten off with a public reprimand. At the next class, the instructor was controlled and polite, and the monk asked no more questions to the very end of training. We were being socialized in chaplain school to live together, so that we would willingly share offices and chapels and help each other at the air bases to which we would be assigned. That was the dream; the instructor's explosion underlined that the tensions among the religious groups still existed under the thin cover of cooperation in the military.

At the training school I was the only rabbi in that summer's class, so I was mostly left to myself. Some of the Christians, both Catholic and Protestant, were alumni of the same seminary or they had encountered each other at denominational meetings, but even this camaraderie seemed to be the kind of friendship that exists among people on a cruise ship or a long train ride. At the end of the journey we would be scattered worldwide, in one of hundreds of air-force installations. The path of wisdom was to remain detached and to be sufficiently pleasant to everyone else so as not to make problems that would find their way into your record. All of us had learned, during the very first few days at Fort Slocum, the meaning of the dreaded initials ER—that is, effectiveness report. Superior officers graded their juniors at set intervals, or when either rank was about to leave for a new posting. These ERs were the principal guide in choosing assignments for the officer under review. Any trainee who got out of line, in the opinion of the member of the training faculty who wrote the report, would very likely find himself assigned to some base in the middle of Greenland or to some forward air strip that was constantly being strafed or bombed. Independence and fighting for principle were noble words, but "keeping your nose clean" was a way of living longer and better. Before the six weeks of training were over, most of us had learned the fundamental lesson of self-preservation in the military: don't buck your superior; on the contrary, bend every effort to make him look good—unless you hanker for the solitude of Outer Slobovia.

Somehow even I managed to learn, and by the last week of training school it was evident that I had made myself insignificant enough, and pleasant enough, that I would not be ordered to some hellhole. I was sent to Mitchell Air Force Base in the middle of Long Island. This airfield was a transit point for airmen and officers who would soon be on their way to foreign duty. Though I was told that this posting would be brief, at most a few months, Phyllis and I, nonetheless, moved from Manhattan to a small house we rented in Long Beach, not too far from Mitchell Field. I soon became comfortable with working in the same office, desk by desk, with a Protestant minister who was the more or less permanent chaplain for the entire base. We shared the time, amiably, of an enlisted man who did the typing for both of us. Our relations were businesslike and pleasant, free of trouble, because essentially we left each other alone. The base chaplain knew that I was marking time until I was ordered overseas. I knew that the base was too small to have any substantial Jewish population among its less than two thousand inhabitants. There was no need for a Sabbath service because most of the people on base were permitted weekend passes. I did get to intervene a few times for soldiers who needed compassionate leave, to go home to close relatives who were very ill. The most important thing that I learned in the few months at Mitchell Air Force Base was not to eat lunch at the officers' club. There, junior officers seemed to spend their time cozying up to commanders who might advance their careers. I expected only to serve out the two years for which I had enlisted, so I was not looking for promotion. I took to eating lunch at the sergeants' mess. It soon even dawned on me that, in the military, the greatest asset is the goodwill of sergeants and corporals. A sergeant at Mitchell Field once said to me, "If we are with you, you can stretch a weekend pass into ten days away, for we will cover for you; if we hate you, you will be brought up on charges for being even five minutes late."

What most surprised me in my first months in the military was the total absence of even a hint of anti-Semitism. In Nashville, I had experienced the strong southern respect for the cloth, but I was reminded in a hundred ways that I was a Jewish rabbi. In the military, the unique insignia that I wore on my jacket, the ten commandments, seemed to create a protective shell around me. My word as a chaplain was eliciting more attention and more respect than could possibly come with my very junior rank of first lieutenant. After a while, I understood what was happening. The military forces had recently been desegregated, in 1948, by President Truman's executive order. The commanders knew that their careers were on the line if they failed to foster equal treatment for Negroes. Jews were an even more sensitive matter. Generals, and most of the middle-rank officers, had served in the Second World War. Everyone vividly remembered the horrors that the Nazis had inflicted on the Jews. Most officers were genuinely helpful, but even the repressed anti-Semites knew that it was prudent not to become known as Jew-baiters. Someone might complain to your superior, and the complaint would be recorded in your next ER. Under this protective cover, I lived my two years of active duty under the most favorable circumstances that a Jew could encounter in America. It was a kind of Shangri-la.

In the late fall, I got the order to go overseas. I had expected to be sent to Japan, to the divisions of the United States Air Force that were helping to fight the war in Korea, so the assignment to Europe was a pleasant surprise. It was even more delightful that my destination was the Riviera, in the south of France. I was directed to travel to the American air-force headquarters in Europe, near Frankfurt, Germany, where I would be given orders to proceed to an installation that was being created near Marseilles. I was to be the deputy staff chaplain of the EAMF. No one had ever heard of this command, so it took some research to decipher the initials and learn that the headquarters of a European Air Materiel Force was being created, at a small town in southern France, to supervise all the supplies that would soon start arriving through the port of Marseilles. This channel would supplement the existing supply route through Cherbourg. The assignment to this new command was an extraordinary piece of luck, but, alas, the dream would not be realized. While I was at sea during the last days of December, on my way to Europe, a subcommittee of Congress had been sniffing around in the Pentagon's budget. They discovered the project to create the EAMF. Congressional investigators quickly figured out that maintaining two supply routes would be more expensive and less efficient: the units in the field would often not know through which port the materiel that they required had arrived. The investigators soon found the real reason for creating the EAMF. Several of the senior generals in Europe wanted an American headquarters on the Riviera so that they would have frequent reason to visit the facilities—and enjoy the after-hours pleasures of the region. The committee summoned an assistant secretary of defense from the Pentagon, who agreed to abort the European Air Materiel Force.

When I arrived in Frankfurt on January 2, 1952, I was ordered, instead, to London, to be Jewish chaplain to the Third Air Force (fighter planes) and the Seventh Air Division (bombers). Together, these two commands contained over thirty thousand American air-force personnel, scattered in some thirty bases all over England. The news that I would spend the next year and a half of my military career based at Third Air Force headquarters, on the outskirts of London, was astonishing and even overwhelming. Phyllis was an only child, and her parents had been visibly upset when she decided to marry an American and live thousands of miles away. I knew that, because England was not a combat zone, married officers could bring their wives to join them. When I got through on the telephone, later that day, to Phyllis in the United States, I kept her from being too emotional by telling her the news in the form of a bad joke: I said that other people had been ordered to Korea to fight the Communists; I was being ordered to London to fuss with my in-laws. But my attempt at humor failed.

Phyllis only forgave me because my voice on the telephone proved that I was alive. The military transport in which I had crossed the Atlantic had been at sea during one of the worst storms of the century. A merchant ship that was thirty miles behind us had broken in two. One half of that ship, the bow, had remained afloat for days, and its captain almost succeeded in bringing it to shore in Ireland. The harrowing story was front-page news in the United States all that week. The captain of our transport tried to turn the ship around, to rescue the sailors on the sinking half of the merchant vessel, but we almost capsized. I had not known how bad the storm was, for I had been so miserably seasick until the last day of the journey that I spent nine days lying on my bunk, to keep myself from vomiting. Each day I forced myself to stand up to light Hanukkah candles at a ceremony that was attended by the thirty or forty Jews on board, but I could not wait to stagger back to my bunk. When we finally entered port in Bremerhaven, Germany, I was so glad to see the shore that I even suspended my visceral dislike of Germany, but it returned in less than an hour. As soon as we disembarked, the five junior officers with whom I had shared a cabin walked toward the nearest refreshment stand. The man behind the counter was a middle-aged German who spoke no English. I was deputized by the others to order the drinks from him. He responded by telling me how glad he was to see American soldiers arriving in large numbers. We would finally do together what we should have done during the Second World War, march against the Soviet Union. I wanted to ask him whether the Americans and the Germans would then cooperate in reopening Auschwitz, but I was too upset. I was stammering and choking, trying to answer this ex-*Wehrmacht* soldier who was still eager for war. I walked away from him toward the train for Frankfurt, where I would pick up the orders that would get me out of Germany.

After one night in Frankfurt, I was sent to London on an air-force transport plane that flew every day from the European headquarters in Rhein-Main to Northolt, the airfield on the edge of London that was now used by the American air staff in England. The offices of the Third Air Force were in a set of two-story buildings nearby. I reported to the chief chaplain, a Southern Baptist minister named Roy Priest. He received me with military correctness and then sat me down to explain to me that I would be in a somewhat unique situation. Personnel who were Jews were scattered in small handfuls, so I would have to be assigned high enough in the military "table of organization" so that I could receive travel orders to visit all of the bases in the command. Therefore, even though I had the lowly rank of first lieutenant, I would work out of headquarters with a room in his suite, and I would be given the title of assistant staff chaplain. Chaplain (Lieutenant Colonel) Roy Priest understood that my main responsibility was to the Jews in the military in England, but he would expect me to carry out some duties in his office.

He did not tell me that day, but he wanted to be rid of two problems, one because it was burdensome and the other because it might cause him trouble and block the promotion for which he longed to full colonel. The burdensome duty was dealing with servicemen who wanted to get married to local women. They could not do so without military permission, because, once married, the new wives had the automatic right to a permanent visa to the United States. The decision on such permissions was made by the office of the staff chaplain, which advised the commanding general. The staff chaplain wanted nothing to do with these irritations, and so, in classic military fashion, he gave it to his lowest-ranking assistant. Most of the prospective brides were decent young women, but some were ladies of the evening. I was assigned the task of interviewing the loving couples. The chaplain's office had an open line to Scotland Yard, the police headquarters for London, so I was on that telephone several times a week. As the months went by, several of the ladies showed up two or three times, with different soldiers. Soon, I could not walk through central London, even after hours and in civilian clothes, without being greeted by women who recognized me and said, "Hi, Chaplain."

The other task to which I was soon assigned had no name, nor a precise definition. Whenever an issue arose in which the chaplain's office might be irritating the commanding general, or any base commander, the staff chaplain somehow arranged that I deal with the question. It did not matter whether anyone got annoyed with me, because I was not staying in the military. So, when our office was late in producing its part of the plan for evacuating American civilians from England if the Cold War with the Soviet Union began to heat up, I was sent to pacify the general's office and to suggest, without saying so outright, that the delay was caused largely because of my inexperience and lack of training in military planning.

Because I undertook these unpleasant assignments, I was given a generous reward. As chaplain to the Jewish personnel, I was usually working on weekends. Sometimes, I went to one of the bases for the Sabbath, and when I was not traveling, I always kept open house in London. In exchange, my boss allowed me compensatory time off in the middle of the week. All day Tuesday, and on Wednesday morning, I sat in the reading room of the British Museum doing research for my doctoral dissertation on the French Enlightenment and the Jews. This was a precious opportunity, because Thomas Carlyle had collected thirty thousand pamphlets from the period of the French Revolution. These texts had all been sold to the British Museum. In this treasure trove, I found some petitions by Jews in France to the Revolutionary Parliament; several of these texts did not exist in any other library.

It was even more important to me that I often worked in the reading room beside Yaacov Talmon, a Polish Jew who had survived the Holocaust and was then a junior member of the history department of the Hebrew University in Jerusalem. In 1952 Talmon was finishing his research on the book that would make him famous, *The Origins of Totalitarian Democracy*. The conversations with him in Hebrew and Yiddish seemed worlds away from the bureaucratic chaos in my office in Ruislip. Talmon had come to the central idea of his life: that totalitarianism had not descended entirely from religious inquisitors and upholders of the absolute power of kings. He had become convinced that liberalism itself was one of the roots of totalitarianism. The dominant message of the Enlightenment had been that the world can be improved by human effort; society could be a happy place if the limits that had long been put on human freedom by the laws of the state, and the rules that religion ordained in the name of God, were replaced by a secular culture of universal values that would include all of humanity. In this dream of perfection, Talmon had discovered a threatening corollary: those who refuse to be reformed, and therefore do not fit into the brave new world, should be excluded; they might even be destroyed, for the greater good of mankind.

In the conversations in the courtyard of the British Museum, I told Talmon how much I agreed with him. It seemed to me that he was making a very contemporary point: that in our day the enemies of freedom were not only Nazis and Fascists; they were also Communists, who had no qualms about doing away with counterrevolutionaries. Lenin and Stalin were the heirs of the men and women who had used the guillotine during the French Revolution to achieve the "regeneration" of society by chopping off the heads of those who did not fit. I once told Yaacov Talmon a very American story, which supported his argument. Supposedly, a Communist agitator, standing on a soapbox in Union Square in Manhattan, pronounced that "come the revolution, not only the rich but the proletariat, as well, will enjoy strawberries and cream." A listener raised his hand and asked, "But what about me? I don't like strawberries and cream." The speaker responded, "Come the revolution, we will make you like strawberries and cream."

But I had trouble with Talmon's arguments. I noticed that he hardly mentioned Jews anywhere in the draft of his book. He answered that he wanted his argument to be read as a rethinking of some of the major themes in modern history and not as a parochial defense of Jewish feeling and interests. I answered by insisting that his book was an outcry against all those who wanted a world purged of dissenters and strangers—and that the Jew had long been the most pervasive, and persecuted, nonconformist and alien. Hitler had murdered them for being Jews, and Stalin had sent Jews to the gulag, or to their deaths, for adhering to their religion or being suspected of Jewish nationalism. I told Talmon that, despite himself, he had written a very Jewish book. He, a Jewish refugee from Poland, was providing the historical basis for the assertion that freedom was safe only in a plural society. Who needed pluralism as much as the Jews, who had just suffered the greatest of all their disasters from Nazi ideologues?

These conversations with Talmon made me think more deeply about the doctoral thesis on the Jews in France in the eighteenth century on which I was working. I was already convinced that, in the nineteenth century, the countries that had given Jews equal rights had never really emancipated the Jew as he is, in his own right. Even in America, where the ties between the state and the majority culture were loosest, at least in theory, Jews were still expected to make themselves worthy citizens by adopting the somewhat secularized Protestant culture of the majority. I was beginning to wonder whether assimilation could ever really secure the place of Jews in society. Many of those whom Hitler had murdered were model Germans, proud veterans of World War I. Many of the Jews whom Stalin had shot or sent to Siberia were paragons of Communist behavior. Some of the early Socialists had been anti-Semites, who kept insisting that Jews were bad by their very nature. In some of the pamphlets in the Carlyle collection, radical Jacobins, the most proletarian element among the makers of the French Revolution, kept harping on the innate wickedness of the Jewish character; it could not be cured, so society had to defend itself by excluding them. I had even found that some of the same arguments had been used to counter the demand for equality of the Negroes in Hispaniola, the Caribbean island under French rule. A large, even dominant, school of opinion among the makers of the French Revolution held that Negroes were, by nature, intellectually inferior and incapable of governing themselves.

In these conversations in the courtyard of the British Museum, I suggested to Talmon that I would one day write a book on this theme. Twenty years later, over tea in his apartment in Jerusalem, Talmon reminded me of this conversation. He had read my book *The French Enlightenment and the Jews*, which was published in 1969, and he was pleased that I had spent years reading all the discussions of the "Jewish question" that I could find in eighteenth-century French literature and collecting as much as I could of the political debates of that time. I reminded him that I had insisted, when we first met in London, that there was a Jewish subtext to his own magisterial study of the totalitarianism of the left. Even then I was aware, with pain, that equality had never been offered to the Jews completely and with a whole heart. The notion that Jews were inherently different—"enemies of the human race," in Voltaire's words—had never died.

My work at the British Museum and the conversations with Yaacov Talmon were my personal business, a kind of hobby for my days off from work. Even the administrative chores in the chaplain's office seemed to be charades, games in which I was substituting for my boss, who was an incarnation of the culture of the regular army: don't make waves and you will eventually be promoted. I encountered real life, and I began to take my job seriously, during my first tour through the military bases. The purpose of the American presence was a forbidden subject, but it was clear that the thirty thousand airmen in England were a forward position in the Cold War with the Soviet Union. The essential American force was the bombers that could carry nuclear devices. The deepest secret in England was the precise location of the bombs with which these planes would be armed in case "the whistle blew," but it was common knowledge that these devices were somewhere, in highly protected depots, very near the runways of the main American bomber bases. During my first weeks in England, a liaison officer from the Royal Air Force described England as the unsinkable aircraft carrier that the Americans were using to intimidate the Russians. The flying time from American airfields in East Anglia to Moscow was far shorter than the flying time from Moscow to New York. American bombers could be escorted by protective fighters most of the way to the Soviet Union. Soviet bombers would have no such fighter cover if they went out over the Atlantic or over the North Pole on the way to attacking the United States.

We, the Americans in uniform, were therefore in England manning a forward position in defense of the United States, but the official reason for our presence was that we were participating in the defense of Great Britain: if the Soviets dropped bombs or, much worse, the bomb, on a British city, that would be the trip wire for a nuclear response by the United States. We were allies, weren't we? Most of the British officers whom I met did not believe the American promise. They did not think that the United States would risk the incineration of New York, Chicago, and Washington if the Soviets took out an English city. They irrationally wanted the United Kingdom to be free from its dependence on the United States. When I first heard this opinion, I thought that it had the sound of appeasement to which the British had been wedded until the very outbreak of the Second World War in 1939. They had kept cheering Neville Chamberlain, who did not want to go to war to protect the Czechs from Hitler's assault. In time, I began to wonder whether there was not some truth in what these Royal Air Force officers were saying. Great Britain was still in deep economic trouble with severe food rationing. The government was surviving with help from American loans and grants. The American Air Force was in Great Britain because the government could not refuse any serious American request. The British public knew this, and therefore an unrelenting current of anger buffeted the American allies who were supposedly there to help defend Great Britain.

The deepest and most negative tide, in the early 1950s, in the relations between the peoples of the British Isles and the Americans was the sense of loss and even despair that pervaded British society. The British resented the unraveling of their empire, which had begun most visibly in 1947 when India was granted independence and Clement Atlee's Labor government surrendered control over Palestine in an ignominious retreat. Everyone knew that there was more to come, that more and more colonies would be peeling away to become independent. Great Britain was being reduced to the rank of a second-rate power. It was dwarfed by the Americans and the Russians and even envious of the defeated Germans and Japanese, who were beginning to make remarkable recoveries from their defeats. Many of the British kept telling themselves that they had been broken by the enormous casualties that they had sustained in war, and by the almost total drain on their resources, because the United States had left them to fight alone against the Germans for two crucial years, in 1940 and 1941. I heard over and over again in London that America had come out of the war with casualties that basically did not dent its population and with an economy that was on the upswing in large part at British expense. This anti-Americanism was present in all classes. The poor blamed the Americans for their poverty; the upper classes were convinced that the Americans had planned, and even schemed, to replace them as the world's rulers; the intellectuals took refuge in defending their supposed cultural superiority against the "barbarians" from across the ocean. To be an American in military uniform in London in the early 1950s was not always a very happy posting, even though I was often forgiven, personally, for being one of them.

The anti-Americanism was sharpened by what was going on then in American politics. In almost every conversation, two subjects inevitably came up: the racial segregation that still existed almost totally intact in America, and especially in the South, for none of the Jim Crow laws had yet been abrogated; and the antics of Senator Joseph McCarthy, who was then flinging accusations of Communism at hundreds of writers, artists, diplomats, and even soldiers. McCarthy reached a climax in the spring of 1952 by accusing no less revered a figure than General George Marshall, who had been chief of staff during the Second World War and was then serving as Truman's secretary of state, of being soft on Communism. In these conversations in England, I was quickly given personal absolution after I told that I had almost become the target myself of an investigation by the rogue senator and his staff, but my British friends vehemently attacked American society as racist, anti-intellectual, and dominated by witch-hunters. I countered that Joe McCarthy was a temporary madness from which the United States was in the process of recovering, as Britain had recovered from its romance with appeasement in the 1930s. There was no possible defense of American racism, but I did point out, over and over again, that the Negro and Asian minorities in Great Britain were then very small. The English could pride themselves that racism was absent from their society, but I had no doubt that that there would be much more racism in Britain if there were greater numbers of Negroes and Asians in the country—and, indeed, twenty years later there was such an upsurge in bigotry.

The distaste in Great Britain in 1952 for the "American Army of Occupation," for racial segregation in the United States, and for McCarthyism was not surprising, but it was astonishing that a large majority of the British public was against General Eisenhower and for Adlai Stevenson in the American presidential election in November 1952. I had imagined that Eisenhower was well regarded in England because he had gone to substantial lengths not to ruffle the British during his years as supreme Allied commander of the combined forces that invaded Europe, but the large majority of the newspapers in England sniped at Eisenhower. They considered him to be dull and much too conservative. His opponent, Adlai Stevenson, was described as an intellectual who might just as easily have graduated from Oxford or

Cambridge. He appeared to be very much like the majority of English politicians, of all shades of opinion, who were educated and polished. Eisenhower, on the contrary, was deplored as an unsophisticated soldier from Kansas. The shock of the landslide for Eisenhower, which was widely expected in America, was unnerving in England. I was to stay at my military post in London for another eight months, but I was ever more aware that the English were becoming more anti-American. I was less likely, after hours, to wear my uniform.

But the frictions with the British were marginal to my life. I had no responsibility for the health of the relations between Americans and Brits. I spent most of my time with the troops. Every day I came back to the flat in Bayswater to tell Phyllis how intrigued, often elated, and sometimes upset I was by what I had found in my office or in my visits to the various air bases outside of London.

One day my boss sent me to a small air base in southern England, near the coast, where there were two chaplains, one Catholic and one Protestant. The age of ecumenism had not yet dawned. Each of these two clerics was equally intransigent in maintaining that only he spoke for true Christianity and that the other was misleading the faithful and taking them to the doors of hell. These two chaplains shared an office, a secretary, and a chapel, but they were no longer on speaking terms. Since their quarrel had become a public embarrassment, the base commander asked my boss to intervene, but he had no military authority to command clerics to disregard the dictates of their faiths. Chaplain Priest sent me to investigate. I invited these two angry servants of the Lord to come to lunch with me, but they sat in stony silence. Finally, my troublemaking impulse took over and I said to both of them, quite flatly and seemingly seriously, that I had heard that they were quarreling over the question of which of their traditions was the true heir of Christianity. I told them that, as a rabbi, I believed they were both wrong and I was waiting for them to "see the light," give up the ancient Jewish heresy, Christianity, and join the one true synagogue. They swallowed the bait; both of the clerics became very voluble; each could hardly wait his turn to hurl "proof texts" at me that, so they insisted, demonstrated that the New Testament was the correct and only heir of the revelation in the Hebrew Bible. I had put them on the same side as

Christians, and they could not walk away from the table to resume ignoring each other. An uneasy peace was restored, and I returned to the office in London in amused triumph.

Wherever I went, I always visited the infirmary on the base. The facilities also took care of the RAF liaison officers who were assigned to each of the American bases as representatives of the host country. On one of these visits I found a British flight lieutenant with the very Scottish name of MacTavish on the list of patients. His chart indicated that he was a Jew. This piece of information startled me, so I hastened to his bedside. He was not at all welcoming, and he soon told me why. In the British military there is "church parade" every Sunday. Those who belong to the majority, the Church of England, remain in place, to take part in a religious service conducted by an Anglican chaplain, and all others fall out to go to a religious service of their own faith. The least acceptable alternative was to write yourself down as an atheist. Mac-Tavish was a vehement nonbeliever, but he had chosen to identify himself as a Jew; he was sure he would not be encountering rabbis at any Royal Air Force bases, and thus he would not be bothered by religion. MacTavish had not reckoned that the Americans would dredge up someone like me to comfort him.

For some obscure military reason, the American air-force detachment at Orly Field in Paris was under the command of the Third Air Force in England. I was, therefore, obliged to fly to Paris occasionally to visit these airmen. I did not resist duty because it meant spending a day in Paris. These trips always went smoothly until the day when I came off the plane to find a jeep waiting for me. The driver was instructed to rush me directly to the office of the American commander at Orly. I was nervous, imagining that some infraction of regulations had caught up with me, and I even had dark visions of being court-martialed. When I arrived, the colonel received me very cordially and told me immediately, in a worried tone, that he had a problem with which he hoped that I could help. The major function of his detachment was to keep the air-force planes flying, so he had to have a maintenance and repair crew available around the clock. One of the maintenance crew was Jewish. This young corporal had claimed the right, as a religious Jew, not to work on the Sabbath, and he had even asked to be released from duty at noon on Friday so that he could go into Paris to prepare himself for all the Sabbath rituals and traditions. The commander had responded by granting him the time off but the corporal was asked to be on duty on Sundays. He refused, claiming that there were additional, post-Sabbath celebrations in Paris on Sunday. He could not be back for duty until Monday morning. The commander was eager to be completely respectful of religion, and especially of the minority faiths, but he had the uneasy feeling that he was being fooled. I asked to see the corporal in question. He had been summoned in advance and was waiting in the next room. It did not take more than a few sentences for the truth to come out. The corporal was not particularly religious. He had a girlfriend in Paris, and this Romeo was using his supposed commitment to religion to get weekends off to spend with his Juliet. I said little to the corporal, for he knew that the game was over, but I did go back to the colonel to apologize that a claim for special consideration, whenever possible, was being abused. The next day, when I came back to Orly to return to London, the colonel told me that he had reassigned the offending corporal to an air-force base in Greenland—but that was not the end of the story.

Events had happened so fast at Orly that I never had time to take off my coat. The Jewish chaplain's insignia on my military blouse (the Ten Commandments) were covered, so the corporal presumed that the hard-hearted Chaplain Hertzberg who had called his bluff was some anti-Semite of German extraction. Two months later, I found a complaint on my desk, forwarded from the Pentagon, in which the congressman from the young man's district, a senior Jewish figure in the House of Representatives, Emanuel Celler, protested against the role of Hertzberg, clearly some German American anti-Semite, in sending this fine upstanding young man, from an excellent family, to icy hardship duty near the Arctic Circle. I happened to know the congressman, so I wrote him a personal letter, not through channels, telling him the story. I added that goofing off was a time-honored military practice, but that pretended piety should not be used in such schemes. I do not know whether Mr. Celler sent my letter on to the corporal's family.

I found it quietly inspiring, over and over again, that anything special that I needed for the Jewish personnel was always made part of the normal business of the American command. The lengths to which the air force went was remarkable. In the spring of 1952, on the eve of

Passover, some of the food came ready-made from the Jewish Welfare Board in the United States, which generously supplied the needs of Jewish service personnel all over the world. However, hundreds of eggs had to be boiled in cauldrons that had never been used for any other purpose except preparing food for Passover. New dishes had to be found on which to serve the Seder feast, to conform with the injunction that only vessels that had never held any food with leaven could be used for this solemn festival. The supply service located some unopened crates of dishes and pots in one of our warehouses in England. Two days before Passover one of the sergeants in the supply depot, moved by great goodwill, decided to open the crates and send them through a dishwasher so that they would be shiny and clean when we picked them up. In the strictest Jewish ritual, this act of goodwill made the dishes unfit for use for Passover, because Passover dishes had to be cleaned separately from other dishes.

When I found out less than twenty-four hours before the festival, I was beside myself. The officer in charge of the supply depot calmed me down. He telephoned air bases all over Europe until he found that there were some unopened crates of dishes and pots at an American base in Germany. He immediately sent a plane to pick them up. They were in hand by morning. The major told me very cordially on the telephone that he did not understand these Jewish ritual concerns, but he regarded it as his duty to help us conform to our traditions. The Jewish airmen were just as inspiring. Phyllis had feared that she would have to cook hundreds of eggs for the Seder all by herself and that we would have to set the tables by ourselves, but we were wrong. Twenty or thirty airmen who came to London for the festival found us at our flat and volunteered to help. The camaraderie was so great that those who put together that Seder in London formed themselves into a kind of club, and they stayed in touch with each other for years to come. Even after the connections withered, I have occasionally been approached at the end of a lecture somewhere by a somewhat familiar person who embraces me as one of the "Passover irregulars" from London in 1952.

There were no women in American air-force uniform in England in those days, but one civilian woman did an enormous amount of work in helping to prepare that Passover Seder. She was beautiful, very young (less than twenty), and very much in love. We had just met her, for she had come to London from somewhere in New Jersey to be with her boyfriend, Abe Bresnick, who was a corporal in the American military police in central London. Her parents had objected to her making the trip, because they suspected, quite correctly, that the young couple would immediately get married in London. The parents thought that she was too young to be married, and anyway, if there was to be a wedding, they wanted it back home where they and their friends could be present. I telephoned the parents to tell them that, despite their objections and any arguments that I could muster for delay, this young couple was going to get married. The parents agreed, reluctantly, that it would therefore be better if I married them in a proper Jewish religious ceremony. The wedding took place a few days later in our flat. It was jammed with some thirty or forty friends of the bridegroom. The tallith that I wore every morning when I said my prayers was held over their heads as the ritual canopy that united them, and the wedding feast was whatever Phyllis and I could quickly put together and spread out on a couple of tables.

I had a far more difficult time with the parents of a young lieutenant from the Midwest. The parents were the pillars of their synagogue and community, so they were especially upset that their son had fallen in love with a young woman who danced in the chorus of one of the musicals on the stage in London's West End. A chorus girl who had not been born into the Jewish faith was doubly unacceptable. The family's rabbi wrote me a long, pained letter asking my help in breaking up this relationship. I answered that I could only promise to meet the couple; I could not agree simply to be the agent, sight unseen, of the family's fears. The lieutenant and his girlfriend came to see me. I found him to be a decent human being, very much concerned with not hurting his parents, but he was deeply in love. The young woman seemed to be a very upright person. She did dance in a musical, but she was not a "chorus girl." On the contrary, her mother accompanied her to the theater and waited every night until the end of the show to accompany her home. The couple had been introduced by a mutual friend, and when I met them, she did not know that he came from a wealthy family. She told me that she was eager to take instruction with a view to converting to Judaism, and he added that she could study seriously, for they were in no hurry to get married; he was obligated to stay in the air force in London for two more years.

I wrote an account of this conversation to the parents, but they responded, in anger, that I was too soft on their son; I was encouraging him toward this unsuitable marriage rather than helping to stop it. They would not accept my opinion that these two young people really cared very deeply for each other, and they wanted to live a decent, religious, and public-spirited life together. I would not turn them away. Someone I knew agreed to teach her, and, two years later, after I had gone from London and left the service, she was formally admitted to the Jewish faith and they were married by my successor. This "Jew by choice" became one of the leaders of the Jewish community in her part of the Midwest. A few years later, I heard from others that her husband's parents were proud of the couple. But when I gave a lecture in the early 1960s in a city very near to the small town in which this family lived, the happily married couple came to see me, but the parents were "too busy." I am not sure to this day whether they were still angry with me for not having done what they wanted or whether they did not have the heart to come and admit that I had done them a favor.

I even had to perform a ritual circumcision. A boy had been born to a Jewish couple at an air base where there was not a single Jewish doctor who might perform the ritual. The parents telephoned me in London, so I asked one of the "reverends" who performed ritual circumcisions to do the honors. He accepted, but he added that the trip would take him the whole day—and he wanted portal-to-portal pay. The amount required was beyond the means of the young lieutenant who was the father, and it would have more than bankrupted the very small chaplain's fund at my disposal. I suggested to the parents that if they could get one of the surgeons at the base hospital to put a safety clamp on the child, it would be safe for me to do the actual circumcision. On the eighth day of the baby's life, I drove my jeep to the hospital and strode in with a box containing a few bottles of wine and some Jewish soul food such as herring and lox. Many pictures were taken of the ceremony, to prove to the grandparents that the traditions had been followed as best they could be. A few copies were sent to me. The one that I liked best caught me looking at the baby in some bafflement. Perhaps I was wondering whether I would ever have to explain to him why he had wound up being the first—and, in the event, the only—child whom I had physically brought into the "covenant of Abraham."

My two years in the military were, to my surprise, a very happy time. In effect, I had no superiors because a chaplain is not really subject to the military chain of command and a Jewish chaplain, who was the only rabbi in American uniform in Great Britain, was almost totally free to make his own program. The officers and men whom I served were not the military equivalent of a conventional congregation. There were no boards and committees to persuade or contend with. On the contrary, the military personnel were grateful, very visibly so, for every act of concern by the chaplain.

There were, of course, malcontents and seriously troubled people among the airmen, but these were a small minority. The great majority were upbeat. They had every hope of finishing their enlistments and going home to an America in which they would find a good life. The United States was the dominant and, by far, the richest country in the world. I heard almost no talk of larger social ideals or of any purposes beyond their individual careers. These airmen came overwhelmingly from lower-middle-class families. They still had fortunes to make, and they were happy that an expanding America was waiting for them. I heard even less from them about religious piety or about knowledge of the classic Jewish texts. Most had attended Sunday school or Hebrew school for some years, and, without exception, they had enjoyed becoming Bar Mitzvah, but their Jewishness was defined by ethnic feeling and by attachments to the ways of their folk.

Sometimes I wondered whether what they knew or felt as Jews would be enough to sustain their children. I liked them, and I was glad to be with them. They evoked from me a protectiveness that I had not known was within me, but I was not hopeful that I could ever evoke from them a passion for Jewish learning. In mid-1953 I left the air force and returned to my post as rabbi in Nashville. I came back more concerned about the problems of my congregants than I thought I could be—and more distant from their culture than I had ever been.

The eighteen months in London as air-force chaplain had emphasized for me how comfortable I was in this international capital,
where "everything" was happening. I could not imagine spending the
rest of my life in a smaller, out-of-the-way town such as Nashville. I
knew that I needed to find a job in some larger place, so I went looking.
Most of the congregations that I saw were not really located in places
that were better for me than Nashville. One synagogue in a very large
town with a substantial and involved Jewish population voted against
me. The majority of its board decided they wanted a rabbi who was less
obviously an intellectual. I waited for two years until the offer of a pulpit in Englewood, New Jersey, a growing suburb only minutes away
from New York City, was made. It took a year for me to be persuaded
that I ought to move to Temple Emanu-El of Englewood. I guessed
that I could survive, and even do some good, as the rabbi of the congregation. I was willing to take my chance at finding a place for myself in
the life of the New York metropolitan area. Nonetheless, a sentence by
Oscar Wilde kept running through my head: "The only thing worse
than not getting what you want is getting it." Maybe this bit of irony
and even cynicism would apply to me—but I did not think so.

In my personal life, in the summer of 1956, my wife, Phyllis, was then twenty-seven and our two daughters, Linda and Susan, were very young children. Linda was less than three; we had brought Susan with us in a bassinet, at the age of a few months. I knew that I could not allow myself to be so busy in the work of the congregation that I would neglect Phyllis and the children—but it was soon apparent that I was no different than so many of the workaholics of my generation. Too much of what I did in the congregation, especially in the early days in Englewood, was at the expense of the family. Like many of my contemporaries, I keep trying to atone to my children for those years by being extravagantly devoted to them. Now, in my later years, the grandchildren always come first.

In those years rabbis worked and were judged by the standard of "success": one passed the test if by midcareer one had become the rabbi of a thriving congregation with which one had good relations. I had no doubt that I would succeed in helping to increase the membership of the congregation (it rose from three hundred to six hundred families in three or four years) or that new buildings would be built, but I was shaken by very deep doubts. I was not troubled by the usual ills of the contemporary clergyman. I was not suffering from the classic midlife crisis of the twentieth-century cleric who wakes up one day and wonders whether he believes in God. My break with fundamentalism had occurred twenty years earlier, but I had found my way toward the Jewish God, the God of our ancestors, whose presence I sensed in my life every day. Sometimes He comforted me; sometimes I wrestled with Him, and sometimes I even defied Him, but I never doubted that He is here. I was not on the way to substituting psychoanalysis, or pastoral counseling, or the "social gospel," for the God of Abraham; and several decades later I firmly rejected spirituality, the practical Kabbalah, and all the other then current nostrums. I had arrived in Englewood, a very near suburb of New York, believing in myself as a rabbi, but that was the problem.

I knew in advance, after ten earlier years in two congregations, that my understanding of the rabbi's task would bear little resemblance to that held by some of my congregants. I remembered very vividly what my father had said in Philadelphia in 1944 when he installed me in my first pulpit. He had warned the congregation, and he made very sure that I would understand that he was talking very directly to me, when he coined the metaphor that the rabbi ought to be the town clock, who determined what the time was for everybody, and not a pocket watch whom individuals could manipulate. His teaching had been reinforced for me more recently when I read the obituaries in memory of Stephen Wise after his death in 1949. Almost everyone quoted the letter that he wrote in 1906 when he turned down the call to be rabbi in Temple Emanuel in New York because the board wanted to control what he would say and do. Wise had rejected the post with proud disdain for the conditions that the lay powers wanted to impose. He had written them,

> A rabbi is not to represent the views of the congregation but to proclaim the truth as he sees it . . . there may be secession on the part of some members . . . but even schism . . . [is better than] an attitude of the pulpit which never provokes dissent because it is cautious rather than courageous . . . time serving rather than right serving. The rabbi is not to be the spokesman of the congregation, or the message bearer of the congregation but the bearer of a message to the congregation.

It was inevitable that I would follow after my father and Stephen Wise. I would always be in sharp conflict with those who wanted a bland employee rather than a leader as their rabbi.

My battle to be the rabbi in Englewood on my terms began a year before I was even offered the appointment. I first met the leaders of the congregation in the spring of 1955, but this encounter became, almost immediately, something other than an interview of an eager candidate who was hoping to be chosen to be their rabbi. On the contrary, most of the evening was spent in debate between me and the committee. The congregation had then been in existence less than thirty years, so some of the founders were still involved. They had created a synagogue in which they, the lay leaders, could do as they wished. Their worship services for Sabbath and the High Holidays were constructed by a committee of the board. I was shown their homemade Sabbath prayer book and their version of the service for the High Holidays. Those who had edited these texts were members of the group that was sitting in the room with me that night.

I looked at the prayer books and talked with the committee for a while. Soon I asked a very blunt question: what do you need a rabbi for? It is clear that your previous rabbis have not been allowed to decide questions of religious law and practice—you do that yourselves—so what is the rabbi supposed to be doing? After quite a lot of talk, including some sharp exchanges among various members of the interviewing committee, I finally understood the answer. They were divided among themselves; they hoped that a new rabbi would find some way of uniting them. Of course, they wanted him to do this work gently and gradually, without hurting any feelings. I responded that it could not be done. "Gradualism" was a slogan that grated with me as I had heard it innumerable times in Nashville, where I had been the rabbi for almost a decade. It was the suggestion that people of the White establishment had been making to the "pushy" Negroes who were insisting that racial segregation must end. Supposedly, it would happen gradually, but in 1955 the schools were still segregated and so were the buses and the toilets. The only way to effect change, in social policy or religious practice, was to do it abruptly, on the basis of fundamental principles. In American society as a whole, segregation in education had just been outlawed, in 1954, as unconstitutional by a unanimous Supreme Court in its judgment in *Brown v. Board of Education.*

It was equally clear to me that the synagogue in Englewood could find direction only if it accepted the discipline of one of the major religious denominations of American Jews. The congregation had begun by defining itself as more liberal in its religious outlook than the Orthodox synagogue in town, but the people of Temple Emanu-El had never been able to make up their minds what shade of liberal Judaism they belonged to. I told the interviewing committee that I could consider leaving Nashville and coming to Englewood only after the synagogue had sorted itself out. I suggested that the leaders of the synagogue had first to accept the discipline of Conservative Judaism so that the encounter between their new rabbi, whoever he might be, and the laity would occur within a frame of reference that everyone accepted.

At the end of the evening several of those who had been at the meeting took me out for a cup of coffee. They told me that they had already interviewed some twenty candidates. They flattered me that I was the unanimous choice of the committee, but they begged me to be "more flexible." By then it was nearly midnight and I was tired enough not to be able to find a gracious way of responding. Instead I asked a very blunt question: what has happened to the several rabbis whom you have had as your spiritual leaders through the nearly three decades in which the congregation has existed? Obviously, they had agreed to be "flexible," and, even more obviously, this flexibility did not help them survive in the congregation. I added that I could not be the rabbi of a synagogue where, essentially, I had no religious authority. I left that midnight meeting certain that I would never hear from Englewood again.

In the next few months I continued to look for an appointment back in the Northeast, but I heard from none of the posts that attracted me. The one rabbinic appointment, in Canada, that I did want rejected me in a split vote in its board. They found me to be too much the intellectual and too little the backslapper, and even less like the rabbi of their dreams, whom they wanted to resemble the chief executive officer of a substantial enterprise. But one day I was astounded by a call from Englewood: they asked to talk to me again. Would I please fly to New York as soon as I could? They were willing to meet my terms. A few days later, I was back in the same room in which the contentious discussion had taken place nearly a year before. In the interim they had interviewed a dozen more candidates, but they could not agree on any one of them. The bulk of the committee had kept coming back to the conversation with me in the spring of 1955. They had come to agree with my argument that the congregation had to stop being a do-it-yourself establishment; it needed a set of rules like those that almost all other synagogues obeyed. The renewed offer of the rabbinic post contained no sweeteners. All the other conditions of the contract were exactly the same as those that they had offered me the year before, but the definition of my role had changed profoundly. They had accepted that I should be the authority who would define the ritual and ethical standards governing the congregation.

Despite the victory, I could not bring myself to accept the appointment on the spot. I wanted to go back to Nashville to talk with Phyllis and with several friends in town. I needed the advice of Manuel Eskind, who had been the president of the West End Synagogue for almost all the years that I had been there, and of Jennings Perry, who was my mentor in the intricacies of southern life and national politics. A good bit of my uncertainty was rooted in the fact that the congregation in Englewood was still worshiping in a private house in which the living room had been extended to provide space for one hundred fifty people for Sabbath services. Plans were well advanced to build a new building, but only part of the money had been raised. I would be leaving Nashville, where the congregation was well housed, well off, and stable, for Englewood, where I had to create over again what I was leaving behind.

As I was ambivalent, the committee in Englewood decided to send its two best "salesmen" to Nashville. These were Meyer Halpern, the president of the synagogue, and Fred Thomases, his closest friend, who was the major power among the trustees of Temple Emanu-El. They came to reassure me, and especially my wife, that they would stand loyally with me—that they would both be true to their words until the end of their days. They enthusiastically insisted that the new building would be erected on schedule, within a year, and that the congregation as a whole would be transformed by the new energy that I would bring. Their visit convinced Phyllis and me that we should accept the appointment. Meyer and Fred were clearly two people whom we could trust. They went back the next day holding an agreement in which I accepted an initial appointment to be rabbi in Englewood for three years beginning in the summer of 1956.

My first serious battle took place within days of our arrival. I was again confronted by some of the lay leaders who wanted to continue to define the religious program of the congregation, without benefit of clergy. I thought that I had slain this dragon a year earlier, but it still lived. Part of the agreement that Meyer Halpern and Fred Thomases had worked out with me was that the congregation would retire all of its homemade prayer books and use the order of service that was then accepted in the overwhelming majority of Conservative synagogues. I had, in fact, ordered such prayer books, but, some days after Phyllis, the children, and I arrived in Englewood, I was again challenged to relent: could I not use the prayer books to which the congregation was accustomed for at least one more year until they would gradually learn to accept the new regime? I repeated my arguments against gradualism, but I realized that I was not winning hearts and minds. My voice became very quiet and controlled. I knew myself well enough to be aware that I could be argued out of positions that I announced at the top of my voice but not those that I expressed very quietly. I said to this delegation, We have an agreement, so let's stick to it.

So, that very first High Holiday we worshiped as an avowedly traditionalist congregation. I had inspected the kitchen of Emanu-El to make sure that it would henceforth be kosher by the strictest standards. And I had made sure that the facilities we were going to build into the new building would be in conformity with the rules of the Jewish religious tradition, albeit with the understanding that we would interpret the rules in the spirit of the middle-of-the-road denomination to which we now adhered. Conservative Judaism was more flexible than the strictest Orthodoxy. We had joined the Jewish version of a "High Church Episcopalian" denomination—that is, to be deeply traditionalist, but with some tolerance for a bit of liberalism both in religious practice and in theology.

After the initial rush of settling into Englewood was over, I had the time to reflect on what I had wrought. To my chagrin I realized that I was in some ways no different from the members of the lay committee that had been fashioning the religion of the congregation before I had come on the scene. They wanted a congregation in which they could feel comfortable. For them, that meant that they would hear some of the melodies that still rang in their ears from their earliest days on the Lower East Side of New York. At celebrations, such as Bar Mitzvahs and weddings, they wanted to eat food that could have come out of their mothers' or grandmothers' kitchens. But they did not want to be bound by the strict and precise rules of Jewish religious law. I wanted a synagogue that would adhere to Jewish practice, even as I insisted on the freedom to change some of the rules, and especially those that discriminated against women. I wanted to be able to explain the Bible as containing records of the encounters of our ancestors with God but not as a text that was literally true in every word.

So, what was the difference between me and the lay leaders of Temple Emanu-El? At the time I thought I was refighting the age-old battle for rabbinic authority, but I really did not understand the nature of the battle as it was unfolding. The tension between the congregants and me had their roots in a difference in backgrounds. The congregants who wanted to cling to their homemade prayer book and their kosher-

style kitchen were carrying forward the folk Judaism of their not terribly well educated forebears. I wore as a badge, often too defiantly, my
descent from many generations of rabbis and scholars. My emotional
center was rooted in the deeply Orthodox way of life in which I had
been raised. I was willing to move from it only to the degree that I
needed to accommodate what I had learned and accepted in the wider
Western world, in the domain of college and university. I was going to
remain as obedient as possible to the Law, even as I had come to suspect
that the Law itself was mostly manmade and even as I could no longer
accept some of its injunctions. My congregants wanted a version of
Judaism that made them feel warm; I wanted to define a version of
Judaism in which I could believe.

These issues simmered beneath the surface in my early days as rabbi
of the congregation. Initially, we were much too busy with the new
building of the synagogue. We actually moved into that structure right
before the High Holidays in September of 1957. The floor was still bare
concrete with no carpet to soften it, and we sat on folding chairs, but we
were elated to be in a sanctuary of our own.

The architects who had designed the building kept repeating that
they expected to win some important international prize for their orig-
inality. They had not gone the fairly conventional route of putting a
dome over the synagogue. It soared upward with lots of clear glass
framed by wooden girders. This synagogue was supposed to symbolize
the tent that Moses and the children of Israel had carried with them for
forty years in the desert on the way to the promised land. From the very
first moment that I became aware of the architectural plans, they made
me uncomfortable. The ancient tent of meeting had been constructed
primarily out of cloth and not out of wood and glass. I could not imagine that Moses and the children of Israel had carried acres of wood and
glass with them during forty years of wandering—but I had more
immediate, pragmatic worries. I was concerned that the building might
leak, that the wooden girders would expand and contract with the sea-
sons and thus rain would fall upon us: we would have to sit inside the
sanctuary under umbrellas! These doubts were swept aside by the architects, who asserted that the wooden girders had been specially treated
to remain firm and unmoving. Unfortunately, my fears were soon justified. The new building was haunted for a number of years by leaks, until

its signature, the wooden "tent of meeting," had to be taken down and replaced by a more mundane, lower roof.

In the years that followed I had to work on a transition that we did not even define as it was happening. I had come to the congregation when it was moving beyond its origins as an out-of-the-way, small synagogue for the neighborhood to become a busy and sizable institution. The number of children in the religious school doubled and then redoubled. Even though we had appointed professional leadership for the school, I regarded it as a major responsibility to remain closely involved. I taught a group of teenagers some of the easier texts in the Talmud, and I had a hand in choosing teachers for the school to make sure that they would be role models for their students. But I took great pains to respect the leadership of the principal of the religious school, Nat Entin, who was also the cantor of the congregation. He belonged to a then newer school of educators who were entranced by the educational efficiencies that had just become available through the earliest, first-generation computer-like machines and other gadgets, which supposedly made learning easier. I belonged to the old-fashioned school, believing that one child and a machine does not make a lesson. Learning is imparted when a caring teacher is in the room with children and teenagers. Nonetheless, I kept my peace and even fought for the budget that paid for these innovations.

Unfortunately, this self-restraint did not help the personal relations between Nat Entin and myself. He felt constrained by having to deal with me at all. After several years, he announced that he would prefer to work directly with the lay board of the synagogue. Nat Entin was both the cantor and the religious-school principal, so he chafed at being condemned by age-old Jewish practice to remain subordinate to the rabbi. When his request was denied by the board, he resigned. I regretted it at the time. When I have looked back on these events of more than four decades ago, some unhappiness remains within me. The closest that I have ever come to being able to understand this fight was through the simple insight that some people are inspired, and condemned, by temperament with the need to be number one. This is particularly true of musical soloists, such as cantors, and of those who regard themselves as innovators in any field.

The largest trouble within the congregation that I ever brought upon

myself was caused by the discretionary power that I had acquired to forgive some or all of the payments owed to the temple by people who
came to me pleading poverty. These encounters were always private.
Usually the decisions that I took were not questioned, but one of these
rulings did explode in my face. Dues had been forgiven for a teenager
who had been for years a good student in our school and was now continuing further studies with a small group under my guidance. This
young man, however, was found by a financial officer of the congregation to belong to a very rich family. This lay leader of the congregation
was outraged that I had been giving the young man's mother a "free
ride" for several years and that I had again written down on this
teenaged boy's registration that he was on the free list. The financial
secretary who had found this notation was very soon in my office in a
roaring huff. I explained to him that the family situation of this
teenager was much more complicated than he knew. To be sure, the
teenager's grandfather, his mother's father, was quite wealthy, but the
grandfather was very angry with the youngster's mother, because she
had married out of the faith, and the immediate family lived in poverty,
hand to mouth. The teenaged boy who was in our school could not
appeal to his grandfather to make some contribution to the synagogue
in appreciation of what we were doing for him because the grandfather
was too embittered. The financial officer of the congregation simply
refused to think about any of this. All that he saw was a rich old man
who was not paying his rightful dues. I agreed, but I insisted that we
could not make his defenseless grandson the victim of our just demands—and so, by fiat, I said that this young man would remain in the
religious school. The lay leader who had challenged me remained, on
the surface, a warm friend of mine, but fundamentally our relationship
had soured. He could not bear the thought of being overruled.

That day I was more than a little bit downcast because I knew that
I had lost a friend and supporter—but some years later, when this
young man was in his last year of college, I discovered that the authorities in the heavenly court seem to have both a long memory and a
sense of humor. The late 1960s and early 1970s were the time of student rebellion. In some of the colleges one of the expressions of that
unrest was the insistence of the students that they participate in
choosing the candidates for honorary degrees. One day in the spring

of 1970 I received a telephone call from the president of Lafayette College. He told me that they were inviting me to accept an honorary doctorate at graduation time that June. I was pleased but also surprised, so I asked him, Why did you choose me? He replied that a young man whose name I immediately recognized was president of the senior class and that he had taken the lead in suggesting my name for this honor. Of course, I accepted without hesitation. Since that first honorary degree more such honors have followed, but the very first at Lafayette has remained uniquely precious. I had earned it not by discovering a new principle in physics, or by writing the "great American novel," but as the reward for defending and befriending a young person.

In my first years in Englewood I behaved very foolishly. The established practice of newcomers to a community was to make themselves secure by annoying as few people as possible. I did the opposite. I would not let the principal of the religious school get rid of children whom he found inconvenient, even disruptive, so I upset not only him but a number of parents who preferred that their "normal" children not be upset by the oddballs in their classes. I provoked a battle about the finances of the temple, and the result of my victory was that we taxed the rich to help the poor. I have never found many among the rich who enjoyed paying more taxes or higher synagogue dues to pay for programs for the poor. Whenever this issue had to be fought out again, some of the elected officials of the congregation opposed me. The reasons that they gave did not matter; what really bothered these lay leaders was that their power was limited because I kept intervening. I do not think that any of the members of the board of trust had read *Murder in the Cathedral*, T. S. Eliot's play about Thomas à Becket. The point of that drama is that the priest's much beloved old friend, King Henry, had become his most vehement enemy. Henry asked his entourage, Who will rid me of this troublesome priest? I soon made some of the congregation leadership feel the same way. I just could not see a different path before me. Despite all the charm that I could muster, and all the innumerable cups of coffee over which I explained myself to people who were upset by what I was doing, and all of my prayers, I had no choice; I was trapped. But what trapped me?

I found that I could occasionally deviate from some ritual injunction in the canon of rabbinic teaching, but I could not move one inch away from the moral outlook of the Talmud. It does not matter how exactly you define your theological beliefs or even what high-sounding principles you assert, God's ultimate demand is that each of us do his best for specific people, for individuals, and especially for those who are weak. To derive a career advantage from looking away when the weak and the friendless are being despoiled is an unforgivable sin. It was a sin that my father and mother had never committed. They knew that God had commanded them to defend the defenseless. Every time that I wanted to "get smart" and "get along," I was restrained by the example of my parents, by the tradition that their parents had handed down to them. I was the next generation—imperfect and far from holy—but it was impossible for me to walk away from the pain of the poor. So I fought battles that a more worldly-wise young man would have avoided. Only now, many years after the beginnings of my career, do I understand why I have kept quoting the explanation in the Talmud of the life of Joseph in Egypt. Here he was, in the court of Pharaoh, subject to all the temptations of a glittering pagan society, and yet he did not forget the Hebrew that he had spoken in his youth in his parents' home or the values by which they had lived. Englewood was not the glory of ancient Egypt, but the lesson remained the same.

To be sure, I was not enlisting for the first time in Englewood in the age-old battle between prophets and kings, and later between Talmudic sages and political leaders, and later still between rabbis and Jewish magnates for the control of the community. I was still on the side into which I had been born many years before. I was reaffirming that I would never budge from the party of the classic rabbis. My ancestors had never thought of themselves as the employees of the laity of their community. They worked for the good Lord as they understood His will, and they had been signing themselves for many centuries as His servants who happened to dwell in whatever town they might be living, and studying, and teaching. It was particularly important for me, when I finally came to greater New York, the largest Jewish community that the world had ever seen, that I make it clear to myself even before it became evident to others that I was the servant of my Jewish conscience—and of no one else. I was not quite alone in this conviction, but too many rabbis lived in fear for their careers. In my first years in

Englewood I would often tell my father about the hot water in which I often landed. His invariable reaction was to ask, So what can they do to you? The worst that they can do is fire you, but, fortunately, we are living in America. It is a big country with many possibilities. Surely you could always make some kind of a living selling shoes. For the rest of my rabbinic career, whenever I was in hot water, my joyous mantra was that I could always change careers and sell shoes.

But as soon as I could, I did take out an "insurance policy." I found a way in 1960, during my fourth year as the rabbi of Temple Emanu-El, to get the board of the synagogue to vote me life tenure. What I was granted was the equivalent of professorial tenure, with the specific understanding that I was as free as a tenured professor in academe to make the case for my convictions.

Some of the leaders of the congregation were astonished at this request, and one of them, Max Grobow, even offered to pay me, from his own pocket, $10,000 a year more than I could get elsewhere if I only would withdraw the request for life tenure. I asked Max why this mattered to him, and he answered that "so long as the board retains the power to reappoint you or to let you go, we are the boss. The moment you have life tenure, we are no longer the ultimate power in the congregation." I congratulated him for understanding the situation as clearly as he did. Then I added that I would continue to battle for life tenure in my job precisely because I wanted to be free from the fear of the board.

What gave me strength and, yes, the leverage with which to insist on life tenure was an offer that had come to me from one of the major synagogues in the Midwest. This was a Conservative congregation that was as dominant in its region as the Reform Temple Emanuel was commonly acknowledged to be in the New York area. This Midwestern synagogue had been through some difficulties with its clergy. The leaders wanted to make a fresh beginning so they invited me to visit with them and, almost immediately, offered me the post of senior rabbi. I really wanted to stay in Englewood, as I enjoyed the life of New York, but this offer was a glittering one. I could have easily made peace with being the rabbi of this legendary synagogue.

On the way back to Englewood, I decided that I would call the leaders of the board and tell them the truth. I was tempted to leave, but there was one thing in the gift of the congregation that would keep me in Englewood: being voted life tenure. Inevitably this unexpected request caused a lot of commotion, but within less than two weeks the board had to vote. The result was life tenure for me and, at the age of thirty-nine, with hopefully many years of work ahead of me, I was now free of the usual abrasions of the rabbi in a pulpit. I was free to tell the truth as I saw it.

D espite all the promises to myself, and even to others, that I would stay out of the public arena until the congregation itself was made stable, I could not quite keep away from the international scene. On reflection in later years, I realized that I needed to find a role in the politics of the Jewish people worldwide because I had not forgiven myself then—and not yet, even to this day—for my good fortune in being safe in America during the years in which Hitler persecuted and murdered Jews with impunity. I had taken part, at some distance, in the battle for the state of Israel and had even gone there for several months in 1949 when the war with the Arabs was essentially over, but that did not absolve me. I needed a role in which I would make a difference, a real difference. Therefore, when I arrived in the New York area in the summer of 1956, I accepted an appointment as chair of the international-affairs committee of the Synagogue Council of America. This was a loose association of the rabbinic and lay bodies of the three Jewish denominations in America: Orthodox, Conservative, and Reform. Its function was limited, by the will of the constituents, to representing the Jewish religious community as a whole in external affairs. When I took the appointment, I expected that it would not amount to much, but it did not turn out that way.

In October 1956, Israel chose to take part in a war that no one expected. The military situation in its part of the Middle East had been heating up for two separate reasons. Gamal Abdel Nasser, the leader of Egypt, had nationalized the Suez Canal, which was critical to the positions of France and Britain in the Middle East. At the same time, Nasser had been conducting a "war of attrition" against the newly created state of Israel by allowing the fedayeen (Palestinian Arab guerrillas) to infiltrate across the border between the Gaza Strip (which was under Egyptian control) and southern Israel. In secret talks the Israelis and the French and British agreed to coordinate military operations against Nasser. The Israelis moved south and west to conquer the Gaza Strip and the whole of the Sinai Peninsula; the French and British invaded Egypt by sea to seize back control of the Suez Canal. The British and the French soon withdrew under an ultimatum from the American president, Dwight David Eisenhower, but the Israelis remained in place in the Sinai and on the eastern shore of the Red Sea. Nasser portrayed himself in Egypt, and in the whole of the Arab world, as the heroic victor over the two major Western powers, but he could not reopen the Suez Canal without getting the Israelis out of the Sinai Peninsula, so he appealed to the United Nations to get back that territory. There was an impasse for several months. The Israelis would not even think of withdrawing unless they had an absolute guarantee that guerrilla warfare against them would cease.

The arena for the diplomatic battle between Israel and the Egyptians was in New York, at the United Nations. Almost everyone who might influence either the Israelis or the Egyptians was set in motion to persuade one or the other side "to be reasonable," whatever that might mean at any specific moment in these torturous discussions. That winter I was very much surprised to find that I was one of the many who were thought to have some influence.

My peer in the Protestant community in America was Ernest Gross. He was chair of the international-affairs committee of the National Council of Churches and had been an ambassador of the United States to the United Nations in the late 1940s, working together with Warren Austin when the partition of Palestine was voted on in November 1947. Gross was a very serious diplomat with very broad contacts; I was a beginner who knew the leaders of Israel, many of them very well, but I did not have Gross's connections or any part of his experience. He soon invited me to meet him to discuss what we could do together to help defuse the crisis. From the first moment of our acquaintance Gross treated me with extraordinary courtesy. He taught me how to behave in diplomatic circles without ever making it obvious that he knew that he was training a beginner. We began a friendship that lasted to the end of his life.

The pressure kept mounting on Israel to withdraw. Gross arranged for him and me, together with one or two of our associates on each side, to meet with the top officials of the United Nations. We convened on the thirty-seventh floor of the Secretariat building in the office of Andrew Cordier, who was then the undersecretary general for political affairs. Dr. Ralph Bunche, who had won the Nobel Prize for getting Israel and its Arab neighbors to sign a set of armistice agreements that ended the hostilities of 1948–49, was in the room. This was the very day, February 17, 1957, when John Foster Dulles had summoned Abba Eban, Israel's ambassador to the United Nations and to Washington, to the State Department to give him what amounted to a dressing-down. He told Eban that the Israelis had to get out of the Sinai Peninsula and return to their own borders. The delegation from the Synagogue Council did not know, that day, of this meeting in Washington, but we did understand that Israel could not possibly retreat without assurance that the guerrilla war against it would not start up again across the Gaza border.

It soon became clear that this meeting had been called because the United Nations Secretariat was prepared to inject a new element into the diplomatic mix. Andrew Cordier proposed that a United Nations force, made up of contingents from several neutral countries (I am not sure whether he actually specified that they would come from Yugoslavia and India) be interposed on the border between the Gaza Strip and Israel. These "soldiers of peace" would be the assurance to Israel that it would not again be attacked. Ralph Bunche seconded Cordier's remarks by adding the proviso that these troops could never be removed without the approval of Israel. To make sure that we got the point and transmitted it correctly and in full force, Bunche added, with considerable emotion, that Israeli negotiators had dealt with him at very close and intimate quarters just a few years ago when he was the intermediary in the armistice talks between Israel and its Arab adversaries. The Israeli leadership had reason to trust him, and he was giving his word that this buffer would never be removed without Israel's consent. I then asked the obvious question: "Gentlemen, so what do you want us, three rabbis from the American Diaspora who do not make Israel's policy, to do?" Cordier was prepared with an answer, in which he was supported by my new friend, Ernest Gross: "You do know the responsible people in the Israeli government. Please go talk to them, conveying what we have said and promised." I replied that I would talk immediately, the next morning, with Golda Meir, the foreign minister of Israel, who was then in New York, to convey to her both the content and the atmosphere of this conversation.

I had been particularly impressed with the gravity of the occasion because people on the U.N. side kept shuttling in and out of the room to a much larger office next door. No one pretended that they were doing anything other than informing Dag Hammerskjöld, the secretary general, and getting further instructions from him. It occurred to me, even when I was still in the room, in the heady atmosphere of talking directly with the principal associates of the secretary general, that this meeting had been held to "turn my head," to make me an advocate in my conversation with Golda Meir. I did retain enough presence of mind, even as I breathed this very rarefied air, to tell Mr. Cordier and Dr. Bunche that I could only promise them that I would convey the message in all its nuances but I did not have the power to twist Golda Meir's arm.

I left the meeting in the middle of the afternoon and headed for a telephone to arrange to see Golda Meir. Within an hour Ernest Gross had already telephoned me to find out if I had accomplished anything. On later reflection, I was persuaded that he knew about the pressure that John Foster Dulles was putting on Abba Eban that very day and that his taking me to the United Nations was part of the same endeavor. The secret, if it even was a secret, was out by the next morning. The newspapers were announcing that Abba Eban had seen the secretary of state and had immediately caught an airplane to Israel to report to the prime minister, the redoubtable David Ben-Gurion. That morning, as Eban was en route to Israel, a very angry Golda Meir let me come to see her at her hotel in midtown Manhattan. She even ordered up a pot of coffee for the two of us. Golda Meir already knew, of course, what Dulles had said to Eban. The only thing that interested her in my account was Ralph Bunche's promise that the United Nations military force would never be withdrawn without Israel's consent. She was more than skeptical that this promise would be kept, and she made no secret that she was opposed to any Israeli withdrawal. The most that she agreed to do in response to my tale of the adventures of Arthur Hertzberg on the thirty-seventh floor of the United Nations was to send a coded message to the prime minister. By the next day the press of the world knew that David Ben-Gurion had decided to pull back. He did not want a diplomatic confrontation with a not particularly friendly government in Washington. Ben-Gurion put the best face on the withdrawal. He announced with satisfaction that he had received a promise from the United Nations that the fedayeen raids would stop.

My rather minor role in this crisis came to a climax ten years later during the Six-Day War of June 1967. Israel had not been able to stop Nasser from demanding the withdrawal of the United Nations troops on the Israeli border. The departure of the Indian and then the Yugoslav contingents were the most immediate signals for hostilities. The keeper of the United Nations promise, Ralph Bunche, was by then a broken man, having suffered a major family tragedy. Neither Bunche nor the new secretary general, U Thant, was willing to keep the promise that the United Nations had made in 1957: that it would never withdraw the U.N. troops from the Sinai without the consent of Israel. It has even been said (I am persuaded that this assessment is reliable) that Nasser more than expected the United Nations to forbid him from pushing the peacekeepers out. Nasser was blustering before the Arab world, expecting that he would be able to say that he wanted to fight Israel but that, while he wanted a fight, the U.N. had tied his hands. But the U.N. failed to remember its role in this script, so the Six-Day War took place.

Golda Meir was then out of office, but she was sent posthaste to New York to rally American opinion, and especially American Jewish opinion, on the side of Israel as it faced this Arab threat. Within a day or two of her arrival, the Zionist movement had a public meeting in New York. I was on the dais among the dignitaries. As Golda Meir saw me ascending the stairs leading to the platform, she walked toward me, her face a mask, which must have been the one she wore as a young woman in Milwaukee when she was a kindergarten teacher about to chastise some unruly child. Golda Meir did not waste a second on any of the amenities of greeting. She simply looked me straight in the eye and said, "That was a very bad day's work you did ten years ago." The messenger of that day was remembered as guilty of bringing a message that she had not wanted to hear.

The hectic days of diplomacy in mid-February 1957 were not followed by more political high drama. That would come some years later, when I became an active participant in defining and defending the position of the Jewish people as a whole in international affairs. I did not miss the pressure and the excitement of those few days in February 1957. On the contrary, immediately after Israel agreed to withdraw from the Sinai, I went back both to the congregation, to a normal, everyday life, and to my study, to finish my first book, an anthology of Zionist thought. I had begun the book in Nashville and had brought the bulk of an unfinished manuscript with me to Englewood. There was to be a long introductory essay to explain why modern Zionism had appeared on the world stage and what difference it had made, which was followed by writings of major Zionist thinkers. When the telephone stopped ringing after the political crisis was over, I returned to my desk with a sense of eagerness and of urgency. I had become tired of writing the book and could not find the zest for finishing the task, but my short and intense flight in the political stratosphere had reminded me that the problems that I had set before me some years before—to explain the meaning of Jewish experience in the modern era—were very real and very immediate. I had to address them.

In the early 1940s, while I was still a student in the rabbinical school of the Jewish Theological Seminary, I had been given permission to take some courses at Columbia University under the guidance of Salo Baron, who was then the premier scholar of Jewish history and especially of the modern period. In Baron's classes and in his doctoral seminar for graduate students, I soon found the fundamental problem that I felt compelled to confront. In the past two centuries the Jews had entered, at least in part, the world of the Gentile majority. This did not happen in one grand moment in which European society granted the Jews political and social equality. On the contrary, this history was one of many battles, in many places. Sometimes Jews found ways to enter the majority culture long before they were granted the political rights of citizens. There were more anomalies and discontinuities in the journey of Jews from the ghetto to some equality, but this complex history could be summarized in a few short, fundamental questions: what changes were demanded of the Jews as the price they had to pay for being allowed into the majority society? What changes did making room for the Jews require of the majority? What did either group do when it found that it was not willing to pay the price for change or, even more painfully, when it concluded that the other party to this transaction had not done and would not do what it promised—that is, when the Gentiles concluded that the Jews would never assimilate enough to be acceptable or when Jews became bitter because nothing that they could do would save them from rejection? I knew very early, as a young man who was no older than twenty-two or twenty-three, that these questions would be central to my life's work as scholar. Even that early, I knew that I would not spend my intellectual career on writing footnotes, even though I would prove, rather defiantly, in several of my books that would come later that I had mastered the technique. But I had no desire to play that game that preoccupied the academic guild. My task would be to think through and answer the very fundamental questions that I had defined for myself.

In the late 1940s and early 1950s I was casting about, as graduate students are wont to do, for a dissertation topic when a project that belonged to my own grand design fell into my lap. Emanuel Neumann, a veteran leader of the Zionists in America, wrote and telephoned me in 1953 asking me to do a book explaining Zionism for future generations, who would probably soon forget the prehistory of the new state of Israel. He offered me whatever help I might need from the publishing arm in America of the World Zionist Organization, and he surprised me by agreeing that neither he nor anyone else would oversee my work for political acceptability. I would be free to choose the sources that I would include in the book, or exclude from it, and I could explain the subject in all of its complexities according to my own judgment. Dr. Neumann, who had once himself taught history in a high school in New York, was totally scrupulous in keeping his promises. He never saw the book (it was published in 1959 under the title *The Zionist Idea*) until I gave him a copy of the galley proofs. After reading them, he said to me that he might have done one or two things differently, but he actually embraced me and thanked me for my work. I knew very well that in the politics of the world Zionist movement Emanuel Neumann had been a redoubtable fighter, and in-fighter, for many decades, but in the realm of learning he behaved with exemplary restraint.

My first task was to read (mostly, to reread) many thousands of pages of the writings of those whom I regarded as the founders of the various schools of Zionist thought. That was actually the easiest part of my work. Just a few years before I had divided my time as a rabbinical student and a graduate student at Columbia between studying the Talmud and reading the Zionist sources. The more difficult, technical task was to translate some hundreds of pages of this material from four languages. By the time I arrived in Englewood, these tasks were essentially finished, but I had not yet written the introductory essay, which turned out to be a short book in its own right. I thought I knew the answers to most of the questions that had been raised by the founders of Zionism, but I kept pondering the unavoidable fundamental question: the basic assertion of modern Zionism was that it would make of the Jews a "normal people." The Zionist endeavor would gather all those who wanted to remain Jews into their own homeland. A new era would begin: the Jews as a national entity would be sovereign and independent, "just like everybody else."

By the mid-1950s it was unmistakably clear that the Zionist dream would not be realized in the form in which it had been dreamed. The bulk of the Jews of the world, especially those in the largest and most powerful Diaspora, the United States, would not immigrate en masse to Israel. The Zionist assertion that Jews in their own state would henceforth live without fear of the Gentiles, that they would no longer be a minority often subject to the will of others as they had been for many centuries in the Diaspora, seemed to me to be doubtful. And yet, the new state of Israel, though a small power not yet certain of the limits of its strength, had already made a profound difference for the Jews of the world. Hundreds of thousands of refugees kept coming to the one place in the world where Jews controlled the government and where, therefore, Jews could not again easily be the victims of anti-Semitism. The holiest places in Israel were its ports of entry—there no immigration official could ever say that the Jewish quota was full.

Yet I was not persuaded that even the triumph of creating the state of Israel was the beginning of a "messianic era" when the lamb, the Jewish people, and the wolves, its enemies, would soon be dwelling together in peace. Being on the edges of the military-political crisis of 1957 made it very clear to me not only that Israel was, and was likely to remain, a small state but that it would be, at least in the foreseeable future, the "Jew" among the states: It would remain in an often marginal place in the political arena. In the last pages of the essay that introduced *The Zionist Idea,* I reflected this somber conclusion. England and France had knuckled under a few months earlier to an order from the United States, and the heroic David Ben-Gurion had withdrawn fairly meekly under the same pressure. Yes, the Zionist vision had created a state among the states, but what did sovereignty mean in a world in which the big powers so easily intimidated the smaller actors on the political stage?

Almost all the Zionist thinkers had insisted that the "normalization" of the Jews would make an end of anti-Semitism. No one expected it to happen overnight, but the notion was widely shared that the sight of a Jewish army and the tales of its valor in the very recent wars of Israel would raise respect for Jews and make anti-Semitism ever less acceptable, at least among decent people. I knew this was not true from my own life in Englewood, a respectable middle- to upper-class suburb that was still dominated by a political establishment of old-line Protestant families. Their prime social expression of their power was in two clubs. One was a place where they played golf together, the Knickerbocker Country Club; the other was a smaller establishment where they ate together and played tennis and swam together, the Englewood Field Club. Our house shared a piece of back fence with the Field Club. Our daughters, who were then very young, under ten, could look across the fence at the swimming pool in which children whom they knew from school were swimming on the hot afternoons of the summer. Phyllis and I had explained to Linda and Susan that they could not go over there and swim because we would not be allowed to become members of this facility.

I chose not to accept this exclusion. From our street, the shortest way to get to the Englewood Field Club was to walk down our driveway and go through an always open door in the fence that marked the boundary between the two properties. One day I telephoned the general manager of the Field Club and told him that I would no longer allow this accommodation. I insisted that an adequate fence be put up so that the separation that the Englewood Field Club had ordained would actually exist. The fence was put up by the Field Club. Thus, I made my point to the local anti-Semites—but as a scholar I had to keep thinking about the causes of this disease. It was part of the larger question that I had set for myself: to understand what happened when Jews and non-Jews encountered each other in the modern age.

In the spring of 1960, Phyllis and I had to face another painful aspect of living as Jews in a supposedly open society. The best kindergarten in the neighborhood was part of a private school that had been endowed by the Morrow family in memory of a daughter, Elisabeth Morrow (a sister of Anne Morrow Lindbergh), who had died young. The headmistress of the school, Constance Chilton, had been born and educated in England, and she still retained both the accent and the way of thinking that she had learned in her youth. Phyllis went to see her to discuss the possibility that our daughter Linda might attend the kindergarten. Miss Chilton was very warm and accepting. She and Phyllis immediately got on well together, and as headmistress of this private school Constance Chilton was farsighted enough to know that more and more of her students would have to come from the growing Jewish population in Englewood and the surrounding towns. Linda was admitted to the school, and she seemed to be content there. Nonetheless, even at the age of five, she sensed that she was in a minority. Most of the others in the class were the children and grandchildren of families from the Presbyterian and Episcopalian churches in town.

Linda said nothing about her discomfort at being kept at a distance by her schoolmates, until the Passover festival that early spring. She knew that we did not eat leavened bread during Passover so we planned to send her to school during the intermediate days of the festival with sandwiches of matzohs. On the very first day Linda came home hungry and very tearful. She had not unwrapped her lunch to eat even one bite of it. She did not want to worsen her situation in this kindergarten by being openly different.

Phyllis and I kept her out of the school for the next few days until Passover was over. We then made an appointment with Miss Chilton.

She immediately understood the problem and was very sympathetic. She offered to do anything she could to make life more bearable for Linda, and she even went to the length of offering her younger sister, Susan, a place in the kindergarten and then in the school when her turn came. When I told her that I would have difficulty affording tuition for the two of them, the response was very generous. The headmistress would make sure that the bills that were sent to us would be in the range that we could afford. Nonetheless, Phyllis and I felt that we had to move Linda in the fall into public school. There she would find a number of other Jewish children in class. The snootiness that even the young seem to imbibe at a very early age would not be so prevalent. We remained friends with Connie Chilton for many years until she retired and left town, but our children went to public school. I did not yet have to answer the question of whether they should go to a Jewish day school because none had yet been created in our neighborhood, but I had to ponder, over and over again, the question of how to raise Jewish children to be themselves in a society that frowned upon their otherness.

One thing I knew beyond the slightest doubt: I could not encourage them to assimilate. That conclusion was seemingly self-evident, because I was a rabbi and a descendant of many generations of rabbis. I would be expected—and would expect of myself—to insist that my children be taught to care about the Jewish tradition and to understand the history and values of our kind. But my experiences as a young father, a scholar of the history of Zionism, and a debutant in representing Jewish interests in world politics had added together to teach me another lesson. The Jew who tries to assimilate is abandoning his own identity in the hope that those who speak for the majority culture will welcome him, or her, and pronounce Jews to be acceptable in their society. But I knew from my own life that this seldom happened.

As I pondered this situation I was saddened—and outraged—by a "discovery." Our believing Jewish ancestors had for centuries appointed the Almighty as their judge and jury. He decided whether His Jewish children were behaving well, in obedience to His commandments, and He determined their destiny. In this more skeptical age Jews had discharged God from His task as their judge and jury. In His place they had put the Gentiles. They would decide whether Jews were becoming adequately assimilated to the way of life of the majority. I felt outraged at my own people, at the moral vulgarity of abandoning awe and trembling before God to accept instead a life of awe and trembling before the admission committees of Gentile country clubs. In the very months in which I was pondering all these issues, I met Horace Kallen, who half a century earlier had first proposed cultural pluralism, in place of the melting pot, as the proper definition of American society. But Kallen's vision did not quickly succeed. Jews were still fighting for acceptance by becoming "just like everybody else." Kallen once said to me, ruefully and bitterly, that the assimilationist Jew is someone who remains forever an amateur Gentile.

It would probably have been easier and more emotionally satisfying to my angry self if I had moved radically in the other direction, toward being part of creating in America a tight little island, a Jewish identity of urban Amish walling ourselves off from the rest of America by living our lives as law-abiding citizens who had very little to do with the larger society, but I knew that I could not do that. In the years since I had landed in New York Harbor at the age of five, I had become too much of an American, too addicted to the tasks of making American society more open to everyone and more generous in spirit. I cared deeply, passionately, for the continuity of the Jewish spirit, but it was from that spirit that I derived the injunction that I had no right to stand by while anyone else's blood was being shed. I had to find sources of energy within my own hurts and disappointments to stand up not only for my own kind but for everyone else.

It would not be easy to live such a life, for there were no existing precedents or sets of rules for how to be a passionately affirming Jew and a caring activist on the larger scene. The only answer to this dilemma that spoke to me I had once heard from Rabbi Stephen Wise. He was once asked which identity, being a Jew or an American, was the dominant one in his life. He replied that he had been a Jew for four thousand years and that he had been an American for seventy-six years—that is, for all of his conscious life. He added that he never felt that he had needed to choose between these unalterable foundations of his life. I knew that I would reach different conclusions than Stephen

Wise, that I would define myself both as an American and a Jew differently on occasion than Wise had, but I was comforted by his basic assertion: one can be both with great passion. Sometimes these identities clashed, but America—my America, the one in which immigrants could remember their past and be shaped by such memories—was strong enough to shelter and accommodate such contradictions.

16

The decade of the 1960s began well for me. Unexpected praise for my book *The Zionist Idea* came from Bayard Rustin, who was then the leading "public intellectual" of the civil rights movement. He told me that he had read the book in one gulp because he had found that, almost everywhere, he could have removed the word *Jew* and put in the word *Black*. Some of the Jewish reviewers went on the attack. They had trouble accepting my basic assumption: that modern Zionism was essentially a secular, even assimiliationist, movement to remake Jewish identity into one of the many modern secular nationalisms; it was not a reaffirmation of biblical religious doctrine that God had given the Holy Land to the Jews. I had asserted that the tie that bound most Zionists now to the ancestral land was not theology but historic memory and the need of much of the Jewish people for a place of refuge, a home of their own. An ironic observation of mine got me into the most hot water. I had noted that many Zionists lived secular lives, on the presumption that the biblical God did not exist, and yet they insisted that He had chosen the Jews and conferred upon us the land of Israel.

My introductory essay to *The Zionist Idea* did not represent a declaration of war on the politics of any one of the Zionist factions. All that

I had done, so far, amounted to a declaration of intellectual independence. I was not in awe of the wisdom of the Zionist leaders. I knew
these people in both Israel and America, for I had already worked with
them for years. I would not accept that even David Ben-Gurion or
Golda Meir, in their new roles as ministers of state in Israel, had
become infallible. I was, therefore, left with my own reasoning and with
what I could learn, and apply, from the sacred texts. I was a passionately
involved Jew, and a Zionist—but I could not belong to any faction or
party. I had to think for myself, and I kept hoping, and not always in
vain, that some others might find some truth in my words.

At the beginning of the 1960s I was defining myself as a dissenting
voice, and not only among the Zionists. On the American scene the
two great issues of the 1960s were the fight for racial integration and the
rising protest against American involvement in the war in Vietnam.
Here, too, I was a dissenter. My analytical essays led me to remain
deeply committed to the battle for racial integration, but I was ever
more insistent that Jews and Blacks were not always on the same side. I
never wavered in my opposition to the war in Vietnam, but I was more
and more disenchanted with various parts of the movement that
denounced the war. These views gave me a reputation as a maverick,
but such reactions to my writing had not yet created any widespread
assumption that I would really act on the principles that I was defining.
On the contrary, it was widely assumed that I would be prudent enough
not to try to lead fights with the institutions and factions that I was
challenging in my writings. I was being dared to prove that I would
stick by my guns. The tests would come some years later, in the late
1960s and early 1970s.

The appearance of *The Zionist Idea* did open the door immediately
to my being taken seriously as a historian and Jewish thinker. The
most serious and significant reaction to the book came from my
teacher at Columbia, Professor Salo Baron. He complained a bit that I
had chosen to do this major project on Zionism and had postponed the
writing of my doctoral dissertation, but he did allow that I said some
good and even true things in the introductory essay and that I had
made Zionism accessible to those who did not read the languages in
which the movement had been fashioned. Baron was nearing the age
of seventy, and his retirement from the faculty of Columbia University

would then be mandatory. He was, therefore, already thinking of how he could be replaced. He concluded that there was no younger scholar anywhere who had his mastery of all of Jewish history. Baron therefore proposed that a medievalist from Israel, Zvi Ankori, be invited to Columbia at the initial rank of assistant professor to cover the area of his competence and that I be appointed, part-time, to teach modern Jewish history. In the winter of 1960 the offer came that I give a course in the history of Zionism in the graduate faculty of the history department. I would thus be in the anomalous position of being technically a graduate student myself but I would be teaching other graduate students. The formal justification was that my dissertation was in the process of being finished; the informal explanation was that I had already published a book that could have been presented as a dissertation if I had chosen to write it in that form. The truth was that Baron wanted to leave Jewish history at Columbia in the hands of two of his disciples, both of whom would, he was sure, continue to look to him for guidance and approval for many years after his retirement. So, in the spring semester of 1961 I began at Columbia at the rank of lecturer in history. I was to stay there for nearly thirty years, most of that time as adjunct professor of history.

In Baron's home I was privileged to meet almost everyone from all over the world who was a serious scholar in Jewish history or worked in the efforts to rebuild Jewish life immediately after the Second World War. In the mid-1940s, Baron was the head of an organization called Jewish Cultural Reconstruction. It had been created to find and rescue the many hundreds of thousands of books that the Nazis had stolen and removed from all the Jewish libraries in Europe. The executive director of this effort was a young scholar, a refugee from Germany, named Hannah Arendt. Before the war she had been the leader in Germany of the Zionist youth moment, Blau Weiss ("blue white," the colors of the Zionist flag), and she had begun as a scholar by writing a dissertation on St. Augustine. In my conversations with Arendt in the 1940s, I found that she was no longer a Zionist and that she wanted to belong to the wider world of the international intelligentsia. She still longed for the intellectual circles in the Germany of her youth, but she had not yet found her own way of dealing with the Holocaust. She did not yet know what it meant for her.

My next encounter with Hannah Arendt was around 1960 when I was deep into the research for my dissertation on Jews and the French Enlightenment. I had been interested by her thesis in the first section of her book *The Origins of Totalitarianism* that modern anti-Semites hated most the assimilated, Westernized Jews with whom they were competing for jobs that the anti-Semites maintained the Jews should not hold because they were "foreign." I made an appointment to come and talk with Hannah Arendt about the work that I was doing on the anti-Semitism of major figures of the Enlightenment in France, in the hope that guidance and insight that she might provide would help me, but unfortunately traffic to New York that day was very bad. I was late for our meeting. She was furious and spent most of the time that we did have in chastising me for being late. Whatever I wrote about modern anti-Semitism in my book *The French Enlightenment and the Jews* owed something to her writing and very little to our conversation. As I left her, I was persuaded that even in exile she had lost nothing of the German addiction to punctuality.

My most serious encounter with Hannah Arendt took place a few years later. She had gone to Jerusalem in 1961 to cover the trial of Adolf Eichmann for the *New Yorker* magazine. Arendt described Eichmann in the dock as a very ordinary figure, a dull little man of no depth who possessed an extraordinary capacity to organize mass murder: the incarnation of the "banality of evil." Almost in passing, Arendt added that this persecution would have been less effective and less deadly if the organized Jewish communities had not cooperated, even in part. It would have been better still had they disbanded. This charge aroused much attention and fury. Arendt was charging the Jews with complicity in their own destruction. She showed little mercy for their powerlessness under the Nazis.

The main counterattack on her was leveled by an old friend of hers, a famous scholar of the Kabbalah, Gershom Scholem. He accused Hannah Arendt of lacking normal and healthy fellow feeling for Jews. I took a minor part in this debate by writing a few paragraphs, which essentially supported Gershom Scholem's critique. Several years later, I was uncomfortable enough about what I had written so that I reread her *Eichmann in Jerusalem*. I found that her critics had been responding to her unfairly, and so I wrote to her that "there are issues to be discussed, and . . . you raised almost all of them, but so far the discussion has not been equal to the searing dignity of the subject, or the seriousness of your analysis, which has been treated quite unfairly by almost everyone, and certainly by me in a few paragraphs." She never responded. Years later, after her death, I found that she had indeed commented on my letter. She had written to her old teacher and former lover, Martin Heidegger, that she had received a letter from me. She pretended that she barely knew of me, identifying me as a member of the Jewish establishment that was now apparently trying to apologize. This was, of course, absolutely untrue. My letter to her was not "official"; it represented no one but me. I remain very sorry that Hannah chose never to have this out with me face-to-face. I would have told her in such an encounter that in my reading of her she still seemed to be troubled by the question of her own survival while so many had died. She was still wrestling with the question of how much of a Jew she could admit to herself that she still was. I later discovered that she had asked Salo Baron to say Kaddish, the traditional Jewish memorial prayer, at her funeral.

My views mattered to Hannah Arendt because by the beginning of the 1960s I had been writing frequently for various journals, and giving public lectures in various places, about the major issues of the day. To be sure, the Eichmann trial in 1961 had put the Holocaust at the center of the Jewish agenda, but the dominant public issue in American society as a whole was the matter of race. The fight for racial integration was one that American Jews could join with enthusiasm. Most of the adults remembered the days only a decade or so earlier when they themselves had been excluded from full participation in American life, so they identified with the battle of the Blacks for equality. The organizations that represented the American Jewish establishment, without exception, were actively and even vehemently on the side of integration. There were many reasons for this unanimity. Chief among them was the lessons of both religion and history that Jews belonged on the side of the persecuted, but there was at least one other motive at play. For the first time in all of their history in America, Jews were not the problem; they were not the object of racial hatred. On the contrary, they were now among the problem solvers. By fighting for the Blacks, Jews were laying claim for a seat at the table among the American elite. This was a transforming moment in the life of the Jews of America.

The organized Jewish community was represented in these battles primarily by two organizations: the American Jewish Committee and the American Jewish Congress. They were then so completely dedicated to the efforts against segregation that nothing else in their agendas—neither the continuing effort to support Israel financially and politically nor the resistance to anti-Semitism—was equally prominent. The spirit of the time in the organized Jewish community was based on the assumption that achieving equality for Blacks in America would mean that no discrimination against Jews could possibly remain. I was not convinced, and I did not suppress my doubts.

In the spring of 1962 I was invited to speak at the national convention of the coordinating body, the National Jewish Community Relations Council, to which all the Jewish organizations who worked in the field of human relations belonged. This invitation was extended because my credentials seemed right. I had been the rabbi in Nashville who had gotten into trouble by being involved in the beginnings of the struggle for integration in the South. I was expected to deliver a ringing affirmation of the responsibility of Jews to take the lead in the struggle for racial equality and to conclude with a denunciation of all the reactionaries in the Jewish community who still held on to some parochial concerns. Unfortunately, I disappointed those who invited me, not only in detail but very fundamentally. I pointed out that Jews and Blacks had different agendas. The Black agenda, then, was that separateness should disappear. The energies of the Black community at the time were dedicated to making an end of that community so that Blacks as individuals could and would become part of the larger American society. The emphasis on negritude among Black intellectuals in Africa and Europe had become important in the 1950s, but it had not yet achieved comparable influence in the United States. Pride in their roots in African culture would blossom among the Black intelligentsia in America in the next decade, along with the attack on the "honkies" by younger nationalists who proclaimed their insistence on Black Power. Even in the early 1960s when Jews were driving hard toward their own integration in America, their agenda was basically different. They wanted to continue to be Jews, connected with each other by memory and tradition. Jews wanted a society in which their children would be free and untroubled in continuing to see life, at least in part, through the prism of Jewish religion and Jewish memory. I concluded that lecture by emphasizing that Jews had a moral obligation to help Blacks, who were still in deep trouble and pain in America, but that we had the right to remember our own specific concerns.

I was weakly applauded. Soon after, however, whispers were going around that I had turned reactionary and even, horror of horrors, treasonable. The leader of those who was putting out these assessments was a senior bureaucrat at the American Jewish Committee, Anne Wolf, who was in charge of their program in human relations. She told me with some vehemence that my views were wrong because they were based on premises that no progressive person could accept. The true aim of progressives was to create a society based on universal ideals that derived from the Enlightenment and the political revolutions of the nineteenth and twentieth centuries. I was introducing confusion into the discussion by telling Jews that their commitment to decency among men and women should be defined by the teachings of the prophets of the Bible and the rabbis of the Talmud.

So, in the early 1960s, my nuanced views of Black-Jewish relations did not fit the angry temper of the times, when you were expected to be either a southern Claghorn or a freedom rider—but these were not the only options. The most neglected front in the battle for desegregation was then not in the South but in the North. Schools were largely segregated everywhere, and housing was almost totally unavailable for Blacks in northern suburbs. These injustices could not be allowed to persist, and the battle against them was soon joined, but in the early 1960s the battles in the South were much more dramatic. Southern governors, such as George Wallace of Alabama, were standing, physically, at the doors of schools to block the entrance of Black students, and their entry into the schools could be forced only by federal troops. Some freedom marchers were being harassed and beaten by local sheriffs, and some members of the Ku Klux Klan committed racist murders that could not have happened unless the murderers were being protected by the police.

By 1962 Black Americans—and their many supporters among the Whites—could no longer contain their anger. The leader of the civil rights movement was now Martin Luther King. He called for a dramatic event, a march on Washington, by hundreds of thousands that would raise the visibility of the protest. A huge multitude of Blacks and Whites gathered together to assert their passion for equality for all. But large public events require planning and budget, especially budget. The "field marshal" who actually organized this event was Bayard Rustin, whom I had gotten to know in New York literary and intellectual circles after I had returned to the metropolitan area in 1956. The two major Jewish participants in the leadership of the projected rally were Rabbi Joachim Prinz, who was then president of the American Jewish Congress, and Abraham Joshua Heschel, a professor at the Jewish Theological Seminary who had become a passionate advocate of justice for Blacks. I did not know Martin Luther King very well, but I had met him years before while I was still a rabbi in Nashville. He and Bayard Rustin, Joachim Prinz, and Abraham Joshua Heschel all called me in Englewood and asked me to find some of the money with which to pay for the demonstration in Washington. I went to some of my friends in the congregation. They surprised me with their willingness to give. I heard the same sentence several times: "I remember being poor and hated as a young Jew in the Bronx. Thank you, Rabbi, for reminding me that, now, it's my turn to help."

After the high moment of the March on Washington, I did stay in occasional touch with Martin Luther King, but the leader of the civil rights movement with whom I had my closest personal connection was Bayard Rustin, who lived in New York. Rustin could usually be found through a local telephone call or two, and he was a charming, ironic, and irreverent friend. Bayard used to tell me tales from the other side, from his neck of the woods, and I would match them by expressing my frustrations that so many of the leaders in the Jewish community were repeating as ultimate wisdom on domestic affairs in America the clichés that they had been given by their speechwriters. Inevitably, we drifted into gossip. Bayard and I both knew that our lunches were part of the education of both of us. His black skin and my Jewish anguish dissolved as we sat across the table. Two men of the same generation were talking with each other about what they held in common.

What Bayard Rustin and I both knew in the beginning of the 1960s had not yet been widely understood: America was experiencing a far deeper upheaval than the change in race relations. This society had reached a historic turning point. The distribution of power, which had remained in place for two centuries, was changing fundamentally. On the surface, the noises and images were those of the battle over the rules and practices of race relations. Underneath the surface, political power was ceasing to be the monopoly of the White Anglo-Saxon Protestants, the element that had dominated society in America since before the founding of the Republic. It had begun to be dispersed among a number of minorities. More than ten years earlier, I had waved off what Jennings Perry was trying to teach me in our innumerable conversations at his home in Nashville. Perry was much less excited about the effort to desegregate toilets, lunch counters, and buses than I expected him to be. He kept harping on one issue: the effective denial of their rights as voters to most southern Blacks. Perry insisted that if the poll tax and all the forms of chicanery that it represented were repealed, the whole structure of racism would fall. Politicians who had been making careers out of defending segregation would now have to court the votes of Blacks. By the end of 1960 I realized how right he was. One night I picked up a telephone and apologized to him for my skepticism a decade or so before.

The turning point in American politics had come in November 1960, when John F. Kennedy won a closely contested election for the presidency over Richard M. Nixon. Here, too, the surface perception was that Kennedy, a Roman Catholic, had finally broken the long-standing prejudice that only a Protestant could be president. But Kennedy had not really surmounted the prejudice against Catholics. He had won the election by assuring the Protestants, and even proclaiming from the roofs, that he would be a "Protestant kind of Catholic"—that is, that his religion would be a private affair and would not have any influence on his political behavior. He portrayed himself as an American who differed from other Christian Americans only in that while they took Communion at Sunday services he attended Mass.

Right after the election, I analyzed the vote that elected Kennedy. I did not publish my analysis (it appeared as a long essay in *Commentary* in October 1961) until Bayard Rustin had read my text carefully and signaled his agreement. I found that the American electorate had split into five astonishing—and easily recognizable—camps. Richard Nixon, who was not as popular among the old-line Protestant elite as Eisenhower had been, nonetheless retained as much of this Protestant vote as

Eisenhower had ever received in his heyday. Kennedy won the election because he received 90 percent of the votes of Blacks, Jews, Catholics, and organized labor. That Blacks and Jews voted for him in such overwhelming numbers was understandable: they were asserting their hopes that they could rise behind this "outsider" to the very highest positions in American politics. The Catholics supported Kennedy despite his liberal politics (the Catholics were not liberal, at least not in those days) and the playing down of his Catholic identity. Kennedy's Catholic supporters were voting for someone who belonged to their kind. Labor voted for Kennedy rather than for Nixon in the hope of moving back from the margins of American politics, where the labor movement had been during the Eisenhower years. Thus, four concurring minorities, each voting at its maximum for the same candidate, combined to produce a slim majority against the existing political bastion of White Anglo-Saxon Protestants.

It was, of course, widely noticed in the Kennedy years that more Jews were being appointed by him to high posts than had happened before under any other president. But this was explained as the immediate result of a government based on "merit"—that is, of appointments to high posts of those who were judged to be the ablest and most competent and not those who were descended from the "right people." In academe the Jews were in the forefront of arguing for the principle of merit. This standard was "good for Jews," who were not the right people, but who were very good at taking tests. But the success of Jews in increasing their visibility in American life was regarded as a triumph of fairness. It took some time before Jews began to sense that they had acquired a share of power in society. They were becoming a new American elite—perhaps even *the* American elite.

The battles and changes in American society were affecting Englewood. The city had long been dominated by the Protestant establishment. The voting balance was tipping because more Jews and Blacks had moved into town. The Republicans had never lost an election in the hundred years since Englewood had been incorporated, but the Democrats were moving ever closer to parity. The focus of the battle became the integration of the public schools. In Englewood the Black residents were still living entirely in a ghetto in the fourth ward; the other three wards, including the third ward, which had become a largely Jewish enclave, were almost entirely White. The housing pattern meant that the schools were, in practice, segregated. The battle of the newcomers against the older inhabitants centered on desegregating the schools. Various proposals were advanced and debated, and sometimes defeated, but the movement was toward creating citywide desegregation of the schools through busing. A secondary element in this battle was the desegregation of housing. It was not always easy to prove the existence of gentlemen's agreements not to sell houses to Blacks, but proposals for building desegregated new housing could be portrayed as threatening the property values of the homes nearby.

All of this came to a climax in the mid-1960s, when it finally seemed possible that the ticket of the Democrats for mayor and the city council in Englewood might win the next election, in 1966. On the Friday morning before the election, Englewood was flooded with a piece of mail that was sent to every house in town. It was purported to be the map of "scattersite" housing—that is, of new construction that would be placed in every block of the city, including its most exclusive (that is, most expensive) neighborhoods. If the Democrats won, so this scare asserted, there would be houses for Blacks in every nook and cranny of Englewood; every family in Englewood would be forced to live next to a Black, or, at very least, only a few houses away.

This mailing engendered a flood of telephone calls. By the early afternoon, an emergency meeting was being held in the First Presbyterian Church, the "power church" in Englewood, where the Republican establishment could be found at prayer; but its minister, Edward Brubaker, was personally a Christian of liberal persuasion. We agreed that we would take vehement exception to this piece of propaganda in our sermons over the weekend. The Christians would have a couple of days to prepare, because their major services came on Sunday morning. I would be the first on the firing line because the largest attendance at Sabbath services in those days was on Friday nights. It was particularly difficult for me because two of the Republican candidates for the city council were members of Temple Emanu-El. They were friends of mine, and they were neither racists or bigots. They had had nothing to do with preparing the offensive mailing, but it had been done by their party and they were inevitably involved in the reactions that this action provoked.

My sermon that night was about racism. As I talked, I became more and more upset by the tactic that the Republicans were using. Soon I found myself going to the limit, and perhaps beyond, in my denunciation of the use of racial fears as a tool in the local election. In the climactic moment of the sermon, I said (yes, I shouted) that my congregation would expect me, as their rabbi, to reiterate the biblical prohibition that Jews should not eat pig. I pounded the pulpit and said that racism is even less acceptable, morally. The night that the sermon was given, it inevitably created some stir within the congregation, but that would have washed down as the "license of the preacher" to use overblown rhetoric. But this angry outburst did not remain a local affair. Someone gave the news desk of the *New York Times* an account of what I had said. It was too late for the Saturday morning paper so it was printed, prominently, in the Sunday edition. The story had thus come to national, and even international, notice.

The immediate result was that enormous pressure was put on my Christian colleagues to moderate their words on Sunday or to say nothing. Edward Brubaker, however, stood firm, even as he used less melodramatic language than I had; within a year or two he was no longer the pastor of First Presbyterian Church. The others who had been at the meeting that Friday said very little on Sunday morning or nothing at all. I remained the man on the firing line. Those who wanted to see the Republicans win the election were annoyed, or even more than annoyed, that I had taken a public stand in politics. By Tuesday night, when the returns were in, the Democrats had won the election by a hundred votes. I have always wondered whether my sermon had made the difference or whether I had actually lost the Democrats some votes. I was later told that some flaming liberals stayed home because they did not want to be "dictated to" by a rabbi. But I do know that this sermon was a watershed in my career in the pulpit in Englewood.

Some of the Jews who were attached to the old-line Republican establishment were members of the board of Temple Emanu-El. They simply could not let this event pass without fighting back. The leaders of this effort were not the two candidates for city council who had actually been in the congregation the night that I preached that angry sermon. The fight was led by two much more powerful people, Abram Lebson and Herman Kahn. Lebson, who was then in his sixties, had lived in Englewood almost all of his life. That meant that he grew up when the old-line WASPs dominated the city. Lebson was a lifelong Republican, and through the years he had become a member of the group that ruled in civic affairs. The other leader of the opposition to my unforgivable radicalism, Herman Kahn, had lived a Horatio Alger life. He had come from the East Side as a young teenager, a dropout from school, to a job as an office boy in Lehman Brothers, and he had risen all the way to be one of the managing partners of the firm. Kahn had a very large following in the local Jewish community, and he was the most vehement right-wing Jewish Republican I had ever met. Each of these two men enjoyed large position within Temple Emanu-El. It was inconceivable to them that they could not get their synagogue to disavow me.

At a hot and lengthy board meeting a few weeks after the election in November 1966, Lebson and Kahn were adamant that a rabbi had no right to enter into any issue that was politically controversial. The task of the man in the pulpit was to be a good pastor and not a participant in battles about public policy. They were shocked to find that the majority of the board was firmly in support of a different principle: the freedom of the pulpit was absolute, and a rabbi had both the duty and the right to speak his conscience. There were people at that meeting who said that I might have overdone it but it was my right to go overboard in expounding a moral value such as the abhorrence of racism. Some days later I took the occasion to talk, separately, both with Abram Lebson and with Herman Kahn. As best I could, I was attempting to remove from the debate any personal bitterness. On the surface, I succeeded: we remained on speaking terms. But there was never any pretense that they had forgiven me. I had done the unpardonable. I had denounced those who had been the local powers-that-be for most of Englewood's history—and those of their spear-bearers who were Jews—and I was getting away with it. I knew that Lebson and Kahn regretted the day five years earlier when I had won the battle to insert life tenure into my contract with the congregation.

CHAPTER

17

I lived through the Vietnam era in the very exposed position of being rabbi of a suburban congregation. In 1963, when the United States began its direct military support of South Vietnam, the American middle class was essentially pretending to itself that the war was a minor incident that would soon end. It did not involve them or their children. I railed against this delusion, and indifference, from the pulpit on the Day of Atonement in the fall of 1963. President John F. Kennedy had sent ten thousand troops as advisors to the army of South Vietnam. The controversy about this action has persisted for many years. Kennedy's defenders have insisted that he sent these troops in order to quiet down domestic political pressure (he did not dare to be open to the accusation that he was "soft on Communism.") but that he intended to take the heat in his second term and bring the American contingents home. That was apparent then only to those few who were in his personal confidence, or who later said that they had been; but I was among the many who knew nothing about such intentions, if indeed they existed. I denounced this action as inevitably leading to a fight that could not be won. The climax of my sermon was an angry assertion that middle-class Americans would be much more upset by the war in Vietnam if their own children were on the line. We would then be asking ourselves the question, Is this war worth the life of my son or brother? I added that then, in the early 1960s, we could still avoid thinking about Vietnam because those who were being ordered into the fight were not our children, who were almost all in college and exempt from military service. I expected that what I said that night would be prodding people to care and reflect, but what I heard immediately was an angry mutter: I was a bloodthirsty ideologue who wanted to send the children of my congregants into mortal danger.

Englewood was not the only place in which I could sense the political mood of those days. I had become comfortable with the personal routine of crossing the George Washington Bridge once or twice a week to teach class in upper Manhattan, at Columbia University. On campus, I could hear the tension rising as opposition to the war in Vietnam increased in the mid-1960s, but the famous sit-in, when hundreds of Columbia students took over much of the campus and made it impossible for normal academic life to continue, did not take place until the spring of 1968. The immediate cause for this outbreak was the decision by the United States government to start drafting those who were of "fighting age." That meant the end of exemptions for college students. Suddenly the war had become real and personal even to the people who had been talking about it with some political passion in the months before. I was teaching on the very morning when the student protest began, and I said to the class as it began to drift out of the room that I would have been much more impressed with their passion for morality and political decency if they had risen up in revolutionary fervor six months earlier, while their draft exemptions still seemed firm.

When the protest began, I was making a distinction between the war in Vietnam, which I had been denouncing for years, and the tactics of the demonstrators. At Columbia, students occupied and trashed the offices in Low Library, the seat of the central administration of the university. They were particularly interested in reading the contents of every locked file, none of which had anything to do with the war in Vietnam. The student protesters knew very well why they had chosen to bring the campus to a halt in the late spring. It was on the very eve of final exams. As they intended, grades in courses could not be given that term; it was impossible to hold exams, and even those instructors who could find a way of grading their students could not register these results with any functioning central authority.

After a week or two of respecting the strike, I joined a growing number of the faculty who chose to teach off campus, usually at home or in the apartment of one of the graduate students. For me the tipping point, when I returned to holding class, came when I heard that the protesters had trashed the office of a young instructor (a totally unpolitical person) and had scattered and destroyed thousands of three-by-five cards that represented the research in which he had been engaged for many years. This was sheer malice.

As the strike went on for many weeks, I found many of the protesters less and less believable and ever less morally acceptable. Stories kept being told of mothers and fathers driving up to the edge of campus to bring their darling sons basket lunches from home or from good restaurants and to make sure that they had enough pocket money. One day I encountered one of these young men about an hour after I had heard him shout "Cossack" at the campus police and at some of the professors who had linked arms so that their bodies stood between groups of demonstrators and counterdemonstrators who had turned violent. I looked at this young man and lost my temper. I said to him that he was using the rhetoric of the young Trotsky but, unlike that Red revolutionary, he was utterly lacking in seriousness. He was not participating in a revolution; his demeanor was that of an adolescent in the midst of acting out. He was shouting his head off in the certainty that his parents would save him from the professors and the campus cops by taking him to a psychiatrist who would then write a letter excusing this outburst as an expression of some as yet unexamined trauma. The end of my harangue was to inform this young "revolutionary" that if he and his comrades kept shouting "Cossack" at those who wanted to stop the unpleasantness, he should be prepared for evoking from the campus policemen and even from the mediating professors the conduct of real Cossacks. I refused to identify the struggle against the war in Vietnam with the antics of spoiled brats angry that it might now be their turn to be drafted.

Facing the student protest at Columbia, I had to make some fundamental decisions. In those days, two priests, the brothers Philip and Daniel Berrigan, began breaking into draft-board offices and pouring blood on draft records. They were setting an example for many of the young of activist revolutionary behavior. Martin Luther King, who moved in those days to take part in the effort to end the war in Vietnam, brought with him the lesson he had taught in the struggle for civil rights: nonviolence. As he had defined his objective in the struggle for civil rights—racial equality—King was fighting not to destroy the existing American society but to make it better. King did not take part in the struggle to end the war in Vietnam because he had become a partisan of the leader of North Vietnam, Ho Chi Minh, as so many of the antiwar crowd had become. King wanted the war to end because it was bad for America.

I had myself come to the same conclusion. One Saturday afternoon, my daughters, who were then in their middle teens, told me that they wanted to march in a local demonstration in Englewood against the war in Vietnam. I suspect that they thought that I would be against this, probably because I would not want them exposed to being attacked by counterdemonstrators. Instead I told both of them that they should take part in the march, and that, indeed, I would be there, too, but I asked of them, do not join in chanting "Ho, ho, Ho Chi Minh." On the contrary, each should carry an American flag to make the point that she was demonstrating in a cause that was good for America. My daughters agreed. They walked in the first row of the march.

In 1968 the draft and the end of automatic exemption did indeed begin to affect the lives of young people in the colleges. Several young men who were nearing their twentieth birthday were being called by the local draft board in Englewood. The question of what to do was soon being put before me, concretely, and emotionally, by young men who had difficult choices to make. No one who came to see me, either alone or with his parents, really wanted to go to Vietnam, but what could they do to avoid being drafted? The options were to flee to Sweden or to Canada, to plead pacifism and thus be assigned to some alternate service (if the plea was believed), or to refuse to be drafted, citing political objections to the war, with the near certainty of being sent to jail. I kept advising those who came to see me not to flee the country because they would be running the risk of becoming permanent expatriates. (Those who fled were lucky that it did not work out that way, because a few years after the end of the war, an amnesty allowed them to return to the United States.) I urged those who refused to submit to the draft that they should say so, forthrightly and honorably. I had no idea of what the long-term consequences might be, but I was sure that they would be less devastating to their futures than taking any of the other options. Most of those who asked my advice did not take it. They or their parents found some wiggle room and managed to avoid the dangers of Vietnam. One of my young congregants did serve in jail; another was sentenced to alternate service; and one or two ran away to Canada. I have never in my life, before or after, been tortured by as much self-doubt as in those days when I had to counsel young men whose futures, and even lives, seem to depend on the conclusions toward which I was guiding them. Sometimes I wondered whether the man who had volunteered to serve in the air force during the Korean War was still alive in me, and whether, even during the war in Vietnam, which I opposed, I had remained more of an American regular soldier than I knew. So, I kept reminding myself that the young people who came to me had their own purposes and their own lives to live. I could not use them for my political agenda, as chess pieces that I could push. Before God, conscience compelled me to give each of them the best opinion that I could offer, in his own interest.

Sometimes, I was tempted to become known as the defiant rabbi who led his young people to become a congregation of draft resisters, but I could not do it. I was put off by the theatricality of the Berrigans, who destroyed draft records, and even by William Sloane Coffin, the chaplain at Yale University, who burned his draft card. I knew and liked Coffin—and still do—but I kept saying to the young men who came to me that he was no role model for children of less well known families. The college acceptances and future careers of his offspring would not be destroyed by his radicalism or by the time that he eventually spent in jail, for the Sloanes and the Coffins were an indissoluble part of the American aristocracy. I kept worrying about those who were less well protected.

Nonetheless the moment did come when I had no choice but to speak out. I took a very public stand on the war in Vietnam at the end of 1969. I entered the international arena not in confrontation with the president of the United States, who was commanding the war in Vietnam, but with an even fiercer antagonist, Golda Meir, the prime minister of Israel, who was then at the very height of her power.

18

The major crisis for Jews in the 1960s was the outbreak of the Six-Day War. Egypt had closed the Straits of Tiran, denying Israel access to the Red Sea, and had ordered out the peacekeeping troops that the United Nations had interposed in 1957 on the Gaza border between Israel and Palestinian guerrillas. On June 5, 1967, Israel launched a preemptive strike on Egypt and four days later it went to war with Syria. Unexpectedly, even Jordan, which had been occupying East Jerusalem and the West Bank since the state of Israel was declared in 1948, joined the war. In the first hours of hostilities, Jews trembled that Israel was about to be pushed into the sea. Even in the Soviet Union, where Jewish concerns were forbidden, everyone, everywhere, was glued to the radio. From all over the Jewish world, young people were volunteering in great numbers to go to Israel and fight or at least to take civilian jobs to relieve trained soldiers who had been called to their regiments. Six days later, when Israel had won its astounding victory (it controlled all of the Holy Land up to the Jordan River, including East Jerusalem and the Temple Mount, as well as all of the Sinai Peninsula), the Jewish world sighed with relief that disaster had not come. Jews were on a historic high as they saw pictures of masses of Israelis who were now free to visit the very heart of Jerusalem, from which they had been barred for a generation.

The Six-Day War caused a major deterioration in the relationship between American Jews and many of their allies in liberal causes. As the war clouds were gathering, Jews expected the liberals, with whom they had been allied in the efforts to end the war in Vietnam and to achieve equality for Blacks, to stand with Jews in their moment of deep fear for the survival of Israel, but this did not happen. Those who had been involved in forging an ever closer relationship with the leaders of the Protestant and Catholic churches of America pressed very hard for support for Israel. Leading individual figures within the various Christian denominations—Reinhold Niebuhr, Martin Luther King, and Alexander Schmemann, among others—were quick and firm in their public commitment to justice for Israel, but the formal establishments of both the Protestant and Catholic churches remained largely silent. In the last days of May, as the crisis was building toward war, almost no statements would be elicited from any of these communions even supporting Israel's right to exist. As soon as the war was over several emergency meetings were arranged between Jewish figures with a large stake in the dialogue and their Christian peers. As individuals (though not as spokesmen for their churches) some of the Christians present had supported Israel's right to life, but the prevailing Christian sentiment in those tension-filled rooms was directed toward the question of Arab refugees and the status of Jerusalem. Israel was denounced as the aggressor in the conflict, and there was general discomfort in being pressed hard by Jews to think differently.

I attended almost every one of these meetings, and I was appalled by the bitterness that the official Christian leadership was expressing. The Jews in the room kept telling the Christians that the existence of Israel was not a negotiable matter for any Jew. The debates became so sharp that Monsignor George Higgins, the executive secretary of the American Catholic Bishops' Conference, lost his temper. He had personally been courageously and consistently pro-Israel, but he was so angered by Jewish pressure on the whole Church to take such a stand that he accused Rabbi Balfour Brickner and me of trying, in the name of our ecumenical ties, to blackmail the Church into supporting Israel.

The situation was just as tense in Jewish encounters with the leaders of the secular New Left. They persisted in regarding Nasser as a pro-gressive third-world leader, and they described Israel as a colonial power and the aggressor in the protracted Jewish-Arab war. There were many young Jews in the New Left. Martin Peretz, who was then one of the leaders of the group, asserted his Zionism and broke away from his peers, but he was in the minority. Almost no one among them took public issue with the very vehement stand against Israel that was an-nounced by the Student Nonviolent Coordinating Committee (SNCC). This was based on the pronouncement by Che Guevara that had labeled Israel as part of the "international ring of crime and treason." At the end of June 1967, the *Village Voice* reported the widespread talk about Israel among leftists, in reaction to its victory in the Six-Day War, "as dominated by mad hawks." Over Labor Day in 1967, a con-vention of the American Left took place in Chicago. Israel was con-demned in one of the resolutions adopted at the meeting as the aggressor. Some of the Jews were uncomfortable with the position that the convention was taking, but no one walked out.

In those days, I was one of those who insisted that Israel could be criticized, that it could be asked to treat the Arabs within its borders better than it had, and that it should move toward making peace with the Arab world as a whole, and especially with the Palestinian refugees. But criticism of Israel, no matter how merited, did not justify its destruction. As early as mid-June 1967, I was dissenting from Israel's euphoria at the extent of its conquests, but I was equally upset with the dire, and supposedly high-minded, hatred that its enemies were pro-claiming. I certainly could not agree with the religious and secular lib-eral leaders who pronounced that they were disappointed that Jewish liberals, like me, could abandon their efforts, even for a short moment, in the great overarching causes of racial equality and making an end to the war in Vietnam to worry about the survival of Israel.

I was angry because it was clear to me that the argument was being framed by the critics of Israel in such a way that only one answer was being implied: religious and secular liberalism both required Israel to disappear. Its very existence was an act of aggression against the Arabs, for the state should never have been created in the land of Palestine. Therefore, all Arab attacks were basically justified. I maintained in return that Israel had been created by an act of the General Assembly of the United Nations in November 1947 as a decision to realize "affirmative action." It was agreed, then, that the Jewish people could not survive without the unusual help of the grant of sovereignty in some part of Palestine and that the world, even the Arab world, could afford this act because the life of Muslim tradition and culture would suffer no unbearable injury if a small part of the vast expanse of Muslim land was made into a Jewish state. I found it particularly galling that my liberal friends and comrades in the battle for racial integration were, without exception, partisans of affirmative action for Blacks, to make up for the many generations of deprivation that they had suffered as slaves but any suggestion of affirmative action for Jews who had suffered centuries of persecution and physical attack evoked near apoplexy from these same liberals. I could explain the strange behavior only by positing the thesis that the leaders of liberal universalism could approve unique measures to right the wrongs of all the persecuted peoples of the world, but not for Jews. I did not condemn all of the liberals. I knew that I could trust individuals whom I had met as we worked together in liberal causes, for some were the finest and the most decent people in the world, but I deplored that side of liberalism that preferred that Jews should simply vanish.

My reaction to the disaffection of the liberals from Israel in the days of the Six-Day War did not make me one of the neoconservatives. Some of my old friends and comrades did take that step. Neoconservatism was the label coined and adopted by Irving Kristol and Norman Podhoretz, both of whom I had worked with as a longtime writer for *Commentary.* Irving had been an assistant editor in the 1940s, and Norman was the incumbent editor in chief in 1967. Not only were they outraged by the betrayal of Israel in its moment of need; they found liberalism to be guilty of spawning the disorderly generation of the 1960s. I shared their outrage, but I could not agree with them that political and social liberalism was to be abandoned. I did not see the conservatives in America flocking to the banner of racial equality or abjuring their own long-standing habits of excluding Jews wherever and whenever they could. On the matter of the libertine ways of the young, I was surprised that my very literate friends Irving and Norman did not remember that F. Scott Fitzgerald and a host of other writers, including Ernest Hemingway, had left no doubt that the country-club set of the 1910s and 1920s had fewer morals than the rebellious young of the 1960s and, certainly, even less concern for the poor and weak. The people whom Fitzgerald and Hemingway described had no empathy for Jews. I refused to believe that Jews could find dependable allies in that part of American society that had almost always excluded them and held them in social contempt.

My old friends among the neoconservatives were startled and even a bit angered by my failure to join them. Without exception, they had not been Zionists even in the late 1940s, when Israel was fighting desperately for its independence and its very existence. Irving Kristol had been a Trotskyite in the 1930s and had been drifting to the right after the Second World War without ever taking part in Jewish affairs. As recently as 1966, just a few months before Israel's travail, Norman Podhoretz had published an essay in *Commentary* entitled "My Negro Problem and Ours." He saw only one solution for racism in America: that Whites and Negroes marry each other freely as they had been doing in Brazil for generations to produce a chocolate-colored America. Indeed, Podhoretz's concern for Jewish issues was so minimal that he managed to omit the Holocaust altogether from his 1968 memoir, *Making It.* Another old friend, Nathan Glazer, a former associate editor of *Commentary,* who had moved as a sociologist to the faculty of Harvard, had written books and articles through the years about the changing social profile of American Jews. His writings always showed a mixture of academic detachment and Jewish concern, but he was never as passionate as he became in June 1967. He was then moving in with the neoconservatives.

I was in the same room with these old companions on that early evening in mid-June 1967 when their own emotions were running high, because they reacted to the near indifference of the New Left to the danger of Israel's destruction by returning, vehemently, to their Jewishness. They were now asserting, without apology, that their being Jews was their primary identity. They expected an old friend and comrade like me to hail their "conversion." I was the "Jewish Jew," who had kept heckling them for their absence from the Jewish community even as I maintained personal connections with all of them. I had officiated at the wedding of Norman Podhoretz and Midge Decter, and Irving Kristol and Nathan Glazer had been the witnesses in 1952 who had accompanied Phyllis to federal court when she was sworn in as an American citizen. They had an even more immediate reason for expecting me to join them. They knew that I was about to publish a book that made the case that the ultimate ancestor of modern liberalism, the Enlightenment in Europe, was ambivalent about Jews. Its most ideological element had followed after Voltaire in pronouncing Jews to be almost completely unassimilable and hopelessly guilty of being the "enemy of the human race." I was tracing the origins of modern secular anti-Semitism to this aspect of the Enlightenment. Thus, in the mind of the neoconservative intellectuals, I had produced the theory on which they wanted to rest their case: that the very source of liberalism, the Enlightenment, had contained an element of distemper with Jews. They were flabbergasted that the long-existing "Jewish Jew" among them, who had now demolished some of the ideological ancestors of modern liberalism, stood aside from their politics.

I was never invited to another meeting. The founders of neoconservatism did not want to hear my nuanced views. Though I had accused the Enlightenment itself of being an ancestor of modern anti-Semitism, I refused to make liberalism the sole culprit, either. The liberals had not made the pogroms in Russia in the early 1880s and they alone had not created the Nazis and sent them to wipe out the Jews in Europe. The ideals of liberty and equality have often been tarnished, and betrayed, by those who had proclaimed them, but these were the only ideals that gave ultimate hope to Jews, to Blacks, and to all those, all over the world, who were excluded and persecuted. Their freedom and their lives would not be guaranteed by trickle-down economics, by giving more money to the rich so that something would eventually flow down to the poor. Self-reliance was a great virtue for those who were well off, but no matter how self-reliant the Jewish slaves in Egypt had once been, it took the active help of God Himself to get them out of slavery and point them toward freedom. I found no substitute in any of the new mantras of the neoconservatives for the Enlightened vision of the Declaration of Independence. To be sure, Thomas Jefferson, who wrote that text, was a slave owner, and, as we learn in occasional remarks in his letters, he was not a great admirer of the Jews, but the universalist ideals that he expressed have become the corrective in American history for Jefferson's own failures. I found hope in this process of change, of America's learning to live up to the ideals that it has professed. I had much less hope in the notion that American society could be made better by joining those who had long made it worse. I did not believe that in gratitude for the accession of new forces—ex-liberal intellectuals—the conservatives would be led to a change of heart and mind.

The neoconservatives were not the only early readers of my forth-coming book, *The French Enlightenment and the Jews.* My critique of the Enlightenment had quickly come to the attention of several of the scholars in the Roman Catholic Church, and the reports soon reached the Vatican. Anti-Semitism had long been a troubling issue because, in the Christian Bible, Jews were blamed repeatedly for rejecting Jesus, condemning him, and then turning him over to the Romans, who cru-cified him as a rebel against their rule. In the Middle Ages the Church had been overwhelmingly and profoundly anti-Semitic, though, on occasion, Jews were protected by some popes and bishops. The most serious contemporary problem for the Church was the charge that kept being repeated by Jews, with untiring passion: that modern anti-Semitism was a direct child of the Christian tradition. Some Jews even kept asking, provocatively, "Wasn't Adolf Hitler baptized a Catholic? Why didn't the Church ever excommunicate the Nazis?" So here in 1967 a Jewish scholar was appearing to say that modern anti-Semitism was created within the Enlightenment, which was itself a secular revolt against Christianity. I was being quoted repeatedly for the next few years as the one who had supposedly saved the reputation of the Church. Catholic writers took pains to assert that I had not granted absolution, as the Church needed none. But, I had done something bet-ter, so some Catholic intellectuals thought: I had severed any connec-tion between Christianity and Nazism. Had not Rabbi Hertzberg said that the Enlightenment was to blame?

It took a few years for those in the Church who were concerned with these issues to realize that I had not given them blanket absolution. I had not said that the hatred of Jews and Judaism that the Church had fostered for many centuries had suddenly disappeared in the nineteenth and twentieth centuries. It most certainly did not. What I argued was that anti-Semitism based on religion was no longer the only source of the great hatred. Elements among the Enlightened had reached beyond

Christianity, back to pagan antiquity, to reintroduce to the West the notion that Jews—and Negroes and other aliens—were defective and even dangerous beings who looked human but were outside the pale of society. I had not simplified modern anti-Semitism by attributing it to one source, the Enlightenment. On the contrary, I had complicated the picture by maintaining that Jew-hatred, this unlovely misbegotten child of the Western tradition, had several ancestors ranging from the father figure of the Enlightenment, Voltaire, back to St. Augustine and other fathers of the Church. Nonetheless, a general impression of my thinking was generated and lasted for some years in the highest Catholic circles that I was inclined to be lenient to the Church and that, therefore, one could "do business" with me. Within a couple of years I became the acceptable leader of the Jewish side in the first official dialogues with the Vatican. I could be talked with because I was not regarded—at least not then—as the enemy.

When the book finally appeared, in 1968, it was a scholarly volume with hundreds of footnotes, in proper scholarly form, published by Columbia University Press. Its sales were not great, and yet the book had considerable resonance. One effect was that I was soon negotiating a full-time appointment at Cornell University. I was asked to leave my congregation and my adjunct professorship at Columbia to become chair of Jewish studies at Cornell University, where no such program yet existed. I declined to consider the move, primarily because starting a new department from scratch without any endowment or secure positions for other faculty seemed to me to be as enticing as the task of building a new synagogue in a community in which I was a complete stranger. I had always dreamed that when I became a professor I would be studying, writing, and teaching, and not fund-raising and institution building. I knew enough about academic politics to be sure that if I did undertake the task that was being proposed to me, a number of people would have an interest in seeing me slip on a banana peel and do myself in. From my many years at Columbia, I knew enough about academics to be sure that professors had more talent at the strategic placement of such banana peels than the usual run of synagogue politicians. Meanwhile, I preferred the devils I knew to the ones I did not.

It is tough to take an unpopular stand. My book was greeted with icy silence in academic circles. I was not then, or ever, invited to any of the conferences on the Enlightenment either in America or internationally. Agents and publishers proposed soon after publication, and in the years that followed, that the book be translated into French, but no French publisher would agree. They did not want to risk tarnishing the shiny image that the French academics and the mythmakers of the French Revolution had constructed for the Enlightenment. This silencing was mentioned at least twice in the literary pages of the flagship newspaper of the French intelligentsia, *Le Monde,* but it made no difference. The book has never appeared in French, but its thesis has been "borrowed" several times by French authors who eventually dared, some twenty years after my book appeared in English, to write revisionist accounts in French of the relation of the Enlightenment to Jews and to Blacks.

Nonetheless, the views that I presented have won the day. My assertion that one root of modern racism is in the most ideological teachings of the Enlightenment has become the accepted view. No one writes about the Enlightenment anymore without having to confront the fact that most of its major spokesmen never confronted slavery. The only possible explanation is that Africans were regarded as an inferior subhuman group, an intermediate stage between monkeys and human beings, as Voltaire himself said. It has thus become much more conceivable that he and others portrayed the Jews as other, as not part of the human race.

The American scholar who first heard best what I was saying, when I published the book, was R. R. Palmer, the distinguished authority on the history of France in the age of revolution who had recently retired from a professorship at Princeton. Palmer wrote a review in *Christianity and Crisis,* a journal that was read by Protestant intellectuals. He commented that I had seen a side of the Enlightenment that no one else had yet defined. What Palmer wrote strengthened me against the attacks of Hugh Trevor-Roper in the *New York Review of Books.* One day, some weeks after Palmer's review appeared, I telephoned him at Princeton and he invited me to tea. We did not talk of my work or even of his lifetime of great scholarship on the origins of modern France. We talked of a far greater subject: that the highest traditions of learning are maintained only if we follow the truth. He added, "The truth may not make you comfortable, but it will ultimately set you free."

The battles that erupted over my views in *The French Enlightenment and the Jews* helped bring me back to Jerusalem. This was, in fact, the most immediate and tangible effect of all the debates. The best-read and most serious intellectual among Israel's policy makers, Yaacov Herzog, read the interchange between Hugh Trevor-Roper and me, and he immediately got my book and read through it with great care. Herzog already had a positive opinion of my writing because he had studied my first book, *The Zionist Idea*, and especially the introductory essay, in which he found an approach to modern Jewish history that he shared. Herzog was the younger son of the chief rabbi of Israel. I had long been linked to Yaacov Herzog because his parents had befriended me in the summer of 1949, when his mother kept telling me that if I would find a proper spouse for her brilliant son Yaacov, she would do the same for me. This became a joke between Yaacov and me that lasted for many years. Yaacov had received a first-class education in both rabbinic and university studies, but he had chosen to become a diplomat. In the late 1960s he was the secretary of Israel's cabinet and the diplomatic professional who was most closely linked to the prime minister of Israel, Levi Eshkol, who had been in office during the Six-Day War and remained prime minister until his death in February 1969. Herzog suggested to Eshkol that I be asked to solve a festering academic problem for the prime minister's office, and Levi Eshkol immediately assented. I had known Levi Eshkol for a number of years, since the mid-1940s, when he came to the United States fairly often on various missions for the Zionist movement. He was an immensely decent, low-key man, poorly appreciated at the time as Israel's prime minister and underrated ever since.

One day in mid-1968, Yaacov Herzog called me from Jerusalem to tell me that he had been "instructed" by the prime minister to go to New York to see me. I was both impressed and curious. In a few days Herzog showed up in my office at Columbia University, but he was not alone. He brought with him a much less polished older man who gave his name as Levitsa. This was the abbreviation by which he was universally known in Israel. He had been the colonel who had commanded the Israeli troops in Jerusalem during the war of independence; his deputy had been a rambunctious lieutenant-colonel named Moshe Dayan. I asked them the obvious question, "Why have you come?" They proceeded to tell me a complicated story that did not add to the reputations of several notable figures. The problem that I was being asked to solve had begun with Nahum Goldmann, who was still president of both the World Zionist Organization and the World Jewish Congress. It had been compounded by Professor Bernard Netanyahu, who was then teaching medieval Jewish history at the still-existing Dropsie College in Philadelphia. Many years before, in the 1920s in Berlin, the then young Nahum Goldmann and an older figure, the essayist and philosopher who wrote in Hebrew, Jacob Klatskin, had undertaken to create, edit, and publish an encyclopedia of Jews and Judaism that they called the *Encyclopaedia Judaica*. Before the Nazis shut that enterprise down, Goldmann had succeeded in finding the money to publish ten volumes in German (the last entry was "Lyra") and two in Hebrew translation. The question of who owned this interrupted enterprise was essentially open, but Goldmann maintained, and no one contradicted him, that he was the heir. He revived the idea of doing the *Encyclopaedia Judaica* in English in the United States, and he proposed that the material already published in German could be used with suitable revisions for a good part of the text. Goldmann had raised some money for this revived endeavor, and he had even persuaded the owners of the *Encyclopaedia Britannica* to be the distributors of this *Judaica* in English when it appeared.

Obviously, so vast an enterprise could not be managed without a formidably learned editor in chief and a staff to help him. It was all the more complicated because only a minority of the scholars whose participation was mandatory wrote English, so the text would have to be translated from a variety of languages, but mostly from Hebrew. The man whom Goldmann found to undertake the task was Bernard Netanyahu. He knew all the languages, for Netanyahu had acquired a deep Jewish education in Europe, where he had been born into a rabbinic family, and he had spent some of his early years as secretary to Vladimir Jabotinsky, the brilliant polyglot leader of the Revisionist Party in Zionism, the activist group that Netanyahu's son, Bibi Netanyahu, would ultimately head on his way to becoming prime minister of Israel. Bernard Netanyahu set to work in Philadelphia and made it the headquarters for the enterprise, but soon disaster came.

The Gentile bureaucrats in the headquarters of the *Encyclopaedia Britannica* followed very un-Jewish rules. Having invested in this enterprise

(I was never told how much money the *Britannica* people had put up in advance), they wanted to see some copy that was promised to them within a year of the beginning of the work. Unfortunately, nothing was available. I cannot, of course, vouch for this story because I was not there, but that is what Herzog and Levitsa told me that day when we met at Columbia. There was no longer any money with which to continue the work in Philadelphia, and so an end had to be made. In desperation, all the material that had been collected in Philadelphia was boxed and sent to Jerusalem. The question remained: was the project to publish an *Encyclopaedia Judaica* in English bankrupt, or could a way be found to continue? It was obvious that the embarrassment of bankruptcy was one that Nahum Goldmann needed to avoid because money had been raised from people who were quite close to the center of the Jewish establishment, both in Israel and abroad. The government of Israel itself would find some of the mud of failure much too close to its own door.

It was becoming clearer to me as the tale unfolded that this delegation, a friend and a heroic soldier whom I had to respect, had come to hand me the problem, or at least part of it, and my guess was correct. The *Encyclopaedia Judaica* was on the verge of total collapse. It had been placed in a program entitled the Israeli Program for Scientific Translation (IPST). This body employed scientifically trained Russian Jews, who had begun to arrive in Israel in some numbers, to translate technical articles and books that were published in the Soviet Union into English, for sale in the United States, Great Britain, and elsewhere. This company was actually making a profit, but hardly enough to enable it to revive the encyclopedia. Herzog and Levitsa asked me to find an American publisher to replace the *Encyclopaedia Britannica* as the major supporter of the *Judaica*, and they wanted me to become centrally involved in the editing of the work. The two emissaries from Jerusalem concluded by saying, with great solemnity, that they had come on the personal orders of the prime minister. He was asking me as a Zionist, and out of my Jewish duty, to become deeply involved in the effort to rescue the *Judaica*.

Levitsa was a soldier, so he pushed me for an immediate answer. Herzog had the advantage of being both a diplomat and a friend, so he was gentler. He gave me a couple of days to think about it. We had lunch alone two days later. I told Herzog that I knew that I could not refuse.

Only two years ago, many thousands of Jews had risked their lives, and some had lost them, on Levi Eshkol's command. All that the prime minister was asking of me was to give some time and some effort, and, no doubt, to show some tolerance for the inevitable unpleasantness that I would have to face. How could I refuse? I was also flattered to be asked.

Very soon, the general manager of IPST, Itzhak Rishin, came to New York to settle with me the details of my collaboration. He turned out to be someone for whom I felt almost instant affection. Rishin had been born in Australia and had edited a Jewish weekly newspaper in Melbourne. He was an uncompromising Zionist. In 1948 he had packed up everything, including his wife, Etti, and two small children, to travel on a tramp steamer to Israel in the very months of its War of Independence. Rishin arrived to no job, so he and his family lived under miserable conditions until bit by bit he found work. Rishin had allowed himself no leeway when he left the security of Australia for the unknown hazards of Israel at war. From the very beginning of our connection, he never ceased hinting to me and lecturing me that I had to give up everything that I had in the United States and come to Israel. His Zionism was nourished by his version of Orthodox religious faith; Rishin was a follower of Rabbi Abraham Isaac Kook, who had been the leading Zionist rabbi in Palestine. Rishin believed in what Kook had taught: that in our time we were living in the antechamber of the messiah, who would appear very soon. Thus, anything that we might be doing to increase Jewish knowledge and the commitment of Jews to their faith was an act that would bring the messiah closer. How could I, he asked me in our first encounter in New York, not join him in producing the encyclopedia?

Rishin told me, very emphatically, that he would stay until I had produced an American publisher for the encyclopedia and had committed myself to working directly on the project. I surprised myself by how short I made his visit. An old friend of mine from the 1940s, when I had first begun to write professionally, Jeremiah Kaplan, had become the head of one of the major publishing companies, Macmillan. Kaplan was not a synagogue person, but he did all kinds of good deeds for the Jewish cause. It was his way of worshiping God. The day after I met with Rishin, I called Kaplan, who asked me to come over as soon as I could. I was in his office the next day and recounted to Kaplan the

major outline of the history, so far, of the *Encyclopaedia Judaica*. He cal-
culated in his head that there was a guaranteed sale of some twenty
thousand copies because in those days the book-buying budgets of all
the libraries in the United States were subsidized by the government,
and every serious public library would certainly have to have the *Encyclopaedia Judaica* on its shelf. He offered an advance of $250,000 on two
understandings: Macmillan would be the publisher in the United
States, and I would agree to be the final editor of all the copy, for all the
many volumes (in the end there were sixteen), before they went into
print. When I reported back to Rishin, he was overjoyed, because the
money that Kaplan was offering would go far enough in Israel so that
he could create a functioning editorial office. He would be able to commission a good number of articles. He knew that he did not have a large
cadre of scholars and editors whose first language was English, so he
was glad that I would help. I offered to be available for consultation by
letter, telegram, and telephone during the year and to come to Israel for
the summer—that is, for the months of July and August—for the dura-
tion of the project. All I asked was that my out-of-pocket expenses be
paid. I would take no money for having been the agent to put this deal
together and no salary for my work. At the end, so Rishin and I agreed,
in a gentleman's agreement, something fairly handsome would be done
in my honor, but that could wait until we had succeeded in producing
the encyclopedia. That promise was never honored.

These meetings, which were held in the early spring of 1969,
involved me in the encyclopedia. Rishin and I soon arranged that I
would be in Israel that summer to help launch the revived endeavor. I
had a very personal reason for wanting to go. Our family was still deep
in mourning for my mother, who had died on January 12, 1969. Her
sudden death had been an enormous shock, for she had always been the
source of all our strength. I was deep in grief for many, many months,
and I blamed myself for not having done more to help keep her in this
world. My father's grief was, of course, even more intense. He was eight
years older than she, and he had always expected that she would be
there to make his life possible until his very end. When I walked
through the door of their home some hours after her death, he said
only, "This I never expected."

As my father was shattered, I hoped that taking him with us to

Jerusalem, in the company of his two granddaughters, would bring him some joy. I guessed wrong. My father was so depressed that not even his grandchildren could cheer him up. One day that summer the recently retired president of Israel, Zalman Shazar, came to tea, but my father stayed in his room. His visible excuse was that Shazar had come to see me and not him, and therefore he had none of the obligations of the host. What he really meant was that he would not allow even the semblance of a happy moment to break into his sorrow for the loss of my mother. He would not betray her memory by rejoining the living. Sad and even nerve-wracking though this was, and especially hard on Phyllis and the children, I nonetheless knew that a great love was emanating from him. I had never seen him hold my mother's hand and never heard, at least in anyone's hearing, a single world of endearment. But I knew how deeply and how permanently, in this world and into the next, they cared about each other. He could not bear to be without her, and especially not in Jerusalem.

I was delighted with the work on the encyclopedia. I was astonished and pleased to discover the high level of seriousness and competence that existed among the editors and the contributors. The entries on the Talmud were being edited, and many were being written, by Menachem Elon, who was then professor of Jewish law at the law school of the Hebrew University, but who would soon ascend to the Israeli Supreme Court. "Kabbalah" was edited by Gershom Scholem, who contributed a book-length essay on the Kabbalah as the lead piece for the subject in the encyclopedia. "Modern Jewish History" was edited by Shmuel Ettinger, who wrote large portions of the basic articles on Zionism, anti-Semitism, and the history of the Jews in Eastern Europe. The editors and lead contributors on other subjects were equally distinguished, and so I spent three summers in a row interacting with many of the major figures among contemporary Jewish scholars. The only one who was not there during the summer was Gershom Scholem, who invariably left Israel in July, mostly to lecture at the Eronos conference on Carl Jung and on his idea that religious archetypes were fundamental to human culture. The major delight of going to the office was the lunchroom. The food varied between bad and atrocious, and the only attempt at elegance were some vinyl tablecloths, but the gossip was superb. Jerusalem was then still a small

town, and it had only two major industries, the Hebrew University
and the government. There was free movement between these two
enclaves, so that people at the luncheon table knew what was going on
everywhere. I listened with avidity, and soon I was even able to guess
which of the rumors had some truth in them and which were trial bal-
loons, or manufactured stories.

As the work continued, I was almost inevitably drawn into writing,
at least in part, some of the major articles on modern Jewish history. I
did the modern section of the long essay on anti-Semitism through the
ages and the account of Zionist ideology in the even longer essay on
Zionism, but the most interesting piece that I did for the encyclopedia
I wrote under pressure and not primarily as historian. I was dragooned
by Itzhak Rishin to write an entry on Jewish identity, when the encyclopedia was already on press and the volume that would contain such
an essay was the next to be printed. Rishin and I had become very close
friends, so I could not refuse, especially since he was, de facto, the editor in chief of the encyclopedia. He called me up in something of a
panic one night and told me that he had to have such an article within
two days. It was a political necessity because Israel was bitterly divided,
and not for the first time, over the issue of who is a Jew. This quarrel
inevitably involved the question of how conversion to Judaism is to be
accomplished and what authority is competent to decide. Rishin told
me he needed an article that would provide historical perspective and
perhaps even help soften the bitterness of the debate. I responded that
I really did not know how I could possibly do a respectable essay, based
on scholarship and not polemics, in the time that we had, but Rishin
was in trouble and he told me quite brusquely that he trusted me to find
the sources and to make some sense out of the contrasting issues in this
embittered and continuing row. I knew that I had been handed an ultimatum and that I had no choice.

I sat down to write almost immediately, and the citations came to
me. I began with the obvious question of why Ezra, who led the Jews
during the days when the Second Temple was being rebuilt, had
insisted that all marriages of Jews with non-Jews be dissolved. Could
he not have solved the problem by asking the non-Jewish partners to go
to a court of three rabbis and be converted according to the halakah—

that is, following the rules of rabbinic law. He had done no such thing because conversion according to the halakah did not yet exist. It was invented later. The proof of that assertion, so I argued, is to be found in the biblical Book of Ruth, where she, a Moabite woman, comes to the land of Israel with her former mother-in-law, Naomi, and chooses to be a Jew. She declares her intention to Naomi and then proceeds simply to live among Jews as her people. The ultimate point of the Book of Ruth is that this Moabite woman, who becomes a Jew by asserting her intention to be one and acting on that choice, is the great-grandmother of the biblical hero King David. I went on to maintain in the essay on Jewish identity that even under the halakah—or, rather, especially under the halakah—the intention of the candidate for conversion is the decisive element, and I more than implied that a solution to the contemporary problem of "who is a Jew" could be found through greater flexibility in applying halakic rules.

This essay was clearly a cross between the history of Jewish ideas about conversion and a not terribly well disguised piece of contemporary polemics. When the encyclopedia appeared, a few months after I had written this essay, I was surprised that I was not the object of counterattack. I first attributed this to the fact that those who might want to attack me from the Orthodox right had probably seen or been told about the article by Ephraim Urbach in the Hebrew encyclopedia, which was being published as a separate encyclopedia. Urbach, a redoubtable Talmudic scholar whose Orthodox credentials were beyond question, had written in the same vein as I, and I was surprised to discover that we had quoted essentially the same sources. More important, it was quickly accepted in the Jewish world that the *Encyclopaedia Judaica* had been composed by many scholars of varying beliefs and backgrounds. The long essays on various aspects of the Bible had been written, without exception, by scholars who accepted "biblical criticism"—that is, they wrote about the Bible as a work not handed down from heaven in finished form but composed within history. Scholem's views on the Kabbalah were clearly heretical by the standards of the Orthodox kabbalists. My heresies about the history of how Jews had managed the question of their own identity were minor by comparison.

The encyclopedia was finally finished in 1971, and I ended my work with a sense of accomplishment and of deep satisfaction. I had made many friends, but, even more important, I had been deeply involved in a collegial endeavor with men and women who were very learned in all aspects of Judaism. We argued and disagreed and then came together, over and over again. My lot had fallen in a pleasant place.

I n the fall of 1969 I had been made a member of the international executive of the World Zionist Organization. It was an unusual appointment because I represented no organized party or faction within the Zionist movement. I could be chosen only if there was general assent by the party representatives who dominated the executive. I was surprised that there was no objection, but it seemed that no one regarded me as a firebrand within the Zionist movement and that the Zionist leadership was looking for the additional strength that a Conservative rabbi and a busy scholar might add. Those who joined in appointing me were not completely mistaken. Even though I had a full and uncontested vote in the executive, I always abstained when party interests were being debated, and I maintained good personal relations with all of my new colleagues, from right to left. Naturally, I was not silent. I spoke my mind on the moral and political issues that concerned me. I had the advantage that I was subject to no party discipline. I quickly grew to like belonging to the Zionist executive, because it gave me access to those who made decisions in Israel and who led the Jewish establishments in the Diaspora. I soon realized that I had fallen into an unparalleled situation: I was both a participant and an observer in some of the high dramas of Jewish life, and, so long as I refused to trim any sails in order to safeguard my reappointment, I had the freedom to say what I thought and to fight, both in private and in public, for the positions that I took.

When I joined the Zionist executive, Golda Meir had just become the prime minister of Israel. By near universal consent, she was also the uncrowned pope of the Jewish world as a whole. Even before Golda and I had a vehement, and soon public, quarrel over Vietnam, I had coined the sour assessment that Jews could be forgiven for having pork for lunch on Yom Kippur or for marrying non-Jews, but they could not be forgiven for doubting Golda's wisdom or rebelling against her authority.

I demonstrated my own sinfulness against Golda in an encounter on the very first night that I sat on the Zionist executive. The meeting was in Jerusalem, and the date was December 31, 1969. That morning, at the opening session of the steering group of the world Zionist movement, the chairman, Louis Pincus, a South African lawyer who had come to Israel some years before, went around the table to ask members from various parts of the world to describe the situation in the lands from which they came. When Pincus got to the United States, three people—Charlotte Jacobson, the representative of Hadassah, the powerful Women's Zionist Organization of America; Ben Halpern, a professor at Brandeis University who was the scholar among the Labor Zionists, the party that had long monopolized power in Israel; and I— took turns in saying that American Jews, and especially the younger people among them, were decidedly opposed to the war in Vietnam. We added that the Israeli government was creating difficulties for us by having moved toward courting the American president, Richard Nixon, by publicly supporting the war in Vietnam. Indeed, just a few days before we had assembled for our meeting, Golda Meir had sent a telegram to Nixon. She was widely known to have obliged the American president because he had asked for her support, hailing President Nixon's defense of a small country, South Vietnam, as proof of his devotion to the security and freedom of other small countries, such as Israel. In the discussion that morning, I countered that equating South Vietnam and Israel was a disastrous idea. The Vietnam War was becoming a lost cause in the United States, and those who were making the case for American support for Israel had to separate it from the cause of Vietnam.

That night the World Zionist Executive had a very festive session in which at least a hundred people crowded into a room that normally seated some twenty people for our working meetings. Golda Meir was coming to spend an evening with us. She was supposed to make a speech, but it did not turn out that way. As soon as she walked in and sat down, it was clear, beyond any doubt, that she had been told about the discussion about Vietnam at our morning session. She began by turning to her faithful subordinate, Louis Pincus (it was his task to keep the Zionist movement in line for her), and asked him to report on what had happened so far in our deliberations. I expected Pincus to give her a brief summary of our earlier discussions, and I had no doubt that she would answer, with her usual vehemence, that she was right and her critics were wrong, but it did not happen that way. Evidently someone had decided to teach me a lesson, so Pincus replied to Golda Meir that Arthur Hertzberg (leaving out Charlotte Jacobson and Ben Halpern) had voiced some objection to her policy on Vietnam, and then he added, "Madame Prime Minister, you are here and so is he, so let him speak for himself." As Pincus was uttering this sentence, an Israeli member of the Zionist Executive, Honi Bergman, representing the Women's International Zionist Organization (WIZO), quickly scribbled a note and passed it to me: "You have been invited to the dance and I dare you to accept." The smart political money was thus being bet on the idea that I would back down and mumble some apology. I passed back to Honi Bergman an even shorter note: "So listen."

At that moment, there was special electricity in the room; Golda had walked in accompanied by a flock of advisors to lend further weight to her presence that night, because she was going to announce a great triumph for Israel: the Cherbourg boats. Five gunboats had been ordered from France before the 1967 war. During the war, however, President De Gaulle had pitted France against Israel and kept the boats in port in Cherbourg for many months. Israeli agents had then quietly persuaded some of those who controlled movement in the port to look away, and the gunboats had slipped out. An hour or two before the prime minister came to our meeting, the gunboats had arrived in Haifa amid great national jubilation in Israel. The Golda Meir who appeared at our meeting was a triumphant warrior, the one who had just given the French a black eye. Who was a relatively obscure Zionist intellectual to dare to stand in her way?

My opening statement was quite brief. I repeated what I had said in the morning and added that the war in Vietnam was, by now, in 1969, abhorrent to almost all of the younger Jews in America. They would not change their view because Israel might have political reasons for supporting this bloody and losing venture. I continued that the state of Israel did not dare, for its own sake, to force the Zionists of America to choose between our Zionist commitments and our devotion to our own children, for whom ending the war in Vietnam could be a matter of life or death. At that moment I looked around the room and I saw one hundred people who were literally sitting on the edge of their chairs. I was unable to restrain myself, for I had gone too far in speaking for the generation that opposed the Vietnam War not to "let it all hang out." My concluding sentence was a simple statement: If I was forced to choose between her and my children, I would choose my children.

A member of her entourage later told me that Golda Meir had come to the meeting to crush me, using the calm insistence of a prime minister who knew better than anyone else because she was in possession of facts that lesser people could not possibly know. But she was angry. Her tone was furious, and she immediately accused me of having misquoted what she had written to President Nixon as well as having misunderstood its content. Her principal assistant, Simcha Dinitz, whom she would soon send to be ambassador in Washington, immediately produced a copy of her cable to the president of the United States. She read from it the opening paragraph, which contained some generalities about her respect for Nixon's commitment to small countries, that they were entitled to security and freedom. When Golda finished reading this text, I challenged her, and I heard a loud gasp from the room. I said very flatly that what she was reading was only part of the cable sent to Richard Nixon, for she was eliding the second paragraph, in which she had equated Nixon's defense of South Vietnam with his devotion to Israel. Golda bristled. Louis Pincus stepped in to say that this discussion had gone on too long; we must turn to the real reason of the meeting, to listen to an account from Prime Minister Meir of Israel's situation on this day of victory over the government of France. The prime minister then gave a celebratory speech. Everyone in the room gave her a standing ovation, but the incident with me was not yet over. I learned two days later that she had gone back to her office to compose a letter, which Louis Pincus received the next morning, in which she furiously denied my allegation that she had told something less than the truth in the debate over her telegram to Nixon. This letter was duly put into the minutes, as an addition to the account of the World Zionist Executive meeting, but I was not told about it then, lest I reply in writing.

The result for me was the reverse of what Golda Meir's cheering section had expected. As the story of the fight made the rounds in the circles of Jewish leadership, I was elevated into a different league. By choosing to quarrel with me, directly and very personally, Golda Meir had raised me from semi-obscurity, where she could have left me if she had governed her temper and simply ignored what I had said that morning, to the status of someone whose views were sufficiently important for the prime minister to address publicly. That night Golda Meir made me an international figure in the Jewish foreign policy debates of that day. But that night was also the last time that Golda Meir took any public position on America's involvement in Vietnam, so this brawl seems to have had some effect.

My ability to anger Golda was far from exhausted by this first battle. A year later I came to Jerusalem, bringing along my wife and our then teenaged daughters, to be a visiting professor in history for a semester at the Hebrew University. For a scholar this semester was an academic feast and a considerable challenge. My colleagues at the Hebrew University were the largest concentration of leading lights in all the fields of Jewish learning. The students were passionately involved in the Jewish history they were studying, because they carried with pride their sense of themselves as the first generation of Jewish scholars to appear after the creation of the state of Israel. Among both faculty and students I formed friendships that have lasted to this day. The older faculty members came from the same cultural roots as I did. The vast majority had been born in Central or Eastern Europe. Most of them had begun within deeply Orthodox families, where they had first mastered the Talmud. They had then moved west into the university world and had ultimately come to Palestine. My life had taken the same path, except that I had been brought to the United States as a small child. My colleagues had fought in the wars of Israel and I had not, but I had been through much the same intellectual and spiritual journey as they. I could not pretend to myself that on the personal level I liked every one of the scholars that I met, but I knew immediately that in the humanities faculty of the Hebrew University I had found my intellectual home.

Even though I thought that I was escaping from public life and politics by taking a sabbatical to teach at the Hebrew University, I really did not want to isolate myself completely from the actions and passions of the day. Again, these involvements brought me into conflict with Golda Meir. As I was finishing the semester, Golda Meir and I again danced the dance that Honi Bergman had dared me to join on New Year's Eve, December 31, 1969.

At the university, I taught not only Israeli students in Hebrew but also a large class of American Jews who had come for an introductory program in Jewish studies, which was given in English. In that second group, I met several young men and women who had come to Israel because they had become disenfranchised from the civil rights movement of the 1960s. The young Blacks had turned nationalist and were chasing out of their ranks the young Jewish ideologues who had been mainstays, both as leaders and foot soldiers, of the movement for racial equality. The buzz word of the 1960s was no longer racial integration but Black Power, and Black Power could be achieved only if Blacks were not led by honkies—that is, Whites. The "honkies" in the civil rights movement were particularly dangerous because they were still partisans of integration, not of Black Power. Several young Jews whom I met in Jerusalem were inspired by the logic of this Black nationalism to conclude that they, too, must do something about the power of their ethnic group, so they came to study and to work at its fabled and historic center, Jerusalem.

The most thoughtful person whom I met in this circle was Edward Geffner. He had found a job in Jerusalem as a street worker with the gangs that were beginning to form among young people who were angry because they could find no jobs and had not been offered any serious education that would make them employable. The mayor of Jerusalem, Teddy Kollek, knew enough about the contemporary scene in the United States—and he remembered his youth in Vienna, where young people without hope went from making disorganized trouble to joining the Nazis—that he created an effort among the city's public services to reach the upset Jewish young people in his town. Some of them were already calling themselves "Black Panthers," in imitation of the Black Panthers who were then making waves in many American cities. The "Black Panthers" in Jerusalem, and elsewhere in the country, were, almost all, children of emigrants from North Africa. They were expressing the bitter resentments of their families at the past twenty years of discrimination. They had had enough of being treated like "Jewish Arabs" or like "Jewish Blacks." Edward Geffner and his then wife, Ellen Joyce, quickly became our friends. Phyllis and I learned from them that Israel, too, was on the verge of experiencing its equivalent of race riots in America. The Israeli government had done very little to offer help, to make these totally alienated people believe that they were not Israel's permanent lower caste.

In June of 1971, as I was preparing to return to the United States after my semester as visiting professor at the Hebrew University, I was invited to speak at the American Cultural Center in West Jerusalem to sum up my impressions of Israel. I accepted very willingly because I needed to sort out for myself what I had seen and felt and learned. The excitement carried me far beyond the praises that I was expected to utter. I did speak with great emotion about the verve and creativity of Israeli society in those heady years after the Six-Day War, but I could not suppress two basic fears. I thought that my love for Israel was beyond question, that I was a member of its extended family, and that I had a right to speak to my brothers and sisters with candor. The last part of this talk reiterated what I had been saying in America and in Israel, in speeches and writings, since June 1967: Israel can find security only if it ends the occupation of the West Bank and Gaza and lives side by side with a Palestinian state. This was not a popular doctrine in those days due to security concerns as well as prevailing high spirits that came with victory. My conviction that Israel could not and should not annex the West Bank, in particular, and the other territories, was not completely scandalous. David Ben-Gurion had said the same as early as the middle of June 1967. In Israel itself, peaceniks were beginning to arise, and so, like quite a number of Israeli intellectuals, I was one of them. Right-thinking people regarded this as a disease that was then limited only to the strange breed of professors.

I also encountered the contrary sentiment: that Israel should retain the territories. In 1967 shortly after the war when I was visiting Israel, I had met up with an old friend, Haim Hoffman, a onetime director-general of the Israeli foreign ministry who had changed his name to Haim Yahil. He was a liberal and urbane man, and he was a secular Jew. His wife, Leni, was a Danish Lutheran who had converted to Judaism and was a historian of the Holocaust. A son had died fighting with the Israeli paratroopers for the liberation of Jerusalem during the Six-Day War. Haim had been transformed by the loss of his son into one of the leaders of those who advocated that Israel retain the territories, that it control "the undivided land of Israel." Some weeks after the war, when I was in Israel, I walked with Haim into the synagogue that is hidden beneath the Old City at the northern end of the Western Wall and where there was already a parchment inscribed with the names of the fallen paratroopers. He had not been there before. We then went to find the spot where his son had been killed; it was simply a place by the side of the road where a bus stop had now been built. Together we said Kaddish at the site of his son's death. Haim Yahil then turned to me and asked, How can we give all this back? He was no religious ideologue, he was claiming no God-given right to the land, but his son had paid the ultimate price, and he, the father, was heartbroken. I replied that a return of territory was necessary to prevent more conflict and more deaths.

What got me into deep trouble was my second warning, about the explosive social gunpowder that the Israeli establishment was ignoring and treating with contempt. In that concluding talk, I summarized what I learned from Edward Geffner and, even more important, from the Jewish "Black Panthers" to whom he had taken me. I said very flatly, without any softening qualifiers, that Israeli society was in danger of race riots, and I did not spare the Israeli establishment, and especially the Israeli government, from some angry criticism. So here I was, a bilingual and bicultural American who dared highlight a social problem that Israel simply did not want to acknowledge.

Even this would have washed down quietly, if the press had not gotten hold of a summary of my remarks. There were no Israeli reporters or foreign correspondents present in the audience at the American Cultural Center in Jerusalem, but Edward Geffner made sure that the bureau chief of the *New York Times* read a two-page summary of my speech. Within a day the *New York Times* carried a story, quoting me as the source for an account of the social tensions represented by Israel's "Black Panthers." I was described as the American Zionist leader who had chastised the Israeli government for ignoring the problem. The incident became sharper because the leaders of Hadassah were leaving the day after the *New York Times* account of my speech for their convention in Jerusalem. These officers of Hadassah began to burn up the wires to Golda Meir's office. Could the Israel they were coming to celebrate be guilty of social neglect? Were riots in the poor neighborhoods possible, or even likely? Here I was again making trouble for the Labor Zionist establishment, which had long regarded itself as the "principal owner" of the state of Israel. Golda Meir decided that this time I was going to be silenced.

Her office tracked me down to tell me that she wanted to see me. I responded that I was on my way to Europe; I would need help to postpone my reservation so that I could wait a couple of days until Golda had time to meet me. In reality, I was being summoned. Within five minutes they called back saying they had booked me on a later plane and that I was to see Golda Meir not in Jerusalem but in Tel Aviv on Thursday, the day when she normally worked in her office in the defense ministry. When I turned up, the scene was totally different from the one a year and a half earlier, when we had had our sharp encounter at the Zionist Executive. I was left to sit alone in a room, waiting for her; there was no one else there even to offer me a glass of water. She strode in without any attendants whatsoever and sat down on a platform at the end of this conference room so that perforce I had to look up at her. I greeted her politely and she nodded back but said nothing, so I broke the silence by asking her which language she wished to speak. She answered unhesitatingly that she, of course, preferred to speak Hebrew. Her eyes conveyed steeliness, tinged with mischief. She was going to prove to this American outsider that he had no right to an opinion because his command of Hebrew would soon not be adequate for him to explain and defend his views. I presumed that she expected that then she would be able to turn on me and say, "So what entitles someone who is essentially semiliterate in the language and culture of Israel to pronounce any opinions?" Golda's own Hebrew was notoriously limited. The wags in Israel had been saying for many years that the reason she thought in such black-and-white, simplistic terms was that the seven hundred words of Hebrew that she used were not enough to express any nuances. Golda soon discovered that she could not back me into a linguistic corner, not least because I had just spent a semester teaching some very critical students at the University in Hebrew, and I had been spending a lot of time socially in the homes of colleagues where Hebrew was the preferred language. After about five minutes Golda burst out in English, "But you speak Hebrew like one of us. So why does an insider like you defame us to the world?" I was in a no-win situation, and the best that I could hope for in this very personal debate, mano a mano, was to come out with some semblance of a draw.

When the battle was really joined, the prime minister readily agreed that more needed to be done for the poor in Israel, but she turned on me and asked me a question that she knew I could not, or would not dare, answer, "Where can the money come from? Are you asking the government to take it from the military budget and thus weaken our defense against the enemies on our borders, or do you want me to take many millions from the government budget for the support of the universities?" I told Golda that I had no expert knowledge of the intricacies of Israel's budget, but I was sure that those who did could find room for enough change to alleviate a threat to social stability. I had not spoken to presume to tell her how to spend the budget of Israel, but I had very definitely said that she could not govern without paying much more attention to the complaints of the poor. I concluded, Let us lay aside, for a moment, the moral issue of justice, and compassion. I am forced to tell you that some of the poor are becoming angry enough to make Israel ungovernable.

The debate soon ended. I had no doubt that it had been a dialogue of the deaf. Golda did not hear a word I said on the substantive issue: she had called me in both to chastise me and to say to the ladies of Hadassah, when they turned up in her office in the next day or so, that she was concerned and that she had even taken the unusual step of hearing me out. I knew as I walked out to go pack my bags for the air journey to Europe and ultimately to the United States that I had simply solidified my reputation as a troublesome Zionist intellectual who could not be trusted to be a "team player." I was even briefly arrogant enough to think of myself as acting in the tradition of the prophets of the Bible about whom the powerful had said, more than once, that "the man of the spirit is crazy" (Hos. 9:7), but I refused to let that thought last more than a moment. I was angry and upset when I had to confront the bad judgment of an Israeli prime minister, but I was not crazy enough to think of myself as a prophet. I was only a worried Jew who kept insisting on thinking for himself. The most I would sometimes allow myself to think was that I was behaving in the image of the little boy who looked at the emperor in his supposedly magnificent new suit and told him that he had no clothes: he was naked.

I fear that these stories of two quarrels with Golda Meir—the stories that dominate in the account of my most intense relations with Israel as a leader in international Zionism and as a teacher at the Hebrew University—convey the impression that this was a period of turmoil and battle, but it was not so. On the contrary, I was able to stand up to the battles; though this was a time of personal stress, it was also a time of contentment and of inner peace. My mother had died in January 1969, and I had spent much of 1969 in trying to cope with my own deep grief and with helping the larger family to worry about my father. My sister Eve and her husband, Azriel, made the largest sacrifice. They came from Silver Spring, Maryland, each weekend, bringing their three small children, so that my father would have some family with whom to sit at the Sabbath table. I would come frequently to Baltimore, and, as always in happier times, he kept arranging to have someone bring him to the railroad station so that he could greet me when I came up the stairs.

My appointment to the World Zionist Executive, a group of some twenty members mostly from Israel and the United States, put me in the middle of often heated arguments about how the many millions that the Diaspora was contributing to Israel were to be allocated. I was personally even more interested in the frequent discussions of religious and ideological questions—such as "Who is a Jew?"—that were inevitably debated within the World Zionist Executive because this body was outranked only by the cabinet of Israel. I was delighted to participate in making decisions about how to work toward the rescue of the Jews of the Soviet Union and where to send them when they came out to freedom, especially if some chose not to go to Israel. So, the issues before the Zionist Executive in the 1970s were important and contentious. I was pleased that I now had a reason to go frequently to Jerusalem. Every time I made the journey I went to pray for my mother in very holy places. I do not know whether my prayers made any difference in heaven, because I was always certain that she had found an immediate place in a very high section in the palace that God had created for the righteous. I found some peace in the thought that my mother had now rejoined the family from which she came: her mother, who had died young, leaving her an orphan at the age of seven, and her father and all her siblings and their families, who had been murdered in the Holocaust. To be sure, we had buried her in Baltimore, the city in which she had lived most of her years. There were no graves anywhere for her murdered family, but I had no doubt that they had found each other somewhere in the heavens high over Jerusalem. Every time that I walked in the city or took the bus to the university, I looked around me and saw the intense and complicated, and often raucous, life of the people who were building the new Jewish state. But I often looked beyond them, my eyes tilting to see over their heads. I saw those I mourned and wanted to remember.

I was happy in Jerusalem in those days because many people made great efforts to be kind and helpful. I had barely known Shmuel Ettinger, the chair of the department of Jewish history at the Hebrew University, before he extended the invitation to be a visiting professor, but I soon knew that he was a great scholar, with an extraordinary capacity for friendship. Ettinger and I very quickly became inseparable. Phyllis and I were frequently the guests for dinner at his home, so we came to appreciate his wife, Rina, who was a professor of cancer research at the university medical school; she was a person of intelligence, warmth, and moral substance.

Ettinger as a historian had become the principal heir to Ben Zion Dinur, the founder of Israeli historical scholarship. The central thesis of the Dinur school of history was that all of Jewish history is the story of the "Jews in their land": of having once possessed it, then being exiled for many centuries, and now returning to their homeland. Ettinger was thus able to write a one-volume summary of Jewish history in the modern era in which he devoted only some six pages to the Jews in America. Yet my friend was so broad in his learning and sympathies that he supported my book *The Jews in America,* which we discussed, knowing full well that it dissented from his views. But he died the year before it was published.

As I spent more time with the Ettingers I was ever more astonished by what each of them told me about their lives. Shmuel was born in 1919 and had grown up in Leningrad, where his father had defied the Bolsheviks and raised his son as an Orthodox Jew and even to be a scholar of the Talmud. In 1935 the young Shmuel Ettinger and his parents and sister received permission from the Soviet authorities to emigrate to Palestine. Shmuel immediately entered the Hebron Yeshivah—and soon he enrolled at the Hebrew University and turned Communist! He was a founder of a Zionist Communist party. When I met him in the late 1960s he was the moral compass of the Labor Zionists in Israel and the statesman of the effort then under way to get the Jews of the Soviet Union to Israel. In the course of this hectic ideological and political biography, Ettinger had never wavered in his total devotion to scholarship in Jewish history, but his enemies, which he had acquired during his political journey, never forgave him for his biography. They denied him some high honors in Israel, but he never talked of these vendettas. I saw in him a man who had begun as a contrarian both in the Soviet Union and in Israel. He had been and was part of the actions and passions of our century—and I quickly learned to love him.

Rina Ettinger's personal history was deeply affected by tragedy. She had begun life in Israel as the daughter of a distinguished medical professor, the head of the Department of Experimental Medicine and Cancer Research at Hadassah Hospital, and of the woman who was the first professor of Russian language at the Hebrew University. Tragedy came on an awful day in 1947 when a convoy of doctors and nurses, more than seventy people, was on its way through the streets of Jerusalem to the Hadassah Hospital on Mount Scopus. They were traveling under guarantee by the British forces, but when the shooting began, the British stood by and did not lift a finger to save them. Arab irregulars cut off the convoy and killed and burned everyone, to the last person, including Rina Ettinger's father. Neither Rina nor her widowed mother (she lived to be over a hundred) ever uttered a single word of self-pity. The only tear I ever saw in anyone's eye was in the spring of 1971 when I stood beside Shmuel Ettinger on one of the lawns of the university at the commemoration of the almost six hundred members of the faculty, staff, and students who had fallen in the wars of Israel.

On the very practical level the person who was assigned by the university to help visiting scholars find housing and integrate themselves into living in Jerusalem was Hannah Gatt. She took admirable care of our family so that we did not see even slight signs of the bureaucracy for which Israel had already become well known. Hannah and her husband, Shimon, a professor of biochemistry at the Medical School, continued to worry about us in all our subsequent stays and visits in Israel, and they give a reception or a dinner for mutual friends every time we come to Jerusalem.

The towering personality whom I met for the first time in 1971 in Jerusalem was Gershom Scholem. He had already retired as professor of the Kabbalah some years earlier, but he continued to dominate the intellectual life of Jerusalem. When he was in the room everyone listened and no one dared interrupt. This attention was a tribute of respect for his unparalleled scholarship—he had literally invented the modern historical study of the Kabbalah—but this awe also expressed fear of his sharp tongue.

As a scholar, Scholem had begun not only to bring the Kabbalah into the domain of Jewish history but to use its message to validate, as precedent, the Zionist revolt against the older Jewish life in the Diaspora. Nonetheless, Scholem had never fully abandoned his respect for the halakah, Jewish religious law, not even when he stopped being religiously observant. As I discovered one Sabbath morning, such affection was very much alive for Scholem to the end of his days. Attending synagogue, I found his name on a small plaque on one of the benches. Later that day, when I asked him why his name was there, despite his well-known nonattendance, he replied, "A Jew might choose not to go to synagogue, but he must retain his place there."

The many sides of Gershom Scholem were quite apparent when I met him for the first time at the home of Ephraim Urbach, a professor of Talmud at the Hebrew University. Urbach and I had first gotten to know each other a few years earlier when we served together on the board of the Memorial Foundation for Jewish Culture, so Urbach gave a party in my honor to welcome me when I came to teach. "Everybody who was anybody" in Jewish studies at the Hebrew University came, including even the by then somewhat reclusive Gershom Scholem. The moment that Scholem arrived, he started to talk about the current gossip in the learned world in Israel, passing comment on every person and event that he mentioned. After about half an hour, he had exhausted the Israeli part of his subject and he began to talk about the Jewish scholars in America. I was soon hearing stories that were out-of-date or simply wrong, so I disregarded the established local custom and interrupted Scholem. I said, respectfully but with a grin, that I accepted his undoubted authority on all matters that concern Jewish scholarship in Israel, but that he had now wandered over into America, a strange territory where I knew the natives better than he did, and would he, therefore, permit me to offer a few corrections?

The rest of the people in the room held their breath while Scholem looked at me as if he were trying to decide what to make of this strange and ill-mannered beast. He then surprised everybody by laughing uproariously and then turning to me to say, "All right, Professor Hertzberg, I am eager to hear the more exact gossip that you have just offered to tell us." At the end of the evening, Scholem made it very clear that a barrier had been broken and that we had become friends. He walked over to me and said that I should feel free to come to see him whenever it was convenient, and he even added that he always had a few people over for coffee on Saturday morning, at eleven, and that he and his wife would be pleased if Phyllis and I would come when we could. As soon as Scholem was out the door, someone told me that this was the hardest invitation to get in all of Jerusalem. I did not understand at that moment why he decided to take me into his circle of friends, and I have never been able to explain it since then, but his friendship was and remained a great blessing for me and Phyllis to the end of his life in 1982, and beyond, in memory.

The saddest event in my life during those months in Jerusalem was the news that came on the telephone one morning several days after the Passover holiday that my father had died suddenly in Baltimore. I was not completely surprised, because he had done something a few days before that was most unusual. He did not wait for me to call him, which I did at least once a week; he called me from Baltimore. In our conversations through the years he had invariably expressed some ironic and even biting opinions on the events of the day, but not this time. He spoke to me on the telephone with warmth, and he volunteered forgiveness for my errors and those of the family and friends who were closest to him. I had the eerie feeling that I was listening to Moses standing on the mountaintop in the last days of his life, looking across to the promised land that he would never enter, but wanting to make sure that those who would live on would continue in his footsteps. I put down the phone hoping that he had some time left to see Phyllis and the children when we returned from Israel a few months later, but I had a deep foreboding that his wish of the past two years that he would be united with my mother would be answered soon. It was. My mother had died on a Wednesday night. She had a heart attack after completing the baking of the challahs for the Sabbath, and we ate those challahs at the sad Friday-night dinner of the weekend of her funeral. She had died in four hours. My father followed the same pattern. He was teaching a class in the Talmud on April 21, 1971, at about 10 P.M. when he had a heart attack, and he was gone by 2:30 in the morning.

As soon as I heard the news, Phyllis and our daughters started to phone the airlines frantically, to find a way of getting me to Baltimore by midday Friday when the funeral would be held. We found a connection through London, and I did get to Baltimore in time to be part of the cortege to the cemetery and to say the first Kaddish for him together with my siblings. I knew, and I had told everyone in the family, that he had forbidden us to follow the ever more prevalent custom of flying his body to the Holy Land to bury him on the outskirts of Jerusalem. When Mother died, I had asked him the question, "Shall we fly her body to Jerusalem?" and he obviously knew that I was asking him about himself too. He answered, without a moment's hesitation, that she should be buried in Baltimore. When I asked him why he ruled that way, he answered that she had lived almost all of her adult life in the city, that she had done much good, and that he presumed in years to come, many people would visit her grave and would be reminded of the virtues by which she had lived. Then, without adding a single word, he looked at me with eyes that did not blink or waver. And so, two years and four months later, we took him to lie beside her. Their graves in Baltimore have become a quiet holy place.

The climactic moment, for me, of the drama of my father's death came not in Baltimore, but, indeed, in Jerusalem, and the central figure was not one of my beloved friends from the inner circle of the Belzer Hasidim who admired and revered my father but from Gershom Scholem. For the very day that my father died, Scholem had arranged for Phyllis and me to be the guests of honor at a gathering that he was giving to welcome me to his circle in Jerusalem. When the news came of my sorrow, Phyllis called Scholem immediately and told him that I would soon be on my way to Baltimore, and so he canceled the party. I came back to Jerusalem after sitting shiva, the seven days of mourning, in Baltimore, and resumed teaching my classes at the university, but I, of course, followed the classic Jewish rules that a mourner does not participate in any amusements. This rule is very strict for the first thirty days after a death, but it becomes somewhat more relaxed for the rest of the year of mourning. On the thirtieth day, very precisely, Scholem was on the telephone. He told me that he wanted to reinstitute the event that had been planned for the day on which I had to leave for my father's funeral, but now that the thirty days of deep mourning were over, he could assure me that this would be simply some conversation over tea or coffee, and, therefore, not in transgression of the rules of mourning. Of course, I accepted the invitation.

A couple of weeks later, on the night of the gathering in his apartment, Scholem greeted me in a way of which only he was capable. He waited for everyone to gather and then he asked for quiet so that he could say a word or two of greeting. He was saying this as he walked from a room behind the living room where most of his books were stored, and he had one hand behind his back. In the hush, Scholem told the gathering that Hertzberg and his family were in his home for the first time, and so he had taken the trouble to find out something about him. He added that he had found what he wanted in the most recent edition of the yearbook of the Leo Baeck Institute, in which I had written a short memoir of my connection with Ernst Cassirer, the German-Jewish philosopher and historian of ideas. Cassirer had died in the spring of 1945 when I was one of his students in a class at Columbia University on the philosophy of Immanuel Kant. The philosophy faculty and Cassirer's widow had asked me, the young rabbi in his class, who had often walked with him on campus, to read the service at the funeral. This story was eventually heard by Robert Weltsch, the editor of the *Leo Baeck Yearbook,* who insisted that I write about Cassirer's thoughts and feelings about his Jewishness during the last days of the Second World War. In order to make me "kosher" in the world of Jewish refugees from Germany, who were the principal audience for this yearbook, some connection had to be found for me to the German speakers among the Jews of Europe. Weltsch had, therefore, chosen to identify me at the foot of the page by nothing else but my place of birth, Lubaczow in Poland. Weltsch assumed that most of his readers would know that the Jewish language of this town in Galicia, which had belonged to the Austro-Hungarian Empire until 1918, was Yiddish or German.

Scholem then brought out from behind his back a slim volume that I recognized immediately. It was a book written by a late-medieval kabbalist Azariah de Fano. My grandfather had found the manuscript in the library of the rebbe of Belz and had published it in the 1890s, giving the place of publication as Lubaczow. Scholem turned to me and asserted that this man was undoubtedly my grandfather. I gulped and agreed. He had established that I came from learned Hasidic ancestors. I looked at him in awe, because he was the only man in the world who could have remembered that in an obscure volume of which copies are very rare, my family name was linked to Lubaczow, the very same Lubaczow that Robert Weltsch had mentioned in identifying me as a graduate student in philosophy in 1945 in Ernst Cassirer's class.

Until we left Jerusalem at the end of June, I said Kaddish at morning and evening prayers at one of the synagogues in the neighborhood in which we had rented a house. I began at a European-style (Ashkenazi) synagogue that was frequented by Romanian immigrants, but I found out very soon that I would not be left alone to say my prayers. Recognizing my American clothes, people kept sidling up to me to offer me black-market rates of exchange for whatever American dollars I had in my pocket. I knew that I could not drive these money changers out of the local temple, so I went to find another synagogue. There was a Sephardi congregation down the street where North African immigrants worshiped. Their rituals were sometimes not the same as those I knew, and their accents in Hebrew were so dominated by Arabic that it took me a while to be able to follow the prayers, but I persisted. The congregants made no visible effort to welcome me, because I was obviously an outsider. Nonetheless, they let me come, and soon I knew that I was part of the scene. One morning they called me to the Torah to say a prayer for the souls of my father and mother. My parents' memory, and their eldest son, who was worshiping with them, had been admitted to the North African immigrants' Jerusalem.

20

I did not begin my career as a rabbi imagining that I would spend any significant part of it in interfaith dialogue. I had learned a fair amount about Christianity in the history and philosophy courses at college (not from the Talmud, in which the early Nazarenes are barely mentioned), but I knew almost nothing about the actual life and immediate worries of the Christian majority. Yet, I could not avoid becoming involved. The question of the Church and the Jews had become a major and very public issue at the beginning of the 1960s. Pope John XXIII was known to be enormously sympathetic to Jews. Not long after he was elected pope in 1958, he began to prepare a churchwide council to bring the Catholic faith into the contemporary world. Perhaps the most painful subject was the historic connection between the Church and anti-Semitism. The deliberations and decisions of Vatican II were expected to cleanse the Church of Jew-hatred, past and present. Jewish delegations and innumerable individuals found their way to Rome, to private audiences with John XXIII, to urge him to continue on his course. These "lobbyists" were able to tell their constituents that they had achieved marvelous progress in the corridors of the Vatican. *Interfaith*, which in America had long meant local relations of goodwill, became an international affair. Soon there were rabbis, and bureaucrats, who had made themselves into specialists as international Jewish representatives not only with the Vatican but also with the World Council of Churches, the coordinating body of the Protestant and Orthodox denominations. The situation was, in fact, chaotic, because those who were representing the Jewish position were in competition with each other and constantly maneuvering to prove that their particular organization had the inside track at the Vatican or in Geneva, where the World Council had its headquarters. The bureaucrats in the Vatican, and even in the less highly controlled World Council, could limit access of people who told them what they did not want to hear. The temptation not to speak up with tough honesty often prevailed.

This chaos bred another problem; when Jews met Christian international leaders, the Jews were expected to know something about Christianity, to understand the sources of the Christian positions. The ability to flatter and cajole, or even to pound the table in anger, was simply not enough. Perforce, the various warring parts of the Jewish community drifted toward forging some kind of unity and finding some scholars to speak for the community, even if each of those who came together in some centralized body really intended to appear in the newspapers, very quickly, with interviews or press releases in which each tried to claim that his particular organization had seized the initiative. To be seen in the United States as preeminent in the field was good institutional business.

At the end of the 1960s and the beginning of the 1970s, I was already so busy that I cannot figure out, as I look back, how I managed to jam everything I was doing into finite days. I had full-time responsibilities at my synagogue, and I remained concerned with all my obligations. I continued to teach at Columbia, where I almost never missed a class. The *Encyclopaedia Judaica* took up my summers and many late nights reading at home, and the executive of the World Zionist Organization required my presence at recurring meetings in New York and at least twice a year in Jerusalem. Nonetheless I did manage another major responsibility, and I cannot even pretend that it was forced upon me as I kept saying "suffer this cup to pass from my lips." On the contrary, busy as I was, with Phyllis and my daughters all complaining that they would now see me even less than before and that I was now trying to kill myself, I accepted the task of being the elected leader of the newly formed International Jewish Committee for Interreligious Consultation (IJCIC). I was now the chair of the body to which the major interests in the Jewish community, both in the Diaspora and in Israel, involved in the diplomacy of Jewish-Christian relations, belonged. The group had been formed in 1967. The prime mover was Gerhart Riegner, the secretary general of the World Jewish Congress, and the chair at the very beginning was Rabbi Joachim Prinz, who was then senior vice president of the World Jewish Congress. In its first year or two, nothing much happened. In 1969 Riegner was joined by Henry Siegman, who was then the executive director of the Synagogue Council of America, the body that then represented the Reform, Conservative, and Orthodox synagogues and their rabbinates in interfaith relations. Together Riegner and Siegman gave new strength and even some authority to the IJCIC. Siegman, in particular, was enough of a fighter to take on the special interests of the various organizations in the field. These special interests seldom involved substantive matters. The organizations fought each other for space and top billing. He was particularly adept at countering Rabbi Marc Tannenbaum, who was the head of interreligious affairs for the American Jewish Committee. Tannenbaum made no secret of the fact that he thought he was the king of the Jewish hill in the interreligious field and he did not intend to yield any of his sovereign right to do as he wished.

For the next several years I had a ringside seat, and I was sometimes called to be referee and occasionally even the enforcer of discipline as I watched the two of them fight. I had this perch because Riegner and Siegman joined together in keeping me in office as head of the IJCIC for three and a half years, until the beginning of 1972. The various competing agencies tolerated me as chairman for several reasons. I had not been involved directly in any of the intense Jewish efforts to lobby at Vatican II, and so I had not gotten in the way of any of the Jewish institutions that were proving how important their work was to the Jewish cause. Yet, it was widely known that I had participated in a series of discreet consultations that took place on the fringes of the Vatican Council.

I remember one such consultation with special vividness. One day in the late 1960s, I had a call from Jerusalem from Mayor Teddy Kollek. We had been friends since the 1940s, when I was one of the many people who worked with him as he gathered help for Israel in the United States before and during Israel's War of Independence. Kollek told me that a group that was fronting for the Vatican was calling for an off-the-record consultation in Rome, in a conference center and not at the Vatican, to discuss a proposal for the governance of Jerusalem. The suggestion was going to be made that the holy places of all the major faiths be governed by an international interreligious commission representing the three biblical faiths. Though this was never said in so many words, it was clear that the Vatican expected to be the leading force in this body. The people who were being invited to the consultation included not only Christians of several persuasions but, especially, some Muslims and several Jews. Kollek made it clear to me that he did not want to sit at this meeting unless he was flanked by two rabbis who would not be rude but were not likely to be intimidated. Rabbi Abraham Joshua Heschel, the rabbinic scholar who had marched beside Martin Luther King in the fall of 1962 at the head of the famous march on Washington, D.C., had already accepted to accompany Kollek, and I was to be the second rabbinic chaperone. I agreed to try to clear my calendar to come, but I was given little time to decide. Within a day or so, Rabbi Heschel was on the phone pushing me not to leave him alone. The implication was that he wanted to appear in his usual persona of a mystic and unworldly religious figure, leaving to me the interreligious infighting.

Nothing much happened at the table except the usual chitchat. It was often high sounding, but, underneath the rhetoric of dialogue and understanding, each of the groups was pushing for its own interests. The Jews clearly did not want to surrender their paramount role in Jerusalem, and the Israelis, who had united the city at great cost in blood during the Six-Day War, certainly did not want an international commission that would work to increase its power while accepting little or no responsibility for the safety of Jerusalem. The two days of talk were essentially an exercise in speech making, and before the end of the first day I was completely bored. The obvious and the predictable were happening before my eyes, but in the middle of the morning on Thursday, the second day of the meeting, I was handed a note and asked to come to the telephone to speak with someone at the Vatican. I was bored no longer.

I found at the other end of the line a very polite monsignor, who was an assistant to Archbishop Giovanni Benelli, the prosecretary of state of the Vatican. The monsignor invited me to meet the archbishop at his office in the Vatican the next day. I was already booked to fly back to New York on the Alitalia flight that left at 11 A.M. That reservation had been made because the plane would bring me to New York early enough for me to get to Sabbath services at my synagogue in Englewood, so I balked at the appointment. After several telephone calls back and forth, the appointment was set for 11 A.M. with the understanding that the Vatican's influence was strong enough to delay the flight until 1 P.M. The next morning, I arrived in Benelli's office a few minutes before the appointed time, but the archbishop was not free because he was being held up by a loquacious, aging cardinal who could not be cut short. Even a powerful archbishop did not dare tell a cardinal that he was overstaying his time.

Finally, my meeting with Benelli began a half hour late. We quickly agreed that we would speak French because neither his English nor my Italian was adequate to the task. So I began by calling him *éminence*, a title reserved for cardinals (he had not yet attained that rank), and he responded by calling me *grand rabbin*, a rank that I would never attain (it exists only in France). Benelli quickly got to the point of the meeting: he offered me a "deal" that would represent a grand resolution of some of the major tensions between the Church and the Jews. He was very much aware that the Jews were eager for the Vatican to give Israel formal diplomatic recognition. He knew equally well that Jews in America were one of the powerful forces in opposition to state aid for parochial education. He confided to me that unless parochial education received subsidies from the American government, the Church would have trouble maintaining the parochial-school network, and thus Roman Catholics in the United States would continue the alarming trend of falling away from any authentic version of their faith. To emphasize for me that this was a serious proposal, he glanced down the corridor to the door of the pope's private apartment, which was a few yards away from Benelli's office, and he told me that if we came to an understanding he would be pleased for us to go together to inform His Holiness.

This offer could not be turned aside with some clever remark. I knew that my reply had to be the truth—and to be believed as truth. I said to Benelli that I had no doubt whatsoever that he could deliver his part of the deal, because the Vatican was a centralized institution with the pope as its monarch. It was within his power to extend diplomatic recognition to the state of Israel whenever he pleased. The American Jewish community was a dissonant community of many opinions, however, and no one had the power to speak for it or to silence those who might be troublesome. It was conceivable that, speaking for some American Jews, I might agree to change policy on state aid for education in return for the recognition of Israel, but no one could guarantee that the bulk of the community would follow such a lead. Benelli heard me with great attention, and he quickly concluded that I was telling him the truth. Obviously, we did not walk down the corridor to the pope's door. On the contrary, as a good host, he walked with me to the staircase that would take me down to the courtyard of the Vatican. A car was waiting to take me to the airport. With the help of a police escort I made it to the plane at one o'clock. The door was closed behind me, and the aircraft took off for New York.

Teddy Kollek had left for Jerusalem the night before. I contacted him from Englewood after the weekend and told him exactly what had happened. He seemed pleased that I had responded to Benelli the way I had. A few days later, he told me that he had given the foreign ministry of Israel an account of the story and that they, too, were content with my refusal to trade for the diplomatic recognition of Israel by offering some dubious support for the Vatican in American politics—support that would then have involved a humiliating and divisive volte-face by American Jews.

In this incident I had made no enemies, but I became known as someone who would take on the Church, without flinching, on some fundamental matters that involved the dignity of the Jewish people. I never safeguarded acceptability in the Vatican by playing down my views on controversial matters. This had begun in the late 1950s when a controversial play, *The Deputy*, by Rolf Hochhuth, a German writer, appeared in the United States in English translation. The author indicted the title character—that is, Pope Pius XII, "God's deputy on earth"—for callousness during the Holocaust. The appearance of this play was the occasion of a bitter debate. I had joined in Hochhuth's questioning of the record of Pius XII, so that the spokesmen of the Church in America knew my views and were perturbed by them. In those years I was especially friendly with a Jesuit scholar, Father Robert Graham, who was a church historian. Graham was embarrassed by the controversy that Hochhuth's play had occasioned, and he wanted to save his own Catholic orthodoxy by helping to defend Pius XII's actions and policies during the war years. Graham accepted an invitation from the Vatican to be one of the principal editors of the documents that passed between the Vatican and the church authorities all over Europe from 1939 to 1945. When Graham left for Rome, we were still very friendly. He was eager to see the documents at the Vatican, and I was equally eager to see the results that would come from the work of a Catholic scholar such as Graham, whom I liked and respected. From Rome he sent me a number of letters, but soon the correspondence stopped. He was obviously not able to tell me anything about his work, and eventually I knew why. The eleven volumes that he helped edit, which were published between the 1960s and the 1980s, represented a Vatican archive that had been carefully expurgated to protect the reputation of Pius XII. Graham was too good a scholar not to know this, and he knew that I would see through this fraud and denounce it. I did not hide my anger at all those who had power and influence in Europe from 1939 through 1945 and who could have made some effort to save my grandfather and all my aunts and uncles and all my cousins—and 6 million Jews like them.

By the end of the 1960s I had acquired a mixed reputation in the interreligious field. I was not pathologically an enemy of Christianity or of the Church, only of some Christians and some churchmen. Like almost all Jews, I was elated and inspired by the papacy of John XXIII (1958–63). He had gone further than any Christian leader before him to end theological anti-Semitism and to demonstrate his very real contrition for what his church had not done during the Holocaust. He was known to have made great efforts to help Jews while papal nuncio in Istanbul during the war, and I knew, from one of the Jews who had been to see him then to ask for his help, that he had broken down in tears when talking of these terrible events. His successor as pope, Paul VI, continued the work of John XXIII in dialogue with other faiths, and he visited the Holy Land in 1964, although he shied away from recognizing Israel. But I was enraged to hear that Paul VI, at a Mass that he said before tens of thousands in Yankee Stadium, allowed as the lesson a passage from the Christian Gospels that condemned the Jews for denying and killing Jesus. Such sentiments were circulating among Catholic intellectuals in America a few years later, during the inner-city riots of 1968, when many White-owned stores in the Black ghettos, shops whose proprietors were often well known to be Jews, were burned down. Rosemary Reuther, writing in the *National Catholic Reporter*, claimed that she had been inspired by these outbreaks of violence to see the very face of the rising Christ in the fires that the rioters had started. I could not get the editors of the *National Catholic Reporter* to disavow this statement, so I resigned from the monthly column that I had been writing for them.

My memory has chosen to blot out innumerable meetings in New York, Jerusalem, Rome, and Geneva that were marked by complicated games of maneuver. The Jewish and Christian delegations circled each other with some wariness, and within the Jewish delegation itself, the battle for center stage never stopped. One meeting does stand out in memory because it represented a profound turn in Jewish-Catholic relations. For the first time in all of the centuries since Christianity had become a separate religion, the Vatican and the world Jewish community, acting through the IJCIC, agreed to have a formal meeting as equals. A delegation from each side would be empowered to survey and discuss the major issues on the agendas of both communities. When the commitment was made to raise the level of Jewish-Catholic diplomacy to this new height, I was overwhelmed by a feeling of deep responsibility and, yes, of great joy.

The meeting was scheduled to take place in the fall of 1971. The Vatican offered to house it in Rome in one of its buildings, but I, very politely, refused. I gave my reason very openly: for many, many centuries Jewish delegations had come to the Vatican to beg for compassion for their troubles or to ask some specific favor. Even in the most recent years, when Jews had lobbied energetically, they had never been admitted to share as equal participants in the Church's discussions about Jews. I asked for a symbol of the new relationship by having the meeting in a neutral city, such as Paris. The suggestion was accepted. The two sides agreed that the gathering would take place in the synagogue in the Rue de la Victoire, which is the seat of the chief rabbi of France. When this gracious acceptance came through, I smiled at the monsignor who brought the news. I joked that I presumed that the prelates and priests who would make up the Vatican delegation would have no difficulty in joining the Jews eating kosher food prepared by the kitchen of the synagogue. This was accepted with great friendliness and good humor.

The Vatican delegation was led by the archbishop of Marseilles, Roger Etchegaray, a person of great warmth and shining decency who obviously cared that relations between Jews and Catholics be based on the deepest mutual respect and ever growing affection. From the Vatican itself, the leading figure who came was another archbishop, of Belgian origin, Jerome Hamer. He was much more tightly controlled than Etchegaray, and it did not take me very many minutes at the table with him to understand why he was behaving as he did. Hamer was very high up, indeed, in the Vatican. He was then a senior member of the group that guarded doctrinal orthodoxy within the Church. He had come to this meeting to make sure that the larger delegation, which contained several priests who were known to be, perhaps, a shade too friendly to the Jews, should not run out of control. After an afternoon of opening generalities and exhortations of each other that we must make progress together, I decided that I could find out what the Vatican's intentions were, and where its red lines in its relationship to Jews lay, only if I had a private, face-to-face conversation with Hamer. Toward the end of the day, I called him aside and invited him to come to my room at the hotel at which I was staying so that we could have a private talk. I was both pleased and amazed when he readily accepted.

When Hamer came to visit that evening, he was in no mood for any of the usual pleasantries. I offered to get some tea or coffee up from room service, but he indicated that he wanted to get right to business. I responded by being absolutely forthright: it was fundamental for building a relationship that each side knew what the basic needs and intentions of the other were. I was prepared to define for him the basic agenda of the Jewish side, and I would be grateful if he told me what the Vatican hoped to achieve in this new relationship with the Jewish people. I paused, hoping that Hamer would take over and describe the Vatican's agenda, but he was too good a diplomat to do that. He very politely said, "You first." I replied immediately, without any hesitation whatsoever, that the Jews, then, in 1971, barely a generation after the Holocaust and the creation of the state of Israel, had two fundamental issues with the Vatican. That the Vatican had not yet extended diplomatic recognition, we regarded as an ongoing downgrading of the state of Israel, a not too subtle assertion that Israel was not quite legitimate. Our second fundamental issue was the long-standing tradition of anti-Semitic teaching within the Roman Catholic Church. We were most appreciative of the basic action in Vatican II as part of its declaration of the attitude of the Church toward other religions: that it condemned anti-Semitism vigorously and unequivocally. Vatican II had forbidden any organ of the Church to teach or spread anti-Semitism, but Hamer and I both knew that much remained to be done. Various parts of the Church had not assimilated the teaching of Vatican II, and "Christ-killers" had not yet been eradicated from Catholic curricula. I added that on the Jewish side we looked forward to working ever more intimately with Christians on problems that affected all of humanity such as poverty, the decline of moral standards in the world, and the protection of the environment, but I reiterated that the two Jewish issues with which we came to the meeting were the ones that I had described.

Hamer replied with equal candor, even though he did hide behind a technicality or two. He told me that the diplomatic recognition of Israel was not on any immediate Vatican agenda. He phrased it by telling me that such action was in the competence of the Vatican's secretary of state, its foreign office, and that he and the entire delegation had been sent to this meeting by the religious interests of the Church. On the matter of anti-Semitism, Hamer told me with great emphasis, and even some emotion, that it was the absolute commitment of the Church to remove every trace of anti-Semitism from every aspect of its life. He could assure me that this concern of the Jewish people would be honored, because it was a deep concern of the Church as a whole. I then asked him the further question, "So, what is your agenda?"

He answered that his delegation had two basic concerns. In the first place, Roman Catholics had been troubled for many centuries that there was no theological parallelism between Judaism and Christianity. It was impossible to think about Christianity without defining its relationship to its Jewish roots. What the Jews knew as the Hebrew Bible was the Christian Old Testament, from the text of which Christians had derived the "good news" of all of the events told in the New Testament. Contrarily, Christianity played absolutely no role in the theology of Judaism. Hamer knew the obvious answer very well: Judaism was no more obliged to take account of Christianity than both Judaism and Christianity were obliged to include Islam in their theologies. Nonetheless, the Church thought it was time for Judaism to develop a theology that perceived Christianity as belonging to religious history and even the theology of the Jews.

Hamer's second concern was the reputation of Pope Pius XII. The Church was very sensitive to continuing attacks on his supposed passivity during the Holocaust, and it knew very well that the Jewish community was overwhelmingly on the side of the critics. He told me that Pius XII had done very much more to try to mitigate the persecution of Jews than he had been given credit for. The Church could not sit by and do nothing while the reputation of the wartime pope was being dragged down. Hamer hoped that as a result of these deliberations, and the relationship that would ensue from them, the Jewish community would change its mind about Pius XII and allow the Church to leave that issue behind and go forward toward a new era of warmth and cooperation. Brilliant diplomat that Hamer was, there was not even a breath of the suggestion that the Church would be much friendlier to Jewish concerns if we abandoned the battle against Pius XII, but, somehow, the suggestion was hovering over the room in which we talked.

It was now my turn to comment. I responded that both of the questions that he had raised were very difficult for the Jewish delegation and that I could give him only a personal reading. I told him first what I expected he already knew. The Orthodox component of the Jewish religious community had allowed the dialogue with the Church to go forward only on the clear-cut understanding that we would work together only on social problems and that we would never discuss theology. This reflected a number of fears, mainly that the liberal rabbis in Jewish delegations would agree in theological discussion to positions that the Orthodox could not countenance, and that in theological discussion the Christian side might bring forth some of the old conversionist arguments that lined Jews up as potential converts to Christianity. I said to Hamer that I believed that this ban would last for a number of years but eventually it would have to fall by the wayside. It was simply inconceivable that we could sit together for a decade or two without trying to understand each other's faith and religious history. Therefore, I could predict that the discussion of the fundamental nature of both our faiths would inevitably take place, but I could not suggest, even in the boldest outline, where such conversations and studies might lead.

On the second, and more immediate, matter of the reputation of Pius XII, I was much less reassuring. Fundamentally, the Church wanted Jews to assent to its estimate of what happened during the Holocaust: that the Church as institution, headed by the pope, was blameless but that, unfortunately, individual Catholics, all too many of them, behaved badly. The consensus of Jewish opinion was the reverse: that many individual Catholics, both laity and clergy, behaved with exemplary decency and courage but that the Church as a whole did not take risks to protect Jews. The Jewish estimate of Pope Pius XII was that his main concern had been to preserve the strength of the Church and to be the main bulwark in Europe against the further spread of Communism. I added that it was conceivable that some of those who were taking part in our dialogue might be persuaded to soften their line toward Pius XII but it was beyond our power, and certainly my power, to silence those many people in the Jewish community who remained unhappy when they contemplated his memory.

Hamer and I soon parted, assuring each other that Jews and Catholics had begun to talk seriously. We would try to build on those issues on which we could find some agreement. In fact, Hamer and I stayed in touch by private letter for several years, until he was raised to an even higher post in the Church, second only to Cardinal Ratzinger as guardian of doctrinal orthodoxy. He was after that no longer directly involved in interreligious affairs, so our connection petered out.

To that initial meeting in Paris of two formal delegations, the Vatican had sent along several priests who were their experts on Jews and Judaism. The most voluble among them was a priest of Czech origin, Father Hruby, who told me that he was a grandson of the late chief rabbi of Prague. His mother, a daughter of the house, had married his father, who was a pious Catholic. Father Hruby had learned Yiddish from his mother, and he spoke it was well as I. He had even studied some Talmud, implying mysteriously that he had found his way to a yeshiva, perhaps in Israel, after the end of the Second World War, telling those he met there that he was the grandson of a very famous rabbi. These credentials made me more uneasy than comfortable. Father Hruby was not speaking as a Catholic. He kept telling the Jewish delegation what our attitude ought, correctly, to be. By the end of the second day, as this meeting was nearing its close, I had a quick word with my new friend, Archbishop Hamer, and said to him very pointedly, "Please, the next time you fellows come to a session like this, bring along Gentile Catholics and not Jewish ones. I should like to hear the Catholics talking for the Church so that they would leave the rabbis to their natural role of speaking for the synagogue."

The next day, I read in the *International Herald Tribune* press releases and interviews with several members of my delegation. Each of them wanted the world to know that he personally had led in advancing the cause of Judaism at this historic moment, but I accepted that as inevitable. I even had no doubt that what they were saying was true, at least in part. Each of the Jewish participants had made connections that would indeed be of some benefit to him and his organization, but together these efforts advanced the discussion. I headed for the airport to fly back to my family and synagogue in Englewood with the feeling that the main outlines of the relationship had been defined. Indeed, they had. In the course of time, the Vatican did recognize Israel, making the point that it was not recognizing the state as a revolution in theology, the "beginning of the redemption," but as a secular entity that had demonstrated that it was a viable political construct. The Catholic Church has gone very much further in banishing anti-Semitism from its teaching and practice, and it continues to struggle with the memory of Pius XII. As I predicted to Hamer in 1971, that battle would not end easily.

We did make some progress, though we did not know it at the time, on the matter of better understanding between our two faiths. Something happened very quietly on the first day of our meeting. The incident seemed unimportant at the moment and even a little embarrassing, but it was nonetheless a harbinger of the journey on which we were embarked: to learn more about each other. In the fall of 1971 I was still in mourning for my father, who had died that spring, right after Passover. I was required by religious tradition to say the Kaddish for him at the daily services morning and evening, and for that a minyan (a quorum of ten men) was necessary. The attendance was adequate at morning services at the Rue de la Victoire synagogue because its authorities had arranged that a few poor people who lived in the neighborhood come every morning in return for a few francs. The quorum was harder to come by in the afternoon because some of the poor who came in the morning were working at odd jobs during the day.

That first afternoon of our meeting, I was scurrying around in the corridors of the synagogue, trying to round up two more people for the minyan. Two bishops who were part of the Catholic delegation happened to walk by and sensed that I was worried. They asked if they could help and I told them I was short two people for the minyan. The bishops instantly offered to join the prayer service. I thanked them with great warmth, as they deserved, and then I explained to them that I was in the same difficulty in which they were: they could not serve Mass to me, even if I wanted to get in line for the wine and wafer, because I had not been baptized a Catholic, and I could not count them to a minyan because they were not Jewish. After this explanation, there was absolutely nothing to do but embrace each other. At that moment, two of the poor Jews who came for a few francs showed up. We went into minyan. I was very moved to see that the two bishops came in with us and stood respectfully, not too far from me, through the service. When the service ended, I thanked the last two to arrive who had helped to complete the minyan and I walked out together with the bishops. I think I saw my father smiling down at the scene.

More was going on inside me in the years 1970 and 1971 than I was willing to acknowledge. My negotiation with Cornell to become a full-time academic did not represent a simple desire to change careers so that I could have more time to think and to write. On the contrary, I had agreed in 1969 to become chairman of the IJCIC, and I had gladly accepted membership on the executive of the World Zionist Organization. These were not the actions of the man whose sole desire, then, was to find ways of withdrawing from the tumult of the world.

As soon as I had made an end of the possibility that I would go to Cornell, I accepted the invitation to come to Jerusalem as visiting professor at the Hebrew University, from January to June 1971. I told myself at the time that this was a move toward concentrating my life around studying and writing, but this account of my motive was self-delusional. I knew very well, beyond any shadow of a doubt, that I could not spend a half year in Jerusalem in the midst of its seething society while staying detached in some ivory tower that I would make for myself. For the first time, I was beginning to confess to myself that flirting with Cornell and then going off on a sabbatical to Jerusalem were both parts of a different story. I had not given up on being the rabbi in

Englewood, but I now thought that my most important work was being done in larger arenas. I would now be attending the regular weekly meetings of the World Zionist executive at the very center of the action, and I would inevitably be taking a direct hand in its decisions about many contentious issues. Would I survive in these debates? I was ever more confident that my views would make some difference.

The first test came in a battle over religious education in Israel. Even if I wanted to, I could not avoid that battle, because there was a presumption about my appointment to the executive of the World Zionist Organization that I would informally represent the interests and point of view of the Conservative wing within the Jewish religious community. In Israel that was a particularly difficult role because the basic cleavage about religion was between the secular majority and a religious minority that was almost totally Orthodox. Public education was divided between governmental schools, which were essentially secular, and those that were controlled by the Orthodox. But a small and growing number of Conservative and Reform Jews had begun to make their permanent home in Jerusalem. These were mostly of American origin, and they had brought their Conservative convictions and practices with them. They had no schools for their children that suited them: the secular schools were too nonreligious, and the Orthodox schools were too Orthodox. The Conservatives were the equivalent of Episcopalians who could not find a home either in a Roman Catholic Church or in the culture of humanists, agnostics, and atheists. There was, however, a provision in the school laws that provided some wiggle room. Parents were allowed to band together and, with sufficient numbers in any school, ask for additional instruction in subjects of their concern. For example, they could ask for classes in violin, or Russian literature, or even the Talmud.

The leaders of the Conservative community in Jerusalem (on this issue, they were represented by Rabbi Moshe Tutnauer) approached me to ask me to help get the school in French Hill, the neighborhood in Jerusalem where most of these parents lived, to introduce additional classes in Jewish tradition and classic texts in the spirit of Conservative Judaism. The obstacle was that the Orthodox element that controlled the religious schools, the religious Zionist party, the Mafdal, was vehemently opposed to any such change. This would open the door to schools under Conservative auspices, and it would irrevocably dilute the idea, widely held in Israel then, that religion meant Orthodoxy. Rabbi Tutnauer had come to me with a simple plea, Never mind the politics; how do we educate our children?

Very fortunately, Mayor Teddy Kollek had become an ever closer friend; in those months we worked together on a variety of matters, and we often had breakfast or lunch together. Equally fortunately, the acknowledged elder statesman of Mafdal was Dr. Joseph Burg, who had been one of the signers of Israel's declaration of independence on May 14, 1948. Dr. Burg and I were somewhat distantly related by marriage, but, more important, I sat right behind him in synagogue every Sabbath morning and, at all the breaks in the service, we engaged in the game of quotation and counterquotation of the sacred texts. Essentially we had declared a draw in this game, attended by expressions of mutual regard and even affection. I asked Teddy Kollek to arrange a meeting, entirely off the record, at which three people would be present: he, Joseph Burg, and I. Within a very few days the three of us were sitting in a hideaway office at the Jerusalem Museum that Teddy seemed to use for discreet meetings.

I proposed to Dr. Burg that if we ignored the request of additional hours of instruction for the children of Conservative Jews, the matter would not go away; it would only fester, and it would very quickly reach the press. I did not think that either the Orthodox or Conservative communities needed a religious battle; passions would be aroused that could only backfire. How, indeed, could the Orthodox win a fight against the Conservatives in the wider court of Israeli opinion if they were denying some Jews the opportunity to raise their children to be more learned and caring Jews? The argument that their leaders would be indoctrinating these youngsters in the wrong variety of Judaism would simply not be accepted by the majority of Israelis. Nor would the Conservatives win if they had to fight a battle to the bitter end against what they would term the "bigotry" of the Orthodox. This would simply help those who wished religious Jews ill to say "a plague on both of your houses." And anyway, so I concluded, the Zionist movement, and now the state of Israel, had always existed by including parties and elements that found each other's beliefs and practices intolerable, but, nonetheless, we lived together as parts of the Jewish people.

I will never forget Dr. Burg's response. He said to Teddy Kollek and to me that he knew that some of his fiercer colleagues and followers would not like what he would do, but he agreed with us that it would be far better to let this proposal become reality than to have a fight. I know that I did not really persuade Joseph Burg that day. He was not hearing me promoting the point of view of Conservative Judaism; he sat there and thought about making the life of the Jewish people as a whole more peaceful and more viable. I had gotten to know Joseph Burg well enough to know that he had spent many years as a master of partisan infighting. That day, I saw a man who rose beyond that to be a statesman and a moral leader.

At the end of this meeting I was elated. I thought that, in the years to come, the religious tensions within Jewish Israel and, by extension, in the Diaspora would be settled by reasonable people who would try to keep the peace so that the Jewish community would not be splintered into warring factions—but I was wrong. Dr. Joseph Burg represented the old-line leadership of the Orthodox believers who were Zionist. By the early 1970s they were in late middle age, and younger elements were pushing to succeed them. The older generation had spent many decades in coming to terms with the secular majority in the Zionist movement, but their successors were not men and women of compromise. They were at war with the infidels within Jewry. The center at which most had received their education was the yeshiva in Jerusalem that Rabbi Abraham Isaac Kook had founded in the 1920s, but which was now dominated by the teachings of his son, Rabbi Zvi Yehuda Kook, who was a much less gentle leader. The younger Kook followed after his father in believing that we were now living in messianic times. He identified the great Israeli victory in June 1967 with the beginning of the messianic era. He taught his followers to push, militantly, for Jews to retain the "undivided land of Israel." His students and disciples were uncompromisingly at war with all those who doubted their messianic reading of contemporary Jewish history.

The followers of Rabbi Zvi Yehuda Kook very rapidly became dominant in the Mafdal. They were pushing aside Dr. Joseph Burg and his generation. In order to survive within his own camp, Burg began to move to the political right. On the personal level, he and I still maintained friendly relations, but otherwise he kept me sufficiently at arm's length that such association would not get him into trouble. The new militant messianists did not totally dominate the religious scene in Israel, but they very quickly acquired enough power to make denying them an ever greater political risk. I had come to Israel believing that I could remain a man of the center, retaining good connections in the Orthodox community. In the course of 1971, the greater part of which I spent in Israel, I learned that this was not true. Personal connections with the older generations in almost all of the Orthodox camps still remained. I could visit the rebbe of Belz and be received with courtesy and warmth, and have a friendly tea at the home of Rabbi Amram Blau of the ultra-Orthodox anti-Zionists, but I could no longer imagine that these personal connections could be used to soften the partisan conflicts. They could not. The times had changed, and, even at the age of fifty, I was already a figure who belonged to an older generation. I would soon be forced into battles that I did not want.

The year 1971 was an early high point in the immigration of Soviet Jews, but the religious status of an increasing number of the families who were arriving in Vienna, the main transit point to Israel or to freedom in the West, was increasingly questionable. Under the rules of the Israeli government, any Soviet citizen who could prove that one of his grandparents was Jewish was entitled to a visa to Israel. This meant that families were arriving on the train to Vienna to be told that some or many of their members, or even all of them, were not Jews by the standards of the halakah. The solution to the problem had been devised very quickly and without fanfare by the leaders of the Mafdal, when they were still of the older generation that preferred to compromise. Some rabbis from this group were sent to Vienna to offer quick conversions to the Jewish faith, en masse, to those whose Jewish identity was questionable. So, in the summer of 1971, I inspected the office that represented the Jewish Agency–World Zionist Organization in Vienna. The day of my visit, an even dozen recently arrived babies were circumcised as the first step in conferring upon them a Jewish identity. This practice was further buttressed by a decision of the new chief rabbi of Israel, Shlomo Goren, who had moved to that post from having been for years the chief chaplain of Israel's defense forces. Rabbi Goren ruled that these conversions in Vienna, including those of adults who had little or no knowledge of Jewish faith and practice, should be encouraged and quickly done for the arrivals from the Soviet Union who had chosen to be on their way to Israel. They would rapidly be absorbed as Jews in an all-Jewish society. However, so Rabbi Goren ruled, those who chose not to go to Israel should not be offered easy and painless conversions; to live as a Jew in the Diaspora, where the majority society was Gentile, would require much more conscious effort and much more personal choice and conviction.

This compromise was unquestioned until Rabbi Menachem Mendel Schneerson, the rebbe of Lubavich who lived in Brooklyn, announced his vehement disapproval in 1970. He maintained that these quick conversions in Vienna represented an abasement of the process of conversion, for such acts were not valid in the law of the halakah. He cast doubt on the qualifications of the rabbis of the Mafdal to make such decisions and to offer their services as the constituent members of courts of Jewish law. The battle was thus joined between a famous and powerful Hasidic leader and the more accommodating Orthodoxy, then, of the Mafdal. To be sure, this setup for religious conversions had been created in Vienna by agreement of the Israeli government and the World Zionist Organization. The religious Zionists of the Mafdal were part of the coalitions that governed both bodies, so one could have expected that they would jump to the defense of the effort in Vienna, but they did not. In the intricacies of Israeli politics, the major players—the representatives of the Labor Zionist Party, which led the incumbent government, and the right-wing opposition, led by Menachem Begin—both preferred not to alienate the rebbe of Lubavich, who controlled some thousands of voters in Israel and much influence in the Diaspora. I took the side of the moderates. I went to Vienna to show support, but the Mafdal party itself was moving to abandon its own creation. It folded the effort in Vienna. No one in the Orthodox camp, even the moderates of yesterday, wanted to be seen as too lenient, as someone of doubtful passion for strict obedience to halakah.

After the Mafdal rabbis withdrew from Vienna, the issue of who had the authority to perform conversions became ever sharper and more embattled. At meetings of the World Zionist executive, I was one of the very few at the table to insist that Jews as a people had to become more accepting of converts. Problems of identity were appearing in ever larger numbers as the rate of intermarriage was rising almost every-where in the Diaspora. In Israel the Orthodox could exercise consider-able control in defining personal status—whether individuals were or were not Jews—but the Diaspora was not dominated by the Orthodox. At one meeting, I even suggested that the rebbe of Lubavich had undertaken this battle not primarily because he was afraid of what might happen in Israel when these quickly converted Russian Jews arrived; he was even more worried about what he saw around him in the United States: conversions and marriages that were much more uncon-trollable because there was no central authority that could enforce its standards. The Jews were faced with a fateful choice: we could become more flexible in matters of conversion and other issues of personal sta-tus, or we could become more insistent on absolute obedience to the strictest interpretations of the halakah.

Where did this new uncompromising agenda come from? I could see several influences converging to create this new Orthodoxy. One was a worldwide trend evident also in Christianity and Islam of "return to the old-time religion." We were living, everywhere, in the shadows of all the vast traumas of the Second World War. Everywhere significant elements were looking for spiritual certainties as their anchor. All over the world liberalism, both in faith and in politics, was held to be a failure, and that old-time religion was being offered as the antidote to the messy world that had supposedly been created by too much religious flexibility. A corollary of this feeling of religious and cultural anger was, almost inevitably, the appearance of revived messianic movements. Among the Christians, the twice-born and those who expected the second coming any day now were ever more vocal. In Islam, even among the intelli-gentsia there was a turning away from secular models of life to a new emphasis on religious revival leading to messianic events; the thirteenth imam, the last representative of the prophet who would announce the end of days, was now being anointed by many. In Judaism the elements who followed Zvi Yehuda Kook were now being joined by the disciples of the rebbe of Lubavich; he was sending many disciples out on missions to turn this time into an era fit for the appearance of the messiah. The battle that had been joined everywhere, in different permutations, was essentially the same basic battle. Most messianists were no longer con-cerned about the destiny of all of mankind or even of all those who belonged to their own faith and community. Except for the followers of the rebbe of Chabad (who wanted to redeem the whole world), the emphasis was on a purified minority. Who cares what happens in the next few years if the messiah will soon appear? What if one must antagonize or even ride over those of too little faith in order to bring about that great denouement?

I opposed these visionaries with great vehemence, and not only in the debates at the table. I went public in the early 1970s, denouncing the partisans of the "undivided land of Israel" by calling them armed prophets, reincarnations of the Zealots of eighteen centuries earlier who had made the revolt in Palestine against Rome and led to the destruction of Jerusalem and the Second Temple in the year 70 because they were certain that they could not lose: God would send the messiah to intervene on their behalf. I kept insisting that I could not believe that God, Who had not sent the messiah to save 6 million Jews during the Holocaust, would now send him in order to guarantee the Jewish possession of the West Bank. I had chosen sides.

The fundamentalists and the maximalists did not really win this fight in the battles of the early 1970s. They overreached. In 1973 they raised, very provocatively, the question, Who is a Jew? They challenged and tried to overturn the long-standing special arrangements under which Jews in the Western Diaspora, and especially in the United States, who wanted to emigrate to Israel, who "were returning to their homeland," would be helped. The decision as to whether a prospective newcomer to Israel was really a Jew was left to the immigration offices of the Jewish Agency–World Zionist Organization. Their special instructions were that anyone who was born a Jew—that is, whose birth mother was a Jew or who had been converted to Judaism by any rabbinic authority (which meant that conversions by Conservative and Reform rabbis were recognized)—should be helped under this law. Encouraged by their success in the battle over conversions in Vienna of Russian Jews, and feeling their oats as a growing power in Israel's complicated politics, the Orthodox right-wingers, declared war on this arrangement. They wanted to change the law in Israel: henceforth immigration offices in the Diaspora would certify a prospective immigrant as a Jew only if he or she could prove that they were indeed Jewish according to the strictest Orthodox halakic standards.

This attempt to change the status quo opened a fierce battle. For the first time since the creation of the state of Israel, almost all of the leaders of the American Jewish community who were not identified with the Orthodox went to war. Enormous pressure was put on Israel's parliament, the Knesset, not to pass such a law. The American Diaspora bluntly refused to let the Israeli political process produce a deal that would cause little upset in Israel, where the Orthodox were in control on matters of personal status, but would have large and even devastating consequences in the Diaspora.

The reason for the outrage was very personal. By the 1970s there was hardly a family among the leaders of the various Jewish national organizations that did not include a convert who had been admitted as a convert by a Conservative or Reform rabbi. The leaders of the United Jewish Appeal, of most of the various Zionist organizations, and even of the synagogue bodies would be in the miserable position that some of their daughters-in-law or sons-in-law would be declared to be non-Jews—invalidly converted—by vote of Israel's Knesset. Some of their grandchildren, who were often being sent to Israel for summer programs or for part of their education, would be told that they did not belong within the Jewish people. This was simply intolerable. The leadership of the American Jewish community, headed by Max Fisher, went into open war with the Israeli religious hard-liners. The Americans were, of course, aided by some of the secular forces in Israel, but there was no univocal and fierce passion in those quarters. The Israeli politicians—at least many of them—in the secular parties had long been accustomed to making deals to quiet down the religious forces, provided the secular politicians could continue to decide such important matters as the nation's foreign policy and, perhaps even more important, the size of the annual budget and which forces and institutions it fostered. But the Knesset did not dare pass the law, and not because it was persuaded that such a decision, defining who was validly a Jew even in the Diaspora, could not be made in Israel. The issue was fought out, quite bluntly, in terms of power. Israel was informed by the dominant Jewish organizations in America that it would be punished by loss of financial and political support. The status quo remained in force: the offices of the Jewish Agency–World Zionist Organization would continue to send immigrants to Israel as Jews even as it knew in advance that the interior ministry in Israel would bow to the Orthodox insistence that some of these arrivals were not Jews.

Inevitably, I could not avoid this battle, and, indeed, I did not want to. For the first time in years, I was not in opposition to the leaders of the American Jewish community. On the contrary, I provided some of the arguments with which they made the case for the Jewishness of many of their families. I cited my article about Jewish identity in the new *Encyclopaedia Judaica* in which I took note of the fact that Ruth of Moab, the first known convert, had not been admitted to the Jewish community by an Orthodox court of Jewish law but she was the great-grandmother of King David. I made the further point, based on my studies a few years earlier of the life of the Jewish community in France and the Rhineland at the end of the Middle Ages, that throughout the centuries rabbinic law had been flexible because it was fashioned to make possible the life of a minority in unfriendly societies. Rabbis had seldom fallen prey to messianic enthusiasm, which would allow them to write off the majority of the Jewish people and accept within its polity only holy sectarians. The last time that many rabbis had fallen into this error had been in the seventeenth century, when the majority of the Jewish people briefly believed that Shabtai Zvi was the manifest messiah, but that dream crashed when he saved his life by becoming a convert to Islam. I chose to belong to that tradition. I disavowed the hard-liners, and I insisted that the Jewish community would have to remain a complicated entity that could survive only by adaptation and accommodation.

Through the 1960s I had been involved in all of the religious issues of contemporary Jewish life, but at one remove, as a thinker and writer. In my eight months in Jerusalem in 1971, I could no longer stand aside. I joined the battles not to defend some bits of turf for the Conservative movement, for the war of religion was now far larger. We who cared, both in Israel and in the Diaspora, were fighting the issue of whether Judaism on a world scale would be dominated by a hard-line minority or would remain a complicated entity that would survive by adaptation and accommodation. I chose the second option. I was a passionate moderate, passionate about keeping all parts of the Jewish world connected and concerned about each other.

22

During those hectic eight months in Jerusalem in 1971 I was ever more aware that my own identity as a Jew was becoming more complicated. I did not hesitate very much that spring when a number of my friends among the university professors joined in signing several ads in support of the nascent Peace Now movement, the movement in Israel against Israel's occupation of the West Bank. These men and women were positioning themselves in favor of a generous peace with the Palestinians. The effort they had launched was directed at public opinion in Israel, but I was not counterattacked in Israel for joining these ads. Yet I was becoming uncomfortable over the question of my identity. This unease became all the more evident as I took account of the positions that I had been taking in the quarrels over religion in international Jewish forums. I had been advancing the views of the moderates, who were a majority in the Diaspora but a minority in Israel.

This personal discomfort became greater as I got involved in the last great quarrel that arose about Soviet immigration. The Israelis, regardless of party, wanted a radical change in the rules under which Soviet émigrés were being received by the representatives of the organized Jewish community. The Israelis—I emphasize that they were nearly univocal—wanted whatever help might be given to these émigrés to be given only to those who were going on to Israel; any Soviet Jew who preferred to go to a transit point in Italy or elsewhere in Europe to wait for a visa for some other place should be summarily cut off from any help by Jewish charities. This position represented, of course, an expression of Zionist ideology: that the proper place of a Jew, and certainly of any refugee on the move, is in the homeland, in Israel. The leaders of Israel wanted all the agencies that disbursed Jewish charity funds to enforce this Zionist demand. There was large resistance in the United States and elsewhere in the Diaspora. Much of it came from the American Jewish Joint Distribution Committee (JOINT) and the Hebrew Immigrant Aid Society (HIAS). These agencies had a long history of caring for Jews, wherever they might choose to arrive in their flights from trouble. The dominant feeling in the Jewish fundraising community as a whole was to oppose the Israeli demand, but that feeling was not quite as strong as it seemed on the surface. Substantial opinion preferred to find some compromise that would mollify the Israelis.

I would not put up with any of this. I went to war with my colleagues in the Zionist executive, and with those agencies that were not willing to give ground. I defined the issues in moral terms. I was not concerned about whether the JOINT or the HIAS remained in business, for I had no doubt that they would redefine their functions even if the Israelis won this battle. I insisted that we who lived in the Diaspora had no right whatsoever to take part in a change of rules that would cut off from help those Soviet Jews who wanted to join us in living in the Diaspora. As the arguments became more pointed, I reminded the Israelis that the international Catholic charity, Caritas, was already helping Jewish individuals who preferred going to Venezuela (their path was made even easier if they chose to convert to the Catholic faith) and the emissaries of the Hasidic sect of Satmar were in every center of the Soviet émigrés to help them come to Brooklyn (especially if they were moving toward embracing the ultra-Orthodox Jewish faith of Satmar). But my basic argument was not prudential. I kept insisting, very vehemently, that we who had become comfortable in America had no right to force others to be Zionist pioneers. I was on the side that won that fight, and I did not regret for a moment—then, in the early 1970s, or later—that I had had a share in beating down the Israeli demand.

So here I was, toward the end of my sabbatical in Israel, having to ask myself the complex question, Who are you? Are you an Israeli intellectual who has joined his comrades in founding the peace movement, or are you a Jew who is defined by the fifty years that he has lived, since birth, in the Diaspora? Indeed, should I stay in Israel or should I return to the United States?

This pointed, and very immediate, question had been building up throughout my months of teaching. It was being made clear to me, in subtle hints and then finally very directly, that I could probably have an appointment as professor of Jewish history in the Hebrew University. The person who was most immediately involved and the most eager to see this happen was Shmuel Ettinger, who was then chairman of the department. The pull to stay was in part that Shmuel and I had become warm and almost inseparable friends, and he was not my only close friend in Israel. It was a wrenching thought that I would be leaving these men and women who had become my "family," to see them only on infrequent visits.

In Jerusalem Phyllis and I had become very attached to Justice Haim Cohen and his wife, Michal. I had met them a few years earlier in Zionist connections when friends among the leaders of the Jewish Agency–World Zionist Organization took me along to a party at their house, but this acquaintance became a deep friendship when we were living in Israel in the first half of 1971. People wondered at the connection, because Haim Cohen, who had been ultra-Orthodox into his thirties, and a celebrated scholar of the Talmud and of all rabbinic literature, had abandoned religion in the aftermath of the Holocaust. He could no longer believe in a God who had permitted these horrors. How could I, who had remained bound by the practices of the religious tradition, have become so close to Haim? I sometimes answered that Haim had broken diplomatic relations with the Orthodox God but I had stayed in touch to continue to fight with Him. Those who got to see us together knew that the deep bond was that we were both descendants of European rabbinic families. His grandfather, who had essentially raised him, had been the chief rabbi of Hamburg, and I was the descendant of generations of Hasidic rebbes. We both loved the texts that we learned in our first education. I found in Haim Cohen a towering moral personality. He insisted in his decisions as Supreme Court justice, or in his dissents, that the law extended equal rights and equal protection to everyone, including the Arabs within the borders of Israel. He was a vehement opponent of Israel's holding on to the West Bank.

An equally close relationship with Aryeh Dvoretsky had begun to evolve in those very months. I got to know him through Shmuel Ettinger, who worked with him on the board of Israel's Institute for Advanced Studies. Dvoretsky, too, like Haim Cohen, was a secularist, but he was steeped in the classic religious tradition, for he, too, had been born in a rabbinic family, and both he and his wife were related to the dynasty of the rebbes of Lubavich. Like Haim Cohen, Dvoretsky was a polyglot, so our conversations would move from Hebrew to Yiddish (Haim Cohen spoke Yiddish because he had come to Israel at the age of seventeen, to study at Rabbi Kook's yeshiva) to English and, occasionally, when we wanted to say something harsh, to German. Aryeh, who had been the chief scientist of the Israeli defense forces, was a pronounced dove who was privately the "grandfather" of those who were then creating the peace movement. I soon knew that Dvoretsky had a piercing eye. He was a world-renowned mathematician, and he also recognized fake rhetoric in any field. This was, of course, also true of Shmuel Ettinger and Haim Cohen. In every conversation, bluffs that each of us had heard were soon demolished.

The moodiest of those who became my closest friends during that semester in Jerusalem was Gershom Schocken. He was then the publisher and editor of—that is, he both owned and ran—the prestige daily in Israel, *Ha'Aretz (The Land)*. I met Schocken first in 1949, when I visited him in my guise as writer for *Commentary* and the *Nation*. He took me to lunch a time or two during that summer in Israel, and we maintained some written connection for a number of years and during my brief occasional visits to the country. Now, in the first half of 1971, we spent quite a lot of time together. About once a week he would drive up from his offices in Tel Aviv, and nearly as often Phyllis and I would drive down from Jerusalem for dinner. Schocken was well known to be a very lonely man. The reason he gave most often was that a newspaper editor who had to decide every day what his editorial policy would be could not afford to have friends.

Schocken arrived in Israel in 1933 because he could no longer continue his studies for a doctorate at Heidelberg. Hitler had come to
power, and Gershom's family, headed by his father, Salman Schocken,
the leading department-store magnate in Germany, soon left. The elder
Schocken bought a struggling newspaper in Tel Aviv and gave it to his
eldest son, Gustav (he adopted his Hebrew name, Gershom, but his
closest friends continued to call him Gustav), to be its publisher and
editor. The younger Schocken had received an excellent education in
Hebrew from private tutors. One of his early influences was Shmuel
Yosef Czaczkes, whom his father had supported when he began his
writing career. Czaczkes was then living in Berlin, and came often to
the house. The relationship remained a deep connection and friendship, which was resumed in Palestine in the 1930s. Czaczkes was now a
foremost Hebrew writer under the name of Shmuel Yosef Agnon; he
would ultimately win the Nobel Prize for literature.

Schocken and I were brought together by the involvement of both
of us in the whole range of Jewish culture, most especially in all the
versions of Hebrew text from ancient times to the present. We shared
a critical involvement, a love-hate relationship, with much of the range
of Western culture. Schocken was a Zionist and an Israeli patriot, but
he had not abandoned the sense of belonging to a universal humanistic culture, at least in its European version. He had not narrowed himself down to Israeli nationalism of the kind that was asserting, "My
country, right or wrong." When his country was wrong, especially in
its treatment of Arabs, Schocken said so in his editorials. When in the
1970s corruption began to seep into the Labor establishment that was
still running Israel, he said so and denounced its falling away from the
ways of the founding fathers. When the rising political power of the
Orthodox confronted Israel with what he regarded as a rolling back of
civil liberties, he was not silent. Someone took the trouble to tell me at
a casual lunch in a faculty cafeteria that my friend Schocken was editing *Ha'Aretz* as if he was the editor of the *Frankfurter Zeitung,* the
great liberal newspaper in Germany in the days of the Weimar Republic when he was growing up. My answer was, Of course, so he should;
he should be editing such a paper for all of Israel. He was a strange bird
in this place, but he was reminding some of his readers of the larger

values with which Zionism had to reckon and among which it had to find its place.

Schocken was an odder man than even his most perceptive critics knew. His carriage was fairly stiff, and he made sure that all hair had been shaved from his head, so he looked for all the world like the quintessential *yekke*, a German Jew who, way down deep, was more German than Jew. This pose was a sham. Gustav sometimes talked to intimates about his childhood in the eastern German town of Zwieckau, in the province of Posen, which had been annexed by the Prussians when Poland was divided late in the eighteenth century. Gustav spoke with emotion about the Hasidic cantor who was his principal teacher in Zwickau, when he was very young. He loved the East European synagogue, to which he went quite often, as he had not liked the much more formal "German-Jewish" temple to which his father was a major donor. It took him a while to impart to me his most interesting revelation: that his father's father had been a Yiddish-speaking Polish Jew who had arrived in Zwickau as a tailor. That placed Gustav Schocken a bare two generations away from the much maligned East Europeans who had become Germans by swimming over the Vistula River at night (hence *wasser Polacken*, "water Pollacks," Poles who swam to Germany) and smuggling themselves in from czarist Russia to the much happier world of the kaiser's Germany. I am absolutely certain that Gustav Schocken lived constantly with his family history. He published poetry in several languages (Hebrew, English, and German) under the pseudonym R. Posen—that is, Robert of Posen (he adopted Robert from the first name of an uncle). As the months went by, I began to understand why his father, who played the German-Jewish hidalgo all his life, had always surrounded himself with scholars and writers whose origins were in Eastern Europe. I even understood why Gustav Schocken made friends with me, a Galician-born American Jewish student of the Talmud.

Gustav Schocken kept pushing me, neither very subtly nor very gently, to stay in Israel. He needed someone with whom he could study the old texts in Hebrew without putting his eyes into the blinders of ultra-Orthodoxy. I countered by saying, So you want a rabbi or even a rebbe for the nonbelievers! He did not deny it, and I was, of course, flattered. These conversations with Gustav made me think most seriously about the growing tension between the ties that bound me ever more tightly to Israel and my need to go back to the United States. I could not avoid the question, Why don't you stay?

The practical reasons were very easy to state. I had come on sabbatical from my post as rabbi in Englewood, and I could not simply write a letter saying that I was very sorry but I was not coming back. I had, at very least, to go back for a year or so and then to return to Jerusalem. I also knew that if I made the shift it would be a hard struggle. Even though I was being paid as full professor, I found that I could not, to use the wry Israeli term, "finish the month." I soon knew that even senior academic figures in Israel survived by working "a job and a half"—that is, teaching part-time elsewhere—and by having their wives bring in a full-time salary at whatever they could do. Some had married women from rich families, and that, of course, made life easier. These options were mostly closed to me. For us as a family to immigrate to Israel was particularly difficult at that point, because Linda would be starting college, having chosen to attend Yale, and Susan had two years of high school to finish. It would have meant sending the children back to the United States so that Linda could be a freshman at Yale and Susan would be someone's houseguest for two years. I knew that this would make staying in touch with the two of them difficult. I also knew very well that, no matter how hard we might try, they would feel a loss of emotional support, the kind that you give your children simply by being there, a support that can never be replaced by others, even by other members of the same family or by very close friends.

There was another equally compelling reason. The position to which I had arrived at the age of fifty in the Diaspora was not transferable to Israel. I could not bring this career with me, because the moment the rumor began circulating that I might be staying, several people who had been cultivating me suddenly dropped me. I was useful so long as they thought I could be an influential friend abroad, but I was a threat to the roles they already occupied in Israel. There was simply not the kind of room in Israel's public or academic life that existed in the wider expanses of the United States.

But what really stopped me was the very deep feeling that I been cooked in a different kettle of fish than the Israelis. I did not know how American I had become until I came to the paradoxical moment when I fell in love with Israel's life, even in all its complication. But I found that the people there to whom I felt instinctively closest were intellectuals of my own generation. It was immediately apparent that they had all been born in Europe as I had. Even though they had achieved commanding positions in the life of Israel, there was still some atmosphere of alienness about them. They were too rooted in the older culture of the Diaspora and too much part of European cosmopolitanism not to stand out as different. Before my eyes I watched Aubrey Eban, the quintessential brilliant Cambridge graduate, rename himself Abba (his Hebrew name) and become a mainstream Labor Party politician. He occupied many roles in Israel's governments, and especially as its spokesman at times of crisis, but he was always thought of as "foreign," and he never rose to even being considered a serious possibility for the office of prime minister. I was aware in 1971 of a youngish writer, Aharon Appelfeld, who had survived the Holocaust as a child and found his way to Israel. He was beginning to write novels with heartbreaking accounts of the Holocaust, and yet he was not an Israeli writer. Many years later, we would share a platform in New York at the hundredth anniversary of *Die Zukunft (Future)*, a Yiddish journal that had been founded in America in 1892. Appelfeld said that day that he regarded himself not as a Hebrew writer but as one continuing the tradition of Yiddish letters in Eastern Europe. In fact, Appelfeld had known no Yiddish when he arrived in Israel as a teenager, but he had learned it there to link himself to the culture that he regarded as most nearly his own.

I had to add to these considerations that deeply involved, indeed possessed, as I was by my passion for Israel, I had also become very much an American. The country in which I had lived since the age of five was going through an age of turmoil over the war in Vietnam and the battle for racial equality, and I simply could not leave these battles behind. I owed much to America, and I had to repay some of my debts by helping my country. At the very end of all these reflections, I consoled myself with the thought that a new class of Israeli intellectuals and especially of academics had been arising: they taught about half of the time in Israel and the other half of the year they spent at some prestigious university abroad. My own time allocations had become not much different. I was spending all the time when I was not obligated to be at the synagogue or teaching classes at Columbia in Jerusalem. The only difference between me and the peripatetic Israelis was that their legal address was in Israel and mine in the United States, but this little witticism ducked the question. I had come to the conclusion that my ultimate identity was simple, perhaps too simple. It was not "Israeli Jew" or "American Jew"; it was simply "Jew." I was a Jew who had been fashioned by the rabbinic and Hasidic traditions, who tried to live by the values of his ancestors in all the several worlds to which he belonged.

And so the day came to leave. We took our daughters to the port in Haifa, from where they were going to embark for Greece, from where they would hitchhike their way through Yugoslavia and Central Europe; and three days later we went to the airport to take a plane to Paris.

During our own journey that summer in Europe, I encountered more sharply than ever before the growing sectarianism within the Jewish religious community. In every town that we reached, I immediately sought out the local synagogue, usually through its rabbi, because I was still in the mourning period for my father, and I participated in the morning and evening services every day. The usual manners of such an occasion are that when a stranger comes and tells those in charge of the synagogue that he is in mourning, he is offered the opportunity and the honor of chanting the service at which he is present. My friends in the World Jewish Congress office in Paris had told the rabbis of the various towns on my itinerary when I would be coming, requesting the usual courtesies. They were not forthcoming. In Amsterdam, these discourtesies came to a point of climax. I called on the chief rabbi of the city, someone whom I had never met but who I knew had been born in a town in Galicia not too far from my place of birth. We sat for an hour or so and spoke the rabbinic version of Yiddish, interspersed with quotations from the Talmud. It was even established that one of his grandfathers had been an adherent of the Hasidic rabbi of Dinov, from whom I was descended. Nonetheless, the rabbi informed me that I could attend synagogue service but that I should not expect to be given the honor of leading the group that was assembled there in prayer. A Conservative rabbi was not acceptable. I had long thought of myself as a nonfundamentalist Orthodox Jew, but the sectarian Orthodox demanded absolute obedience to their most restrictive definitions of Judaism.

In Jerusalem, the differences had not yet become so personal, at least not in the circles in which I traveled. I went to synagogue usually in a place that was frequented by the leaders of "enlightened" Orthodoxy, government servants in high jobs, journalists, and professors—all of whom read *Ha'Aretz* even though it was not the newspaper of the religious. Only the most adamant right-wing politicians tried to suggest by their body language that I was not one of them. I used to visit the headquarters of the Belzer Hasidim, and I was always invited to pray with them; they even, on one occasion, when I had to say special prayers on the second anniversary of the death of my mother, convoked a minyan in the small library of the yeshiva. I was the only one in the room who was not wearing a caftan, but they handed me the ceremonial sash with which one distinguishes between the upper and lower regions, and I chanted and led the service. I had often wondered if Freud thought of the distinction between the id and ego by watching his Hasidic father put on such a sash. Though I knew that even in Israel the various shadings of religion, and nonreligion, were becoming angrier, the incident in Amsterdam rubbed it in as never before. I thought I was going back to the United States to face some of the tensions in American society as a whole, while the Jewish community retained a spirit of tolerance in its own affairs. But in Amsterdam I knew that the crossfire between the Jewish factions in the Diaspora was now increasing to the point of anger. That night I remembered the statement in the Talmud that God does not promise us a peaceful and untroubled life either in this world or in the world to come.

The very first sermon that I gave in Englewood, after my return, upset many people. I had been living in Israel, and not as an American who could only read the *Jerusalem Post,* the local Jewish newspaper in English, which fed visitors, and even longtime residents who knew no Hebrew, the official line. Anybody who read a Hebrew newspaper knew that Israel was ever more bitterly divided. After a few weeks, I was telling my congregants that they should learn Hebrew so that they could read the Israeli press. That was, of course, a pious wish, so I tried another way of getting the forbidden information to them. I wanted to describe, in a leading American Jewish journal, Israel as it really was. The most widely read publication then was *Hadassah Magazine,* which was published by Hadassah, the Woman's Zionist Organization of America. I was then already serving on its editorial advisory committee, so I imagined, in all innocence, that an essay that I would submit would be published without question. I chose to write about the beginnings of the protest movement Peace Now. In the essay I described this effort as a movement being led by people from the universities and by a surprising number of retired military officers. I named names; they were people such as Aryeh Dvoretsky, whom the

Hadassah Magazine readers had been taught to admire. This essay was rejected out of hand. When I protested, I was bluntly told that *Hadassah Magazine* existed to give a favorable image of Israel and that my essay about inner strife did not help the cause. It was nearly ten years before such discussions could turn up in a "respectable" Jewish journal in America.

I persevered and kept reading the Israeli press as quickly as copies of the weekend papers arrived in the United States. Quite often, I would stand on a pulpit or a platform and read the contrasting accounts of the same events put out by the propaganda machines and what one could read in the free and unfettered Israeli press. It was a constant battle to convince some people in the United States that they were being fed fairy tales rather than truth, both by the weeklies that were published by the Jewish charity federations and by the publications and press releases of the various national agencies. Accounts of inner strife in Israel were bad for the campaign to raise money for Israel and were dangerous for the pro-Israel lobbies.

The situation was more complicated at Columbia, where my students were not only Jews but also Arabs, mostly of Palestinian origin. The Jewish students were mostly like their parents; that is, their attitudes were being formed by the desire to not give the Palestinians an inch. The Palestinian students, and other Arabs from all over the Middle East, were saying, over and over again, that the Palestinians and not the Jews were the real victims of the quarrel between them. I was badgered and attacked from both sides. The Jews complained that I had lost something of my Zionism, in, of all places, Israel. The Arabs kept saying that if I was already so critical of Israel's policies of occupation and conquest in the West Bank—and did not speak in glowing terms of the "return to Judea and Samaria," the Biblical names for the West Bank favored by the Israeli right—why did I not take this to its logical conclusion and join with them in wishing for the end of Israel?

The tensions with some of the Jewish students came to a head in the semester after my return, when I taught a course in the history of Zionism. In the very first session, I had announced that there would be a final examination with some choice as to which question each student might choose to discuss ("answer any three out of five") but that one question would be mandatory: make the case for Palestinian nationalism. After the buzz subsided, I addressed myself to the Jews in the room and told them that if they were incapable of understanding Palestinian national-ism, then their Zionist convictions were shallow and could exist only if they closed their ears to the outcry of the other. One woman in the class refused to accept this explanation. She went to the dean of the graduate school to argue that her intellectual and religious freedoms were being infringed on because I was forcing her to answer this question. My response to the dean was to admit that I was practicing coercion, as pro-fessors do, because I wanted all the students to learn something that most of them would otherwise not take the trouble to think about. If the young woman refused to answer the question, she could not get a pass-ing grade in the course. I won this argument, but I also lost it. The answer that she produced on the final examination was such a caricature of Arab nationalism that it reminded me of the way Jews were described in anti-Semitic pamphlets.

A few days later, I had a more comforting complaint from another segment of the class. The dean called me up to tell me that the Arab students had lodged a protest with him, to which I responded with some testiness, And why are they unhappy? After all, they seemed to know in class that I was nobody's enemy but everybody's teacher. The dean laughed and told me that the Arabs had complained because in my lectures I frequently told jokes from which they felt left out because the punch lines were in Yiddish.

I did not live many months on the American scene in the backwash of Israeli politics. By the middle of the winter of 1971–72 I was aston-ished to be invited to join the leadership of the American Jewish estab-lishment. The request came from the one organization that had a long tradition of liberalism and dissent. It was the American Jewish Congress, which had been founded by Justice Louis Brandeis and Rabbi Stephen Wise during the First World War. Its prime purpose then was to fight for Zionist aims against the indifference and enmity of the wealthier Jews from "uptown"—that is, the Jewish settlers in America who had come from Central Europe ("German Jews") a half century earlier. These "uptown" leaders of the American Jewish Com-mittee, which then represented the richest element of American Jews, were essentially opposed to Zionism (because this national movement to establish a Jewish homeland in Palestine would call their American identity into question), so the American Jewish Congress arose in revolt; it represented the working masses against the upper classes. They outnumbered the rich, but the American Jewish Committee had much more money and social position. The American Jewish Congress struggled along fueled by enthusiasm and more than a bit of self-righteous principles. It was led by a cadre of brainy professionals and some notable lay leaders who were associated with liberal and even left-wing causes. Its first president had been Rabbi Stephen Wise, and after his death, the tradition of having a crusading rabbi who was both a Zionist and a leader in liberal causes on the American scene was continued. His immediate successor was Joachim Prinz, who as a young rabbi in Berlin had defied the Nazis. The next president was Rabbi Arthur Lelyveld, who had been the liaison with Christians who were Zionists in the 1940s and who then became the rabbi of a major congregation in Cleveland and a leader in the battle for racial equality in America.

Will Maslow, who was on the point of retiring as executive director of the American Jewish Congress, called me one day and asked me to lunch. He told me on the telephone that he wanted to discuss the presidency of the American Jewish Congress. I responded that I had been involved in the Philadelphia branch of the American Jewish Congress in the mid–1940s but I had become a nominal member since then because this organization did not exist in Nashville, where I went when I left Philadelphia, and I had become too busy in several other endeavors to become actively involved again when I returned to the New York area. Maslow brushed all this aside and insisted that he wanted to see me. I could not refuse an invitation from a man of his eminence. I knew that he had been part of the legal brains in the group in and around the National Association for the Advancement of Colored People (NAACP) and a close associate of Thurgood Marshall in writing the legal briefs that led to the unanimous decision by the Supreme Court in *Brown v. Board of Education* in 1954. Within two days, he and I were sitting at a table in a discreetly hidden dining room at Columbia Presbyterian Medical Center to talk about my becoming president of the American Jewish Congress. My arguments against were obvious, and I thought that they would settle the question: I was not known within the organization, nor did I have any sense of its inner workings. I would need to learn much more than I knew about its major concerns today.

Maslow countered by saying that the organization continued to need a rabbi in the mold of the three rabbis who had been its past presidents. Maslow represented the search committee, which had decided that I was the one to be asked. He had no doubt that we could come to reasonable terms and some compromises, if necessary, on matters of policy, because the search committee knew which sides I had taken in the quarter century that I had already spent in public life. Maslow then added that I could not refuse to lead the major Jewish organization that was passionately attached to both Zionism and social liberalism. As I listened to Maslow say these words, I could not help remembering that I had said these very words to myself as the reason for returning to the United States: American Jews need to be better Zionists by understanding the true problems of Israel, and American Jews need to resist the blandishments of having become well off and being tempted to vote their pocketbooks. They could never allow themselves to forget that Jews in America had begun in poverty and that they had a deep moral obligation to help those who were still poor, especially those whose skin color was dark. Here was Will Maslow sitting across from me; he had given all of his adult life to these causes. How could I possibly not join him for the few years that were the term of office of the president of the American Jewish Congress? I agreed to serve.

Maslow went back to his committee and told them that I would accept if the post were offered. His associates quickly agreed, and so I was nominated and elected the national president of the American Jewish Congress in June 1972 at a convention that was held in Cleveland, the home city of the retiring president, Arthur Lelyveld. This changing of the guard was very friendly, because I had worked with Lelyveld in Zionist causes in the 1940s and both of us remembered that I had always tried to do everything he had asked of me. After a three-day convention I came back to New York to find that Maslow had meant what he said; he had retired as executive director of the American Jewish Congress, although he did keep an office in the building. Those who might want to speak with him or ask his advice could come and see him. The new executive director was Naomi Levine, the first woman to be appointed to such a post in any national organization in which the membership was predominantly male. I soon discovered several things about Naomi: she was nervous about her new job, and she had been told

that I was difficult to work with because I was opinionated and probably a male chauvinist; but only the first charge was true. She made it
clear to me from the beginning that she was a committed Jew but did
not believe in God. She was challenging me, the rabbi, to persuade her
that He (or She?) existed. What she never told me directly I found out
almost immediately. She possessed a brilliant mind and an unfailing
sense of the difference between right and wrong. Naomi and I very
quickly drifted into the habit of spending an hour or two in her office
or mine arguing about God and matters of organizational policy. I
remember the day that all the preexisting barriers fell. I looked at
Naomi one day and said to her that I do not believe that brains have
gender—and at that moment we became not only colleagues but
devoted friends.

But not everyone at the American Jewish Congress was Maslow or
Naomi Levine. Among both the lay leadership and the professional
staff I found some mediocrities or self-servers, but I also found a number of brilliant leaders. Philip Baum, who was then the director of international affairs, was one of the best informed and most devoted forces
in the making of policy for the organization. What the American Jewish Congress had to say in those days about foreign affairs was particularly sensitive because of large and growing conflict in American society
over the war in Vietnam. Baum was on the antiwar side, as was much of
the popular sentiment in the American Jewish Congress, but even on
the issue of Vietnam, there was some hesitancy among its members.
Some feared an American pullout from Vietnam. The United States
might come closer to abandoning the cause of Israel in its quarrels with
the Palestinians. Phil Baum was uncompromisingly and totally devoted
to the defense of Israel's interests, which he saw in black-and-white
terms. He regarded those who questioned Israel's continued presence in
the West Bank and Gaza, and its insistence that not one inch of the
greater Jerusalem could ever be handed back to its Palestinian inhabitants, as misguided, or worse. The thought that it would be better for
Israel to help create, or at least not hinder, the development of a Palestinian state was anathema to Phil Baum.

I thus found myself in an embattled position. In the American Jewish Congress I found considerable sympathy for my dovish views, for
my insistence that only a two-state solution offered any hope for peace,

but there was always some friction. I had, of course, the right to speak my mind, both in internal meetings and in public, but I was often exasperated by the opposition to my being a "peacenik." At one board meeting, I lost my temper. The dominant antiwar position in the American Jewish Congress was expressed by a stampede toward a resolution demanding that the military budget of the United States be cut very radically. This was followed by another resolution asking that the American support of Israel, and especially of its military, be increased by several billions. After this exercise I got up to say that what has been passed was that the United States should have a military budget of $11 billion to $12 billion, of which $9 billion to $10 billion should be used for Israel. As I cooled down, I realized that the people who passed these resolutions back-to-back really did not expect that those who made policy in the White House would pay much attention to their words. The resolutions were intended to demonstrate their emotions, that they were the antiwar people that they always had been and yet they were still the unabashed and unshakable defenders of Israel. They added under their breath, Do not ask us to balance these commitments into a coherent policy.

I soon found another example of such policy making in the "correct" patter of those days about the injustice being done by racial prejudice and the remedies that should be applied. One night at the executive of the American Jewish Congress, two matters were on the table: the firemen in Birmingham, Alabama, and the quarrel about racial preferences for students in admission to medical schools. The Birmingham case was clear-cut for everyone who attended that meeting. For many years, only Whites had been hired to be firemen in Birmingham. The questions on the entrance examination had been constructed so as to enable the examiners to fail anyone whom they wanted to exclude, and they always wanted to exclude Blacks. The remedy proposed was that henceforth every other fireman hired in Birmingham had to be Black. This was affirmative action to redress past injustices. The board enthusiastically agreed to this resolution in a resounding unanimous vote.

The next question was of a young man, James Bakke, who was battling for admission to the medical school of the University of California at Davis. Bakke had proved that a number of students who were admitted to study medicine at the university had lower grades and scores in the entrance exam than he had achieved and that their superior qualification was that they were Black and thus affirmative action came into play. The board of the American Jewish Congress fiddled with this problem for hours. What they really wanted to do was to instruct the legal division to file a brief on the side of Bakke and against the University of California's commitment to affirmative action. But they held back from that course of action, as it would have put them on the same side as some of the most conservative forces in the United States. However, the American Jewish Congress could not agree to oppose Bakke. At the very end of this wearing discussion, my temper had frayed again. I knew very well that I would be losing friends, but I could not shut myself up. I said very bluntly to the board that I understood the discontinuity between the issue of the firemen in Birmingham and the medical students in Davis. Since none of their cousins or relatives in Birmingham wanted to be firemen, they were eager to maintain their liberal stance there through affirmative action. But many of their own children, and the children of their relatives all over the country, wanted to get into medical schools. Here, the principal of merit had to be followed, according to the mainstream of the board, without deviation. I ended my protest with the observation that the enthusiasm for affirmative action for the firemen of Birmingham and the aversion to it in the case of medical-school students in Davis was hypocrisy.

I even added, then, that the moral issues raised by affirmative action were central to the defense of Zionism. We could not possibly make the case for the Jewish settlement in Palestine within the past century, in the teeth of Arab resentment and resistance, without invoking the need of the Jews for a homeland of their own after twenty centuries of being persecuted in every country in Europe and to a substantial degree in the Muslim world. The basic argument for Zionism was that the Jews required an act of affirmative action to make their continued life possible. If we Jews were asking of the world, and even of the Muslim Arab world, that it make some room for a Jewish commonwealth in a small piece of the large territory of the Middle East, did we really have the right to oppose some compensatory damages to Blacks and others who had suffered large and continuing injustice in Western society, and especially in America?

When I finally had quieted down, I was stunned to discover that no one in the room had really asked the question, What is the essential Jewish claim to the restoration of a homeland of their own? The room was not full of religious believers who could reply, "God gave us the land," so their defense of Zionism seemed to me very questionable. My mute colleagues were espousing an interesting non sequitur: "There probably is no God, but He chose the Jewish people for a very special destiny and He gave them the Holy Land." I was not finished with this "lesson" that night. I had to keep repeating this point throughout the six years that I was president of the American Jewish Congress, but I knew that I was not winning many converts. Still, what I was saying at the table was getting around.

The most bitter continuing battle in which I was involved was the struggle to open the doors of the Soviet Union for the many Jews who wished to emigrate. The basic issue was clear: the Soviet regime refused to acknowledge that people had a right to leave their country and go elsewhere. From the Soviet point of view, such a desire was not an exercise of freedom; it was an act of betrayal. Obviously, no one who had been raised in Western democracy could accept this repressiveness, and so the protests had begun early in the 1960s. They had been fueled by growing evidence that there were many thousands of Jews in the Soviet Union who were actively demonstrating their desire to live as Jews and their despair at their inability to do this. In 1949, Gold Meir arrived in Moscow as the first ambassador from the state of Israel. The Soviet Union expected her to be greeted modestly and quietly by the large Jewish population of Moscow, but that was not what happened. When she came for the first time to the synagogue—the one large synagogue that the regime allowed to remain open, under tight control—the streets were mobbed with tens of thousands of people. That welcome was particularly striking and moving because the welcomers were clearly defying the Soviet regime and proclaiming their Jewish loyalties.

The second transformation took place in 1967 with the outbreak of the Six-Day War. Soviet Jews in their hundreds of thousands were glued to the radio to hear the news on the shortwave broadcasts, from Israel, by the BBC and Radio Liberty. The Soviet listeners were fearful that Israel might be destroyed by the combined attack of all its surrounding neighbors and thus the Jewish people as a whole might experience a second Holocaust. Large numbers of the Jews of the Soviet empire had not abandoned their Jewishness. Soviet repression, past and present, had made no difference. These Jewish fears were soon transformed into joy when Israel survived the war in June of 1967. Many Jews insisted on their desire to leave for Israel. To be sure, not all of those who were pushing for exit visas were motivated by burning Zionist feelings. Many wanted simply to get out of the Soviet Union, because increasing anti-Semitism was limiting opportunities for Jews to find places equal to their talents within the economy and, especially, in the professions. But the passion to leave for Israel was the most visible element in what amounted to an uprising by the Jews against the Soviet regime. What made this confrontation all the more pointed and more embittered was the plain fact that the Soviet Union had been the ally and patron of Egypt and Syria in the Six-Day War. The Jews within the Soviet empire were defiantly opposed to their government.

Obviously, all the stirrings toward emigration were noticed by the Jewish communities abroad—in Israel, in the United States, and in the smaller Jewish communities all over the world. The first efforts to help the Jews of the Soviet Union had begun in the early 1960s, when a few young people in the United States organized a lobby to promote the cause of Soviet Jewish emigration. Though it has been frequently denied, I knew from friends in the Israeli government that it preferred not to stir this pot. Israel at the time hoped that it could keep the Soviet Union from siding with the Arabs in the conflict with Israel. The nascent movement to "free Soviet Jewry" was a political embarrassment. Despite this early hesitancy, Israeli representatives abroad later insisted that the makers of the effort for Soviet Jewry were obliged to follow their lead. This became particularly important after 1967, when the Israeli government was forced to conclude that going easy in the quarrel with the Soviet Union would bring no dividends. Indeed, confronting the Soviets over the issue would help to keep them out of any negotiations on the Middle East. They were cast as the biased enemy of Israel.

One day in 1973, early in my tenure as president of the American Jewish Congress, the official in charge of Israel's concerns for the Soviet Union, Nehemiah Levanon, came to see me in my office in New York to tell me what Israel's policy was on matters great and small—and to make it very clear that he expected me to be a faithful and obedient representative of these decisions. I refused to accept this ukase. My chief heresy was the position that I had already taken in the Zionist executive, to insist that the Jews living comfortably in New York, London, or Paris had no right to demand of Soviet Jews that they must all go to Israel or we would effectively sever them from the world Jewish community. Levanon got very angry with me, and I got no less angry with him. This discussion reached a climax when I said to him that I was a citizen of the United States of America and traveled on an American passport. My Jewish loyalties were very deep, but not even senior operatives from the state of Israel had the authority to define them for me. I was not subject to his command. Levanon left my office in a huff, and, even though he remained in the United States for several years more, I never saw him again.

My quarrel with Nehemiah Levanon was an opening skirmish in a larger and ever more pointed fight: how to get even more Jews out of the Soviet Union. The key was in the United States: to persuade the American government to put the demand to "free Soviet Jewry" in a central place in its dealings with Moscow. The leading figure in America in fighting this battle was Max Fisher. He was then the most important Jew in the Republican Party, and he had held or was holding, in the 1960s and 1970s, many of the central offices in the Jewish establishment. Max Fisher was a man of charm and he exuded personal warmth, but he never forgot, even briefly, that his main passion was political maneuvering. He had put himself in the situation of being the bridge between the Republican White House of Richard Nixon, and his successor Gerald Ford, and the Jewish community, both in America and in Israel. Max Fisher was too good a politician and too much a realist not to know that the large majority of American Jews were Democrats and not Republicans. He quickly adopted me. We became an "odd couple": he was very rich and very Republican; I had no money and had remained an unwavering Democrat since my teens—but he was constantly on my telephone to find out what majority Jewish opinion thought about the issues of the day or how far the bulk of American Jews could be pushed or pulled in any direction.

The larger battle, to open the doors of the Soviet Union, became a matter of the highest consequence in American politics. The cause of

Soviet Jews had been taken up by Senator Henry "Scoop" Jackson, and his policies were managed for him by a right-wing Democrat in his entourage, Richard Perle. Senator Jackson led in passing the Jackson-Vanik amendment to an international trade bill. The force of this amendment was to create an annual review of American trade with the Soviet Union that was linked to its performance on emigration. It was very clear that Senator Jackson and those around him were preparing him to be a candidate for president on the ticket of the Democratic Party. He would run based on a reputation as the man who could face down the Soviet Union and even humiliate it from his seat in the Senate. Jackson was already campaigning in 1973, to the right of the incumbent Republican president, Richard Nixon, who had established some kind of working relationship with the Soviet leader, Leonid Brezhnev. The matter of Soviet Jewry was all the more embroiled in international politics because in 1973 Nixon was fighting an ever more bitter battle to retain the presidency; and, as the waves of the Watergate scandal were rising ever higher, Nixon imagined that he could save himself by proving that he was indispensable as the master of foreign policy. Nixon was desperately eager to prove that he could do more for Soviet Jewry, through his connections with Brezhnev, than Senator Jackson could.

Max Fisher was, of course, eager to help the threatened Republican president, so I found myself at small meetings at the White House, usually in the Executive Office Building next door, in the second-floor office of Richard Nixon's legal counsel, Leonard Garment, who had drifted into the informal role of being also his representative to the Jews. Sometimes Fisher and I talked with Henry Kissinger, in his office in the White House as national security advisor, and, on occasion, I had lunch alone with Lawrence Eagleburger, Kissinger's principal assistant, who had become a friend. Eagleburger was that rare public figure who always told me the truth, even when we disagreed. I became convinced that he cared about rescuing the Jews of the Soviet Union because to him it was a moral issue. After much maneuvering, a major breakthrough was made. Brezhnev offered Nixon exit visas for 38,500 Jewish émigrés each year and an orderly and reasonable end to the problems of the "hard cases," of those Jews who had been denied the right to emigrate and had formally opted out of the Soviet system—the "refuseniks." This offer was unquestionably authentic because it had been made by Brezhnev using the direct channel between him and Nixon.

I was together in the White House with Max Fisher when this offer was repeated to us by several of Nixon's closest associates. I was very pleased, because the offer of an annual number of exit visas was more generous than the most ardent proponents of emigration from the Soviet Union had imagined could be achieved. Elated and confident, I went back to New York and asked Stanley Lowell, a vice president of the American Jewish Congress and a middle-range figure in New York Democratic politics, to come and see me. Lowell was then the chairman of the National Conference on Soviet Jewry. I told about the offer that had been described to me in the White House the day before, and I expected Lowell to be pleased and even exultant, but what I saw was a face that became ever grimmer and angrier. It was clear, almost instantly, that he was upset that this offer by the Soviets had been made to the Jews not through him but through Max Fisher and me. He simply could not tolerate that this victory would not bear his name—but he had even deeper reasons for being opposed. These became apparent when he came back the next day and flatly refused the Soviet offer. He was part of the group around Scoop Jackson. They could not afford to let the issue of Soviet Jews die because it would lessen, perhaps even fatally, the momentum of Senator Jackson's nascent campaign for the presidency. Lowell spoke for a group of political figures who were looking forward to running the White House in a Jackson administration. They would not let their aces be trumped by a Brezhnev-Nixon deal.

During my meetings with Lowell I kept my temper, but after he walked out of my office for the second time, having delivered his uncompromising refusal, I exploded. I did not regard myself as the tribune of either Nixon or Jackson. I had no ambitions in American politics. Whatever office I held in the Jewish community had come to me, so I thought, to represent the interests of the Jews and their ideals. For many centuries the legal and moral texts of the Jewish religion had emphasized that "redeeming the captives" was one of the greatest of all the good deeds that a Jew could and must perform. For the first time in my life masses of captives were being offered freedom. I had no doubt that it was my religious and moral obligation to accept the offer. To reject it because it would be inconvenient for the personal and political agendas of a small group of insiders seemed to me to be contemptible and unforgivable.

For the rest of my political career in the Jewish establishment, I could never shake off the suspicion that when colleagues were talking about high-sounding principles I should keep listening for the sounds of their personal ambitions. The day on which I had to convey to the White House the refusal of Scoop Jackson's minions to accept the Brezhnev offer was the day that I became much lonelier and much less trusting of others.

E ven in the midst of the Cold War with the Soviet Union, the morass of the American involvement in Vietnam, and the Watergate scandal, which would lead in 1974 to Nixon's resignation, race continued to be a major and, indeed, the dominant issue in the United States. Jews had been heavily involved for many years, but by the beginning of the 1970s a group of younger Black leaders had appeared who consciously and effectively threw the Jews out of their newer and more militant organizations. The leaders of the Student Nonviolent Coordinating Committee made it very clear—very pugnaciously clear—that they wanted neither Jews nor any other Whites within their group. The more I got to know about the intricacies of this scene, the more apparent it became that in both the Black and the Jewish communities there were people who were trying to make public careers by representing the most uncompromising version of the interests of their constituencies. So I became ever firmer at meetings of the American Jewish Congress and in other forums in denying the usual mantra of the moderates: "Come, let us reason together." If the tensions of the 1970s could be quieted down, it would happen only if the real interests of the combating minorities could be put on the table and compromised.

Without asking any one of my associates, because I did not want what I was thinking to leak, I decided one day in 1973 to invite two leading congressmen to meet with me, in total secrecy, in a hotel room in Washington. The men whom I asked to come were Charles Rangel, the congressman from Harlem who was then the chair of the "Black caucus" in the House of Representatives, and Sidney Yates, from Chicago, who was then the senior Jewish congressman. There was not then, nor is there now, an organized Jewish caucus in the House. Neither of these men had any reason to accept my invitation. I had no personal connection with either of them, but they both knew that the growing antagonisms were serious and that, as president of the American Jewish Congress, I might help them do something to quiet the conflicts between Jews and Blacks. In the course of our talks across a dinner table, we had little difficulty understanding one another. We agreed that the continuing need of the Blacks in national politics was and would remain the welfare state. Only through its welfare programs for the poor could a large number of Blacks live in some minimum decency. On the Jewish side there was one concern that united all the factions of the Jewish community: the defense of Israel. As a lamb among the wolves of the Middle East, Israel needed sufficient American support to be able to defend itself. Therefore, Jews needed friends and allies in American politics who would help to make Israel more secure. The three of us quickly saw the obvious conclusion: let an alliance be made between the Black congressmen and the Jewish congressmen so that each group would vote for the agendas of both sides. Jews would remain committed to the welfare state, even as it meant higher taxes for the middle class, and Blacks would support Israel.

The alliance that was defined that day has lasted for many years. It represented a quiet consensus both among Jews and among Blacks. The large majority of Jews have continued to vote for taxes to support the welfare state even as they have been urged by the Republicans, and especially by the emerging neoconservatives, to vote their pocketbooks. Jews have remained the only community of White "haves" to remain firmly attached, by an average of two to one, to the Democratic Party. This has made the Jewish neoconservatives uncomfortable enough so that one of their intellectual leaders, Irving Kristol, ruefully observed that "Jews make money like Episcopalians and vote like Puerto Ricans."

Countering this remark of Kristol's, I said repeatedly in essays after the last four or five presidential elections that Jews support the welfare state not only for moral reasons but also because they regard it as in their interest. Class conflict has always been bad for Jews, for many centuries and in many different historical situations. The welfare state is a wall against pogroms.

In the Black community, a few prominent Blacks have flirted, on occasion, with the idea of attacking the moneys spent by the United States in support of Israel as a deprivation of the Black ghettos, but almost no one among them has crossed the line of trying to make a political career by fighting Israel. All of the Black political figures who have survived as mainstream politicians have continued to know that they need Jews as part of their coalitions. The agreement between Jews and Blacks to join in the defense of each other's basic concerns has, thus, been a quiet foundation stone of their intergroup politics. Precisely because it was never announced and no one ever took credit for this agreement, it has lasted well. When Sidney Yates and Charles Rangel left that night, I had found out what the founding fathers of the United States meant when they created a democratic government in which representatives were ultimately charged with carrying out the mandate of the people without always consulting the people whom they supposedly represent. The representatives were supposed to act in the best interests of those who had put them in place, sometimes even in ways that they might not immediately approve. Rangel and Yates had behaved as statesmen.

In the next few years the tensions between Blacks and Jews did not disappear, but, though there had been race riots in Los Angeles, Detroit, and Washington in 1968, as well as in Harlem, in New York, the tensions did not get worse. They did not boil over into major, continuing violence. Jews retained a deep awareness that Black rage could be lessened only by helping the poor toward a better life, and Blacks realized that they had hope for the future only if they worked to increase justice within the established social order and not toward destroying it. Some people supported the leaders of the agitation for Black Power, who did want to go to war with the Jews—and especially with their power to support Israel in American politics—but they remained a vocal and visible minority. Despite the tumult of the 1970s, racial war in the United States was not likely. The coolest heads—Bayard Rustin,

Martin Luther King, Roy Wilkins of the NAACP, and many others in the Black community—knew that racial conflict was not in the Black interest. Among the Whites, and especially among the Jews, the weight of statesmanship was on the side of keeping peace by making the life of Blacks better, by opening the way into society.

For Jews in America the perennial issue that would not go away was the conflict between Israel and the Arabs. In this quarrel, public opinion in America remained strongly supportive of Israel, but forces in America, and especially in the highest quarters of the government, were looking for ways to compromise the quarrel, and not necessarily entirely in Israel's favor. At the beginning of the 1970s American Jews were in a new political situation. The government of the United States wanted to push Israel toward peace negotiations with the Arabs. Signals were coming out of Washington that the American Jewish community was expected to support the government of the United States. This pressure was rejected with great vehemence by those who insisted that Israel's frontline position in opposing the Arabs in the Middle East was "good for America," but a more difficult question was being asked: is it morally acceptable for Israel to rule over millions of Arabs who wanted to be free of Israeli occupation?

In December 1969 William Rogers, who was the secretary of state during Nixon's first term, suggested a three-month cease-fire in the fighting that was taking place along the Suez Canal between Egypt and Israel, as a prelude to a peace treaty. The content of that arrangement, in Rogers's suggestion, was to be Israeli withdrawal from all of the occupied territories, while postponing discussion of such hard questions as the ultimate arrangements for Jerusalem and for the future of the Palestinian refugees. For Israel this meant a return to its borders before the 1967 war, and the proposal was therefore widely unpopular. Nonetheless Israel had no choice but to accede to the American suggestion, which it accepted in mid-1970. Nothing came of the Rogers Plan because the Egyptians were using the cease-fire to place more sophisticated antiaircraft missiles in the territory near their side of the Suez Canal. But the Rogers Plan had made it clear that the United States government was opposed to the "undivided land of Israel" and that it took the Arabs' side to deny Israel its conquests during the Six-Day War.

I had gotten into the conflict very early, in the days immediately after Israel's victory in the Six-Day War. Phyllis and I were in Israel in June 1967, and I had spoken and written about my fears for the future of an Israel that held on to territory and population that it could not and indeed should not attempt to digest. Between the Mediterranean and the Jordan River, nearly 40 percent of the population was Arab, and their numbers were growing. The undivided land of Israel, so I pointed out, in speeches and articles in Hebrew that summer, meant that Israel would soon lose its Jewish character and become a Jewish state with a Jewish minority.

The views that I had expressed in Israel I soon transferred to the United States. In the fall of 1967, a conference was announced at the Harvard Divinity School on the next steps that should be taken to end the war between Israel and the Palestinians and the Arab states that had supported them in the Six-Day War. The roster of speakers was headed by Noam Chomsky and Edward Said, both of whom were known to be vehement critics of Israel, and the rest of the speakers were equally one-sided. Two graduate students at Harvard—David Harman, whose father had moved recently from being Israel's ambassador in Washington to becoming president of the Hebrew University in Jerusalem, and Ismail Serageldin, a descendant of one of the most aristocratic families in Egypt—agreed that the meeting as projected would represent nothing more than an organized attack on Israel under the cover of free discussion at Harvard. They approached both the dean of the Harvard Divinity School and the organizers of the meeting to insist that the case for Israel had to be made at that event by someone with substantial sympathy for Israel. After considerable haggling, Harman and Serageldin succeeded in getting agreement that a Jewish liberal who was not automatically a defender of all of Israel's actions and policies would be acceptable. The result of these negotiations was that I wound up one night speaking in a packed auditorium opposite Edward Said, a colleague on the faculty of Columbia University.

Said argued what was then the line of the Palestinians: let Israel become a binational state comprising the entire region of Palestine, as it had been in the days of the British mandate; let the region return to undivided unity from the Mediterranean to the Jordan River. This is what it had actually become as a result of the Six-Day War, but all of the territory was now under Israeli control. Said wanted a state to be freshly created. There would be no special preferences for Jews, such as the right of return for those Jews who were compelled or wished to move to the homeland; no hindrances should remain to block Palestinian refugees from returning to their homes anywhere in this binational state. Said concluded this presentation by speaking, with some emotion, about the supposedly beautiful life that Arabs and Jews had lived together in Palestine in the decades before this supposed idyll was destroyed by Israel's military victory in the war in 1948.

I rose in rebuttal and described this picture of the past that Edward Said had drawn as a fabric of untruths that I was certain he himself did not believe. No doubt he knew that the entire period of the British mandate been a time of bitter fighting, with periods of armed attacks against Jews and of Jewish counterattacks. In fact, relations between Jews and Arabs in Palestine had never been peaceful. The last and most important of the British commissions to investigate the Jewish-Arab conflict, chaired by Lord Peel, had asserted in 1937 that the partition of the land was not a perfect solution, but it was a better solution than continuing war between the two communities. When the United Nations finally enacted the partition of Palestine in November 1947, the reasoning of its majority had been the same: partition is not a pleasant option, but better two states than one state in which Jews and Arabs have already demonstrated that they could not live together in peace. I ended my remarks on that platform by asserting that what Said had just finished saying was a political ploy and not a serious attempt to find some resolution to the conflict. However, I did not walk out of that ring as the matador in top favor with the spectators. Most of the several hundred people in the room belonged to the New Left, both secular and religious. They had come to the meeting to cheer Chomsky and Said, but I felt that I had to be there. Chomsky and Said had to be answered.

What Said heard me say that day, in describing the long-standing and bitter conflict between Jews and Arabs in Palestine, did not silence him. He wrote in the same vein in the winter 1969 issue of *Columbia Forum*, claiming that before 1948 there had been a functioning multicultural Palestine, "which had allowed Christian, Moslem and Jew to live in counterpoint with each other." I reacted to this piece by writing an essay entitled "Palestine: The Logic of Partition Today," which appeared in the winter 1970 issue of the same journal. Over my own signature as an academic, and not speaking for any Jewish organization, I said clearly and without any disguise that peace could be made only if a Palestinian state was created right beside Israel. I insisted that the suggestion that had been made in 1937 by the Peel Commission was still true and would remain so: Jews and Arabs are not in Palestine for love of each other, and there is no ideological compromise that can end their conflict; there can only be an untidy set of pragmatic arrangements that are best expressed through partition of the land and the political-military separation of the two combatants. These views were essentially anathema to the Jewish establishment, both in Israel and abroad, but I could not suppress the truth that I saw.

This essay did not cause my immediate expulsion from the various offices that I held in the Jewish community, because that would have created a public firestorm, especially since the liberal left intelligentsia in Israel would have spoken up vehemently in my defense. Retaliation did come from "defenders of the faith," from the Zionist hard-liners, but not immediately and not publicly. But the day after this essay was published, there was an immediate reaction from a totally unexpected quarter. The chairman of the board of trustees of Columbia University, John McCloy, called me at home, praising my views and asking me to come and have lunch with him as soon as I could. We made the date for the next day at the Faculty Club of Columbia University. I found myself sitting across the table from the man who was then chairman of the oversight committee that rode herd on all the American intelligence agencies and chairman of the board of Chase Manhattan Bank, a financial institution that represented the Rockefellers in the world of big business. McCloy was then, by common consent, the head of the permanent American establishment in politics and economics. He was a man to be taken very seriously, so I sat there and listened to McCloy. He told me that he had asked me to lunch because he wanted me to do something. He wanted me to intervene in the growing international crisis between Israel and the Arabs, and especially the Egyptians. As a result of the Six-Day War, the Suez Canal had remained blocked to traffic because a number of ships had been sunk along its length. McCloy made it clear that this was a problem not only for the Egyptians, who needed the revenue that a reopened canal would bring them, but, much more seriously, for all of the European states, which ran their economies on the basis of Middle Eastern oil. The oil could be delivered only by sending tankers on a long journey around the southern tip of Africa, and this delivery route could be interrupted by a declared enemy of the West, Colonel Khadafi, the dictator of Libya, who could harass some of these ships when they entered the Mediterranean to unload their oil in ports in southern Europe. McCloy then added that this danger could be averted only if the Suez Canal was cleared and reopened, so that the oil tankers would travel much shorter routes from east to west in the Mediterranean and not past Libya, and they would have no trouble continuing quickly on their way to European oil pipelines in Italy.

Israel had remain unequivocally opposed to any proposal to allow the Egyptians and their friends to make the canal navigable, but McCloy insisted that Israel was putting the United States into the difficult position of not being able to guarantee the oil supplies of its friends and allies in Europe. He did not think this was good for Israel. Moreover, Israel would actually benefit, even militarily, by agreeing to this proposal. It could pull back between six to ten kilometers from the shore of the canal, thus keeping it under observation and guaranteeing that it could be easily blocked again by Israeli guns. A reopened canal would guarantee that no military action on the ground could be launched by Egypt against Israel, for the moment that traffic stopped in the canal, Israel would know that a military attack was in the works.

After listening for nearly a half hour in silence, I asked John McCloy the obvious question: So what do you want me to do about it? He answered that he had reason to know that I knew many people in the top circles of Israel's government and army and that he hoped that I would agree to bring his message, forcefully and persuasively, to their attention. Even at that early stage in my involvements in international politics, I knew that this message had obviously been sent to Israel through other people and that McCloy wanted to send me as a kind of reinforcement. Perhaps he imagined that I would not be received, at least not by everyone in Israel's government, as a meddling stranger.

Without hesitating, I agreed to go to Israel, so I asked him, Whom do you want me to see? We both agreed that Golda Meir, the prime minister, would be hard to persuade. He suggested that I go to see the minister of defense, General Moshe Dayan. I told John McCloy that Moshe Dayan would no doubt see me but it was inconceivable that he would not tell the prime minister that I had asked for a meeting with him; I had to ask to see her directly. The next day I arranged through friends who worked in the Israeli diplomatic service in the United States that I would see Moshe Dayan as soon as I arrived, and that I would go on from Tel Aviv to Jerusalem to see the prime minister, Golda Meir, the next day. I did not provide an advanced summary of my conversation with John McCloy, but I did indicate that I was coming bearing some messages from him.

The meeting with Moshe Dayan was quite dramatic, even though it ended not with a bang but with a whimper. I was ushered into a very large room in the offices of the defense ministry in Tel Aviv and not into a smaller, more personal, place in which I had expected to meet him. He was surrounded by about thirty officers. Not a single one of them said a word in the course of the conversation between Dayan and me, but several were taking copious notes. In a few minutes I began to understand what was going on. Dayan was protecting himself. He was making sure that the whole of the conversation was recorded in every detail and, as I soon began to suspect, that all the various elements in the defense department, and perhaps even a few "reporters" who would debrief with other powers in the Israeli government and intelligence community, were in the room. This meeting was an interplay of two public performances: my account of my talk with John McCloy and Dayan's acting out his loyalty to Golda Meir. After I had said what I had come to say, Dayan responded very briefly. He allowed that there might be some merit in the proposal that I had brought from John McCloy, and he even subtly suggested that he was not hearing this idea for the first time, but he very firmly added that the decision would, of course, have to be taken by the prime minister and not by him. I responded by saying that I would be seeing her the very next day in Jerusalem. General Dayan seemed to know that.

As I later told John McCloy, the imaginings of some of his Arab friends that Dayan might break ranks and push for this idea over the opposition of the prime minister was a pipe dream. Dayan had, on occasion, gone his own way, as he had done right after the Six-Day War when he ordered that the Israeli flag should be taken down immediately and not be hoisted again on top of the mosques on the Temple Mount, but he was not going to take on Golda Meir on the question of how to behave toward the Egyptians.

The scene the next day, when I was ushered in to see Golda Meir, was entirely different. She did not have a single aide to accompany her. We were alone in her office. She clearly knew in advance what I was going to tell her; the report of what I had said to Dayan and his assistants had obviously been forwarded to her immediately. Golda Meir had prepared her answer. She paraphrased Winston Churchill when he had said twenty years before that he had not "become His Majesty's first minister to preside over the liquidation of the British Empire." The prime minister of Israel told me, with great emotion, that she had not become the head of Israel's government in order to be the first leader of the new Jewish state to return territory that had been acquired by the valor of Israel's soldiers. She then added that the benefits to Israel in the McCloy proposal were unnecessary and even laughable: what was this ragtag Egyptian army, that Israel needed to be afraid of it? Since I had a long history with Golda Meir of irritability on both sides, I did not bother to restrain myself even in her august presence as Israel's prime minister. I looked her straight in the eye and said that if she continued to repeat this contempt for Egypt's power and for the manhood of its soldiers, she might be surprised one day to find out that they would rise in anger and prove her wrong. She looked at me as if I were mad—and so, without even a show of the usual courtesies, the conversation ended.

Two and a half years later, when the Egyptians shocked Israel, on Yom Kippur Day in the fall of 1973, by moving across the canal and deep into the Sinai Peninsula, I was not surprised that Golda Meir felt personally very guilty for this disaster. When the war was over Golda Meir soon resigned from office, clearly broken and depressed. She could have bought a long armistice with the Egyptians by agreeing to withdraw a maximum of a dozen kilometers, and such a withdrawal would have the changed the map of the Middle East in Israel's favor. She had not. Israel would pay for this stubbornness for many years.

I came home from this journey permanently distrustful of men and women in high places. For years I had been stopped, and sometimes chastised, as I expressed my heresies regarding the reigning official doctrines by being warned, often in mysterious whispers, that those in authority had access to much better information than their critics. Israeli leaders leaned heavily on the near legendary reputation of the state's intelligence services. But how could I continue to believe in Israel's superior information when Golda Meir was so obviously wrong, even in 1971, before the lesson that was taught by the war two years and seven months later, in holding the Egyptian army in contempt? She was not taking into account the effect of the support of the Soviet Union in training and rearming their client in Cairo. Whatever information Israeli intelligence might be bringing to her, Golda Meir was disregarding it because she was acting on shallow preconceptions. Those who thought about strategic problems without prejudice were more likely to see the truth than those who read top-secret dossiers through the eyes of their own illusions.

Several days later, on the long airplane ride back to New York, I kept repeating to myself the statement that Clemenceau had made during the First World War: "War is too serious a matter to leave to the generals." On the basis of my own recent experience I had to add that international politics and the destiny of nations was too serious a matter to leave to the judgment of prime ministers. No one could shirk the task of using his own intelligence and moral judgment.

For me personally, the hours of reflection on the flight back to the United States set the seal on a transformation in my sense of the political role that I had to play. To be sure, I had made some speeches and written some essays between 1967 and 1971 in which I had moved to the side of the doves, to become one of those who advocated compromise with the Arabs and a two-state solution to the Israel-Palestine conflict, but these speeches and writings were still those of an intellectual. I was being dismissed as an academic who belonged to the bleeding hearts. But I also operated in some of the corridors of Jewish power. I was a political figure with the moral responsibility to act on my convictions. I could not put what I said and wrote into some separate box from what I did in public life. On the airplane it became clear to me—uncomfortably clear—that I would have to fight the Israeli government. Its leaders would keep demanding that I keep my mouth shut and toe the line, but I was returning from Tel Aviv and Jerusalem with close and immediate knowledge of how disastrous the line was. I could not avoid doing battle.

But I was still reluctant to go public. I felt that it was right, and nec-essary, to argue for my views within Jewish forums, but that I should not go the final step to break with the policies of Israel's government and its supporters in the Jewish world in the public arena. It took me several years to realize that Israel's political establishment no longer had the power or the moral authority that it claimed to have. These were the years when the governments led by Labor pretended that they were keeping the West Bank in trust until a peace treaty was finally negoti-ated, but these statements were clearly not true. Everybody knew that settlements "beyond the green line" (that is, Israel's borders before June 1967) were being established at great rate, some with permission in the guise of being necessary for Israel's security and others because the set-tlers had the brass to move in and the government of Israel had not the political courage to move them out. So, to cite just one example, some hard-line annexationist ideologues moved into a hotel in Hebron in 1968 supposedly to celebrate the Passover holiday at the tomb of the biblical patriarchs and matriarchs. They remained. Essentially, they forced the government to send soldiers to protect them.

As the ruling authorities in Israel pretended to look away at the cre-ation of more and more settlements, the opposition to these endeavors kept rising and becoming very vocal. What the doves—led by the liberal left parties that combined in Meretz and, later, by dissident reserve offi-cers who founded Peace Now in 1978—were saying was being widely reported in the international press and television. Israel, and the Jews who supported it, had become divided, and the government of Israel had become the spokesman and leader of one of the factions. Israel's successive governments asserted that concern for Israel demanded that every Jew had to support what Israel was doing. The more that this was asserted, the more persuaded I became that I had to be "disloyal" publicly—together with most of the people in Israel whom I greatly admired such as Shulamit Aloni in politics and Gershom Scholem in academic intel-lectual life. I could not be silent, and I could not keep my dissents within the confines of writing essays for Israeli journals or arguing at board meetings of Jewish organizations in Jerusalem or New York.

My growing distemper with the official Jewish line was inevitably noticed in Washington. I was always part of the delegations that the Conference of Presidents of the Major Jewish Organizations kept sending to Washington to meet with the secretaries of state. The meetings became more frequent as Henry Kissinger succeeded William Rogers in that office in 1971 and thus became the only person to combine that office with that of the national security advisor. The whole world knew that Henry Kissinger was a Jew, and that made his meetings more difficult both for him and for us. Dr. Kissinger was representing an administration that wanted a settlement in the Middle East that would not leave Israel in control of the West Bank. No matter what the Israeli government might be saying at various junctures (it sometimes tried to sound reasonable, if only for tactical reasons), the delegations that met with Henry Kissinger were unbending in support of Israeli maximalism. It was no secret from him and his aides that these American Jewish representatives had been briefed in advance by the Israeli Embassy and that someone in the group hastened to debrief with the Israelis after the meeting. He never quite got to say it openly, when all his visitors were still in the room, but he would often explode in exasperation, while their backs were still visible on the way to the elevator, that he saw no point in talking with these people since they were repeating verbatim what the Israeli ambassador, Simcha Dinitz, had said to him the day before.

Kissinger quickly caught on as he listened carefully to the nuances of these meetings that I was not a cheerleader of the official line. He began to invite me to stay behind, usually with his personal assistant, Lawrence Eagleburger, in attendance, to give him my assessment of what the Jewish community was really thinking. In these private conversations, I did not hesitate to tell Kissinger that American Jewish opinion was much more nuanced and divided than the official delegations were describing—but he had trouble believing what I was telling him. One day, after we had become more than casual acquaintances, he told me why. The Jewish periodicals in America, including even *Die Aufbau,* the weekly that was published mostly in German and was read by the older generation of Jewish refugees from Germany, constantly attacked him as a "bad Jew." His retort to these repeated attacks was very basic: he was the secretary of state of the United States and not the foreign minister of Israel. He even added that he thought that the policies he was promoting would soon prove to be better for Israel than its own intransigence. He even told me that he had spoken often with the Israeli ambassador, asking him to quiet the Jewish periodicals and to get them to be more understanding of what he, the first Jew to become secretary of state, was doing. Simcha Dinitz had answered that he did not have the power to control the journals of American Jews. One day, Kissinger turned to me and asked whether I could help. He added that he was on the edge of his nerves every Friday, when he expected, and usually received, a telephone call from his father, a very Orthodox Jew who still lived in the apartment to which the family had first come in Washington Heights, in Manhattan. The senior Mr. Kissinger used to call his son in the middle of the day, after he had read that week's edition of the *Die Aufbau,* and say, "Heinz [Henry's first name on his birth certificate in Germany], how can I go to synagogue tonight after what everyone has read in the paper?"

I soon found an excuse to go visit the senior Kissingers, supposedly for other matters, and, inevitably, the pained subject came up. I told the senior Kissingers that I knew their son well enough to be certain that his love for them had never lessened and that I, the rabbi, was very much aware that Henry was a very caring Jew. I then suggested that I would like to give a luncheon in Washington in their son Henry's honor. It would be a function of the American Jewish Congress, so that, while still in office and sometimes under fire, he would have been honored by a national Jewish organization. The Kissingers beamed and very happily accepted the invitation to come to such a function when it could be given. A couple of months later, when the luncheon actually took place, the whole Kissinger family sat together at a table next to the dais, with my wife, Phyllis, as their host. I had the pleasure of making a short speech about Henry Kissinger. He was visibly moved by this Jewish honor that was being conferred in the presence of his parents.

Through the years Kissinger and I developed a friendship. Many stories come to mind, but the favorite is one that had no relationship to the various political dramas that were the stuff of his career. One day, I walked into Kissinger's office (the inner office in which he worked and not the much larger one in which he received visitors), and he soon saw that I was grinning an impish grin. He wanted to know why I was so amused. I told him that I had found a document that might interest him. When he had first arrived as a teenage immigrant to the United States, he was still an ultra-Orthodox Jew who belonged to that wing of

German Jewish ultra-Orthodoxy that was opposed to Zionism. Someone whom I knew had belonged with the young Kissinger to a youth
group of this community in Washington Heights. These teenagers
published an occasional bulletin in which one or another of the members wrote an essay. The fourteen-year-old Heinz Kissinger had been
the author of an article in which he chastised the Zionists for trying to
return to the Holy Land for secular and nationalist reasons and not
waiting for the messiah to come and return the Jewish people to the
land. Dr. Kissinger shamefacedly admitted that he had once written
such an article, and then he said to me, "But, Arthur, you won't repub-
lish it, will you?" I assured him I would not. I added that no one should
be held responsible for what he wrote at fourteen, especially since life
had taken him in other directions.

My distemper with Golda Meir and my increasing regard for
Kissinger as a concerned Jew had placed me with the defenders of the
Rogers Plan. I was allied with Kissinger's policies of encouraging and
sometimes pushing the Arabs and Israelis toward peace. The tensions
rose many notches in October 1973 when the Egyptians crossed the
Suez Canal on Yom Kippur Day. Within a very few days, Israel was in
dire trouble; it was losing the war. Suddenly, I was not the black sheep
of the American Jewish establishment or the Israeli government. Anyone who had any special connection to Washington needed to be
enlisted. I, too, had a role. I was the increasingly well-known dove and
dissenter, so I could be especially useful. The masters of power in
Washington needed to know that no Jew would stand by while Israel
was humiliated—and in danger.

25

The news that war had begun between Israel and Egypt reached me in synagogue in the midmorning of that Yom Kippur Day. Phyllis came in with a deeply troubled and very somber look on her face, and she walked straight up to me on the pulpit. She had heard that Egyptian soldiers had crossed the canal and that there was bitter fighting on the east side, within the territory that Israel had occupied in 1967. Fighting tears, I felt immediately angry with Israel's leaders for not having taken the offer that had been made them to withdraw from the canal and let the Egyptians make it navigable again for peaceful travel. This was an unnecessary war, which the Israeli army never expected, and the ordinary Egyptian soldiers were fighting because they had to obey orders from their commanders. In a very few minutes after Phyllis had brought me this bitter news, I found a place in the service in which I could make room for a special prayer for peace. There was a large gasp in the congregation when I told them that war had begun and an even larger gasp when I said the prayer not from some set liturgical formulas but impromptu. I prayed for the life and well-being of the soldiers on both sides, emphasizing that the Egyptian attackers were as much the children of God as were the Israelis. I added that we needed to be on the side of life and peace for everyone and not on the side of national chauvinism.

Many, and perhaps even most, of the thousand or so people in the synagogue at that moment agreed with what I was saying. Even the doubters seemed to understand that I represented the moral impulse that had been stated long ago in a Talmudic text: When the Jews left Egypt, Pharaoh, with all his chariots and soldiers, had pursued them and trapped them at the shore of the Sea of Reeds. Miraculously, a path was opened in the waters for the Jews to cross. As the Egyptians tried to follow, the waters closed in again and they drowned in their thousands. Standing in safety on the other side of the sea, the Jews sang a song of thanksgiving celebrating their deliverance. In heaven, the angels joined the celebration. The rabbis had the courage to put in the mouth of God that He chastised the angels, commanding them to be silent: How dare you exult when my handiwork, the Egyptians, are drowning in the sea? I could join no chorus that morning exulting in what seemed then to be the quick and inevitable victory that Israel would win. I could only weep for the dead and wounded on both sides.

That there would be no easy triumph in the image of 1967 dawned on most people by the time Yom Kippur Day was over. Returning from synagogue, we knew that Israel was reeling. Israel had been defending its side of the canal with less than six hundred troops. The prewar assessment of Israel's strategic planners and intelligence services was that the daring attack across the canal that Egypt had executed was inconceivable and that the massing of troops that had been observed for a number of days before the attack was simply a feint or a training maneuver. Therefore, there was little of the army in the forts of the Bar-Lev Line to stop the Egyptian advance. That first day of war, the Egyptians were across the canal and advancing into the Sinai.

Golda Meir and Moshe Dayan were sufficiently discouraged by the following Tuesday (the attack had begun on Saturday morning) that they were on the verge of asking for an armistice and accepting the then front line, which was the high-water mark of Egyptian success. Meir and Dayan could continue the war and turn Israel's fortunes around only if the United States provided large, immediate resupply of Israel's armed forces. The leadership of Israel bet its very existence on the hope that this would happen. Every means of persuasion and pressure that could be mustered on behalf of Israel had to be used.

In the Jewish liturgical calendar, the Thursday and Friday of that week were the first two days of the holiday of Sukkoth, when Jews commemorated their forty years of wandering in the desert after they had succeeded in breaking out of Egypt. I had never in my life failed to observe the holiday, but Israel's situation was grave and even desperate. On the first day of the holiday I informed my congregation that I would not be in synagogue the next day. I had to go down to Washington to help in the effort to secure immediate help for Israel. I shall never forget that day. As I drove to the airport I kept remembering that the halakah permits and even commands the most pious to disregard all of the rules of Sabbath, the various festivals, and even the Day of Atonement itself in order to save a life. The Talmud even asserts that cooking on the Day of Atonement for someone who is gravely ill is a very meritorious form of observing the fast. I was obeying the halakah when I was buying a ticket at the airport that morning. And yet it felt very strange to be giving Talmudic law such an immediate and contemporary definition as I sat in the airplane on the way to Washington.

That very day, Friday, Richard Nixon turned the tide of the war. He gave the order to open, immediately, an air bridge to Israel to supply it with whatever it might need for its defense. Israel's military leaders were now free to hold back nothing that they could use, because they were assured that America would replenish their arsenals. The war was won by the Israelis, but at great cost. Inevitably, the argument soon arose, even as the airlift was barely begun, as to who was responsible for the decision to help Israel generously and without qualification. There were two contenders, Henry Kissinger and Richard Nixon. It was always obvious to me that the question of who formulated the suggestion to give Israel such immediate and munificent help was a secondary matter. The ultimate power to decide was Nixon's, and not that of his secretary of state, so that the order to send the aid had to be put on the credit side of Nixon's ledger sheet. Richard Nixon soon proved that he wanted this credit very badly. He was campaigning to survive the growing Watergate scandal as the great master of American foreign policy. Even as he fumed in private against the Jewish liberals as his most formidable enemies, he wanted to lessen their hostility.

Some weeks after the end of the war, Nixon invited three or four American Jewish leaders to meet him, headed as always by his friend Max Fisher. Nixon made sure that Henry Kissinger was in attendance. This time we sat, not around the table in the cabinet room, but in the Oval Office itself. Almost immediately, Nixon led the conversation to that Friday in October when Israel was close to its breaking point. He turned to Kissinger and said, "Henry, you came to me at that time and you asked for a few planeloads of help, and I understood that you could not ask for more because it was for Israel. I reacted by saying that a few planeloads would not really help and if we were taking a hand in this war, we had better send the amount of supply that would make a difference." Nixon then turned directly to Kissinger and said, "That's correct, isn't it, Henry?" Dr. Kissinger may have had a somewhat different story to tell, but he had no choice but to say, "Yes, of course, Mr. President." Nixon had thus fixed a record in the presence of some leading figures in the American Jewish community, both Republicans and Democrats, that left him as the central figure in saving Israel from defeat.

I did not ever discuss this incident again, not at that time or later, with Henry Kissinger. One did not have to be a great master of human psychology, or an insider in American policy making, to know that Nixon needed Kissinger for his enormous talent but wanted, across the board, to establish that he, the president, was the originator of policy, the diplomatic genius who saved Israel in October 1973 and the visionary who had opened China to trade in 1972. At the very end of his presidency, when Nixon had Kissinger kneel with him in prayer in a semideserted White House, these two men were together, but their agendas were and had been different.

I have little to add to the enormous amount of literature already in print about the military turnabout that stopped the Egyptian advance in the second week of the war, and the hectic rounds of shuttle diplomacy that Kissinger undertook to make an end to hostilities. In the course of those weeks, he made it clear several times to the leaders of the main Jewish organizations in the United States that the Soviet Union was a power that could not be ignored. The Egyptians had been trained and rearmed by Moscow, and the large toll on Israel's air force, its most vaunted weapon, had been caused by Soviet antiaircraft missiles. As Egypt began to lose the war, high-ranking sources in the State

Department kept floating the story (the same one that had first appeared in 1957, during the Suez crisis) that a parachute brigade was poised in Odessa to come to the aid of Egypt. Did the Israelis and their friends want to embroil the United States in the beginnings of a super-power war in the Middle East? There is some doubt now, in 2002, nearly three decades after the Yom Kippur War, whether the Soviet parachute brigade ever existed except as a feint, or perhaps as a figment of some intelligence officer's imagination. But in October 1973 it seemed very real indeed. It was certainly useful to Dr. Kissinger to knock heads together among the pro-Israeli forces in Washington. But he never displayed a satellite photo of the paratroop brigade. It was odd that such evidence was not available, since Adlai Stevenson, at a meeting of the United Nations Security Council, had waved satellite photos in the face of the Soviet ambassador during the Cuban Missile Crisis a decade earlier.

In the course of Kissinger's travels to Moscow, to the Arab capitals, and to Jerusalem, he did patch up an armistice, and he made a set of arrangements in which Israel agreed to give back the western end of the Sinai Peninsula. These arrangements also contained an agreement of American involvement by stationing observers of the truce and, more important, by giving both Israel and the Egyptians substantial American aid to compensate them for the costs of withdrawal and rebuilding. At the end of Kissinger's shuttle diplomacy, the United States was more heavily engaged than ever in the Middle East. The two chief protagonists in the war, the Israelis and the Egyptians, were essentially put on "good behavior." The Americans' stakes were obvious: Washington could neither offend the Israel lobby in the United States nor alienate its principal Arab ally, Saudi Arabia. Neither the Israelis nor the Arabs could be allowed to claim anything approaching total victory. The result of this diplomacy was that while Israel had won by rebounding from its disastrous losses in the first week of the war, it was soon to be chastened. The Arabs had won a major diplomatic and propaganda victory. They were able to say that by the force of their arms they had regained Arab land and pushed the Israelis out of some of their conquests. At the time much of Israel was angry with Henry Kissinger for orchestrating this agreement for disengagement and Israeli withdrawal and for making it crystal clear that the days of euphoria that had followed the Six-Day

War in 1967, and the belief that all the conquered territories could be retained, were over. Kissinger did not become, then, a hero to the Israeli moderates, not because they disagreed with his diplomatic results but because they thought that he was behaving like the proconsul of the American empire, commanding the natives as to what they must do.

The Yom Kippur War had a devastating effect on the politics of Israel. The lava of resentment burned the Pompeii of Israel's Labor Party. This political alignment of the Left had dominated among the Zionists for half a century. It regarded itself and was commonly respected as the group that had fashioned and founded the state of Israel, had proclaimed it under the leadership of David Ben-Gurion, and had won famous victories, from the War of Independence in 1948 to the Six-Day War in 1967. Even the million or so Jews from North Africa who had come to the state after its founding had continued to vote for Labor, though they resented their status as second-class citizens. They were given little preferment in jobs, social services, or education. The state belonged to the Labor Party, and the Jews from North Africa could only hope that this "god" would turn his favor toward them.

The last major remaining symbol of the founding fathers was Golda Meir. She had been tested by this war and had failed. And what was worse, she herself knew that she had failed. Within a very few months, Golda relinquished the office of prime minister and retired to her apartment in Tel Aviv, as a broken person. Precisely because I had warned her two years earlier that some such attack might happen, and had had other fights with her at significant moments in the history of Israel, I felt that it was my duty to go and visit her. She did not wave me off. On the contrary, I was treated to coffee and cake in her living room, and the conversation was the friendliest we had ever had. It opened the door for personal relations that continued and became closer till the very end of her days. A further result of the rapprochement with Golda Meir was that Naomi Levine and I invited her to New York for a special dinner of the American Jewish Congress in her honor. The dinner was made all the more attractive because Henry Kissinger, who had been the target of her barbs for years, had very willingly agreed to speak in praise of Golda that evening. This occasion thus took on the aura of a family festival in which members of the clan who had been annoying each other would demonstrate their mutual affection and their indivisible unity.

There was exactly this kind of atmosphere in the room when the dinner was given in the fall of 1977. Henry Kissinger's parents were there, beaming. At the end of the evening, I walked over to Henry's father and said, in his son's hearing, "I'm sure that this Sabbath you will not be badgered at the synagogue by criticism of your son." The old man's grin became even broader and he half embraced me.

After Golda Meir's resignation in the spring of 1974, the Labor Party now needed to pull itself together and find a new prime minister who would reclaim some of the confidence that had been lost during the 1973 war. It decided to field Yitzhak Rabin, the general who had commanded Israel's armed forces in the Six-Day War and who had been a notable success as Golda Meir's ambassador to the United States. Rabin was elected without much trouble, chiefly because he was then more of a hawk than a dove; that is, the Israeli hard-liners knew that he would defend the settlements that had already been established and that he would probably not stand in the way of putting new ones on the West Bank. Rabin was, in a sense, a unity candidate—so inevitably, we quarreled shortly after he was elected.

During his tenure as ambassador in Washington, from 1968 to 1974, Yitzhak Rabin had unusual acceptance in the Pentagon and elsewhere in Washington because of his enormous reputation as the victor of the Six-Day War. He made it absolutely clear that he regarded Israel's relations with the United States as those of one state to another and that he wanted nothing to do with the American Jewish lobby. He did not want to be a supplicant in the United States asking sympathetic forces in its political life to help him. He was not interested in hearing any advice or in sharing any information. I left him alone, saying on occasion to friends and associates that just as it is never as bad as you think it is, it is certainly never as good as you think it is, but there was no point in tangling with a young general at the zenith of his reputation.

After Rabin became prime minister in 1974, his ingrained attitude of being a commanding general continued. Rabin also had a certain Sabra disdain for the Jews of the Diaspora. The first time that I was in Jerusalem after he became prime minister, I asked for an appointment and was soon alone with him in his office. I told him that I had been in American air-force uniform during the Korean War and that I sought permission as a former junior officer to address the commanding general.

I said to Rabin that American opinion was a major battleground for Israel and that, despite all of his years of experience as ambassador in the United States, he perhaps did not know some of the terrain as well as some of us who cared deeply for Israel but lived and labored on the American scene. Would it not help him if he heard spoken reports regularly from Americans who were on his side? He responded in a huff. He told me that at various points in his career he had refused to listen to reports from some subordinate officers. With his larger vision, he might decide that they were expendable, and he was not going to be deterred by the reports that they might want to give him. I said nothing, but Rabin was far from a stupid man. He knew exactly what I was thinking—that an additional perspective, independent from Israel's diplomats, might be of some use. There was soon, within days, a payback to this discussion. Justice and Mrs. Haim Cohen had remained for years among our closest friends, and Michal Cohen had been to high school with Leah Rabin, with whom she still maintained a warm friendship. The Cohens invited the Rabins for dinner. They were delighted to accept, but then Michal Cohen told Leah Rabin who else would be there and that this dinner was being held so that the new prime minister and I might become friends. The response came back almost immediately: the Rabins could not make the dinner. And so it remained throughout Rabin's prime ministry and beyond.

There was one exception, a couple of years later when a personal scandal forced Rabin out of office. He and his wife were subject to the law, then in force in Israel, that no citizen of the country could keep a personal account in foreign currency abroad. One day when Rabin as prime minister was visiting Washington, somehow, an Israeli newspaper reporter was in the lobby of a Washington bank and saw Mrs. Rabin withdrawing dollars from her personal account. The story hit the press in Israel immediately, and, even though the infraction was quite minor, it led quickly to Rabin's taking full responsibility and resigning his office. The Labor Party replaced him with his archrival Shimon Peres. Leah Rabin soon found that as the wife of the ex–prime minister, and the cause of his downfall, she was no longer in demand at dinner parties in the United States. Michal Cohen called to tell me that Leah Rabin was very downcast. Phyllis and I responded by taking her to the most public occasion that we could think of—a concert of the New York

Philharmonic Orchestra—during her next visit to the United States. This gesture broke the ice between the Rabins and ourselves. Through the years there was a growing warmth in our encounters.

The Rabin government had not been a success. The prestige and authority of the Labor Party was sinking. Rabin represented a second generation, the successors to the founding fathers. Most of his contemporaries among the leaders of Labor Zionism had been born in Israel or had been brought there as young children. They took their position in Israeli society and their dominance for granted, and some of them began to show characteristics of a "new class," like the second generation of the rulers in the Soviet Union and its satellites, who behaved like hereditary heirs to the state. Rabin himself was personally honest, and he remained so till the end of his days. He never lived the high life or took personal advantage of his position, nor did he leave his family much of an inheritance, but that was not true of some of his contemporaries. Scandals broke that were far more serious than the technical problem with the regulation about holding foreign currency abroad, even in small amounts. A minister in the Labor cabinet committed suicide rather than face the accusation that he had lined his own pockets, a leading banker went to jail in total disgrace, and there were a series of other unpleasant incidents.

Many people looked back to the founding fathers of Israel through the haze of memory. Ben-Gurion had gone off to a kibbutz in the desert in southern Israel, and he was usually pictured walking or working in a pair of shorts. The men and women of his generation were equally austere. I suspect that Golda Meir never possessed more than two or three dresses, because those were the only ones I ever saw her in. The one for everyday wear was black. I even was with her at a formal party or two where this black dress was ornamented with a bit of costume jewelry. But the next generation did not suggest that they still longed for the austere kibbutz. On the contrary, they lived in ever plusher apartments in Tel Aviv or its plush suburbs, and they became part of the growing society of Israeli entrepreneurs and big businessmen, almost all of whom made their fortunes through their close connections with the government.

In the few years after the Yom Kippur War the internal politics of Israel were radically transformed. Both the government in Washington and the leaders of the American Jewish organizations were stunned by the results of the election in 1977, when the Labor Party was turned out of office for the first time in Israel's history. It had simply never occurred to anybody that this era could end, so that neither the American diplomats nor the Jewish organizational presidents and senior bureaucrats knew the men, and the few women, who would lead the new regime. Nowhere—not in Washington among the diplomats, not in New York among the Jewish organizational types—was there a contingency plan for how to deal with Menachem Begin, the victorious leader of the Likud Party, and those whom he would bring with him into office. I was in a different position. I had made a point of visiting Menachem Begin in the Knesset whenever I was in Israel. When he came to New York, I extended to him the courtesies that were due to the leader of the opposition. I had acted this way not with any political foresight but because I had always thought that all the leaders of Israel, in all the various factions, belonged to one family—a quarreling one, but a family. One did not allow personal relations to wither over political difference. I kept suggesting to friends in American political and diplomatic circles and in the Jewish organizations that what was necessary now were two seemingly contradictory approaches: having been treated as practically nonexistent outsiders for decades, Begin and his associates would react to the proffer of friendship; however, those who would do political business with the new regime should not flatter but, rather, tell the absolute truth. It was particularly important for the American Jewish establishment, which had for so long simply followed the lead of the Labor government, to learn, quickly, to disagree when necessary with the new right-wing government, but with respect and dignity. These transitions were never made, either by the government in Washington or the Jewish leaders in New York. Washington bullied the Likud, and the Jewish organizations mostly fell over each other flattering and fawning over the new regime.

It is too easy to explain this shift simply as reflecting the need of American Jewish organizational leaders to keep their union card as "regulars" in support of Israel's government; a deeper motif was coming to the surface. A minority among the Jews in America had long been hardliners, but they had been driven into semisilence in the years when the Labor Party was in power. This element consisted of several groups: Most of the Orthodox had been moving toward messianic dreams; they were convinced that confrontation with the Arabs was a necessary preamble to the coming of the messiah. Another group consisted of Holocaust survivors and their children. There were many who could not bear the memory of Jewish powerlessness during the Nazi years. The use of Jewish power in Israel was a recompense for the past. This tough stance did not convince the majority of the moderates in the Diaspora, but there was some re-echo of the pride in power in the hearts of many who regarded themselves as political moderates. Begin evoked large admiration in the Diaspora. Here was a leader who was standing up to the Arabs in the region and to the not very sympathetic Gentiles in Washington.

The inevitable implications of the shift to the political right among American Jews was best understood by a very controversial young rabbi from Brooklyn, Meir Kahane, who was the founder and the leader of the Jewish Defense League. Kahane had appeared on the scene during the race riots of the late 1960s, and, in the face of some anti-Semitic incidents, thereafter, to create a counterforce against the enemies of the Jews. Kahane soon moved to Israel to participate in its politics. He maintained, without disguise, that the Palestinian Arabs should be forced to leave the territory of the "undivided land of Israel." Kahane was denounced as a warmonger and even a racist. But he was right. If the basic premise of Jewish policy became to hit back at the Palestinian Arabs and to regard them as interlopers in the ancestral Jewish land, the safety of the Jews would require removing them, gently if possible, from the land. Those who were getting some kind of emotional release from the use of Jewish force had to ask themselves: where does this lead? I could not abide the political fuzziness of the American Jewish response to the ascent of Menachem Begin. I insisted that he who says Begin is, inevitably, asserting Kahane.

Many explanations have been given in the very large literature that has appeared in the past twenty-five years about this part of Israel's history, and many "causes" have been blamed for the downfall of the Labor Party in the election of 1977. But my own view was much simpler than the usual explanations. What had happened was best explained by a Chinese metaphor and, very comparably, from the politics of the Book of Kings in the Bible. In the Chinese version, a regime is finished when it loses the mandate of Heaven. In the Hebraic version, when God has decided that the incumbent king has been an unfaithful servant, it becomes time for a change. He confers the leadership of His chosen people on someone who, He hopes, will behave more nearly in His spirit. Two substantial elements in Israel's political life no longer believed in the divine right of the Labor Party to govern. One of the rebellions originated within the traditional constituency of the Labor Party and even represented some of its staunchest supporters in the middle class and among the intelligentsia. These people were recoiling from the corruption of the new class; they wanted a return to the pristine Zionism of Israel's early years. The other group that rebelled wanted no such return to the past. It contained many tens of thousands of immigrants who had come in the late 1940s and early 1950s from North Africa. They no longer believed in Labor's propaganda that they ultimately would be the beneficiaries of its economic policies. They did not see their situation improving, because the Israeli economy, which was dominated by the state, was being good to those who could manipulate their connections but little was left over for those who were not within the charmed circle.

As I reacted to Begin's election, I had to admit to myself that I was breaking with the American Jewish establishment. The dominant mood at that moment in 1977 was to pretend, or even make oneself believe, that American Jews could go on supporting a moderate, liberal Israel that desired a reasonable peace with the Palestinians. I knew that this was not so; I had no doubt that Begin and the people with whom he was coming to power really believed that they could achieve the "undivided land of Israel." I was moving beyond the limits of what my constituents in America, even those who belonged to the organization of which I was president, the American Jewish Congress, would really support. I had to finally admit to myself that I drew my strength from other sources than some immediate public opinion polls or even the democratic process of organizational elections. I had been raised among people, whether the Hasidim of my youth or the scholars of my young adult years, who assumed as a matter of course that they had views of their own and that these views mattered. Very early on, in my first encounter with the new state of Israel in 1949, I had refused to accept the notion that the government of Israel was now the supreme authority in Jewish life. I was old enough to have worked with such people as Stephen Wise, Abba Hillel Silver, and Nahum Goldmann. They were as much the founders of the state of Israel, and leaders of the entire Jewish world, as Theodor Herzl and David Ben-Gurion. I finally discovered that I belonged to those who knew that leaders come and go, that policies change as the needs of the Jewish people change, and that I was not one of those who wanted, or needed, for those who held power at the moment to like me or be satisfied with the amount of obeisance that I showed them. I was the descendant of ancestors who made decisions, in-season and out-of-season, based on their sense of what they thought was right and, yes, whether in the long run it was "good for the Jews." In the spring of 1977, I understood why I had been drawn to the last great survivor of the founding fathers of Israel, Nahum Goldmann. He carried with him the certainty that he, and he alone, made up his mind and neither an Israeli government nor a seeming consensus in the Jewish world could silence him.

Ruefully, sometimes sadly, and always defiantly, I knew very clearly now that I always belonged to these older Jewish figures. I was afraid that I was the last of the breed. On occasion, I consoled myself in this loneliness by thinking, as usual for me, of the teachings of two traditions. Rousseau had taught, in the eighteenth century, a distinction between the "will of all" and the "general will." The will of all defines the values and political direction of a majority of the people at any moment, but it is almost always a temporary majority. The general will means the long-standing and continuing values of a community, even if these values do not always command the assent of a majority. The leader, so Rousseau asserted, speaks for the general will. The Talmud taught that we must obey the majority, as the Bible prescribes, but we are commanded not to follow the majority when its decisions contravene our moral conscience. At that point we must take the risk of standing with the few, or even standing alone. In 1977, it was clearer to me than ever before that I had to act on my own, clearly and unmistakably.

The Israeli election of 1977 had been a hard fight between the Likud Party, the collection of various factions which supported Begin's ultranationalist view that the Jews were entitled to the undivided land of Israel, and the Labor Party, which was more moderate without being at all clear as to what its ultimate plan for peace with the Arabs was. But the political drama of that election campaign was in the appearance of a new party, Dash (the Democratic Movement for Change), under the leadership of one of Israel's most famous archeologists, Yigal Yadin, who had previously been one of the central military figures in Israel's War of Independence in 1948. The fact that he had been raised in the Labor Party gave him a particular appeal: voting for the new party he had created was not seen to be a betrayal of the fundamental political tradition of the Israeli state. The Dash Party could be imagined as an act of restoration of the true values of Labor, which had been traduced by the new class of politicians who were now tainted by both the perceived defeat in the Yom Kippur War and the various corruption scandals. In this election Yadin's party received enough votes to gain an astonishing fifteen seats in a Knesset of one hundred twenty members. But the results of the election could be added up in several quite contradictory ways. Yigal Yadin thought that his party of fifteen would now lead the Knesset and that he had an unlimited future in which he would become, perhaps after the next election, the head of a much larger party and probably prime minister. In the meantime he was being courted by Menachem Begin to accept the office of deputy prime minister in a Begin-led cabinet. Another possible reading of the election result was that all of Yadin's fifteen mandates came from the traditional voters of the Labor Party and that his numbers and those of the Labor Party, taken together, were exactly the same as the size of Labor's own Knesset delegation in the previous election. Therefore, he would do better for the country and even for himself if he joined with the Labor Party in a coalition government that would reform Israel's politics.

I happened to be in Israel right after the election and was immediately enmeshed in the political maneuvers of Labor, Likud, and Dash as they jockeyed for seats in a new government. I was on friendly terms with all the principals—with Shimon Peres, who had become Rabin's replacement as the head of the Labor Party; with Menachem Begin; and even with Yigal Yadin, whom I knew least but with whom I was connected indirectly. William Foxwell Albright, my mentor at Johns Hopkins, had been a close friend of Yadin's father, Professor Elazar Lipa Sukenik, who had been the leading figure in biblical archeology in Palestine in the middle decades of the twentieth century.

My involvement in this haggling came to a climax one night at dinner in Tel Aviv at the home of Zalman and Ayala Abramov. Zalman Abramov had been for many years a steadying hand in Israel's interparty politics, and he had, indeed, served several times as the deputy speaker of the Knesset. Abramov himself belonged to a small middle-class party, the Liberals, but he was universally regarded as a trustworthy friend of all the groups. Zalman Abramov invited Shimon Peres and Yigal Yadin to dinner for the express purpose of talking through the political situation with a friendly outsider. Peres was eager—indeed, well-nigh desperate—to persuade Yadin to come with him in a Labor-led coalition government. I was very soon aware that Yadin did not believe that joining forces with Peres would advance him toward his personal goal of becoming prime minister.

In the discussion I told Yadin very bluntly that I had known Menachem Begin for many years, that I did not have the slightest doubt that Begin could and would outmaneuver him in all the games of political infighting, and that Yadin's dream of eventually succeeding Begin as prime minister was not realistic. There was not only Begin to consider; there were all the long-hungry political types of the Likud who now would sit at ministerial tables. They would make no allowance for an archaeologist and a former general who was a political amateur. Yadin did not like what he was hearing, but I persisted. I even went to the length of saying, in Peres's presence, that I did not think that he would be living in the Garden of Eden in a Peres cabinet, but on balance I urged him to take that option and not to enter a Begin coalition government, with people who were not at all like him or the voters who had given him his fifteen seats.

I failed. Yadin left the dinner table convinced that a very bright future was before him if he entered into government with Begin. And so a political revolution was made. Menachem Begin was at liberty to believe that he had become prime minister not on the basis of the votes of the resentful but because Israel was genuinely elated to follow his lead, that the true aim of a Zionist state was to rule over all the land from the Mediterranean to the Jordan River. Yet again, the Jews from North Africa had been used by Israel's political leadership. They had gone unmentioned during the dinner at the Abramovs. They were of no great concern to either Yadin or Peres, while for Begin they were simply a stepping-stone to achieving his territorial goal, the undivided land of Israel. By no stretch of the imagination could I hope that the Arabs would be treated with any real equality either. What was I to do?

26

W hat was I to do? How would I behave after Labor was turned from power? I had to answer this question sharply and decisively far sooner than I expected. Menachem Begin formed a coalition government with Yigal Yadin and the religious parties in the spring of 1977, and he was almost immediately planning a visit to Washington. Such a trip had become an important rite of passage for a new Israeli prime minister. Begin's journey was beset with tensions. It could not be compared with the trip of a new British or French prime minister who had just won an election putting his party back into power and was seeking to warm up already established ties with America. Begin and the new Carter administration were wary of each other. American Jews were in a troubling bind. They could not suddenly change direction and become ardent supporters of Begin's zeal for the "undivided land of Israel," but they also could not go into opposition and renounce the habit of treating the Israeli prime minister as their secular pope. The leaders of the American Jewish establishment had become accustomed to being received in Jerusalem with ceremony, and such rituals persuaded their constituents that they had a close relationship with the leaders of Israel and that their advice was taken most seriously in Israeli government circles. This routine was much more difficult to maintain now that the new prime minister was a figure whom many of them barely knew and whom most had long snubbed.

I found myself very much in the middle of these complexities, because I was in Israel in that summer of 1977 when Begin was packing his bag for his first visit to Washington. I was there, in part, because I was attending some meetings arranged by the American Jewish Congress, but I was there primarily as the bearer of a message from President Carter and his national security advisor, Zbigniew Brzezinski. I had known Brzezinski for some years because he was professor at the School of International Affairs of Columbia University, where I also taught, part-time. We lived in the same town— Englewood, New Jersey—and his children were occasionally in my synagogue to attend the Bar Mitzvahs of their Jewish classmates. It was not unusual for me to encounter Brzezinski at the front door, waiting to drive his children home after services. We had not become close friends from these encounters, but we were comfortable with each other.

Almost immediately after Carter assumed the presidency in January 1977, I had gone to Washington to visit with Brzezinski in his office at the White House. The organization of the White House was still so chaotic that he and I were stuck waiting for one another on what turned out to be the two sides of the same door because the secretaries did not know how to tell each other that I had arrived for the appointment. When I was finally ushered in to his office, it was the very room that Henry Kissinger, his perennial rival, had occupied. Brzezinski knew that I had spent a fair amount of time with Kissinger, so he remarked that there had been some changes made. I replied, Yes, you are now the national security advisor. But Brzezinski pointed with some pride to the different look of the office because he had rearranged some furniture. The ensuing conversation was, inevitably, about the Israeli-Arab conflict. Brzezinski was not apologetic for remarks that he had made before taking up his post in the Carter administration that there would be no peace before a Palestinian state was created. I was not outraged by this heresy. Brzezinski was left with the impression that I had not changed my views in recent years: I had remained a dove, a peacenik. We agreed to talk some more.

That happened again, in a few months. After Begin took office in Israel, I knew that I would soon be traveling to Israel, so I went to Washington to see Brzezinski. He told me that he suspected that Begin would be coming to meet with Carter to try to bring the Americans around to his view that the whole of "the undivided land of Israel" was nonnegotiable: it belonged to the Jews. Brzezinski then said that the warrant of the Israeli hard-liners was the biblical promise that God had once given the Jews. He then reminded me that Jimmy Carter was a convinced and pious Southern Baptist and that he himself was a believing and practicing Roman Catholic. It was obvious that each of them had different understandings of the biblical texts that the Jewish hard-liners liked to quote. He added that we also had to take into account the Muslim view. It would therefore not be useful for the first encounter between the new president of the United States and the new prime minister of Israel to become bogged down in biblical exegesis, trapped in religious issues about which neither the Jewish nor the Muslim Arab protagonists could ever agree and about which the deeply interested Christian world had views of its own. What could usefully be discussed was the matter of Israel's security. Brzezinski knew that President Carter (Brzezinski offered that he was of the same mind) would take the most generous view possible of Israel's security needs, if "security" meant allowing Israel to maintain lookout points and a few strongholds on the West Bank to prevent attacks. But he was emphatic that the United States could not be pushed into supporting an expansionist, nationalist, and ultimately religio-mystical Jewish ideology to allow Israel to retain the occupied territories. I asked Brzezinski whether he wanted me to say all of this to Begin when I met with the prime minister. He replied that he thought that my repeating the bulk of this conversation in Jerusalem would be helpful.

Several days later, Phyllis and I arrived in Jerusalem. I found that Menachem Begin had not yet moved into the prime minister's official residence but was staying in a suite at the King David Hotel. I asked his secretary to make me an appointment, and without delay I received an invitation to tea. It was a friendly session in which Begin and I resumed a well-established habit of speaking with each other in the most intimate of all the Jewish languages, Yiddish, the language in which we had both been raised. It had the atmosphere of an informal family reunion—but every time I tried to tell him what Brzezinski had said to me on his own behalf and Jimmy Carter's, somehow, the subject changed. A few days later I returned for tea and tried again to convey to Menachem Begin what I had heard at the White House, but he again avoided the subject. By that point I felt that I had a responsibility to deliver the message, and so I called his principal aide, Yehiel Kadishai, and said to him, with a little exasperation, that his boss had to permit me to speak my piece. And so there was a third round of tea. This time the atmosphere was more formal and noticeably colder. The language used was no longer Yiddish, because I wanted to report what I had heard from Brzezinski in the language in which I had heard it. Begin listened, and he did not look very happy. He responded by ending his long-standing habit of calling me "Reb Avraham"—that is, by my Hebrew name and my religious title—by switching instead to "Professor Hertzberg." To this now alien being, Prime Minister Begin said that he would of course come to Washington and make the case for Israel's security needs, but he had the political and, more important, the moral obligation to explain to President Carter that the people of Israel had elected him because they wanted the land of Israel to remain undivided under Jewish sovereignty. He would, in fact, take some time with the president to explain Israel's position from his ideological perspective. As I heard Begin out, it became clear to me why he had been avoiding what I had to tell him. Obviously, messages similar to mine had already reached him from Washington. I left my third tea party with Begin with the somber feeling that he and Jimmy Carter would not get along.

Begin had one more shot to fire across my bows. As he organized the group that would accompany him to Washington he thought that his hand would be strengthened if some leaders of the American Jewish community accompanied him on his journey. He therefore invited me to join his party. Obviously I was invited not because of my views but rather to demonstrate to Washington that even people like me who were not right-wing loyalists would rally to him in the cause of Jewish unity. He would repeat this maneuver through his years in office, a maneuver that his successor, Yitzhak Shamir, developed into an art form. I refused to go. Formally, I gave as my reason that I could not show up in the United States walking off the prime minister's plane, a few paces behind him, without raising the question of what my identity was. Was I an American who cared deeply about Israel, or an Israeli who happened to travel on an American passport? But Begin and his entourage understood what I was really saying: a Jew could be deeply and passionately concerned for Israel's welfare, but he would not equate that concern with the Likud's hard-line politics. On the contrary, he would be an advocate of compromise with the Arabs.

But others made different choices. The then chairman of the Conference of Presidents of Major American Jewish Organizations, Rabbi Alexander Schindler, had been selected for that post because he was widely known to be a liberal and a dove. Under Begin's pressure, Schindler announced that the organized American Jewish community was committed to supporting any incumbent Israeli government. Begin was the elected prime minister, and Schindler would support him through thick and thin. Schindler, who was also then in Israel, boarded the plane and flew to Washington as a member of Begin's party. Two contrasting positions about the relationship between the American Jewish community and Israel's hard-line new government had thus been defined. One side was Schindler, and many other people following his lead, who would go along with whatever the government might say or do, putting the best face on policies that I knew they privately could not accept. For the next several years, in fact, the American Jewish establishment kept pretending to itself and others that Begin's hard-line positions over the West Bank and the Golan Heights were merely "tactical," that he was negotiating in a Middle Eastern bazaar trying to secure Israel's future, and that he was really not the anti-Arab ideologue that he seemed to be.

The other position was defined by me the very day Begin was elected. Though I spoke for no organized group of American Jews, I was certain that my view represented the general will. The Washington correspondent for *Ha'Aretz* had tracked me down and asked for a reaction to the startling defeat of Labor and the victory of Menachem Begin's Likud Party. I replied that I was not a hostage to any Israeli political party, neither to the mainly dovish but defeated Labor Party nor to the hawkish and victorious Likud. I remained steadfast in my concern for the security of Israel. This meant in actual practice that I left room free to differ publicly and even vehemently with Israel's leaders in the name of Israel's ultimate interests.

Although it remained an abiding concern, Israel's future and all of the politics it engendered actually occupied only a small proportion of my time. Throughout these years I remained very involved in, and busy with, a synagogue of some six hundred families, was a teacher at Columbia of classes on modern Jewish history, and, above all, found myself the often worried father of two young daughters who were growing up within the upheavals of their day.

All seemed serene on the surface in Englewood, but I was beginning to feel that some undercurrents of deep discontent were already in existence within the congregation and that some storms might be brewing. The essence of the matter was in the changing demography of the American Jewish community. The trends were reflected exactly in Englewood. The people who had brought me to Englewood in 1956 were then, on average, ten years older than I, so that twenty years later, in the mid- and late 1970s, some had died and others were heading toward retirement and even moving away. Those who were replacing them in the synagogue or in leadership roles in the town were by now my age or younger. The older generation that had begun to fade out were, almost without exception, the American-born children of immigrants from Eastern Europe. The newer generation, at the beginning of middle age, represented, more and more, the grandchildren of the immigrants. They no longer understood Yiddish or had any immediate sense of what the world of the Jews in Eastern Europe had been like when their grandparents were young. They had waited a long time to assume the roles of their elders, and I was now, in their minds, one of those elders whose dominance impeded their ascent. I was especially in their way because I was the rabbi with life tenure, who could not be voted out of office or silenced and who continued the bad habit of speaking out every Sabbath from the pulpit and often vetoing decisions made by the board in the middle of the week. The tactic that this new group soon invented was to give up trying to control the synagogue but instead to take over the reins of Englewood's Jewish Community Center. They worked very hard, and very expensively, to make it the dominant Jewish institution in town. It became an enterprise dominated by its lay board, which decided its policy and instructed the professionals on its staff to do exactly what the board wanted.

I reacted to this current by going on the warpath. After some years of intermittent squabbling, the climactic moment came when a new building for the center had been erected in a more elegant section of the neighborhood and was about to be dedicated. At that point, the lay board was fearful that not enough new members would be found for their very expensive new institution unless it was opened on the Sabbath for such recreational purposes as the use of its athletic facilities. No one argued that this is what Jews ought to be doing on the Sabbath; but they would, at least, be together in a "Jewish environment." What the board was really saying was that their definition of a Jewish community center was a place where Jews could be together while ignoring the synagogues and flouting the restrictions and values of the religious tradition. This institution represented the new American Judaism: secular and ethnic, not religious and learned. Indeed, at one point during the years of controversy over the center, I had suggested to its founders that part of the land be used as an educational park to house all of the Jewish day schools in the area regardless of denomination. I was summarily told that this did not belong within the vision of what they were creating. I suspected that what they meant was that schools would bring with them educators and rabbis who, Heaven forbid, would have notions of what should be happening in the center and whose very presence would undercut the authority of the younger element who were leading the project.

In the matter of being open on the Sabbath, I was bitterly opposed by the lay board. Since the builders of the new Jewish Community Center were the most active and potent community force in those years, none of my rabbinic colleagues, including the rabbi of the Orthodox synagogue, had dared to oppose them. I sent the message out that, on the first Sabbath that this enterprise would be open, they would find me at the front gate picketing and the newspeople and their TV cameras would be tipped off in advance. This stopped the plan to open the Jewish Community Center's doors on the Sabbath in its tracks. It was a demonstration of exactly the kind of power that the new boys on the block could not control and that they could not abide. The people whom I had cowed into submission saw this event as a further battle in a power struggle between personalities within the community. They did not want to understand that we were fighting about basic religious values. I could not allow the Sabbath to be desecrated.

I won the fight, but I knew that I had not changed the minds of those whom I had beaten. The older generation with whom I had begun still remembered something of the tradition of Eastern Europe, which included respect for the religious authority of the rabbi. The younger generation looked upon the rabbi as an employee, to perform certain functions. They would call on the rabbi when they needed him, but he was not to bother them until then. Religion had been transformed. It offered not moral guidance, but peace of mind or pleasing ceremonies. My father, the classic rabbi, had no doubt that he existed to teach his people how to live as good Jews. I was increasingly dealing with congregants who wanted to tell me how to make them feel good. By the middle 1970s, I was becoming ever lonelier.

The measure of how much the times were changing was in the suddenly revived memory of the Holocaust. In the immediate aftermath of the Second World War, American Jews did not want the mass murders in Europe to be much mentioned in public, although privately the trauma was often discussed. Even the survivors who came to the United States joined for the next two decades in the quest for equality and normalcy for Jews in the larger American society. As late as 1961, I invited the then struggling Elie Wiesel to give a lecture summarizing his semi-autobiographical novel, *Night*, but, despite much effort, I could not get twenty people to come to listen even though there were many more than twenty Holocaust survivors among the congregation. Several years later, when I spoke in commemoration of the Warsaw Ghetto uprising during Passover week of 1943, the father of the young woman whose Bat Mitzvah was being celebrated that Sabbath went to the board of the synagogue to complain that I had ruined a happy family occasion by bringing up so sad a topic. But in the mid-1970s I discovered that in my own synagogue school and all over the country the main subject of the Jewish education of the young had become the Holocaust. I was astonished, but I soon understood why this radical reversal was taking place.

American Jews were very worried about their children. They had bet the future on pride in Israel. Their children and their children's children would be glad to continue this glorious identity—but by the 1970s, a generation after the state of Israel had been founded, American Jews were becoming very nervous. The rate of intermarriage between Jews and non-Jews was rising to one in three among young adults, even in the families of the leaders of the organizations that had the greatest zeal to raise money and to apply political pressure on Israel's behalf. It had become common knowledge that pride in Israel was not enough to guarantee Jewish loyalty of the young.

At that point the leaders of the Jewish establishment chose to play another card: they would evoke the memory of the Holocaust. The prime motive was guilt. American Jews had, by and large, made it in America in the generation since the end of the Second World War. They no longer needed to suppress the memory of the Holocaust. They could begin to think about these horrors and even, for the first time, to ask some questions: could we have done better to help save our relatives? Could the United States have done more? In atonement for what Jews had failed to do a generation earlier, they were ready to evoke the memory of the dead—how they died and how they had lived before they were destroyed by Hitler. The delayed evocation of the Holocaust was the necessary, and inevitable, beginning of a painful catharsis. Another motive was forcing the evocation of the Holocaust in the 1970s: the fear of assimilation. The young had to be told that no Jew had a right to leave the battlefield against Jew-hatred on which Jews had been arrayed century after century. It did not matter what any individual professed of the ancient Jewish faith. The enemies of the Jews made no distinction and neither could the Jews. We were all in this fight together.

But it was difficult to evoke anti-Semitism as a serious threat in America in the 1970s. This was the very decade when the last barriers against Jews were falling. Jews were now competing equally for all the opportunities available within the American economy and in the institutional power structures, such as the universities and the government bureaucracies. How does one tell younger Jews that they are to live in fear of anti-Semitism when they have been admitted to one of the Ivy League schools from which their fathers and uncles (their mothers and aunts had not even dreamed of applying) had been rejected just a generation earlier because they were Jews? The ingenious answer was to remember the Holocaust. The young were suddenly being told that, even though anti-Semitism had ebbed in America, they had to remember that the Nazis had appeared in a supposedly civilized country, in Germany. It remained conceivable that they might reappear elsewhere. Jews in America had to remain on guard so that "it might not happen here."

At the end of the 1970s and into the 1980s, the community as a whole joined in the creation on the Mall in Washington of the Holocaust Museum. This is the single most expensive public building that the Jewish community has ever erected in America. This building was the national cathedral of American Jewry's Jewishness. But it did not take many years for the community to have to face the fact that yes, indeed, the Holocaust had to be remembered, but remembering the Holocaust would not necessarily keep Jews "on the reservation." The demographic evidence kept increasing, and becoming undeniable through the 1980s, that one could teach the Holocaust in the religious schools of the various synagogues and then teach it again in the burgeoning Jewish study programs at the colleges and the universities, but this would not stop the substantial traffic of those leaving the Jewish community.

The Jewish establishment tried not to know these facts or heed this judgment, and the official, tamed intelligentsia who appeared regularly at the annual meetings of the Jewish organizations, such as the American Jewish Committee and B'nai B'rith, kept offering reassurance that all was peace—or, as Dr. Pangloss had said in Voltaire's novel *Candide*, that all was for the best in the best of all possible worlds. To be sure, some of these people knew that I was writing and saying that all was not going well, but they kept it on the margins, describing me as a minority of one, a gadfly and more than a bit of a crank, thereby ensuring that I would never be asked to speak at any of the ever more nervous gatherings of self-congratulation. In the mid- and late 1970s, even while head of the American Jewish Congress, I was effectively blackballed from "speaking truth to power." Fortunately, some journals continued to print my views.

By the late 1970s I was ever more aware that the Jewish organizational types, especially in the United States, were tired of hearing my critical voice, but I also began to tire of them. The first clear sign of this came in the late winter and early spring of 1978. My closest counselor at the American Jewish Congress, Naomi Levine, told me that under the accepted practice and precedents, I could not be elected to a fourth term as president unless I was supported by a two-thirds majority. She told me that there was no doubt that a majority of the membership of the organization supported me and was even proud of the positions that

I had been taking in both international and domestic affairs, but that a two-thirds majority was now doubtful. This was all the more pointed a problem because Howard Squadron, a lawyer who had a lifelong involvement in the organization, was eager to be the next president. His campaign argued that the organization had gone on long enough— from its founder, Rabbi Stephen Wise, to its incumbent president, myself—being headed by rabbis who were public figures and regarded as somewhat larger than life. The time had come, Squadron maintained, to elect a leader who belonged to the warp and woof of the organization. I had been much too involved in Zionist affairs and too little concerned with the liberal domestic agenda of the American Jewish Congress for their liking.

Naomi Levine told me that I could surmount all of this if I spent some time politicking within the organization. I refused. I said to her that I sometimes had to do that as a rabbi in a congregation where I had to soothe hurt feelings, but that was a professional obligation that I assumed when I chose to be a rabbi. I told Naomi that I had absolutely no desire to involve myself in such an endeavor as a ploy in political games. Naomi argued that if I did, I could retain the power position of president of the American Jewish Congress for many years, as long as I liked, but I responded that I had no such political desires. I soon understood that what I was sensing within myself reflected the beginnings of a withdrawal from the cut and thrust of public life. So, in mid-1978, at the annual convention of the American Jewish Congress, a candidate whom I had publicly favored as my successor, a very brilliant and learned man, Rabbi David Polish, was defeated by Howard Squadron.

That year was also the time when my nearly ten years of membership in the executive of the World Zionist Organization came to an end. I had served two five-year terms, but the powers-that-be among the leaders of the World Zionist Organization decided that I should not be reelected. During the years that I served on the executive, I represented no party or faction. The easiest thing to do was to make an end of the possibility that any members elected as individuals in their personal right could henceforth belong to the executive. That avoided any discussion of my ever more public and independent views on almost all of the major issues that were being debated in the Jewish world. It was much easier for the parties to deal with each other in the art of political horse-trading: you approve our candidate for chief bureaucrat of the finance department and we will support yours for head of the department in charge of settlements. Yet, I left the World Zionist Organization executive with some relief—and with surprise that I had survived for ten increasingly hectic years.

Nonetheless, even as I was leaving both the American Jewish Congress and the Zionist executive, I was far from through with Jewish public life. I still retained the office of vice president of the World Jewish Congress to which I had been elected in 1975. How I got to be vice president was in itself a strange story. At the international convention that year in Jerusalem, the Likud Party, the right-wingers led by Menachem Begin, offered to support me if I would run for chairman of the executive board of the World Jewish Congress. This was a very strange suggestion, because they well knew that my views were different from theirs. I soon understood that my candidacy was being hatched in order to embarrass Nahum Goldmann. He had just finished constructing a balanced ticket, with the agreement of the dominant Zionist parties, which was to bring in his friend Philip Klutznick as chairman of the executive board. The Likud politicians had counted votes and decided that, with their support, I had enough independent strength to beat Klutznick. Nahum Goldmann knew this, too, and so there was an impasse. I invited myself for coffee at his flat in Jerusalem and told him that I had no desire to be the candidate of the Likud; as Dr. Goldmann well knew, I was in agreement with his moderate views and not with Likud's hard-line nationalism. Goldmann came up with a political formula. He went to a meeting the next day of the Zionist parties, which had agreed that there would be five vice presidents of the World Jewish Congress, representing their various factions, to suggest that a sixth be added, or else an unpredictable person, Hertzberg, might be tempted to upset the applecart by running for the second-highest office in the World Jewish Congress. The scare worked, and so Goldmann acquired me, a very friendly associate and a political disciple, near him in his last years of acting as the recognized Jewish leader of the Diaspora.

Goldmann made almost immediate use of me. He had passed the age of eighty, and he no longer had the energy to fly around the world as he used to. The outlying Jewish communities in Asia and in Australia and New Zealand had not been visited by a ranking representative of the World Jewish Congress in years, so he sent me on a trip around the world that summer to refresh relations. For the next several years, whenever Nahum Goldmann was in New York, or I was in Jerusalem, we spent much time together. I supported his plans to go to Cairo to see Sadat and to Moscow to see Brezhnev, even though the Israeli government successfully vetoed both journeys. They were putting Goldmann out of business as a major figure in the diplomacy of the Jewish world.

Our relationship became so close that Goldmann wrote in his final autobiography (there had been several earlier ones) that he wanted and expected me to succeed him as president of the World Jewish Congress. I banked on that promise. Having served at the next-to-highest rungs in the ladder of organized Jewish life, I hoped to reach the top—but it was not to be, thanks as much to my own doubts as to the efforts of others. Somewhere deep in my heart, I suspected that this would happen, and, even deeper, I was not sorry for it. All the time I knew that I would be miscast, because the presidency of the World Jewish Congress demanded skills that I did not have. I was not at home in the Byzantine art of organizational compromises, and I knew that raising the money to keep the World Jewish Congress going was a task that would soak up most of my energies. I had to accept that, by temperament, I was a soloist, probably even a loner, and certainly not a manager of complicated institutions. These inner hesitations and doubts were the real reasons that I did not become the president of the World Jewish Congress.

The story has been told elsewhere, but only in part. What is well known is that Nahum Goldmann retired as president of the World Jewish Congress in 1977 and handed on the post to Philip Klutznick. Goldmann told me that this was being done for a brief time, to redeem a personal promise that he had made to Klutznick, but that I would in the not too distant future be elected to the post. The question came to a head sooner than I expected, because in 1979 Philip Klutznick was appointed secretary of commerce in Jimmy Carter's cabinet. Klutznick hastened to call me to ask me to take over as acting president as long as he was in the cabinet, with the understanding that he would return to office in the World Jewish Congress when his political term was over. I accepted this invitation to keep the seat warm for him, but then the explosions came.

The World Zionist Organization had veto power over any candidate for president of the World Jewish Congress. Its officers insisted that that included the appointment of an acting president. I could have dealt with the question by getting on an airplane to Jerusalem and making some political promises to my enemies, but I refused. I counted votes and came to the conclusion that with the support of the still largest party in the World Zionist Organization and the World Jewish Congress, the Labor Party, I had the votes to prevent a veto—but I was wrong. The showdown meeting took place not in Jerusalem but in New York. The casting vote was in the hands of the Labor representative, Akiva Lewinsky, but he managed to find out that morning that he had a cold and did not feel well enough to come to the meeting. I soon discovered that Labor had made a decision to go with the Likud in return for a few political goodies, knowing full well that this would make an end to any possibility of my becoming acting president and ultimately president of the World Jewish Congress. I was not beaten by Menachem Begin's veto. I was beaten by the betrayal of the Labor Party, which was supposedly pleased with the political positions for which I had taken many risks and had, thereby, earned the enduring political hostility of Menachem Begin and his associates. Oddly enough, or not so oddly, my personal relations with Begin continued; we respected each other for acting on principle. I had no such good feelings about the Labor politicians who sold me out. A few years later, when his wife, Aliza, died, I wrote the very depressed and ill Menachem Begin a note of condolence, and I was surprised and very moved to get back very soon a note from him, in his own hand, thanking me in the warmest terms for my concern and my personal affection.

At the meeting in which I was vetoed, Edgar Bronfman was put into position to take over the leadership of the World Jewish Congress. The most important quality that he brought to his post was the security that he needed nobody else's patronage. In his own right, he was a major figure in international business. Very soon after he came into office, he had occasion to go to France to see its president at the time, Valéry Giscard d'Estaing. There had been some anti-Semitic incidents in France, including an attempt to bomb one of the synagogues in Paris in which two people were killed. The president of France wanted to demonstrate his concern by receiving Edgar Bronfman. The president's office had arranged for pictures to be taken of this encounter, and never mind what results, in terms of greater safety for Jews and Jewish institutions, this meeting might produce. Edgar Bronfman said, very forthrightly, to the president of France that he wanted to forgo the pictures because he had already had his picture taken with presidents of countries. He had come not for ceremonial purposes but to achieve some practical results. I heard him speak to the same theme some years later, in the 1990s, when he was leading the battle to force the Swiss banks, and those in other European countries, to account for the dormant accounts of Jews who had almost certainly died in the Holocaust. At a press conference to explain what he was doing, Edgar Bronfman warned, in a very strained voice, that the bankers and governments with whom he was fighting had best remember that he represented a Jewish generation that was different from the one before: his father had helped lead the world Jewish community in the 1930s when Jews were under murderous attack and they were themselves weak, ever weaker, and very frightened; he spoke for the next generation, which had gained strength and dignity, and he would take no insults and no disregard from the bankers who thought they were the masters of the world. They were not, and he would not rest, until he had made them own up to their misconduct.

I had known Edgar casually for years, but now in the work of the World Jewish Congress, I soon came to know him well. He was a pleasant surprise, because he was never pretentious. He always wanted to learn. Bronfman did not claim to be steeped in knowledge of Judaism, but he worked at learning Hebrew and classic Jewish text even as he led the World Jewish Congress.

The assumption of the politicians who had combined to defeat me was that I would slam the door in anger and complete my exit from organized Jewish life, but they were to be disappointed. The very first thing that Edgar Bronfman did, at the end of the decisive meeting, was to have a private conversation with me in the next room. He asked me not to walk away but to stay close to him. I readily accepted. This conversation began the transformation of my role in the world Jewish community from that of an activist to that of a thinker. Bronfman took advice from many sources, and he heard my unvarnished views at fairly frequent four-eyes conversations—but he always decided for himself.

27

D espite being edged out of the World Zionist Organization and the American Jewish Congress, I was not yet through with politics. Indeed, the most bitter and notorious of my political confrontations took place at the end of the 1970s and the beginning of the 1980s.

The striking political event of the past years of the decade was the visit by Anwar Sadat to Jerusalem in November 1977. In his speech to the Knesset he offered "no more war." He asked the Israelis to move toward compromise and peace with his own country, Egypt, but also with the Palestinians. He clearly expected that a settlement of these quarrels would bring peace to the region as a whole. After Sadat left Jerusalem, the diplomatic meetings between Egypt and Israel began, but months of discussions led nowhere. Jimmy Carter was persuaded that the only way to advance the cause of peace was to invite Sadat and Begin to Camp David and to lock these leaders and their delegations up in the compound until they reached an agreement. It took eleven days of intensive bargaining before some "white smoke" appeared from the chimney.

The three principals and their delegations then came back to Washington to celebrate the achievement. Some fifteen hundred people were

invited to be present at the signing of the agreement on the lawn of the
White House. Dinner was given that evening under a huge tent. Both
the senior bureaucrats of the Conference of Presidents of Major American Jewish Organizations and the social secretary of the Israeli Embassy managed to forget to put me on the guest list. But this was an
occasion for those who cared about Israel and not simply for Begin loyalists or for those willing to pretend to be loyalists. Several of my friends
who were senior Israeli Embassy officials in Washington felt, as I did,
that I should be there. I must confess that I wanted to annoy some of
those who had banished me by turning up. My friends in the State
Department were willing to oblige, so they added me to their list of
invitees. That day, I was both on the White House lawn and at the
evening dinner. At dinner, Begin, Sadat, and Carter were at a table
together, ringed by Secret Service people, and a special pass was
required to approach it. An Israeli friend had the wit, and impudence,
to suggest that I might wish to congratulate Begin in person. Being in
possession of the required special pass, he took me to Begin. I congrat-
ulated Begin very warmly, and sincerely, on this great achievement for
peace. It was the only time in our many meetings that he looked flustered, barely able to stop himself from asking, "How did you get in
here?" So that he did not have to ask, I volunteered the answer that I
had friends in the State Department.

A few days later at a meeting in New York I learned, beyond doubt,
that the Camp David agreement was both less and more than it seemed
to be. I knew that it was less because Menachem Begin came to New
York to address a very large meeting of his supporters among American
Jews. I made a point of attending, and my hair almost stood on end.
The media had reported, and Washington had been repeating, that all
settlement activity in the West Bank would cease until the issue had
been reviewed in negotiation between Egypt and Israel. Everyone took
this to mean that Begin had promised to stop increasing Jewish settlement in the West Bank indefinitely until there was agreement on the
dimensions of Palestinian autonomy. Speaking publicly before a large
Jewish audience, with the press in attendance, Begin pronounced that
the Camp David agreements had obligated him to suspend settlement
activities for thirty days and no more; thereafter, he would be free to
resume building settlements as he pleased. Begin's words did get around

but did not, to my surprise, occasion another meeting of the principals. Sadat, in particular, did not cry out that he had been misled. The contrast between what Begin was saying, and what he had purportedly agreed to, made me suspect that the real deal at Camp David was not the one that was being advertised to the world. I soon found out that my suspicions were correct.

As I was known to be totally politically independent, I was invited, in 1980, by the government of Egypt to visit Cairo, to give a lecture at their training college for diplomats. I accepted quite willingly, not because I wanted an Egyptian forum in which to disagree with and criticize Begin's politics, but because I thought it would be a step toward opening up a broader dialogue between Jews and Arabs. This was an invitation that was made all the more attractive because a dear friend, Roy Atherton, had just left the post of assistant secretary of state for Near Eastern Affairs to be posted to Cairo as American ambassador to Egypt. He and his wife, Betty, offered to house Phyllis and me as their guests in the ambassador's residence.

Upon our arrival in Cairo, I made a point of immediately calling the Israeli ambassador, a man who was Israel's first-ever representative to an Arab state. Elihu ben Elissar sounded both puzzled and annoyed to learn that I was in Egypt at the invitation of the Egyptian government and as the houseguest of the American ambassador. He made no secret on the telephone that it would have been much more "proper" had I been in Egypt at the behest of his government and under his management. I replied that I would not have been invited to speak at an Egyptian government institution if I had been perceived to be no other than a representative of the then prevailing Israeli political orthodoxy. As for where I was staying, what was the problem with accepting hospitality from my own government? I added that he need not worry about what I was going to eat, since Atherton had a young Orthodox Jew on his staff, Dan Kurtzer (now, in 2002, United States ambassador to Israel), who, together with his wife, was looking after our kosher requirements.

As a contribution to Jewish-Arab dialogue, my trip to Cairo did not go well. I did get to give a lecture at the Egyptian foreign ministry's diplomatic training school, but nobody seemed particularly glad to have me there. The students listened but did not ask any questions. In my talk I suggested that a firm peace had to be based, in the first place, in a far greater understanding on both sides of the other's thought processes and that this could start only if the two countries' scholars and students were able to talk to each other. The chilly reaction to my lecture under-lined for me that the hinterland for Egyptian scholars and intellectuals was the Arab world as a whole, and not the West. They felt that they had no need to learn about Israel and that they would never forgive those who wanted to establish relations with Israelis. But during my few days in Cairo I learned the truth about the Camp David accords. They were indeed not what they claimed to be: less, because there would be no Israeli withdrawal from the West Bank; but also more, because the commitment to peace in the Sinai ran very deep indeed.

Very good friends though we had become through the years, I had never asked Roy Atherton any questions about his involvement in the Camp David negotiations when he was a principal advisor to Jimmy Carter, and I did not ask him any such questions in his own home. He did, however, introduce us at dinners to a number of leading Egyptians. I did not ask direct questions, but I listened to the Egyptians very care-fully and especially to their underlying premises. Before the end of the week they had left me in not the slightest doubt what the deal at Camp David had been: the Egyptians were promised the return of every inch of territory that they had lost during the Six-Day War and had failed to regain in the Yom Kippur War. The Israelis had been willing to agree to this because Menachem Begin and his associates did not regard the Sinai as part of the "undivided land of Israel." Begin's reward was that the Egyptians, in effect, allowed him to do as he pleased with regard to the Palestinians. Never mind that the Camp David accords supposedly connected progress on the solving the Palestinian issue with returning the Sinai by stages to Egyptian sovereignty. That was mere verbiage. What the Egyptians cared about was getting back what they regarded as their own. They had no intention of breaking off that process, at any point, to express anger at the Israelis for the sake of the Palestinians. It was clear that the Egyptians never had any intention of establishing a "warm" peace with Israel, but neither did they intend to go to war with Israel for the Palestinians. Therefore the "cold" peace that had been established—the exchange of ambassadors but not of people—was, from the Egyptian perspective, the perfect formula.

When I returned to the United States I knew that I would have to put on record what I had learned in Cairo. I imagined that any journal interested in Israel would hasten to publish such a story, so I sent my essay on the Camp David accords to Martin Peretz, who had become the owner and editor of the *New Republic*. I did not know then that he had become an Israeli hard-liner. The manuscript managed to languish on his desk for a few weeks, long enough to make it clear to me that he had no intention of publishing it. I therefore telephoned an old acquaintance from a dozen years earlier, Robert Silvers, at the *New York Review of Books*, whom I had come to know when I had debated Hugh Trevor-Roper in its columns over the role of anti-Semitism in the Enlightenment. He reacted by asking to see my report from Egypt the next day, and he published it immediately. Remarkably, nobody took issue with the essay, but the winds blowing from Jerusalem were quite cold. I was the political equivalent of the child who told the emperor that he was wearing no clothes—but in this version of the story I was the one who felt the chill.

The policy makers in Jerusalem were much more annoyed by the venue in which I had published the essay than by what I was saying. They very well knew that it was true because the foreign minister of Egypt, Mohammed Ibrahim Kamel, had resigned immediately after Camp David, citing this very issue. He was outraged that Sadat had agreed to a pact that, despite its rhetoric, was marginalizing the Palestinians. To have published my essay in *Ha'Aretz* would have been annoying, but tolerable: it would have kept the discussion within the family. I might have even gotten away with printing this essay in some American Jewish publication in English. But here I was, an undoubted insider, revealing "family secrets" to a large and foreign audience. Unless I agreed to shut up in the future—and this essay proved that I would not—the politics of the Jewish people could not be kept as the private, tightly guarded knowledge of the Jews. My critics were right. This essay was the springboard for many more that I wrote in the next decade, mostly for the *New York Review of Books,* in which I denied, over and over again, the official versions of events that came out of Jerusalem. I was a particularly troublesome commentator because I kept proving that the American Jewish community was not united behind the expansionist doctrine of Menachem Begin and his even more hard-line successor, Yitzhak Shamir.

Angers were simmering between the policy makers in Jerusalem and me for the next couple of years, but open warfare had not yet broken out. The final pretense of civility collapsed in the summer of 1982 following the Israeli invasion of Lebanon. Phyllis and I were again in Israel for an extended visit, because I had been invited to be a fellow at the Institute of Advanced Studies at the Hebrew University in a group that was examining the origins of Jewish nationalism. I was therefore in Israel from January through August 1982, so I was present when the war broke out on June 6. The rationale that the defense minister, General Ariel Sharon, gave for invading Lebanon was the need to defend civilians living in the Galilee and to retaliate for a terrorist attack that had left the Israeli ambassador to London, Shlomo Argov, critically wounded. In Sharon's version, PLO rockets from across the Lebanese border were being fired into northern Israel; he was defending the Galilee by marching into Lebanon, up to forty kilometers north of the border, in order to push these PLO rockets out of the range of Israel's northern frontier. For a few days this rationale for military action was accepted by all of Israel's newspapers, but very soon all of Israel's major dailies, including *Maariv* and *Yediot Ahronot,* both of which had avowed right-wing sympathies, were contradicting Sharon and stating flatly that he had ordered his troops to advance beyond the forty-kilometer line. Soldiers were informing their families that they had orders to march on Beirut and that they were indeed approaching the city. Few in Israel doubted that Sharon had hatched a grander design than the one he had announced. He intended to chase the Palestinians out of Lebanon and to turn Lebanon into an Israeli protectorate under the rule of the Christian Phalange Party and its militia, whom Israel had long supported covertly during the civil war in Lebanon between Muslims and Christians. Sharon may have kept Begin somewhat in the dark about his ultimate intention (this issue is still disputed), but it is beyond doubt that Sharon knew from the beginning where he was going. He did not blunder into Beirut by accident.

Israel's conquests in Lebanon very soon became a show. Seats were on offer in reasonably well-guarded minivans to see the sights. I was included in one of these trips because of my continuing connections with the World Jewish Congress. It was a very peculiar journey. We began by stopping just north of the border, at Beaufort Castle, where

Begin had visited just a few days before. Then we headed north on narrow mountain roads. We eventually had lunch in the very busy city of Tyre, on the coast. We had gone beyond the limit of forty kilometers that the pass in the hands of the driver had prescribed, but our accompanying officer was adventurous and not too disciplined. He was a fortyish teacher at the Hebrew University, in the philosophy department, who was himself a political dove. He was completing a tour of his reserve duty, and by the next day he expected to be back in his classroom in Jerusalem. The officer suggested that we ignore the limit and take the car as far as we could get, preferably to Beirut. The passengers in the minivan agreed, and so off we rode, north.

We saw some very strange sights. Every mile or two there was an Israeli checkpoint, and not very far away we could see an encampment of soldiers and a tank or two. In the middle of the afternoon we encountered a small military formation that consisted entirely of students from an Orthodox yeshiva. We stopped to talk with them and found that they wanted to say the prescribed afternoon prayers but there were only eight of them. They asked that two of us join them to make a minyan to say the prayers. So there we were, standing with these young men under the shadow of a tank, chanting the service in which at the end we pray to God that He should make peace both on high and on earth. When we got into the van and went a bit farther north, we saw an even stranger sight. We were driving along beside a beach in strong sunlight where some dozens of people were sunning themselves. On the right of the road, we could see the ruins of a village that had been shot up very recently. I soon figured out the explanation of this sight: the sunbathers were Christians, whose political party had welcomed the Israeli advance. No harm had come to them, and they continued to be protected.

It was late afternoon when we finally got to Beirut. The Israeli advance had stopped in the suburbs on a high ridge. The presidential palace at Ba'Abda was in Israeli hands, but Arafat and his PLO fighters were in West Beirut in the port area. Israeli guns were pounding them. We in the minibus were received with some deference, because only VIPs would have been permitted to come this far, and we were even given tea and coffee by the artillery officers commanding the battery of guns. I felt as if I were part of a stage set, but I was very uncomfortable. I could not forget for a moment that the shells that these guns were firing were killing or maiming people as they landed. I managed to find a member of Israel's foreign service, Moshe Arad, with whom I had become friendly in Washington when he had been the Israeli Embassy spokesman; he was, at that moment, the diplomat assigned to accompany Israel's military commanders in Lebanon. I told him about my concern for the safety of the mother of a colleague at Columbia University who had refused to move away from her flat in the outskirts of Beirut. Moshe Arad promised that he would make her safety a concern of his; she would be protected until the Israelis left. I could not linger there, and I started to urge that we turn around and go back. And so we did.

It was very nearly dark when we started the return journey, and eventually we got lost. By eight o'clock that night we were on a dirt road in the middle of an encampment of Arabs, both Lebanese and Palestinians, who had been pushed out of their homes just a few days before by the war. We did not talk of it to each other, but several of us were beginning to be nervous. Here we were in an isolated minivan, among hundreds of Arabs, and all that we had as protection was a nonprofessional soldier with one gun in his hands. But the Arabs in the tents on the beach onto which we had wandered were not in the mood to fight or to take revenge for their plight. On the contrary, they wanted us out of their way as soon as possible, so a couple of them gave us directions to get back to the main road. Within an hour or so we reached Metullah, the first town on the Israeli side of the border.

I came back from this journey prepared to not believe a single thing I would hear from official sources about the war in Lebanon. The situation dragged on through the summer, and it was essentially unchanged by the time I left in late August. The Reagan administration decided to evacuate the PLO from Beirut in August. By then I was already in Englewood.

One day in mid-September the news came over the wires that a massacre was in progress in two Palestinian refugee camps near Beirut, in Sabra and Chatilla. Israeli troops were in the vicinity. They did not participate in the massacre, but they did nothing to stop it. It was known within hours that the gunmen were members of the militia of the Christian Phalange, the group that General Sharon had been busy installing as the new rulers of Lebanon. The Christian Phalange knew that it no longer had demographic parity with the Muslims in Lebanon, and it wanted to scare at least some of them out of the country. Hundreds were killed that day, and the television pictures that began to appear by the next day showed dead bodies strewn around, including those of women and children. There was immediate outrage all over the world, and especially in Israel. While the assault on the inhabitants of Sabra and Chatilla had been taking place, an observer phoned the highest official whom he could reach, the then foreign minister, Yitzhak Shamir, who waved the news off as unworthy of his attention. In the next several days, the outrage in Israel rose to an unprecedented climax. That Saturday night, one day before Yom Kippur, there was a rally in protest to which four hundred thousand people came. The center of Tel Aviv resounded with the outrage against the conduct of the Israeli government. This protest forced the appointment of a high-level commission to investigate what had happened. The result of this inquiry, reported some months later, was a decision that Ariel Sharon had to leave the post of minister of defense.

During the week following the massacre, the leaders of the American Jewish establishment tried, ineffectively, to maintain that these murders at Sabra and Chatilla had been carried out by a Lebanese party, the Christian Phalange, and that the Israelis bore no responsibility. No one in the United States really believed this nonsense, not in the face of the vehement protests in Israel itself. On Thursday afternoon of that week, as the protest movement in Israel was gathering pace, I was contacted by Tamar Jacoby, who was then deputy editor of the op-ed page of the *New York Times*, whose political convictions were then liberal. Tamar asked me to write an op-ed piece that would be printed in the Sunday edition. The editorial page of the *Times* would normally be seen in Israel the following day, because it was printed in the *Jerusalem Post*. On this occasion, however, it would be seen a day later, on Tuesday morning. Yom Kippur began on the Sunday night of publication, so there would be no *Jerusalem Post* on the Monday morning. I had very little time to write the piece, because the Sunday op-ed page was locked up early on Friday. I got up at four that morning and wrote, by hand, what I had to say. The title that the *Times* gave the piece was blunt: "Begin and Sharon Must Go." I accused them of having behaved like the police in czarist Russia. These representatives of the czar almost never participated in beating up Jews or murdering them during a pogrom. They simply stood aside and let the mob do all the terrible things it wanted to do. I expressed unbounded horror at the notion that the leaders of a Jewish state could behave that way. I noted, "Menachem Begin may not resign next week, but he has lost the power to govern effectively. A Prime Minister of Israel can survive blunders at home, deep strains with the US and disagreements within World Jewry, but he cannot remain in office if he has squandered Israel's fundamental asset—its respect for itself and the respect of the world."

The lasting effect of this essay was that it added cubits to my stature in the political and academic communities in the United States. I was now definitely the Jewish insider who would tell it like it is, whether in print or on a lecture platform or on television. To some degree I had set the seal that day on being the Jewish and Zionist countervoice.

This role was necessary because the war in Lebanon had permanently changed the landscape of the Middle East and had forced a painful realignment of Jewish opinion all over the world. In Western opinion, Israel had long been favored as the representative of the people that had been victimized for centuries and had very nearly been destroyed by the Nazis and their collaborators. The wars that Israel had to fight had been presented to its people and to world opinion as wars of necessity, of defense against enemies who wanted to destroy it. Such a description, of brave little Israel standing against those who would destroy it, was even used to describe the opening of the war in Lebanon: Israel was defending itself against shells being lobbed across the northern border. But soon it could no longer be claimed that this was a defensive war at all. It was a "war of choice," as Sharon proudly proclaimed it. It was a military action that Israel had chosen to launch in order to improve its position in the region and to make Lebanon a protectorate. The Jewish world now had to account to itself and to all the world for the carnage of a war that was not an act of self-defense.

In Lebanon, while Begin remained silent, Sharon had behaved like the military leader of a small warlike state using its weaponry to gain advantage. There were no ready slogans or clichés in the older Zionist rhetoric with which to defend this attempt to become "like all the nations of the world." Jewish opinion was visibly split by this change in Israel's behavior. Many took the view of "Israel right or wrong." Jews had to display their unconditional love of Israel by supporting its actions. This was the official message that was being beamed out to the Jewish world from Jerusalem, but the Jewish world was restless. No amount of Jewish loyalism could convince American opinion that Sabra and Chatilla had been a good and blessed enterprise. The basic trouble with the image of Israel as a military power enforcing its will was that it stood in the way of the cherished image of Israel as the only democracy in the Middle East. Democracies cannot have clear consciences and let their armies stand aside while massacres are being carried out on their watch. The authorities in Jerusalem might still force an appearance of united Diaspora support of their policies, but it was becoming increasingly clear that this was appearance and not reality. Worldwide Jewish opinion, which had been so united in 1967 out of fear for Israel's future and then in exultation of its victory, was now in 1982 utterly divided.

The change in Israel caused serious rethinking by Americans. The Arabs were still quite unpopular, and Israel still commanded the respect and affection of most Americans, but a substantial element was beginning to agree that the Palestinians were victims. The editorial boards of the major American newspapers were now describing the Palestinian sense of hurt and loss in sympathetic terms. The Israelis were now seen to be conquering rather than defending. The dominant mood in the West, and especially in the United States, was that peace needed to be made and that there were two obstacles to its realization: one was, of course, the intransigence of the Arabs, but the other was the unwillingness of Israel's dominant right-wingers to give back what Israel had taken in the West Bank. The Jewish defenders of Israel took refuge in the argument that the Israeli government of Menachem Begin, who was followed by Yitzhak Shamir, who took over as prime minister in 1983, was really committed to compromise and that its annexation of East Jerusalem and the Golan Heights was simply part of a tough negotiating posture, but when the time was right for compromise, Israel's government would make large concessions.

I denied this pipe dream in essay after essay and speech after speech. There was no ambiguity to be found in what Israel's right-wingers were saying in Hebrew at home. I regarded it as a moral duty to make an end of this charade, for I kept returning in memory to the day in Jerusalem in 1977 when Menachem Begin had told me bluntly that he was going to go to Washington to tell Jimmy Carter that Israel had elected Begin's new government in order to retain the whole of the "undivided land of Israel." Begin never pretended that he was simply being a tough negotiator. Yitzhak Shamir was even blunter.

I was now inexorably and very publicly in opposition, but I could not really be cast out of the Jewish establishment. I simply had made too many friends in the forty or so years in which I had been integrally involved in public life, and I did still hold one major office, that of vice president of the World Jewish Congress. So, when the World Jewish Congress held a meeting in Jerusalem of its international executive in 1983, Yitzhak Shamir, who had just become prime minister, followed precedent and received all the officers in the cabinet room. As we took turns in walking around the table toward the prime minister, he shook hands with every one of us. A photographer took a picture of each of these encounters. When my turn came, he shook my hand and turned his back on me, in one extraordinary motion. All of my colleagues in the room were appalled, but I recognized this gesture for what it was. He was excommunicating me.

Shamir could not successfully anathematize me, for he underestimated the size of the constituency for which I spoke. I was strongly supported by Meretz, the left-wing Israeli party of peace, which had ten seats in the Knesset; by many in the Labor Party; by the bulk of the academic intelligentsia both within Israel and in the Jewish world; and by the opinion of Israel's friends in the wider society who wished that it would be more accommodating to the aspirations of the Palestinians. Yitzhak Shamir and his associates were dazzled and even blinded by talented and clever middle-aged Jews who had become neoconservatives and who had made a connection between their American politics and the views of the Israeli right-wingers. Seen from the prime minister's office, there was little doubt that Norman Podhoretz and Irving Kristol, and their younger followers, were moving the American Jewish community toward the political right; the liberals were being defeated, and I, and the likes of me, were becoming irrelevant. The only trouble with this interpretation was that every election in the 1980s demonstrated that the American Jewish community was remaining resolutely liberal. It voted for the Democratic Party by two to one, and it preferred peace in the Middle East to occupation of the West Bank. A "high priest" who tries to excommunicate someone whom he does not like had better take care that he is speaking for the overwhelming majority of his people.

Some months after Shamir's snub, I was again sitting across the table from him at an executive meeting of the World Jewish Congress, and the argument between us resumed. This time I let my anger show. I told Shamir in the iciest tone that I spoke for more Jews than he did. He responded with furious silence. I had been publicly rude to the prime minister of Israel, and I was not in the least bit sorry.

28

In June 1981 I turned sixty, and a dinner was given at the synagogue to mark the occasion. On the surface it appeared that this was a celebration that pointed to my continuing as the rabbi for many years to come, but I was looking for a way to retire. I had less and less energy, and less and less patience, for the day-to-day politics and abrasions of congregational life. By then, I had served nearly forty years as a congregational rabbi, and I had heard the all too usual complaints too many times. I was indeed guilty of practicing a kind of triage in my work: I had little tolerance for those who wanted to assert their influence, and even power, to command some of my time for reasons that I regarded as self-serving. I wanted to protect my energy for those who needed help, rather than attention, and for those who wanted to come to learn rather than to make a show of themselves. As I was reaching the sixties my inner balance had tilted, and I could no longer pretend that I did not know that this had happened. I felt that I was paying too large a price for putting up with the day-to-day nonsense that came with my position as the rabbi of a major congregation, although I still liked the possibilities for doing good that such a post afforded me. But the price for these possibilities was rising. I remember telling a friend who was a physician that when patients became annoyed with him, they could go elsewhere. When congregants became irritated with me, they stayed and complained or joined the board of the synagogue to strengthen the anti-Hertzberg forces. It seemed to me that it was no longer emotionally possible for me to fight in the political trenches of Temple Emanu-El. I would be telling less than the truth if I did not add that I felt that I had outgrown these battles.

I had tried to avoid facing the need to leave the temple by accepting an invitation for a scholarly sabbatical in Jerusalem in 1982, but I returned with an even greater sense of alienation from the chaos of the congregation. It came to a head one day when I discovered that one of my supposed friends in the membership, who was also a fervent Israel loyalist, had become so outraged by my telling uncomfortable truths about the Lebanon war that she actually telephoned the New Jersey office of the Anti-Defamation League to ask their advice as to what to do about me. They told her that there was nothing that they could do, and they advised her to suffer my heresies in silence because I was too big a fish for the Anti-Defamation League, and so for her, to catch. The woman in question was an ardent reader of *Commentary*, which had just run an article that had denounced both Abba Eban and me as "functional anti-Semites."

Increasingly, I longed for the quiet of teaching, reading, and writing. I had never relinquished my commitment to learning and to thinking about the problems of our time and their relation to the destiny of the Jews. This was the career that I had kept alive, to be my home when I decided that I had paid my dues to public life and the congregation. Although I had begun to think very seriously about retiring, I took no immediate steps in that direction because I had no clear vision of where I would pursue such a career after I left the synagogue. Then without any preliminaries, Ronald Green, professor and chairman of the department of religion at Dartmouth College, invited himself to my office at Columbia the spring of 1984. He told me that he and his colleagues had been looking for many months for someone to teach Judaism in their department, but that they had room for only one person, so they needed somebody who would be able to teach both ancient and modern Judaism. They had seen many candidates, younger people who had just gotten their doctorates, because the authorities at Dartmouth had initially

limited the job to the rank of assistant professor. Ronald Green knew
that the post could not easily be filled with a recent Ph.D., so he asked me
to become visiting professor to give them time to extend their search. I
declined, for I had just returned to Temple Emanu-El from a sabbatical
and could hardly ask for another. I then surprised Ronald Green by
telling him that all of my life the jobs that had proved to be good for me
had come unexpectedly, which meant that the portents for this one were
favorable. I would be delighted to come to Dartmouth if he could offer
me a full professorship. Green agreed to go back to Dartmouth and ask
for additional money to enable them to appoint me. Within very few
days I was invited to visit the campus and spend the day meeting members of the department. They were very welcoming. The president of
Dartmouth, David McLaughlin, was particularly warm; it was he who
had ensured that the funds were available for a full professorship. I
returned to Englewood and called a meeting of the officers of the congregation to announce my retirement as of the spring of 1985, giving
them ample time to ensure that the transition would be in good order. I
never experienced any withdrawal symptoms, as I maintained many
friendships and contacts within the congregation even as I spent half of
each year at Dartmouth. Soon I could look forward to waking up in the
morning and going to my office in Thornton Hall at Dartmouth, where
I could close the door and write.

In a few months I took long-accumulated vacation time and spent
the spring of 1985 at my new post, usually returning to Englewood for
the weekend. One Sabbath morning as I was walking to synagogue I
encountered a woman who had been a member of the congregation for
many years. She stopped and looked at me with a face reflecting puz-
zlement and wonder. Quite soon she could no longer remain silent, so
she asked me, "Why are you still doing this? You're no longer the rabbi,
so you don't have to." I answered that now that I was no longer the rabbi
of the congregation, I was trying to find out whether I really meant it. I
remembered this conversation recurrently during my first years at Dartmouth. I was now going to find out what I really cared about. As a professor I had the obligation of teaching my classes, but I was otherwise
free to do what I wanted with my time. I was curious myself where I
would be putting my energies. I found out about myself in those wonderful six years at Dartmouth. I discovered that I really did intend to

write (the results were two books and dozens of essays) and that I had told myself the truth when I was wrestling with the question of whether to stay in Israel: I cared with all my heart about all the questions that a Jew would ask himself, but I cared just as deeply about the health of American society as a whole and about helping to make an end of hunger and of war all over the world. I dreamed that the move to Dartmouth College would be a signal that I was leaving public life and that I would henceforth be busy with teaching and writing. But the change was not absolute: I could not absent myself from the problems about which I cared.

Under the cover of scholarship and intellectual pursuits, I kept being invited to international functions where politics was often more important than the announced content of the meeting. This happened to me in the fall of 1985, when I was asked to come to the headquarters of UNESCO in Paris to help celebrate the eight hundred fiftieth anniversary of the birth of Maimonides. My name had been proposed to the organizers of the meeting by the European office of the World Jewish Congress, in the full awareness that I would understand and take part in its announced purpose to celebrate Maimonides as the great figure who appeared at the point in time, in the twelfth century, when Jewish, Arab, Christian, and Greek culture interwove, but that I would be useful in dealing with the not too hidden political issues. Amadau Mahtar M'Bou, the director general of UNESCO, was running for reelection, but he was being attacked fiercely for his strong bias toward the third world and for the extravagant budgets with which he used money that came from Western governments to finance a bloated staff, largely from Asia and Africa. He wanted this meeting on Maimonides very badly to suggest that he was not biased against Jews.

In mid-December 1985 a group of scholars who came from Algeria, Morocco, Senegal, Nigeria, Saudi Arabia, Kuwait, Iran, and the Soviet Union, and, of course, from Israel, France, and the United States, assembled at UNESCO. Most of us had never met, and our basic premises were in sharp conflict. Several of the Arabs claimed Maimonides for Islamic culture and even insisted that he had converted and left Judaism. Dr. Shlomo Pines, from the Hebrew University in Jerusalem and a widely respected authority on Maimonides, countered very sharply that Maimonides' writings were full of counterattacks on the teachings of the Prophet. In this debate I witnessed the first round in what has become a continuing battle between, on the one hand, many of the representatives of Islamic culture who keep trying to deny that Jews have any place in the history of the Holy Land and the Middle East as a whole and, on the other, the Jewish scholars (and almost all the others) who find such claims to be bizarre. These arguments continued through the conference without resolution, but at least the debates and the arguments were polite. The content of the discussions seemed less important in December 1985 than the fact that scholars from countries to which Israel, and increasingly Jews, were anathema were sitting amiably with each other and lunching at the same tables.

My strangest political subtext was the encounter with Vitaly Naumkin, who came representing the Soviet Academy of Arts and Sciences. Naumkin was not a medievalist but a linguist who knew Arabic extraordinarily well. From the very beginning of the meeting he worked at cultivating me, and I kept wondering why he was doing it. I soon found out through friends in the Israeli diplomatic establishment that their "book" on Naumkin included information that he had spent several years quite recently training PLO fighters in camps in Kuwait, that he was probably of Jewish origin, and that he held fairly substantial rank in Soviet intelligence, which was then still called the KGB. I decided that I would put Naumkin through some "strange" Jewish experiences. Twice in a row, I took him to dinner at the ultra-Orthodox restaurant that was run by the Chabad emissary in Paris. I had no doubt that Naumkin knew that there was more elegant food to be had in Paris, but I thought that he should suffer a bit for his unrestrained eagerness to get close to me, who was, formally, the leader of the Jewish delegation. When the meetings ended, we agreed to stay in touch. I did not imagine that this gracious way of saying good-bye would soon have serious political content, but it did.

Half a year later, in late August 1986, Naumkin was in touch with me through the telephone, by letter, and by fax to urge me most insistently to come to Moscow immediately as the guest of the Academy of Arts and Sciences. It became clear very soon that this request was a cover for the real purpose of the invitation. In September Mikhail Gorbachev, the new ruler of the Soviet Union, would be on his way for his first tour of the United States. He and his aides were afraid that the visit would be a fiasco. Tens of thousands of demonstrators who sympathized with the plight of Soviet Jews, and especially of the refuseniks, were going to be out in the streets in New York and Washington, and wherever else Gorbachev might go, to demand that the Soviet Union free the Jews who wanted to emigrate. That summer everyone in the Soviet establishment who had any connection with Jewish figures of consequence in the United States invited them to Moscow and asked each, in turn, to help quiet the tempests that were being prepared for Gorbachev's arrival. Without exception, each of these worthies answered that he had not the power to shut off the protests. At the very end of the summer, with Gorbachev's visit just a few short weeks away, it had become the turn of Vitaly Naumkin to produce "his Jew," me, in the hope that I might find a way to save Gorbachev from embarrassment. I exacted as the price of my coming that I would give a lecture on Zionism at the Soviet Academy—at a time when it was forbidden to speak publicly of Zionism—and Naumkin cabled back that this condition was accepted. They were even willing to brave the protests that came from several of the Arab embassies in Moscow, led by the Syrians, when the news got around that the Soviet Academy was going to be "dishonored" by a lecture on Zionism by a known supporter of this forbidden movement. Thus, I was certain that my hosts were in the mood to listen very carefully to any political advice that I would give.

By the third morning of my visit, I was in the offices of the Soviet foreign ministry, meeting with the deputy minister of foreign affairs and his principal advisors. I repeated what others had said: no one could order the protesters to be quiet. But I suggested that, nonetheless, the problem could be solved. I told my hosts that they were foolish to keep the most prominent refuseniks in what amounted to house arrest in Moscow, indefinitely, because the refuseniks had nothing else to lose. They were speaking frankly and bitterly to everyone who came to visit them—and the Soviet authorities did not dare to cut off such contacts because then they would be accused of the crime of gagging their critics. I suggested that they should simply let twenty or thirty of the refuseniks out immediately so that when Gorbachev came to the United States he would be in a position to say that his government was taking a new and much more liberal view of the question of the emigration of Soviet Jews. He would be able to point to the fact that he had already let out the most difficult cases, and he could add that he would go back home to take a new look at all the rest.

The officials to whom I made this suggestion were not high enough in the Soviet government to be able to respond, but within thirty-six hours I was told that the suggestion had been accepted and that the most prominent refuseniks would be given their exit visas before the weekend. Suddenly on Thursday and Friday of that week the world press was carrying the strange news that longtime "prisoners of Zion," led by Ida Nudel and Yosef Begun, would be on their way out of Moscow within a day or two. I knew that the pressure on the Soviet government to let such people leave had come over and over again from the American and other Western governments, and, of course, from Jews all over the world. Without this constant prodding, the pain of the Jews of the Soviet Union would have been forgotten. But I had the opportunity to make the case to the Soviet authorities that it would be best for them to accede to this pressure if they wanted a friendly reception for Gorbachev in America. Other people had been the major figures in raising the dog that had growled at the Soviet authorities for years. I had the privilege of sounding the last bark.

Despite trips to UNESCO and the high politics of the visit to Moscow, the move to Dartmouth had basically achieved my purpose in changing careers. Most of the time at Dartmouth I could settle in, day after day, and think through some of the larger questions that had been troubling me for decades. Inevitably, I turned first to the students whom I was teaching. They were interestingly different from those I had known forty years earlier when I had been the Hillel director at several colleges in New England. The scene that I remember from the 1940s could be described in stark terms. Anti-Semitism was alive and well, and it was particularly at home in the academy. Professors who were Jews barely existed, and Jewish students, especially the few who were admitted to the most prestigious colleges, knew that their advancement depended on how well they behaved as amateur Gentiles. The few engaged in Jewish worship tried hard to be inconspicuous. In the intervening forty years the situation had fundamentally altered. The quota against Jews in the Ivy League schools and in comparable colleges all over the country had been largely destroyed.

This process had begun at Columbia University, where in the 1940s

Rabbi Stephen Wise had mounted a credible threat to go to court to cancel Columbia's tax exemption: he maintained that it was not serving the entire American community because it was restricted against Jews and other minorities, and so Columbia University was not entitled to any more consideration than the tax laws gave to a private club. Columbia backed down and abandoned its most notorious quota, which limited the access of Jews to medical school. In the early 1960s at Columbia, many still felt hampered by being Jewish; they were afraid that many avenues were still closed to them, but this complaint was lessening. Discrimination was ebbing. At Dartmouth, in the mid-1980s, everyone seemed confident of the future and untroubled by anti-Semitism. It had even become fashionable to be Jewish—at least, so it seemed.

But the scene was not quite so idyllic. It was flattering that within a year or two after my arrival at Dartmouth the number of students taking my courses in Jewish studies had grown from less than twenty to many times that number, making my classes among the most popular on campus. However, as I got to know the Jewish student body better, I found that it split into almost equal halves. Half were emphatically Jewish, mostly in an ethnic sense; the other half, who were listed as Jews, simply did not project themselves as such and were even resentful when any attempt was made to bring them into Jewish life on campus. I encouraged one of my students, Jevin Eagle (he was among a line of assistants who were very helpful with my writing and scholarly work), to write a senior thesis on the quality of the Jewishness of his fellow Dartmouth students. Half of them willingly answered the questionnaire he sent out; the other half of the recipients resented the questions and declined to answer them. The half that did answer reported that there was some member of their family, usually a grandparent, who would be very upset if he or she married out of the faith, but even among this more involved half, only one in ten was certain that he or she would never marry out. At the end of the decade, in 1990, an elaborate population study that was commissioned by the Jewish Federations found that the rate of intermarriage had risen to one in two from the one in twelve that it had been thirty years earlier. This did not surprise me. It was consonant with what Eagle had found at Dartmouth.

Culturally, Jews had become a kind of new priesthood among the writers and intellectuals. The great intellectual gods of the era were Freud and Kafka. A host of writers who were consciously Jewish such as Arthur Miller, Saul Bellow, and Philip Roth were the gold standard of American writing, which meant that Jewish subject matter was "in." The immigrant Jewish ghettos had become as much a region that American writers evoked for their readers as the counties of the deep South that had been portrayed by William Faulkner, Tennessee Williams, and Thomas Wolfe. This changing cultural atmosphere had contradictory results. If Jews were now an American elite and no longer a persecuted minority of recent immigrants, it was also easy to move out of being Jewish into some other American realm, because the external constraint of anti-Semitism had been removed. At Dartmouth, a generation earlier, two Jewish fraternities had existed because Jews had not been admitted to the fraternities that dominated the campus. The old graduates whom I met still remembered those fraternities with a mixture of longing for their coziness and anger for being forced into them. The younger people did not know of them because they had gone bankrupt. Jews were now being pledged by the fraternities—and sororities— which were open to everyone whom they might choose to invite.

A minority of Jewish students, those who were most intensely concerned with being Jewish, were different from those that I had known in the past. Their Jewishness was not primarily ethnic, expressing itself through Zionism or resentment of anti-Semitism. They were trying to find their way toward some learning in Judaism. A number were searching for a religious identity. The Jewish ethnicity and the pro-Israel activities in which they had been raised by their parents were not sufficient for them. Around them on campus were groups of Christians protesting against the shallowness of American consumer culture by joining growing groups of those who were being born again, rediscovering their faith. Some Jews were on a parallel journey. The most intense students who came to my classes were becoming more observant of Jewish tradition. On the major Jewish festivals, and especially on the High Holidays, hundreds turned up for services.

What I found most striking was the story of the daily prayer service. One of the students had tragically lost his father, and he wanted to say Kaddish, the memorial prayer, at least once a day at a formal service or, he felt, he would have to leave school and go back to the New York area, where he would have no trouble finding a synagogue. I put the question up to the students whom I had gotten to know and they instantly volunteered to meet every afternoon at four o'clock to create the minyan in which the student, Gary Katz, could say Kaddish for his father. It worked. The minyan continued every day without interruption. Gary, who soon became another of my assistants, finished college with a summa cum laude, went on to Harvard Law School, and was eventually a law clerk for a federal judge and then for the chief justice of Israel's Supreme Court. He spent an extra year in Israel studying Talmud. His personal journey took him toward becoming an Orthodox Jew.

One of the women who attended that minyan, Susan Shankman, went on to rabbinical school at the Hebrew Union College, the seminary of Reform Judaism. As I stood with these students in a makeshift synagogue of a small room in the student center, it was clear to me that the Jewish future in America could be guaranteed only by more study and more piety. We could not depend on domestic anti-Semites or the conflict in the Middle East to compel Jews to be Jewish. They would have to want to be, and only the learning and the faith of their fathers, as they understood it in their own day, could help them feel authentic as Jews and as human beings.

This struggle to redefine oneself as an American Jew was not limited to students. The issue was not just how to be a Jew in the new, much more open, America. It was how the Jew, no longer much preoccupied with self-defense, was to be an American. Was he or she to join the conservatives, who proclaimed that they were the keepers of true Americanism, or should Jews continue to belong among the liberals? One of the most interesting journeys of self-definition was navigated before my eyes by James Freedman, the new president of Dartmouth, who was elected to that post in 1987. Freedman had been the president of the University of Iowa, but he was raised in Manchester, New Hampshire, by schoolteacher parents who came from Brooklyn. His coming to Dartmouth was both a "return of the native" and proof that America was now much more open than in his father's day. In the 1930s, when his father graduated from college in the midst of the Great Depression, he could find no teaching job anywhere except in a high school in Manchester. The son was now returning to New Hampshire to become president of the state's Ivy League college. Jim Freedman and his wife, Sheba, quickly became friends, and Phyllis and I got to hear something of their biographies. Both had been raised by parents who were sufficiently observant of the Jewish tradition to keep kosher at home and never play down their Jewish loyalties. Very soon after his arrival at Dartmouth, Freedman announced that he wanted to get both faculty and students to work harder at academic pursuits; he wanted Dartmouth to live down its long-standing reputation as a party school.

Freedman was a very proper gentleman, but he had the bad habit of reading ten or twelve books a week, and he did not seem enthusiastic on the occasions when he attended the obligatory football games. His critics were right as they muttered under their breaths, or out loud after a few beers, So now we've got a Jewish intellectual.

The saga of Freedman's presidency came to a head in the turmoil that was created by the *Dartmouth Review.* This periodical had been making much noise on campus for some years before Freedman came to town, but the *Review* became louder and rowdier after he assumed the presidency of the college. The paper was very busy finding "liberals" on the faculty and attacking actions of the administration, and statements in class by professors, that did not conform to its right-wing views. The paper was widely distributed, free, all over the campus. Its appearance became a day of glee for those who were on its side and a day of discomfort and fear for the majority that found it offensive. Freedman tried to defend academic freedom and the civility of discussion at the college, but he was answered by the *Review* with a cartoon that depicted him in the uniform of a Nazi officer. The climax of these attacks was the republication by the *Review,* on the eve of Yom Kippur of 1990, of the introduction to Hitler's *Mein Kampf.* Representatives of the *Review* stationed themselves outside the doors of the college chapel, where the Jewish services were being held, and handed copies to the worshipers.

These attacks rallied the campus in near unanimity against the *Dartmouth Review.* A rally was soon organized that was attended by over three thousand people, the large majority of both the students and the faculty. The only time in my six years at Dartmouth (from 1985 to 1991) that I asked for a public role was when I volunteered to take part in the program of that event. Every group on campus that felt injured by the *Dartmouth Review* was represented, from the Black students to the Gay and Lesbian Alliance. I spoke first and excoriated the backers of the *Review*, especially the conservative foundations that paid its bills, and William Buckley and Irving Kristol, whom the *Review* claimed as advisors and patrons. The main point of my speech was that I remembered the tactics that were used by the Trotskyites and Communists in the 1930s, when small Trotskyite and Communist papers appeared on a number of campuses and especially at City College of New York, where the young Irving Kristol edited the Trotskyite weekly. The tactic was to make outrageous charges against the administration and some members of the faculty so that the furor tied up the campus in the direction in which these journals wanted to push. Now, sixty years later, the approach that had been honed to control discussion in ultra-left-wing directions was being used by some of the same people, who had now become the icons of right-wing politics, to instruct the young to be equally outrageous in the pursuit of right-wing purposes. The politics had changed, but the method was the same. When James Freedman arose to speak, he was uplifted by the size of the crowd and by the emotion he had heard expressed by others on the program. He delivered an impassioned but statesmanlike speech about the need to defend the freedom of speech in our society. The platform from which we all spoke was on the central green of the college, perhaps thirty yards from the building on the quad that commemorated Dartmouth's most famous graduate, Daniel Webster. Freedman evoked his memory when he called for the need of the college to remain faithful to his teaching of free speech and respect for others. The very future of American society depended on our fidelity to these commitments.

This meeting was widely reported all over the country. On campus it represented a major turning point. The *Dartmouth Review* was constrained to apologize for the offensive cartoon, and it turned down the volume of the attacks that it had been mounting on those whom it had been vilifying. After this rally, Freedman felt freer to pursue his desire of creating a more studious campus in which values could be examined in civility. I was glad that I had been asserting my identity as an American by standing up to the *Dartmouth Review* from my first days on the faculty, and I was, indeed, quite surprised that I had not been singled out for counterattack. The large rally in 1991 established that the campus community as a whole ultimately would not tolerate being bullied.

One of the main reasons for leaving the rabbinate for a professorship was that I was assured that I would not have to deal with academic politics. Despite that assurance, I could not quite avoid the intrigues that seem to be the daily business of a college town. I was saved from getting involved not by my own wisdom but by the concern of a professor at Dartmouth who had quickly become an especially precious friend. He was not a great scholar, though he could have been; heartaches in his family had preoccupied him for years. Tim Duggan was chairman of the philosophy department, and he soon took me under his wing to keep me from making more trouble for myself than I needed to. He knew the intricacies of academic politics at Dartmouth and especially the unfailing rule: never reveal, even by implication, the opinion that much of the faculty tended to be more devoted to sitting on committees that concerned themselves with "governance" than sitting in their studies and writing books. He once held my hand down by force at a faculty meeting to keep me from asking to speak, because he suspected, correctly, that I would give voice to this complaint. I was going to suggest that governance is best left to professional administrators and that professors should spend their time on scholarship.

One afternoon at my house when the conversation was uninhibited, Tim wanted to know what the source was of the affinity between an Irishman of blue-collar origins (he had gone to college and on to his doctorate on the GI Bill) and a rabbi's son whose native language was Yiddish. I answered, without any conscious thought behind what I said, that for every Jew who had lived through the Hitler era, one question was embedded deep within him: who among my non-Jewish friends would risk his life to hide me or my children or grandchildren if the Nazis ever dominated America? The bond between Tim and me, so I told him, was that I had no doubt that he would. After he left that day, I sat with the remains of my drink and wondered why this question had never left me, and why it was ineradicable. At the end of many minutes of reflection, I finally understood that Tim Duggan, and all of the other non-Jewish friends whom I trusted, had become the answer to the teacher at Johns Hopkins who had warned me in June 1940, in that time of great fear, that I should not come to his door asking for refuge. The existence of Tim Duggan reassured me that the child of four who had run away from those who wanted to beat him up in the town of his birth, Lubaczow, was not alone.

After a couple of years at Dartmouth, a project that I had postponed for nearly a half century became mandatory; I had to write a history of the Jews in America. At first glance it seemed unnecessary, because libraries had been written, and books were still being published, that extolled the glories of American Jewish achievements. The most recent had come out in the mid-1980s, written by Charles Silverman, a well-known journalist. His volume, *A Certain People*, was given to me for review, and so I read it with particular care. Silverman belonged to a long line of authors who had described American Jewish life as a success story with an untroubled future. I took strong exception to that view, because what I had seen of three generations of Jews had frightened me. Jews were indeed successful, but Judaism was in trouble. I had known this very early in my life. My father had taught it to me in the 1930s. During the depression he said, over and over again, that these Jews wrestling with poverty might, and probably would, become much better off, but they would not be able to buy food for their souls. The problems that money could solve were not the real problems. My father kept insisting that American Jews had not brought with them the resources of Jewish learning on which to base a serious religious culture.

In searching my files, Phyllis found two small blue notebooks, the kind in which we used to write exams at the Jewish Theological Seminary. In them I had written the first few pages of a book about the disastrous spiritual poverty that threatened the future of American Jews. So my discomfort had deep roots. When I decided that I had finally to write a book on this theme, I did not even think twice when I characterized my work with the subtitle *The Story of an Uneasy Encounter.* I regarded the history of American Jews as a success story, and I insisted that the success of the immigrant minorities in finding their place in America, whatever that place might be, was a central element of American history. But Jewish history has a different central concern: what has happened to the Jewishness of these immigrants? Was Irving Berlin, who became America's most successful songwriter, even as he left the Jewish community, the model for American Jews? Did the success story breed Jewish continuity or did it produce assimilation?

As I sat, hour after hour, and day after day, working away at this book (at Dartmouth, where so much of the evidence was around me, and where I had the time, the library, and the student assistants to labor with me), I had to answer some more fundamental questions about the Jews in America. Who were they? Where did they come from? Even before I arrived at Dartmouth, I had come to one fundamental conclusion, and I had argued it in an academic paper that I had given in 1981 at the international convention in Jerusalem of the World Union of Jewish Studies. In that paper, I established that the immigration of Jews to America from its very beginnings, and especially in the era of mass migration after 1880, was no different from that of any of the other large streams of populations that had come to American shores. The Irish who had arrived in America in the mid-nineteenth century were the poorest of the poor. The Germans who had come at the same time, and the Italians who had come a half century later, were poor farmers. The Jewish immigrants were the poorest and the least-educated element within their European Jewish communities. They had been mostly petty artisans or people of no particular skill or trade. None of these waves of immigration had brought with them a large number of educated people, because the middle class everywhere tended to have sufficient connections to survive in the home country. Even the Jews in czarist Russia, when the pogroms in the 1880s drove thousands from their homes in the villages, did not necessarily leave for America. Nearly 2 million did leave, but many others, those who were better off and who had family connections, moved within Russia to the bigger cities and away from the legally mandated Jewish ghetto, the so-called Pale of Settlement. I concluded in that paper that the American Jewish community represented the masses without the classes. These immigrants provided a very weak religious and intellectual foundation for American Jewish life. The Jewish culture of the Catskills, which has been celebrated by battalions of comedians who were once bellboys in the Borscht Belt, and the catering establishments in the cities at which Bar Mitzvahs and weddings were celebrated, did not represent continuity from the whole European Jewish past. At most, it was the version in America of the culture of the Jewish poor in Europe, not of its high culture, either religious or secular, which a small minority had brought with it. The American Jewish intelligentsia that began to invent itself at the turn of the century at City College of New York had as its model not Jewish thinkers, scholars, and rabbis from Europe but their college teachers in New York. Their "old country" was not the East European shtetl; it was the Lower East Side.

As I was writing the book on the history of the Jews in America, I became ever more aware that I was a minority of one. When the book appeared in 1989, it was greeted with hostile reviews, especially in the weeklies and magazines that catered to the Jewish community. I had not gloried in their success story but had instead pointed to the uncomfortable truth that American Jews had not yet found a way of guaranteeing the continuity of their culture and traditions. The most pointed attack was written by Arthur Goren, a professor of Jewish history at Columbia University, who had come back to the United States after many years on the faculty of the Hebrew University of Jerusalem. Goren was given many pages to write a review essay in the *Journal of the American Jewish Historical Society*, the quarterly that represented the scholarship of the Jewish historical establishment. Goren was upset that I had scanted the main point of American Jewish experience, the success story, and he insisted that the future of American Jews was rosy. He saw no clouds on the horizon. By the time this review appeared, the results of a famous population survey, the assessment of American Jewish demography for the year 1990, had just been published. The striking and upsetting conclusion of this study was that the rate of intermarriage had climbed to over 50 percent. This result cast a pall upon Jewish discussion. A community that was losing so large a portion of its population was in trouble. Never mind that American Jews were owning many Jaguars and Mercedes, as well as Lincolns and Cadillacs. The 1990 population study established that these expensive cars did not make Jews happy. They were worried that their children and grandchildren seemed to care less and less about their Jewishness.

I did not reply to Goren's review, in part because I have almost never answered reviews and in part because I simply did not regard the journal in which he wrote as the place in which the debate needed to be aired. I had learned from my father not to reply to reviews. I had come to him many years earlier, crestfallen after a negative review of one of my pieces of writing. He was absolutely unperturbed. He reminded me that "with yesterday's newspapers they wrap fish; books remain and they stand on their own merits." I did, however, find the opportunity to renew my attack on Goren's complacent view of American Jewish history two years later. The Columbia University Press published a paperback edition of the book, which gave me the opportunity to write a new preface. In it, I maintained again that the Jewish success story in all its supposed "uniqueness" was really a part of American history, as the arrival of the Jews had been; it was part of the story of the "huddled masses" from all over Europe coming to America to better themselves. The only reviewer who actually understood this point was the anonymous essayist who wrote for *The Economist*. He knew that I had put my finger on the dirty secret of American Jews: in the very midst of their success, they were in danger of evaporating as a distinct group and a distinct culture.

What I had written about American Jews was troubling to many others who did not belong to the Jewish community. By the 1980s and 1990s, ethnic studies were growing like weeds after a rainstorm all over America. Chairs in Jewish studies, or concentrations in Jewish studies, or even departments in Jewish studies were part of the same landscape as African studies, Native American studies, Hispanic studies, or, for that matter, women's studies. Everywhere these disciplines thought of themselves, or were cast for the role by others, as being cheerleaders for ethnic revivals. One did not get tenure in one of these shops by letting the side down. My book on American Jews supposedly broke this taboo. I did not think so, and do not think so now. On the contrary, I was insisting that American Jews, to save themselves as Jews, had to put their energies into deepening their knowledge of their own culture and tradition. I sniffed at Jewish studies programs that had five courses on the Holocaust, three on contemporary novelists who loved (or hated) the Catskills, and one or two on the theory and practice of klezmer music. I wanted to know how such Jewish studies could be taken seriously when they were bereft of Talmud and Maimonides. For me the climax came one day, about the time that my book was published, when I discovered that in several places in the United States, programs of Jewish studies were headed by tenured professors who knew no Hebrew.

Those who studied the classic texts were ever more confined to the Orthodox community and to the yeshivot, but what was being taught in the programs of Jewish studies almost everywhere was "Judaism-lite." It therefore meant that serious links to the classic Jewish texts had become the monopoly of religious fundamentalists. I kept chafing with the desire to rescue the Talmud, a great enterprise of religious reform and revolution, from the hands of the fundamentalists, who had persuaded themselves, and almost everyone else, that they were its true owners. They could get away with this only because so many of those who led programs in Jewish studies had chosen to be so trivial. In the first half of the twentieth century those few who taught Judaism and Jewish history in the American universities and in the Reform and Conservative seminaries had been learned in the classic rabbinic texts. The next generation strove to be relevant and contemporary. "God is dead" was a fashionable assertion in Christian theological circles, so it appeared in Jewish versions. The quest for mystical experience was enticing to Americans of all persuasions, because it made them feel better at a time of turmoil over the Vietnam War and racial tensions in American society, so professors of Jewish studies followed suit by teaching "introduction to the Kabbalah." There were, of course, numerous conferences in the late 1980s and early 1990s to discuss what to do to create a caring Jewish community. The conferences were seeking "meaningful Jewish experiences," by which they really meant something Jewish that could be packaged as pleasant or, at the very least, intriguing.

I was glad that my lot had brought me to as pleasant a place as Dartmouth. There I was able to write in my office with the feeling that I was putting a message in a bottle and that in due course it would wash up somewhere, without the discomfort of arguing with those who had no ears to hear. And yet, my pessimism, and even occasional despair, and my revulsion at the shallowness of American Jewishness were not total. Indeed, my spirits even lifted a little during my years at Dartmouth. I found that some of my students were hungry for the very values and learning that were so important to Jewish continuity. Among those who seemed indifferent, I found here and there some smoldering embers of Jewish seriousness that could be stoked. As I lectured on other campuses and in the larger Jewish communities around the country, I kept hearing discontent at what was available and hunger for what ought to be. I began to think back on the whole history of the Jewish tradition, through the ages during which it was fashioned, and I was struck by an obvious truth: at no time has biblical-prophetic-rabbinic Judaism been the religion and culture of the majority of Jews. On the contrary, the Bible is the record of constant struggle against idolatry. At one of the great climactic moments, when the Prophet Elijah confronted the priests of Baal, he stated parenthetically that in all of Israel there were only seven thousand individuals who were "all the knees which had not knelt to Baal" (1 Kings 19:18). I did not arrive at the hope that one could save the majority of the Jews of America from assimilation, but I did begin to believe that a strong minority would develop a vigorous and deeply grounded passion for Judaism in its most authentic forms.

The people whom I got to know, and to love, were themselves wrestling, each in his or her own way, with the central problem of Jewish existence in our time: how does one affirm oneself as a Jew and as an American? How does one see life through Jewish eyes and make one's decisions on the questions of the day on the basis of one's own traditions while being part of America? My own conclusion had become that this very conundrum was the deepest meaning of the American experience. This new society, supposedly the "last best hope of man," had been constructed so that an East European Jew like me, a rabbinic traditionalist, and a Buddhist from Korea could be and were American. Equally American was a Chinese colleague at the university who sent her children home for the summer with their grandparents so that they would be rooted in Chinese culture. Such intensities were what each of us contributed to the many voices that were heard, and that spoke to each other, in America. I kept thinking that Americans of Italian extraction needed to give to the rest of us more than a taste for pizza. They needed to remind us of Dante and Mazzini, and they could not do so unless they themselves knew and loved such great sources of their identity. Jews needed to contribute to America something other than bagels and Borscht Belt humor and, for that matter, something other than our profound distaste for anti-Semitism. We needed to find a home in our inner selves for the prophets of the Bible, the rabbis of the Talmud, and the builders of the early kibbutzim in the land of Israel. As I sat at Dartmouth and regained some hope for the Jewish future, I realized more and more that this was not my problem alone. All Americans of whatever origin had to solve for themselves the same question: the definition of their personal identity and how to relate to all other identities within America.

Quite surprisingly, during my second year at Dartmouth, I was invited back by Temple Emanu-El to be the officiating rabbi for one of the two parallel High Holiday services. The first year after my retirement, I had come back to Englewood and sat in the congregation along with all the other worshipers, for the politicians on the board of the synagogue had decided that they wanted a clean break. I was not surprised, because I knew that strong rabbis eventually create the desire in some congregants to be free of such authority. But this decision not to ask me back did not sit well in the congregation. The unrest about it became very pointed and very powerful, because those who had remained in the synagogue during my nearly thirty years as their rabbi were a self-selecting group, and they were firm in their convictions. In their overwhelming majority, as they demonstrated to the board, they wanted to keep hearing what I had to say, as I applied Jewish teachings to the social and political problems of the day. In the late fall of the following year, a letter arrived inviting me to return as rabbi, alternating between the service in the main synagogue and the overflow service for those who could not be accommodated in the synagogue itself. I accepted the invitation. I was pleased that what I had been preaching had not been soon forgotten. At the end of the service that Yom Kippur, though, I told the congregation that this was the last time that I would share in the conduct of the service. My successor had the right not to live in my shadow. Let the congregation that I had fashioned become a memory.

That Yom Kippur Day, in 1986, when I gave what amounted to a farewell sermon, proved not to be the end of a lifelong involvement in organized religion. On the contrary, after a couple of years out of the pulpit, I had a new perspective on religion at the end of the twentieth century. Within the West, and especially in America, religion had long meant Christianity. Jews had been fighting for their place within a society that was dominated by Christianity; they were rewarded by the halting acceptance of a new definition of America as a Judeo-Christian society, but there was great turmoil in interreligious circles over the assertion by the World Council of Churches that the mission to Jews to bring them to Christ remained a prime objective. This purpose had been reaffirmed by the World Council of Churches in Amsterdam in 1948, as part of their reflection on the Holocaust: converting the Jews would be the Christian atonement for not having protected the mass of them from the Nazis. The National Council of Churches in America, the umbrella group of the Protestant denominations, followed suit in the early 1950s by repeating the classic Christian notion that the mission to convert the Jews was a key obligation of Christians.

I denounced the Amsterdam declaration in 1948 as an obscenity. What right had those who stood by while 6 million Jews were being murdered to offer their religion, which had allowed them to do too little to save Jews, as balm for the survivors? In America a redoubtable Protestant figure, Reinhold Niebuhr, had suggested a way out of this uncomfortable confrontation. He offered a theological idea that had first been suggested a generation earlier by the Jewish thinker Franz Rosenzweig: the two-covenant theory. This thesis asserted that the biblical God revealed himself in a covenant with the Jews as depicted in the Hebrew Bible and then in another covenant with the Christians as depicted in the New Testament. Each of these covenants was equally valid, and each was definitive for its own community. It was fashionable and correct for a theological liberal in the 1950s to hail Niebuhr's restatement of Rosenzweig's two-covenant theory. I was such a liberal, I admired Niebuhr as a teacher and a friend, and I revered the memory of Franz Rosenzweig, but I could not agree with either of them. I thought that the two-covenant theory was provincial. What about the many hundreds of millions of people who were Muslims or Buddhists or who belonged to some other faith? Were we to presume that they had been left for the Christians to convert and that otherwise they were bereft of divine light? It was clear to me that the many religions would have to coexist in practice and they would have to accept in their theologies that God spoke through each and all of the traditions. I published these reflections in *Christian Century*, the journal that was most read among liberal Protestants. I was surprised to discover that I was not counterattacked. Evidently, the intelligentsia of American Protestantism did not believe that the world as a whole was a missionary field, a place for Christian evangelism.

At Dartmouth, I went to work every day to my office at the department of religion where an expert in Chinese culture and the most characteristic of China's religions, Taoism, was two doors down. Right next to him, the professor in residence was an ex-evangelical minister who was now teaching and studying Hinduism. My office adjoined the study of the only woman in the department. She was less and less concerned about the subject of her graduate studies, philosophical theology in America in the last century, and more and more involved in feminist thinking. The most intriguing figure on the floor was Charles Stinson, whose office was right across from mine. He was a scholar of Christianity who was spending his life in writing the definitive study of one of the founders of theology in England, the Venerable Bede. Inevitably, Charles Stinson and I examined each other, while pretending to make jokes about how much of the fine points of his work I could understand. I soon found out that Charles read voraciously and was remarkably well informed about the religious scene worldwide. He had very critical judgment about everybody's religion, including his own, and yet Charles went to church regularly and was, in a very private way, a believer. This combination of learning, breadth of interests, and critical judgment appealed to me, so we became fast friends. Our many conversations helped me think again and more deeply about the reaction that I had had to the debate in the 1950s that religion is more than the tension between Judaism and Christianity.

Tim Duggan and Charles Stinson were not the only ones about whom I had come to be certain that they would risk their lives, if necessary, to hide my children and grandchildren. The woman who managed the office that took care of both the religion and philosophy departments, Sandy Curtis, became equally dear to Phyllis and me. We were soon convinced that she too belonged to that minority that would, without hesitation, stand up against evil for the good.

I was challenged to put these ideas into practice very soon, by an invitation to take part in a major interreligious encounter. The World Wildlife Fund was going to celebrate the twenty-fifth anniversary of its foundation in Assisi in August 1986. The then chairman of the World Wildlife Fund, Prince Philip, believed that the defense of the environment was a cause about which major religions of the world cared, or ought to be reminded that they care. Over some opposition in his board, he decided to invite delegations from as many of the major religions as possible that would agree to come, even though they would have very little time to prepare. Martin Palmer, an Englishman who was his advisor, organized an "alliance for religion for conservation" to carry out this purpose. To find Jewish representation, Palmer went to the central office of the World Jewish Congress in Geneva. The general secretary, Gerhart Riegner, suggested that I be invited since I was the ranking officer of his organization who was a rabbi. Prince Philip soon asked me to come to Assisi to help define the issues on which the various religious communities and the World Wildlife Fund could cooperate. The religious organizations easily agreed that each should publish a declaration, based on its own sources, to the effect that the defense of the living planet was an obligation for all believers.

The climactic event of the meeting was a joint ceremony at which each of the faiths would contribute something of its tradition. This event was especially moving and dramatic because it was held in the Basilica of St. Francis of Assisi. It was preceded by a very colorful procession through the city by delegations from each religious tradition. We had no trouble finding a common platform because the religious leaders had been housed in the monastery of St. Francis, the home of the leaders, worldwide, of the Franciscan order, where we had studied together for two days. The results of these deliberations were a commitment to make environmental concerns central to the work of each of our denominations throughout the world, in the many thousands of congregations and houses of prayer.

This concluding service in the basilica was solemn and jubilant, but it was not without problems. The other religions, especially the Muslims and the Jews, were uncomfortable with the many crosses in the basilica, so the Franciscans in charge behaved with incomparable respect and magnanimity. Part of the basilica was partitioned off, and no one who sat in that part was under a cross. We were made to feel as equals in a building that is an important Christian shrine. Thanks to their willingness to accommodate other traditions, I was able to come to the basilica that day with a Jewish prayer shawl over my shoulders, to represent my community. I remained under the prohibition of not saying formal Jewish prayers in this setting, but I wanted to take part. I found a solution that would meet my Jewish obligations and that would allow Judaism to be visibly represented on this grand occasion. I brought along with me the most elegant shofar (ram's horn) that I possessed. When the procession arrived at the basilica, I stood on the steps to receive the hundreds who were arriving. There was a formal pause, and I sounded some of the traditional calls on the shofar, those that had been used on every occasion since the Jews began their journey from slavery in Egypt to call people to prayer. I then joined the procession, cradling the shofar under my arm, and entered the basilica. As this was happening, I heard a member of the Muslim delegation, a muezzin (the one who calls Muslims to prayer), standing on the forward edge of the roof of the Basilica, proclaiming the call to prayer in Arabic. The head of the Muslim delegation said to me at the end of the event that he was grateful for my example of sounding the shofar at the door of the church, which enabled him to find a similar solution for the Muslims. Indeed, I later learned that many others, including Prince Philip, had been much taken with the shofar.

This involvement in the celebration in Assisi was not for me a single ceremonial occasion. Involvement in the work of conservation continued through the years and allowed me to come to know many of the leaders of the other religious delegations and to remain in contact with them. I became much more understanding of the other traditions, and those with whom I worked from all over the world learned to think of Jews and Judaism in a new way. Jews ceased being, in their minds, some remnant from a very ancient people, the history of which had ended in biblical times, or a small and supposedly powerful ethnic group in modern times. We were being thought of, more and more, as a vibrant world religion with concerns that were similar to those of all the others: the defense of the physical world and the defense of the defenseless, all the defenseless, everywhere.

I had not abandoned or put in the shade one iota of my concern for Jews in special danger, in lands in which they were being persecuted, or the continuing difficulties for the state of Israel, but I became more committed than ever before to working with others to help the poor, all the poor. One day in the middle of a meeting in London, when I sat among representatives of the Eastern faiths (they wore torn sandals or were barefoot), I suddenly understood why I was learning to care so much. In every child in misery all over the world I saw myself at the age of nine walking to school with holes in my shoes.

Memoirs are sometimes confessions. They can appear to be honest and balanced accounts, warts and all, of the life and times of the author. Yet, without exception, memoirs share one characteristic: even at their most self-flagellating, they remain briefs for the defense. Now at the end, I must put aside narrative to reflect on the large questions of my life. Did I find solutions to the problems and concerns that have troubled me?

My longest battle has been to find a place within the traditions into which I was born. This quest has been portrayed over and over again in the past two centuries as the problem of the Jew who leaves the supposed safety of the ghetto of his birth and ventures out into the possibilities, but also the insecurities, of the majority society. This experience has, of course, colored my own biography, but it is not my basic story. I learned fairly quickly to cope with a different language than the Yiddish of my childhood and with the customs, manners, and outlook of the new society. What shook me very early was the contrast between the religion and values that were being taught by my parents and the world in which I attended school and college. My father made sure to teach me the rabbinic texts that a rabbi of the old school had to learn, but he knew that he was not succeeding in making me into a religious fundamentalist. He hoped that his example would be enough of an education, and, in many ways, it was, but it did not persuade me that God had sat on top of the mountain dictating every last line of the first five books of the Bible, word by word, to Moses. And yet I revered my father, and I soon realized that he was a great scholar and great spirit who belonged together with the greatest men and women whom I came to know at various points of my life. He could be very temperamental, and sometimes he was wrong, but never on a moral issue.

My answer to the religious tension between my father and myself over fundamentalism was to read the Bible, and especially the Talmud, and to understand the rabbinic tradition that descends from it in historical terms. These texts are the records of the soul of the Jews straining, age after age, to hear what God might be saying to them as they struggled toward decency and justice. My father and his father before him, and all of our ancestors, had defined a tradition that I had to study. I could argue with it on occasion, and sometimes, in the very name of what my father had taught me, I could rebel against it. As the decades went by, I arrived at the conclusion, for me and those who would hear me, that the inherited rabbinic law had been unfair to women and had treated them unequally. I had to assert the equality of men and women before God and in His service. But my father had taught me to be a questioning Jew, sometimes even a rebellious one—but within the tradition. I shall always remember the scene on the afternoon of Yom Kippur when he stood before his Hasidic congregation in Baltimore and pronounced an indictment against God Himself for his misconduct during the Holocaust. That day he even said that Jews have been the bearers of God's teaching for a long time, and they have long suffered for telling the world moral truths that it did not want to hear. Let us now, he said, choking on tears, take the Torah back to Mount Sinai and ask God to give the honor, and burden, of being its bearers to some other people. But my father remained a pillar of the faith.

The more I thought about my own problems, the more I realized that these were questions of no great novelty. Some sons want to break from their fathers, as Abraham did when he broke the idols of his father, Terah, and heard the voice of God ordering him to go to a new country. Other sons are almost exact copies of their fathers, as the patriarch Isaac was, as his life is retold in the Talmud. I have come to realize that I had more nearly followed the tradition of Joseph. When Lilith herself in the guise of the wife of Potiphar, his master, tempted him, Joseph was restrained at the very last moment because he saw before him the image of his father. At every turning point in my life, I have no doubt heard something of the thunder that once rang around the Jews who stood at the foot of Mount Sinai, but I am not sure, perhaps because my ears are more than a little out of tune. What I know is that I have seen at every moment of my life the image of my father and my mother. What would they have done? What would they have regarded as the right and the just? I have always felt saddened by those—and I have known so many—who have been searching for other values and for other senses of belonging. You need not be a carbon copy of your forebears, but you dare not obliterate the connection. That would mean obliterating yourself.

Sometimes when I was growing up, I regretted that our home was not more American. I have for many years been ashamed of the moment in my freshman year at college when I found an invitation for my mother and father to come to the home of the dean for a reception for the parents of undergraduates who had made the college's honor role. I did not deliver that invitation. My mother spoke a heavily accented English, and my father never spoke it at all. Their clothes and demeanor seemed to me to be alien and not American enough for a reception at the dean's house. They would probably have chosen not to go this party, but I made the choice for them. At that moment, I still wanted the protective coloration of seeming to be not far different from anyone else. But in the next several years at college, I found out that I was irretrievably different, that I belonged to a very small minority. I began to discover in my late teens that I would have no trouble dealing with well-bred non-Jews. They were who they were. Their inner strength rested on their pride in their ancestors, so they understood my sense of myself as the descendant of rabbinic scholars. I had greater trouble with my fellow Jews.

My father thundered much more about the faults of the Jews than the misdeeds of the non-Jews. He concluded that the American Jewish community was dominated by immigrants, who came from the poorest among the Jews of Europe, and by their children, who had been raised in the values and outlook of their parents. Jews had come to America, as had the bulk of all the other immigrants, to succeed. Very few had come to transplant their culture and religion into a new land where they would be free to cultivate their values and their learning. My father had not come to the United States to take a chance on getting rich. He had resolutely refused to sacrifice any of the laws of classic Judaism, which he obeyed; nor did he abandon his studies of the holy books. He had left Poland in 1923 because he could find nothing, not even a small rabbinic post, that would enable him to support his family. He went to New York to build a bridge for us, but he never gave up his essential identity. My father, and my mother with him, lived as if they were still in the very center of East European rabbinic life, and they made no concessions to the hundreds of thousands of their Jewish contemporaries who were renouncing this background. We lived by our values inside the boundaries of the little patch of Galicia that they had transplanted to America.

My own identity became clear to me one day in my senior year when I read *The Education of Henry Adams,* that classic reflection on his tension with American society. Henry Adams, the grandson and great-grandson of American presidents, had written his memoir in the early years of the twentieth century. Adams's theme was his distemper with American society in the gilded age. It was a materialist time, when America was dominated by the new men and women who had arrived at the top of society through their new money. Adams was furious that the tradition from which he sprang, formed by the generations of his family who had dedicated themselves to public service, was dying out. Henry Adams thought that he was the last of them. The Hertzbergs were not the Adamses, but Adams's pessimism and sense of loss were infectiously appealing.

In that class in American history, I read for the first time an even more famous book than Adams's, Alexis de Tocqueville's *Democracy in America,* which that French observer of early America, two generations after the Revolution, had written in the 1830s. Tocqueville found that the new Americans reflected their immigrant origins. From the very beginning, in the seventeenth century, two kinds of newcomers had arrived in the United States: the overwhelming majority were the poor from Europe who came to the new land with no objective other than that of getting rich. A small minority, consisting primarily of the Puritans in New England, had come to establish a new heaven by the light of their religion on the new earth of America. From its very beginnings the fundamental social tension within America had been fashioned by the struggle between Puritans and their descendants on one hand and the arrivistes who emerged from the not particularly literate mass of the poor of Europe on the other. Tocqueville had unwittingly described the position of Jewish traditionalists like my father as they tried to deal with the mass of the Jews who did not come from rabbinic learning. I had to wrestle with my contemporaries to try to make them hear the values that they never knew. But I knew that I had to persist. I had to make myself be heard, to be the kind of Jew that I had been raised to be. I could only hope that I would persuade some people to hear me out.

I was confirmed in this self-understanding because I soon found the same outlook in what remains for me the saddest book about American Jews ever written in America. Its author was the Yiddish writer who was famous under his nom de plume, Sholem Aleichem. The Sholem Aleichem that I know is not the creator of Tevye in the sentimentalized version in *Fiddler on the Roof.* The book of his that I read and reread in the 1930s was his last, unfinished, novel, *Motel Peyse, the Cantor's Son.* It was first published in 1915 in installments in the great Yiddish daily, the *Forwerts* (the *Jewish Daily Forward*). The book ended abruptly, for Sholem Aleichem had died before writing the final installments. The hero, Motel Peyse, comes to America from a shtetl in Eastern Europe, and he finds himself very much lost in the new land. He thinks that he will find an anchor in the company of earlier immigrants who had come from his own town, so Motel Peyse goes to the synagogue that these townsmen founded when they arrived. He expects to be treated with some respect because he is the son of the very learned cantor in the great synagogue of the hometown and he has himself studied the holy books for years. He finds that the greatest scholar among these immigrants, an older man who had been highly respected in Europe, is being treated with neglect and contempt. When Motel Peyse protests, he is told by the leaders of the congregation in New York that this is a new world and that they are not bound by the older traditions of respect. Here, "money talks." Motel Peyse walks away from this synagogue and goes looking in New York for people like himself, but he is not very hopeful that they will be many.

Sholem Aleichem's death meant that we do not know the outcome of

Motel Peyse's search. Does he find an environment for himself in America or does he remake enough of the community so that he can live within that minority? We do know that there were hundreds of thousands of mourners at Sholem Aleichem's funeral, but I am far from sure that the mourners understood all that Sholem Aleichem had been saying to them. To be sure, he was one of them, because throughout all his work there is an ongoing protest against capitalism. Sholem Aleichem was always on the side of the workers, both in Russia and in the United States, as they demanded equal treatment. But there was another side to Sholem Aleichem: he abhorred the abandonment of the inherited Jewish values and especially of respect for learning in the ancient and classic texts. He had come to the United States once before, in the first years of the twentieth century, and he had found that he could not tolerate the rough-and-ready, disrespectful environment that the immigrants had created, so he left and returned to Russia. He came for the second time before the outbreak of the First World War as the situation for the Jews was getting worse under the czar and Russian society as a whole was becoming ever more unstable. Even so, Sholem Aleichem was not certain that he would stay, because he was still dubious about the American Jewish scene, and he explained why in *Motel Peyse, the Cantor's Son.*

The hero of this novel reminded me very much of Henry Adams. Thinking about Adams and Motel Peyse helped me at the beginning of my journey as an adult—but I knew that I did not have Henry Adams's option of defining my life by aristocratic disdain for the society around me. I was too much of a Jew for that. I therefore spent my career fighting to change what I could not tolerate or, at very least, to establish that I could live within this America of "money talks" and never surrender my deepest values. Thus, at the very beginning of my career I had shaken off the idea that I should judge myself by what had become the conventional values of the majority community in America or by the accepted nostrums that dominated among American Jews. I would face the questions of where I belonged by myself.

Soon I had to answer a new question: what does it mean to be a Jew in the Diaspora after a Jewish state has been created? Is one authentically an American while there is the counterpull of Israel? Does one have a right to opinions that sometimes amount to a casting vote on the policies of Israel, or is one obligated to follow the line that Israel's government lays down? Is Jewish identity now, in the era of the state of Israel, religious or secular? Has the creation of the state of Israel begun a messianic revolution, a total remaking of the identity of Jews?

As early as 1949 I denied that the state of Israel was a "messianic event." All the Jews worldwide were not about to leave for Israel. The new state would add strength to the Jewish community and would thus make the Diaspora into a stronger and more lasting entity. Decade by decade, essay by essay, and book by book, I have increasingly insisted that every Jew has a right, and in fact a duty, to think about the nature of Israel's life and its policies. Such opinions have every right to be heard. Jews, a people with a questioning tradition, could not be put in the strange position that they could and should be vocal and influential on every issue before them, but they suddenly should become silent about their most immediate concern, the life and values of Israel. I was repelled by the widely used slogan that American Jewish groups on "missions to Israel" kept repeating, "We are one." Few of those who shouted this slogan had children in Israel's army. They were tourists in the dangerous lives of others. Further, we are not one, because each Jew has to define for himself to what element of Israel's life he is attached.

My links with Israel did not include automatic political obedience: I was largely in opposition to the dominant policies. I found myself restating this view year by year, as repeated attempts were made to silence me from Jerusalem and by its lackeys in New York and Washington. I insisted that we in the Diaspora could represent the best interests of the Jews worldwide—never mind the political and moral foolishness that governments in power might be proclaiming. I was no biblical prophet; I had no such delusions. But I also had no fear that I was committing treason by denouncing what I knew was wrong and foolish, and I laughed off the label of "maverick."

And yet, I accepted the most basic religious assertion that to live in America is, indeed, to be in *galut*, in exile. This had nothing to do with personal safety, because Jews in America were ever less fearful of anti-Semitism, while armed opposition by the Arabs to the Jewish presence in the land of Israel was becoming more murderous. American Jews were in *galut* because only in Israel did the very rhythm of life, even for the nonbelievers, reflect Judaism. Only in Israel does the working week begin on Sunday and end on Friday. Only in Israel does public education, whether secular or religious, require all Jewish students to study the Bible. Only in Israel does life run in Hebrew. To be sure, modern Hebrew is ever more a different language from biblical Hebrew, but it is not quite so different that the links have been severed. One can live the Jewish religious calendar in the Diaspora, and one could impart classic Jewish education, but these require effort and an act of resistance. One is always confronted by choices: how much do you separate yourself from the majority society, and what are you willing to join of the practices of the majority? And by what standard do you make your choices? This untidy, continuing tension is the hallmark of Diaspora existence.

However, I have always been sure that Jewish existence in America need not be poor or stunted simply because it is being lived in the Diaspora. Most Jews have lived in the Diaspora for at least two thousand years. After the Bible and the Mishnah, which is the basic text of the Talmud, everything else that the Jews have created was fashioned somewhere in the Diaspora. The more important of the two ancient commentaries on the Mishnah was conceived and written in Babylon. Maimonides, in the twelfth century, wrote much of his work in Arabic, under the influence of one of the high moments of medieval Islamic culture. In the eighteenth century, Elijah, the Gaon of Vilna, wrote his definitive commentaries on much of the Talmud in Lithuania, under Russian rule; and his contemporary and rival, Israel ben Eliezer, the Baal Shem Tov, founded the Hasidic movement in the nearby Ukraine. For that matter, every one of the Zionist ideologists did his thinking in the European Diaspora and within the context of European society. I cannot accept, today, that the encounter of millions of Jews with American democracy means nothing to the Jewish spirit or that, for the first time, Jews have run culturally dry and can survive only on what they might borrow from the new Israel.

What has happened in recent decades is the reverse. The Diaspora is ever more aware that watching Israel, being its fan club and, on occasion, its protective armor, is a moral necessity but also that Israel is not the salvation of Diaspora Jews. The Jews will survive as Jews in New York and Kansas City, and London and Melbourne, and especially in Moscow and St. Petersburg, if they commit themselves to Jewish learning and the practices of the Jewish religion. These age-old concerns are, as always, the central questions of Jewish existence.

In the past sixty years, the central religious issue that has gnawed at almost every Jew is the Holocaust: how can God, who is described as loving and merciful, have stood by while 6 million Jews and many more millions of people of other faiths were murdered by the Nazis and their helpers? Theologians have tried to justify the ways of "God to man," but without exception they have failed. This could not have happened as punishment for the supposed sins of the Jews, because no sin that this people had committed warranted the extermination of 6 million individuals, among whom at least a million and a half were children. Some of the theologians have maintained that God was somehow in eclipse, or He was absent, while the Holocaust was happening, but what right did God have to go on vacation while my grandfather and his family were being murdered? Other theologians tried to absolve God of responsibility by saying that He is master of the good in the world but evil is made by men and women using the power of free will and free choice. At this thesis about a "limited God," I screamed back that every classic Jewish text tells us that God is the master of both the good and evil in the world. Did not our ancestor Abraham demand of God that he prove the justness of his decision to destroy the wicked in ancient Sodom and Gomorrah? I have been reading "Holocaust theology" for over fifty years, and, from right to left, from very orthodox to very liberal, I have found it empty and sometimes even obscene. Most of these "theologies" agree that Jews were guilty of some sin or failing for which they were punished. Since this makes little sense even to the most doctrinaire theologians, a new theory has now arisen. It is promoted, in particular, by the former Sephardic chief rabbi of Israel, Ovadiah Yosef: by their death the 6 million atoned for their sins in previous incarnations. To such a "theology" I would prefer atheism.

Very early in my career, in the summer of 1949, I was in the presence of the Hasidic rebbe Aaron of Belz, a major figure among the Hasidic leaders of prewar Poland who had survived the war. He was, as I have told earlier, more eloquent in absolute silence than all these theologians. Aaron of Belz refused to speak with me of my grandfather and my uncles who were his very close friends, but he also would not speak of his wife, his children and grandchildren, all of whom were killed. He regarded their deaths as mysteries of a divine will that he could not explain. What had happened was so overwhelming that he could not even bring himself to say memorial prayers for these martyrs. But the rebbe Aaron of Belz did find the strength to spend the rest of his life in the Holy Land, rebuilding as much of what had been destroyed as he could by re-creating the court of his Hasidim and, above all, the house of study in which they could continue to ponder the holy books. For Rebbe Aaron of Belz, the way to affirm God was to re-create these institutions and the values that the holy texts taught. I know that the rebbe never read in Greek mythology, but like Sisyphus he was going to roll the rock up the mountain again, and again the rock was going to keep rolling down on Sisyphus. But Rebbe Aaron persisted.

I left him that day in 1949, thinking about the great sage of the Talmud, Rabban Yochanan ben Zakkai, who did not ask the Romans after the destruction of the Second Temple to give Jerusalem back to him so that he could rebuild it and return the Jews to the world that existed before the year 70. He knew that could not happen, so he asked the Romans, instead, to give him the possibility to rebuild Jewish learning and reestablish the practice of the Jewish religion. As I left my meeting with the Belzer rebbe, I remembered a line in Shakespeare where Marc Antony, speaking the eulogy for Julius Caesar, bitterly asserts, "the evil that men do lives after them; the good is often interred with their bones." In the quiet certainty of the rebbe, I found that something much different was true: evil will eventually be defeated; only good lives on. The Jewish religious answer to the Holocaust is not to produce theological theories of one kind or another, supposedly to give us hope. We find our hope, as we have found it over and over again, by refusing to be defeated. Like Job, we simply start over again.

Inevitably, I thought many times about the privilege of my encounter with the rebbe of Belz. Eventually, I came to a very strange thought. The rebbe was the quintessence of East European Hasidic piety and wisdom. He looked like a figure of two centuries ago, but suddenly he seemed very American to me. The rebbe was teaching that faith can express itself only in acts of rebuilding—which is exactly what the founders of America, those who had defined its essential spirit, had said in their own rhetoric. The rebbe would not have understood if I had tried to explain to him that he was a man whose outlook paralleled that of the makers of the American Revolution: we cannot bring perfection to the world—only God can do that in His own good time—but we can never stop trying to make the world better.

For years I had been seeking the fundamental common ground between my Jewish faith and my American identity. I found it in my meeting with the sad but undaunted rebbe. I knew whence my father and mother had taken their courage. They had taught me how to be a Jew. After the encounter with the rebbe of Belz, I finally saw that my ancestors had also taught me how to be an American. I had followed after them: I had become an American by refusing to assimilate.

So what is the moral of my story? I now know that the deepest intellectual influence in my life was the study of the Talmud. It has, of course, been my guide on thousands of abstruse questions of morality and of Jewish religious law, but the most important lesson that I have learned from its immense text of thousands of folios and many tens of thousands of pages of commentary is that the rabbis of the Talmud would stop in the middle of defining their own convictions and ask the question, always, What if the premises of our opponents could lead us to a contrary conclusion? I heard such an attitude in a famous sentence by Oliver Cromwell, the lord protector of England during the Puritan revolution in the seventeenth century, who probably never read a page of Talmud. He threw out the Long Parliament in England, saying to them that in all their certainty that they, and they alone, knew God's will, they should bethink themselves that they might be mistaken.

There are at least two lessons in this attitude. One cannot affirm one's own certainties without understanding the counter-certainties of others. I have learned to doubt, and doubt again, those who speak in the loudest voices of religious, intellectual, or political authority. I am especially on guard against those who tell me that they are possessed of a unique pipeline to God, whose true teachings only they understand, or to those who pronounce in the affairs of man that they have secret information that gives them a superior right to decide. My own experiences have been that the self-proclaimed prophets are almost inevitably raising their own choices, or prejudices, to the level of revelation. I am even more certain that in the realm of public affairs those who say that they know better, especially if they are presidents or prime ministers, simply do not. The decisions on the large questions of public life, and for that matter one's own conduct, can only be based on our morality and our conviction, often painfully reached, as to what is the path of right.

It is a very painful business to have to keep thinking and rethinking all the serious issues of life, but it is far more painful to wake up at the end and have to say, "I was not myself; I was only a poor carbon copy of other people." My ancestors were not. Each plowed his own furrow. They have left me no other choice. In a painful book after the Holocaust, Victor Frankl described the attraction of Fascism and Nazism as helping people flee from freedom to certainties that relieved them of thinking for themselves; but we do not dare take this option. Our humanity is in the difficult mix, always, of what we decide is the truth and of the tentativeness and self-doubts that we must always allow to remain.

My most important lesson was the one certainty of which I have the least doubt. It was perhaps best stated in the nineteenth century by Ralph Waldo Emerson, a descendant of American Puritans who had revolted against his religious heritage and become a Unitarian. Emerson knew very well that "every man is a charabanc (a conveyance) on which all his ancestors ride." I knew this even before I encountered this judgment of Emerson's. I knew it from the Talmud. Always, and especially if one differs with an ancient authority, one must cite him and then state one's own view. The proper form is to add, respectfully, "and perhaps I did not plumb the very depth of his understanding." It is a well-known cliché that the older children get, the likelier it is for them to see that their parents are not empty or stupid. I have gone through many worlds and many journeys; I have not learned to agree with every word of my Jewish forebears, but my respect and reverence for them is the foundation of my being. I have brought them with me into the very modern and contemporary world in which I live.

ACKNOWLEDGMENTS

This book was written for all its readers, but especially for my daughters, Linda and Susan; their husbands, David and Stephen; and their children, Rachel and Michael, and Michelle and Derek. In the writing, this text moved away from autobiography toward a memoir. It became an account not of my personal life but of my religious, political, and intellectual journeys. I hope that all those who read this text will have some sense of what I learned from my journeys.

My daughters each read the first draft with their customary incisiveness. My oldest friend, Melvin Sykes, and my friend of sixty years, Eli Ginzberg, moved me to define more clearly some of the issues that I have raised. As he has done for the past twenty years, Mark Friedman read this manuscript critically, and he corrected a number of errors. For this book, as for the several that have come before in the past decade or so, Edgar Bronfman volunteered to be the "first editor," and he has discharged that task with remarkable thoroughness.

On the more technical, professional level, I am very grateful to everyone at HarperSanFrancisco who has been involved in seeing this book to publication. The editor, Liz Perle, was and remains a critic, a goad, and above all a very supportive and wise friend. Her principal assistant, Anne Connolly, has made all kinds of technical problems easier and more manageable. Lisa Zuniga, the production editor, has presided over a highly competent job of editing while making sure that the basic character of the text has been retained. Joseph Rutt designed this text with skill and devotion. Kathi Goldmark has been working hard on bringing this work to public attention; she has been doing this job so gracefully that she made a friend of the author.

Much of this book was written at home. I am very grateful to Merline Buddo, who runs our house, for the wisdom and the diplomacy with which she has safeguarded my writing time. My secretary and assistant for the past twenty years, Carol Ivanovski, sits with me day after day to correct and correct again until we are satisfied with the final draft. My younger friend, Andrew Apostolou, and I adopted each other more than ten years ago, and, since then, he has been at my side as I have fought my way through to the final drafts of the last several books and especially of this memoir.

Since 1991 I have been teaching at New York University as the Bronfman visiting professor of the humanities. This post was made possible by Edgar Bronfman, who persuaded the Samuel Bronfman Foundation to fund it, and by Naomi Levine, the executive vice president for external affairs of New York University, who suggested my name to the university. Naomi and I have discussed the various parts of this book often and intensively. I continue to be enriched by her help and her friendship.

I owe the greatest thanks to my wife, Phyllis. She has been particularly supportive in the past several years, as I withstood several bouts of bad health. Phyllis has kept me going through two major operations and helped me return to writing. She has never wavered in her conviction that the way for me to get well is to not give in to illness. This book exists because Phyllis insisted that I had to complete it.

My ancestors used to conclude each book that they wrote with a prayer: *The work is concluded, and may it add to peace. All praise to God, Creator of the world.*

תם ונשלם שבח לאל בודא עולם

Aaron of Belz, 210–12, 456–57
Adams, Henry, 451, 453
affirmative action, 358–60
Ahavath Israel synagogue, 127–31
Albright, William Foxwell, 52, 53-54, 68-69, 71
Aleichem, Sholem, 452–53
Americanism: anti-Semitism at odds with, 38-39; desire of Nashville synagogue members for, 169–70; finding common ground between Jewish faith and, 448–58; Kaplan's views on, 106–7; self-recognition of, 348–51; struggle over, 11-12, 20-24, 28-29; tension between Bar Mitzvah and, 30-33. *See also* assimilation
American Jewish Congress, 354–65, 405–6
American Jews: connection between Israel and, 204; in danger of losing Jewish identity, 440; Holocaust memory used by, 403–4; impact of Yom Kippur War on, 389–92; as main Jewish community, 148–49; racial integration supported by, 267–75; rising rate of intermarriage by, 403–4; secular/ethnic elements of new, 402; Six-Day War and, 282–86; struggle to redefine oneself as, 431–47; writing history of, 437–40; Zionists among, 98–102. *See also* Jewish identity; Jews

American politics: civil rights movement and, 267–75; Israel-Carter administration relationship and, 396–97; Israeli-Arab conflicts and, 369, 377–80; Jewish-Black alliance in, 367–69; on Soviet Jewish immigration, 360, 361–65; sympathy for Palestinians and, 420–22; Vietnam war and, 276–80, 300–302
Amsterdam declaration (1948), 444
anti-Semitism: as abuse of power, 38, 43; Christianity and, 39–44; encountered in Nashville, 183–84; evident in Western intellectualism, 62-65; French Enlightenment and, 266, 286–90; invocation by American Jews (1970s), 404–5; military lack of, 219; during the 1930s, 34-37, 38-44; "normalization" notion on ending, 258; postwar continuance of, 145–46; pressure on Jews from subtle forms of, 115–19; Western intellectuals and, 135–36. *See also* racism
anti-Zionists: among Reform Jews, 132–33; in Nashville Jewish community, 179–80
Arab nationalism, 353–54
Arad, Moshe, 418
Archer ("the other") image, 144
Arendt, Hannah, 265–67
assimilation: distaste for those abandoning Jewishness for, 144–45; doubts regarding